WHAT OTHERS ARE SAYING ABOUT THIS BOOK

This is not just one more "christianized" self help book on self-esteem. Beginning with God's design in our creation as divine imagebearers, it diagnoses the full gamut of spiritual and emotional factors which deface that image and produce a sense of worthlessness and low self-esteem. Best of all it contains the divine prescription—practical suggestions for restoring it so we can stand tall as God's redeemed children. It is the integration of Scripture and psychology at its best.

David Seamands
Pastor, Counselor and Author

A landmark book on self-esteem and the Christian life. Important reading for anyone wanting to improve his/her sense of self-worth from a Christian perspective. Easy reading, thought provoking, practical and encouraging. Reading it would be a significant step towards building a healthier and happier marriage and family.

H. Norman Wright
Christian Marriage Enrichment

Rarely does a book come along that has within it the power to transform lives. . . . This book doesn't talk about fixing up the external you—instead the focus is upon allowing the Holy Spirit to take the information and apply it to your heart, changing you from the inside out. I believe that there is a special anointing on this book that enables the reader to leave the past behind and embrace the full liberty of becoming more like Christ. We began using Dr. Day's book as a textbook for our Discipleship classes in 1996, I have been privileged to watch year after year as lives have been transformed by it's teaching.

Cheryl L. Harper
Dean of Students, Capital Bible College, Sacramento, CA.

I'm so glad for Larry's book. He makes the connection between biblical fidelity and personal reality. His discussions of the image of God are right on target. He has gained enormous wisdom as he has applied the image concepts in many lives over his years of counseling. Now the fruit is available for all of us. This book is God'"s gift to all of us who want to see healing in hurting people.

Gerry Breshears, Ph.D.
Professor of Theology, Western Seminary, Portland, OR

"A truly biblical approach to understanding your worth. Dr. Day teaches us how to quit looking at ourselves with clouded vision and begin to see ourselves the way God himself sees us. The result can change your life."

Lew Davies
Former host on KPDQ Radio in Portland, Oregon

"You have written a very needed book! These concepts are life changing to me. Magnificent truth! I'm thankful to be able to recommend this book at my seminars. It is over-due!"

Joanne Wallace
Speaker and Author of *Starting Over Again*

"I know of no one better equipped or skilled to write and speak on self-esteem than my friend, and fellow conference speaker, Dr. Larry Day."

Dr. Dale E. Galloway
Former Senior Pastor, New Hope Community Church, Portland, Oregon

"I am so thrilled with the information in the book that I want others to benefit also. It is life-changing information. . . . *Self-Esteem: By God's Design* should be in every Christian book store. It would eliminate having to buy a lot of self-help books because it says it all."

Chris M.
Washington

"I've described your book as the most practical manual for mental health and spiritual growth I've read. . . . This book is a must for every Christian's library."

Gayla W.
Montana

"This book has been an encouragement to me personally, and I trust, also will be to my ministry. . . . I hope to put into my preaching some of these concepts to help my people grow in their Godly image."

Pastor Denis
Oregon

Self-Esteem:
By God's Design

A Journey to Worth and Identity

Formerly titled *By Design and In God's Image*

Larry G. Day, Ph.D.

Dr Larry Day
Psalm 139:13-14

SELF-ESTEEM: BY GOD'S DESIGN
Formerly titled *By Design and In God's Image*
©1992, 1994, 2004 by Larry G. Day, Ph.D.
Published by Mt. Tabor Press
P. O. Box 33524
Portland, Oregon 97292
503-231-0202
www.drlarryday.com

Printed in the U.S.A.

Grateful acknowledgment is made for permission to print the poem, "My Own Best Friend," by Marty Fuller. Used by permission.

Unless otherwise indicated, the Scripture quotations are from the New International Version of the Bible, © 1973, 1978, 1983, 1984. Published by The Zondervan Bible Publishers. Used by permission.

Other Scripture quotations are from the New American Standard Bible (NASB), © 1960, 1962, 1963, 1971, 1972 by The Lockman Foundation. Used by permission.

Those marked KJV are from the King James Version of the Bible.

Cover design by Bruce DeRoos
Cover Photo by Joe Felzman of Joe Felzman Photography
Edited by Bron Day
Typesetting by Debbie Johansson

Library of Congress #94-075900

ISBN 0-9635021-1-5

This book may be ordered directly from the author by writing to the publishing address or by calling (503) 231-0202.

Third Printing
Revised Edition

Dedicated to my wife Gail:
a great traveling companion whose love, encouragement,
support, and affection has enriched my life beyond words.

Dr. Larry Day speaks at churches, schools, conferences and retreats. He also conducts self-esteem seminars based on his book *Self-Esteem: By God's Design*. For further information write or call. He would be delighted to hear from you.

Dr. Larry Day
Box 33524
Portland, Oregon 97292
(503) 231-0202
www.drlarryday.com

ABOUT THE SYMBOLISM OF THE COVER DESIGN

The front cover is a collection of items that symbolize being on a journey.

- The old key unlocks doors and opens life to new possibilities.
- The candle provides the light needed to see our way in life.
- The compass gives moral and spiritual direction so we can have an accurate sense of where we are going.
- The map is the area in Wales where my wife's family lived before they immigrated to Vermont. In the late 1800's, her great grandfather traveled west with a wagon train and settled in Idaho. The map symbolizes the big picture showing where our adventure begins and the journey we take to arrive at our final destination.
- The old Bible is the instruction manual containing the information needed to live life well.
- The Coptic cross from Ethiopia represents all that Jesus Christ accomplished on our behalf.
- The cross is resting on an old Hebrew prayer book signifying the importance of prayer in our daily lives.
- The pearls represent the parable Jesus told about the merchant who sold everything he had to purchase a pearl of great value. Jesus is the merchant who sees you and me as pearls of great value to him.
- The smaller coin is a Roman coin that is almost 2000 years old. Look closely and you can see the image of the Emperor Constantine on the coin. Just as the coin bears the image of Constantine, so we bear the image of our Creator.

Acknowledgments

A person completes a project like this only because of the many people who quietly and significantly contributed their part. I want to thank them for helping me make this book a reality.

- My mom and dad, Edie and Foggy, for their stories and for the love and encouragement they always gave their oldest son.
- My brother, Bob, and his family, Sandi, Cherice, and Lora for helping me with the computer and for the early typing of the first manuscript.
- My brother, Bron, and his family, Debbie, Misty, and Derek for encouraging me to put into print what I teach.
- My son, Kent and his mother, Mary, for their stories that made the book alive and real.

I want to give a special thanks to those who helped with the original production of this project. I am grateful for their efforts on my behalf. Dick Sleeper, Randy Demlow, Steve Halliday, Rachael and Marty Bogan, Robin Georgioff, James Scott, and Mike Petersen.

I also want to thank the current people who helped me revise and update this edition of the book.

- My wife Gail, whose creative energy and imagination helped the book reach the highest quality possible.
- My kids, Kent, Talitha, Tabatha and Tim whose enthusiasm about the message of this book continues to inspire me to do more.
- Bruce DeRoos, whose creativity and cooperation in designing the cover was an example of God's image shining through his craft.
- Debbie Johansson, who patiently worked with me typing and retyping all the revisions we made.
- Joe Felzman, whose photographic skills are displayed in the beautiful cover of the book.
- Ake Lundberg, who helped me greatly to get the book printed.

Finally, I want to thank my clients and those who have attended my self-esteem classes, who have taught me more about life than they will ever know.

Contents

Introduction

I am excited about sharing with you my ideas on self-esteem. It was 1966 when I first became personally and professionally interested in the relationship between self-esteem and Christianity. My interest was born out of my own painful feelings of a inferiority. In my search for answers to ease my pain, I began to discover a new way to live that is described in this book. Over thirty-eight years of study, research, and personal experience have shaped the ideas and conclusions I will be presenting to you.

The central message of this book is that our worth and identity ultimately rests in the belief that each one of us is made in the image and likeness of God. Both the Jewish and the Christian faith have always held the view that the origin of human-kind is directly linked to a creative act of a personal God and that God purposefully and specifically (by design) created human beings *in His image* (Genesis 1:26-27). What I will be emphasizing is that the ultimate basis of a secure and healthy sense of worth is directly related to the level of *accepting, understanding,* and *experiencing* the truth of our being Imagebearers of God. This one truth explains *why* God has placed such great value and worth on human life; *why* God loves each one of us personally. It explains *why* Jesus Christ loves you and me and willingly gave His life to become our Savior.

Discovering the relationship between self-esteem and being created in God's image has changed my life profoundly. Many years ago as a freshman in high school, I accepted Jesus Christ as my personal Savior, and this produced the first major change in my life. It secured my salvation and brought me into a personal relationship with God. Learning more about the Bible and the Christian life helped me morally and spiritually to make better choices in the way I lived; but deep inside, my negative feelings about myself remained unchanged. It was not until I saw myself as a human being made in God's likeness that these feelings began to change.

Gradually, as my view of myself began to center around being made in God's image, I experienced a subtle but positive transformation taking place in my feelings about myself. My faith in God and Jesus Christ slowly deepened and became more real and solid; and my Christian life became more understandable, exciting, challenging, and enjoyable.

One of the most exciting lessons I began to learn was *I could be a real human being and a happy Christian at the same time.* For years, I had felt ashamed about being human. It was like having leprosy; I knew I had it, but I didn't want anyone else to know about it. Now, I could be both a healthy person and a happy Christian.

This leads me to tell you about a major assumption underlying this book. It is my belief that there is no contradiction between good mental health and the Christian life. If God made mental health and Christian living incompatible, God would be cruel. God, as the Author and Source of life, would not design a conflict between them. If He did, we would be forced to choose between being a psychologically healthy person but not a Christian, or being a Christian but not a healthy person.

If we are suffering from psychological problems or if we are unhappy in our Christian lives (aside from medical causes like low thyroid etc.), it is due to the lack of good information or the misinterpretation or the misapplication of either psychology or Christian teaching or both. If in God "we live and move and have our being" (Acts 17:28), then psychological health and a mature Christian life will integrate and work together in harmony; both will be life-giving. Just as God created the law of gravity, the laws of aerodynamics, the laws of nutrition, he also created the laws of mental health. As with the other laws if we violate them, we will pay a price. If we learn about them and follow them, we can become healthy and happy.

I am aware that many books have been written on the subject of self-esteem. Our world has undergone tremendous changes in the past six decades and we have not escaped the impact of these changes. As psychology began to study self-esteem and investigate its influence on a person's sense of well-being, many in the Christian Community welcomed these findings. But there was also a growing disagreement in other members of the Christian community that said our focusing on self-esteem was unbiblical and humanistic. They said it was wrong (if not outright anti-Christian) for people to become concerned about how to improve their feelings of self-worth. They claim that the gospel of self-esteem has replaced the gospel of Christ.

In contrast, many in the secular community believe that self-esteem affects every area of a person's life. They emphasize the importance of developing a positive and healthy self-image. They claim that many of society's problems could be solved if people would learn to love and respect themselves and then pass this love on to others. They teach that religion, especially Christianity, has been a negative force against the development of a positive self-concept.

The tension between human dignity and worth on one hand, and human sinfulness on the other, has often left many of us caught spinning in a revolving door with no way of escape. Both positions claim to be right and are calling us to choose their side. How can we decide which way to go when we feel caught between choosing either (1) self-actualization or salvation, (2) focusing on self or focusing on God, (3) human goodness or human depravity, (4) self-esteem or Christ-esteem, (5) loving self or loving God?

To relieve this tension, this book represents a third position. When the subject of self-esteem is understood correctly, psychology (mental health), philosophy (ways to understand our world) and Christian thought will arrive at a point of harmony and integration. The worth of human life in general, and self-worth specifically are intrinsically linked to our being made in God's image. It will show how human worth and human sinfulness can be better understood and balanced. It will show how self-esteem and salvation are two separate issues, both interlinked but dealing with totally separate concerns. To help you understand this, I will present material from ardent atheists as well as the most respected leaders of the Christian faith.

I have attempted to be both philosophical and practical by presenting these ideas from a comprehensive Christian world view; yet making it warm and personable enough to be encouraging and inspiring as to the possibilities for your life. Three words summarize my attempt to do this: **Affirmation**, **Permission**, and **How-to**.

Part I, *Not by chance, but by Design*, is the affirmation section. In chapters 1 through 10, I lay down the biblical foundation for a renewed sense of self-worth and dignity that comes from our being Imagebearers of God. I will talk about WHY it is okay for us to develop and enjoy a healthy sense of self-esteem. This can help us begin to be set free from the emotional and spiritual imprisonments of the past that have kept us locked in a poor sense of self-worth.

Part II, *And in God's Image*, is the permission and how-to section of the book. God as our Creator has given us eight unique human abilities as gifts of his likeness: feeling, choosing, thinking, communicating, self-awareness, moral-awareness, spiritual awareness, and creativity. These are the marks of His image in each one of us. These are what make us a person even as God is a person. As you read chapters 11 through 26, I encourage you to give yourself permission to accept these gifts as personally yours. These abilities were designed in your inner being and by accepting them and giving yourself permission to practice them, you can begin to grow, heal, recover, and change in ways that are exciting and rewarding. You can learn how to live more successfully in becoming the person God designed you to be: as a whole person in a quality relationship with God and others. These chapters will deepen your appreciation for what it means to be made in God's likeness while also equipping you with the skills, tools, and perspectives to help you become alive and real and healthy as a human being.

Some of you will find these ideas are just what you have been looking for. You have been growing and changing as a Christian, but you may have felt uncertain or alone in the process. I hope you will feel supported, encouraged, and strengthened in your growth by what you read.

Others of you may find these ideas new and different. They may not be as familiar to you as the ideas you now believe about life, psychology, and Christianity. I have tried to be sensitive in presenting these perspectives because I know how new ideas can be unsettling and disturbing. Take from the book those ideas that help you in your personal growth and leave the rest on the shelf that reads, "I need more time."

Some of you may believe in another religion or you may not have any particular religious faith at all. I wrote this book in a manner I felt would respect your position yet encourage your growth as a person by gaining a better understanding of the relationship between the Christian faith and psychology. Obviously, I hope it encourages your faith in Jesus Christ and I would be less than honest if I did not say so. Nevertheless, I have covered the subject with enough breadth that you should find it interesting if you are curious about how psychology and Christianity fit together in affirming the worth of human life and building a healthy identity.

This book has been designed, not merely to be read, but to change lives. I wrote it with the hope that you can tailor-fit the material to your personal life. If you want to change, I believe this book will help. It requires a purposeful effort on your part for you to be successful. If you want the changes to come easily, you will be disappointed. Yet, with God's help, with each new decision made, and each new thought or action repeated, a new and healthier you will begin to emerge. The awkwardness of your new beginning will eventually disappear and new life attitudes and habits will become natural. They say it usually requires at least twenty-one days of conscious effort before we can expect to see any significant changes in developing new feelings, attitudes, and behaviors. I encourage you to be committed to your journey for healing, growth, and change. I encourage you to trust in the love, mercy, and power of God and to be confident, as Paul was confident, "that He who began a good work in you will carry it on to completion until the day of Jesus Christ" (Philippians 1:6). May you become more like the person God created you to be. Let the Journey begin.

Dr. Larry Day

PART I

Not by Chance, but by Design

Then God said, "Let us make man in our image, in our likeness, and let them rule over the fish of the sea and the birds of the air, over the livestock, over all the earth, and over all the creatures that move along the ground."

So God created man in his own image, in the image of God he created him; male and female he created them. . .

God saw all that he had made, and it was very good.

Genesis 1:26-27,31

The discovery of the self-image is one of the most important finds of this century. For, though we may not realize it, we all do carry with us this mental blueprint or picture of ourselves. . . . Furthermore, all our actions and emotions are consistent with our self-image. You will act like the sort of person you think you are.

Maxwell Maltz,
The Magic Power of Self-Image Psychology [1]

———— ⊱⊰ ————

The conscious and unconscious feelings you have about yourself constitute your self-image. It is important . . . that we do not deceive ourselves, and that we recognize the deep inner feelings planted there long ago . . . Why bother? Simply because self-honesty is essential to honesty with God. We cannot know God any better than we are willing to know ourselves.

Cecil Osborne,
The Art of Understanding Yourself [2]

———— ⊱⊰ ————

The greatest barrier to achievement and success is not lack of talent or ability but, rather, the fact that achievement and success, above a certain level, are outside . . . our image of who we are . . . The greatest barrier to love is the secret fear that we are unlovable. . . . This, in simplest statement, is the importance of self-esteem.

Nathaniel Branden,
Honoring the Self [3]

CHAPTER 1

Self-Image:
Our Hidden Pictures of Ourselves

"Who me? I can feel good about myself? I can learn to like myself and see myself as a person of worth and importance? You've got to be kidding!"

Sometimes it sounds like a cruel joke to be told we can feel good about who we are. We know how hard it has been to cope with the painful feelings of not liking ourselves, of feeling like a failure, or feeling that we are unimportant, not needed, or unloved. If someone took time to talk with us, we could tell them what we have tried to do to feel good about ourselves. Sometimes it worked and we felt better for a while. Then something would happen and we would be right back where we started. Those old familiar feelings would be triggered by an unwanted failure, an unexpected rejection, or a sharp criticism, and it would ruin what started out as a pretty good day.

Years ago a seventy-six-year-old man came for counseling. He was a strong, rugged-looking man who had been a carpenter all his life. He was painfully self-conscious as he seated himself in my office. A look of apprehension reflected on his weathered face as he began to talk about his concerns. Several times he stated, "I don't know why I can't do anything right any more. I am just a good-for-nothing." Before the session was over, I asked him to explain how he came to see himself in such a negative way. He told me that as a boy he worked with his perfectionist father who was also a carpenter. For years he had endured his dad's anger and frustration with his performance and was verbally put down with the statement, "You good-for-nothing. . . ." In time, his dad's opinion became deeply imbedded in his young mind and heart and it became his own. Sadly, its destructive force was to be felt for a lifetime.

Maybe you could tell a story of how something happened or how someone said something or did something that shaped your self-opinion. Negative reactions, the disapproving silence, or the disgusted facial expressions of people around us speak volumes. The cumulative effect during our growing-up years contributed to the formation of our self-image. As impressionable children or teens, we observed and experienced the world around us. We tried to make sense of it all, especially as it related to our importance and value as a person. In time we began to develop certain feelings (felt-opinions) about ourselves based on our perceptions and interpretations of life. Like this man, many of us come to some inaccurate conclusions about ourselves—that we were unwanted, unloved, or nobodies. Others of us felt we were dummies, nothings, or nuisances. To better understand how we came to feel this way, we need to answer two questions: (1) What is self-esteem?, and (2) How does it develop?

Thoughts about Self-Image and Self-Esteem

People talk about self-esteem in a lot of different ways. Words like "self-image", "self-concept", "self-identity", "self-worth", "self-respect", and "self-esteem" have been used interchangeably, yet each can carry a distinct meaning. When I use the word "self-esteem," I think of a *core felt-belief that is formed in our hearts about our worth as a human being.* It is more than just what we like or don't like about ourselves. This relates more to our self-image. Self-esteem is much deeper than that. It deals with whether we like ourselves *at all;* whether we respect and love ourselves for being alive. *Do we value ourselves as a human being?** To help us appreciate the richness of the word "esteem," let's look at a list of synonyms:

- to value
- to prize
- to hold dear
- to honor
- to respect
- to think highly of
- to love

- to appreciate
- to cherish
- to treasure
- to admire
- to like
- to be fond of
- to care for someone or something[+]

When applying the term "esteem" to our own lives (self-esteem), it means to value oneself, to care for oneself, to like oneself, to respect oneself. It is the development of this perspective about ourselves that brings us to the more personal definition of the word "self-esteem."

---

*For the purposes of easy reading, I will be using "a person . . . they" rather than "a person . . . he/she." You may make the word "they" be masculine or feminine as it feels comfortable to you. I will also mix plural with singular, such as "we . . . person." I apologize for any grammatical discomfort this may cause, but I feel the benefit is worth it.

Pictures in Our Hearts

Simply stated, self-esteem is a deeply felt self-picture we carry in our heart. It is a self-opinion, a self-attitude, a self-impression we have come to feel about ourselves. This self-picture is formed from our perceptions, experiences, and interpretations of the things that happen to us in our daily life. From this information we make a *value-judgment* about ourselves which can be either positive or negative. If our conclusion is a positive one, we feel good about ourselves; but if it is negative, we feel bad and we begin to not like who we are. All of us build our earliest self-opinions from the experiences in our childhood and teen years.

Maxwell Maltz was a well-known plastic surgeon who tried to help people feel better about themselves through improving their physical appearance. In his book, *Psycho-Cybernetics*, he wrote:

> Self image is our own conception of the "sort of person I am." It has been built up from our own *beliefs* about ourselves. But most of these beliefs about ourselves have unconsciously been formed from our past experiences, our successes and failures, our humiliations, our triumphs, and the way other people have reacted to us, especially in early childhood. From all these we mentally construct a "self," (or a picture of a self). Once an idea or a belief about ourselves goes into this picture it becomes "true," as far as we personally are concerned. We do not question its validity, but proceed to act upon it *just as if it were true.*[5]

It is natural for us as children to develop our sense of identity and worth from our understanding of what makes a person good or bad, loved or unloved, wanted or rejected, a somebody or a nobody, pretty or ugly. Where we so innocently make our most serious mistake is in the *interpretation* of this information.

Often our interpretation and resulting conclusions about ourselves are LIES. They are not accurate. Unfortunately, these lies are taken to heart and remain there unquestioned and unchanged until brought into the open, questioned, and corrected. All kinds of people with whom we come in contact each day influence the shaping of our self-opinion. They all have expectations as to how we should act, think, believe, and feel.

Gradually, we begin to try to MEASURE UP to their expectation in order to feel loved and accepted by them. We begin to attach our worth (our identity) to what we do and to how we please people. Inevitably, something "bad" is going to happen and we interpret it personally in a negative way and a negative self-opinion is born. I have found that these deeply felt self-opinions are generally formed sometime between the ages of three and sixteen. They can form as the result of a single incident (like an embarrassing moment) or because of the cumulative effect of something happening in our life (such as learning problems).

As children, we were more aware of our feelings than of our ability to be logical and rational. Because of this, *our self-picture(s) becomes crystallized deeply in our heart as a felt belief, a conviction that is very resistant to change.* Self-pictures can generally be identified by the kind of "I am" sentences we carry in our heart. It is what we say about ourselves when things go wrong: "I am a dummy," "I am a nobody," "I am inferior," or "I am bad," and we mean it! From that moment on, we turn against ourselves. We begin to dislike the person we *feel* we are.

So, Where Did We Go Wrong?

Our "I am" sentences reveal how we feel about ourselves *as compared* to some external standard of measurement. The criteria we use to decide whether we like ourselves or not can have far-reaching consequences in our lives. One of the nation's leading advocates on self-esteem is Nathaniel Branden. He makes this connection central to understanding the development of our sense of self-worth. In his well-known book, *The Psychology of Self-Esteem*, he wrote:

> There is no value-judgment more important to man—no factor more decisive in his psychological development and motivation—than the estimate he passes on himself. . . . The nature of his self-evaluation has profound effects on a man's thinking processes, emotions, desires, values and goals. It is the single most significant key to his behavior. *To understand a man psychologically, one must understand the nature and degree of his self-esteem, and the standards by which he judges himself* (italics mine).[6]

If the standards we use to determine our sense of worth and identity are based PRIMARILY on what we do or fail to do, accomplish or fail to accomplish, or who we please or fail to please, we will eventually run into trouble. We will suffer the consequences of using unfair standards to determine whether we can like ourselves or not. That's what happened to Mary. Let me tell her story.

The Bad Little Girl

Mary was a darling five-year-old, blue-eyed, blonde. One day she and her three-year-old brother decided to play hide-and-seek. Mom and Dad were missionaries in Mexico and the family's adobe home was only half completed. Specific instructions had been given to both children that they were not to climb the ladder Dad had resting against the house during his work. Like normal five-year-olds sometimes do, Mary decided to climb the ladder anyway and hide from her brother in the new house. She was successful, but when her little brother followed, he fell and was knocked unconscious.

While waiting for the doctor, Mary ran away and hid in a dry irrigation ditch next to her home. For what seemed like hours, she sat there feeling scared and totally alone, all the while *talking to herself* about what a terrible thing she had done. Over and over again she thought, "If only I would have done what Mom and Dad told me to do, none of this would have happened. It's all my fault. *I am a bad girl.*"

The felt-picture of "I am a bad girl" crystallized itself permanently in her heart. It was an innocent yet destructive interpretation and conclusion about the goodness of her entire personhood. Who she was and what she did merged into a single felt-picture that was both painful and long-lasting.

Her brother recovered, but the hidden damage to Mary's self-esteem was already done. Once the lie became embedded, any future disobedience, failing, or short-coming only reinforced her belief about herself. To over-compensate for feeling like a "bad person," she tried to be the nicest person anyone would want to meet. She tried to prove to herself and everyone else that she was not as bad a person as she felt she was. Being nice to people had its rewards, but it did not solve her problem. In her heart she still felt the same. As time passed, she also felt she was a bad Christian, eventually a bad wife and finally a bad mother.

Self-Worth and Identity Based on Doing

Like Mary, our failure to overcome our negative feelings about ourselves is the result of trying to derive our worth and identity from primarily one source: WHAT WE DO. As children we are all little philosophers trying to make sense of our ever expanding world.[7] Gradually, we develop our personal world view about how life functions. DOING begins to represent all those ways we *think* we can earn or prove we are somebody. It fails us because our self-picture represents a philosophical conclusion we made about ourselves, about our existence as a person. It symbolizes what we believe about *being human.*

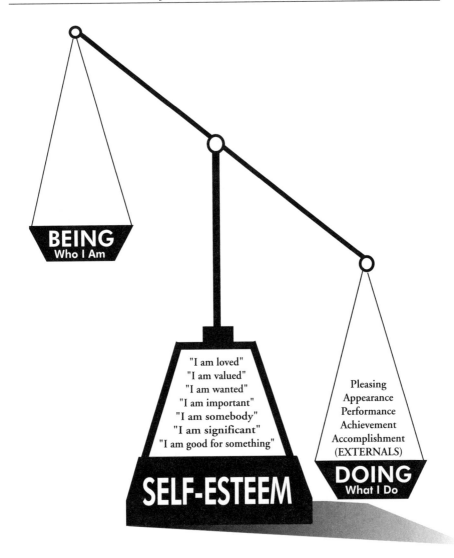

If our conclusions about our worth are inaccurate or lies, the results will be psychologically and spiritually damaging. In our attempt to fix the pain, we will try to, *do something,* (legal or illegal, healthy or unhealthy) to make ourselves feel like we are somebody. Unknowingly, we become even more committed to measuring our self-esteem by the standards of ACHIEVEMENT, PERFORMANCE, SUCCESS, ACCOMPLISHMENT, PLEASING PEOPLE, AND PERSONAL APPEARANCE. The above diagram illustrates how *out of balance* we can become when focusing too much attention on DOING as the primary standard of measurement for establishing our sense of worth and identity.

The scale becomes imbalanced when all our attention becomes focused on *measuring up* to these external standards. Only when we feel we are doing well, performing successfully, achieving important things, pleasing all the right people, or are attractive looking do we feel we are okay, important, or somebody. But, if we fail, our sense of esteem diminishes and we are right back where we started.

If we continue to compare ourselves to others, we will swing back and forth between either feeling superior or inferior to them. Our sense of worth fades in the light of their "greatness." We find ourselves numbered among the ordinary of the world and it feels terrible. Comparing, striving, and proving, or quitting, not trying, and giving up become the trademarks that characterize life in our inner world.

People who look upon our outward appearance, our outer manifestations of success or failure, would be surprised to find how our inner world is filled with confusion, fear, self-doubt, discouragement, insecurity, and pain. They can't see how desperate we are in our attempt to feel better about ourselves—to feel that we are valued and loved, that we are somebody. Like a hamster on a treadmill, we can become tired of working so hard, but we don't know how to get off. We are afraid to stop trying, so we find other things we can do to try to feel better about ourselves or to numb the pain, like using drugs, sex, or alcohol. Let's look at some of the most common ways people try to earn their sense of worth and identity.

Suggested Reading

1. Maltz, Maxwell. *Psycho-Cybernetics*. Prentice-Hall, 1962. and *The Magic Power of Self-Image Psychology*. Simon & Schuster, Inc., 1964.
2. Branden, Nathaniel. *The Psychology of Self-Esteem*. Bantam Books, 1969.
3. 1 Samuel 16:7; Ecclesiastes 3:11-14; Isaiah 28:10; 40:28; 45:12; 66:1-2a; Jeremiah 10:12; Matthew 23:5-7,12; Luke 9:46; 22:24-27; Ephesians 6:9.

Man's need of self-esteem is inherent in his nature. But he is not born with the knowledge of what will satisfy that need, or of the standard by which self-esteem is to be gauged; he must discover it.

Nathaniel Branden,
The Psychology of Self-Esteem [1]

Because the human being is created in the image of God, the will to dignity is the irreducible, psychological, and spiritual nucleus around which the life of the human soul revolves and evolves. The need for dignity, self-worth, self-respect, and self-esteem is the deepest of all human needs.

Robert Schuller,
Self-Esteem: The New Reformation [2]

Human worth in our society is carefully reserved for those who meet certain rigid specifications. The beautiful people are born with it; those who are highly intelligent are likely to find approval; superstar athletes are usually respected. But no one is considered valuable just because he is! . . . Personal worth is not something human beings are free to take or leave. We must have it and when it is unattainable, everybody suffers.

Dr. James Dobson, *Hide or Seek* [3]

CHAPTER 2

─────────∿ড়৶৶~─────────

We Have Been Weighed
on the Scales of Self-Esteem
and Have Been Found Wanting

Marty's aqua-blue eyes filled with tears as she talked about a painful childhood memory she no longer wanted to remain hidden. Forced by circumstances to decide between despair and rejection on one side or anger and determination on the other, she chose the latter. Marty was twelve years old when she made this decision.

This all started a few weeks earlier when Marty went home after spending the night with her grandmother to find she had a new step-father and two new half sisters. It came as a total surprise! Her mom didn't tell her about the marriage until after it had taken place. Overnight, her family changed from two people to a five-member family.

Feelings of shock, fear, disbelief, confusion, and excitement rushed in simultaneously. As the weeks unfolded, those feelings gave way to feelings of inferiority and insecurity. She desperately wanted to fit in, to belong, but instead found herself excluded from the inner circle of the other four family members. Like Cinderella, she felt rejected and not as important as the other girls.

As the pain deepened, she came to a turning point in her life. She would either have to give up and accept that she would never be good enough to belong or she would have to prove to them and to herself that she was better than all of them. *I'll show them*, she said to herself. *I'll show them that I am not only as good as they are, but that I am even better!* Twenty-five years later, she had proven to everyone but herself that she was one of the best. She had a college degree, a good husband, two wonderful sons, a nice home, lots of friends, and a successful career.

She was striving to be the best wife, mother, Christian, and business woman she could be, but what a price she was paying. The final blow came when she began to realize that all her efforts were falling short. Like wolves around a wounded reindeer, the feelings of anxiety and insecurity hounded her daily. She realized she no longer had the energy to hold them at bay, but to give in would be catastrophic. She feared she would become the very thing she dreaded most—an unwanted failure.

Like Marty, we are most ready to find an answer to heal our pain when we are stripped of the facade of our external proof of our worth. When we stand alone before our Creator we can begin to learn that our worth is already given to us by God; we are loved, valued, and wanted because we are created in His Image, *not* because we are doing all the right things.

Like the ugly duckling who came to like himself and appreciate that he was a swan, we can begin to learn how to like and appreciate who we are as Imagebearers of God. Slowly, we can began to experience the freedom that comes from no longer being driven to prove our worth. So let's look at what we try to do to prove we are somebody—that we are worth loving.

Let Us Count the Ways

I have traveled in over thirty countries around the world. I try to learn what each culture uses to prove you are an important person. I am convinced that struggling with self-worth is universal and that every culture, as well as every religion, has its beliefs about what gives us status and prestige. People have described to me countless ways they have tried to feel like they are somebody. Let me list some of the more common ways. Do you recognize any as your own?

1. *Marital Status*. Husbands and wives often attach their worth to their spouse. Many have had their self-esteem devastated by rejection and divorce. The rejection was even more painful if their spouse was involved with another person. Many teenagers and single adults are also looking for someone to date or marry as proof they are desirable and wanted—they are looking for someone to affirm their worth. In some cultures, the man's status is based on how many wives he has and how many cows or pigs he paid for each.

2. *Children*. It is not uncommon for people to attach their self-esteem to children, both in how many they have and in how they behave. Parents, bragging about their kids' accomplishments, sometimes put undue pressure on them to excel to build up their own egos. But many fathers and mothers have had to detach their self-esteem from their children when their son or daughter chooses a way of life that rejects what their parents most desire for them.

3. *Academic Success.* A great number of teenagers and adults with normal intelligence feel inferior to others who are more highly educated. They compare their grades or degrees to others and conclude they are inferior to them. Attaching self-esteem to educational success has brought unnecessary pain to many who are talented and bright.

4. *Career.* I wonder how many families have been sacrificed on the altar of a man's or woman's career because they measure their worth by career achievements and promotions? Family life suffers greatly if a person's worth is primarily linked to the prestige and status of success at work. Anxiety, stress, pressure, and depression often come to those who attach their importance to the corporate ladder. Many have felt like complete failures when they realize they are unable to achieve the desired level of success that would finally prove they are somebody. Retirement can also impact self-esteem. After retiring from a high position in a corporation, a man experienced a severe depression and loss of identity. He told his minister, "I don't know who I am anymore. I don't have any stationery."

5. *A Clean House.* Idealistic and well-intentioned young brides sometimes attach their self-image to keeping a perfectly clean house or to being the perfect wife. As children are added to the family, her already busy day is made more hectic. Dust and scattered toys can wreak havoc on the self-esteem of a perfectionist.

6. *Popularity and Fame.* Many teenagers and adults have achieved fame and glory only to find them hollow measures of self-worth. Their journey to the top was challenging and exhilarating, but once fame was achieved, the only direction to go was down. As popularity declined, so did their sense of self-esteem.

7. *Money and Income.* Bank accounts and paychecks have often been used as proof that we are somebody important. Self-esteem attached to the dollar improves with earning power. But if one's income declines because of a career change, physical disability, or aging, self-esteem can experience a serious blow.

8. *Material Possessions.* People sometimes measure their importance by the quality or quantity of what they own: the size and worth of their home, a certain kind of car, designer clothes. Eventually they discover that material possessions are inadequate to provide a lasting sense of importance. An accident or the death of a loved one can minimize the importance of material things compared to being alive. A charming seventy-five-year-old lady in Arizona once said to me, "Larry, you have never seen a U-Haul following a hearse have you?" I have to admit, I never have.

9. *Athletics.* Self-esteem and athletic accomplishments have been interrelated for thousands of years. Laurel wreaths, blue ribbons, gold medals, and trophies are seen as measures of personal accomplishment and significance. If winning is proof that "I am somebody," defeat can be demoralizing. Intense competitiveness is often driven by a desperate search for self-worth.

10. *Ability to Please People.* All their lives people have worked to gain the approval and acceptance of their parents, friends, spouses, or employers. If they could only make everybody happy, then they would know they are all right; they are a good person. Feelings of anger, frustration, failure, and despair come when they realize they will never be able to win that final approval. No matter how hard they try, no matter what price they pay in physical, emotional, or spiritual health, they will never be quite good enough.

11. *Ability to Please God.* When self-esteem becomes linked to pleasing God, the consequences can be disastrous. Sensitive and thoughtful religious people, including Christians, have become crushed under the weight of a sense of guilt and failure. They feel God is deeply displeased with them and they see no way to escape. God expects or demands perfection and they continually fall short of these standards. Striving for God's approval to earn one's worth is an unbearable burden.

12. *Bible-Reading, Prayer, and Church Attendance.* Many Christians try to improve their self-esteem through strict adherence to religious practices. Their dedication is sincere, intense, and passionate. Peer pressure in their church also reinforces the behaviors *expected* of a "spiritual" Christian. But by focusing on external behaviors, they eventually find themselves feeling spiritually superior to others and become worn out by the constant effort it takes to keep measuring up; or they feel spiritually inferior when compared to others and they live in a continual state of discouragement. Many teens and adults have had to rebuild a new Christian faith and a new sense of self-esteem after feeling like complete failures.

13. *Friends.* Feeling important is often connected to the number of friends one has or to who those friends are. Everyone wants to be liked by their peers, and friends are proof that they are somebody. The loss or betrayal of a friend is naturally painful, but it is even more devastating if that friend was used as a measure for one's sense of self-worth. Name-dropping is a common strategy used by those who link self-esteem with knowing famous people.

14. *Travel.* Globe-trotting has made some people feel they are somebody special and being a jet setter puts them in the group of "important people". Frequently, those who have not traveled feel inferior to those who have.

15. *Physical Appearance*. Physical shape, beauty, health, and strength are often used as measures of self-esteem. All cultures put a heavy emphases on physical attractiveness. However, if one is born with physical defects or if overeating, injury, disease, or aging resculptures a person's appearance, feelings of self-esteem can wither and die.

16. *Sexuality*. Sex is such in integral part of human life and is frequently used as a measure of self-worth. Many teens and young adults determine their value and self-acceptance based on maintaining their sexual innocence and purity before marriage. If they engage in sexual intimacy or intercourse before marriage, voluntarily or involuntarily, not only do they lose their sense of innocence or virginity, but they also experience a loss of self-esteem. This is one reason why rape, incest, and sexual molestation are destructive to a person's sense of worth. It violates the very core of their being with a behavior that has been given great significance in determining one's worth, value, and goodness.

There are others who feel like they're somebody depending on how well they perform sexually. Living up to the characteristics of a "good lover" makes them feel significant. But if they think they are sexually inadequate in some way, their self-image suffers. People try to affirm their worth by being sexually active. That's why sexual promiscuity and infidelity (as well as sexual difficulties) almost always have self-esteem issues involved.

17. *Developing Our Talents and Abilities*. Everyone has various interests, talents, and abilities and we are encouraged to develop them. But highly talented and gifted people can easily link self-esteem to their talents and make their efforts to develop them a double burden. Some people have "trashed" their giftedness to be freed from its weight.

Self-Esteem: The Proverbial Roller Coaster Ride

It's amazing what we will put ourselves through in our efforts to earn our worth, to feel like we are somebody. Each of us have tried our best, using hundreds of different ways to improve our feelings about ourselves, only to find they eventually let us down. You may have used some of those listed above, or you may have developed unique ones that you tailor-made from your culture, family background, and personal experiences. But whatever we have tried, we make one major mistake—and it costs us dearly. When we measure our worth primarily by the standards of performance, accomplishment, achievement, pleasing, and appearance, *we rely on measures that will ultimately fail us*. All measures of self-worth based on DOING are external and temporal. They are defenseless against the changes brought by time, circumstances, or other people's choices. Our sense of worth and identity can be destroyed by failure, rejection, accidents, sickness, aging, or a host of other assailants. Like a house built on sand, self-esteem built *primarily* on external measures of importance can be washed out from under us with devastating consequences. Something can happen in life that tips the scales of esteem against us and we are found wanting.

If we are to be a healthy, happy Christian, we cannot build our sense of worth primarily on what we do, who we please, what we possess, how we look, what we accomplish, or any external standard. If we do, our sense of well-being will be like the proverbial roller coaster ride. One week we feel great about ourselves: we are doing everything we are supposed to do, we are liked by the right people, we are accomplishing something worthwhile, and we are living the Christian life as we should. But the next week we feel terrible because everything we do seems to go wrong: the kids are misbehaving, our spouse is complaining, our boss is unhappy with us, our boyfriend or girlfriend or spouse has decided to dump us, or we have failed to live up to the expectations of our Christian life. On top of all this, we are getting old, fat, and ugly.

Yesterday we felt like an important and valuable person. Now we feel worthless, like a nobody, a total failure, an ugly fatso.

Our Self-Esteem Shapes Our Daily Lives

It is not hard to see how our sense of worth and identity can have a profound impact on our daily lives. If we have over-emphasized external standards—performance, accomplishment, achievement, pleasing, or appearance—as the primary reasons for liking ourselves, when something "bad" happens to us (and it always does) we go in one of two directions in trying to "cope with it."

We become discouraged and don't want to try anymore; so we GIVE UP. Once in awhile we may put some effort into trying to overcome something that really "hurt us," but any failure in our effort or any criticism from others and we go back to our attitude of "I quit," "I can't do it," "It doesn't do any good anyway."

The other direction we may choose is to pour ourselves into proving to ourselves and others that we are somebody. We find something we can do to try to fix what we feel about ourselves. We OVERCOMPENSATE in our efforts to EARN or PROVE our worth. We become trapped in a performance game, but we can't quit. To do so is to become the very thing we hate. So we keep striving, working, pushing ahead only to become more tired. The emotional swing from feeling loved, important, wanted, valued, or significant to feeling inferior, rejected, worthless, insignificant or a nobody becomes old quickly. The following diagram shows this dilemma.

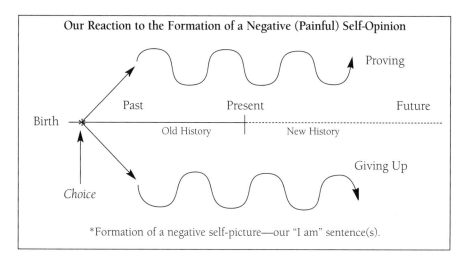

Our Reaction to the Formation of a Negative (Painful) Self-Opinion

*Formation of a negative self-picture—our "I am" sentence(s).

It is time to change when we become tired of the painful roller coaster ride. But is there a better way to determine our self-esteem, a way that makes DOING secondary? I am here to tell you there is a better way to measure our personal worth and value that can bring healing and change throughout our life. It is found in the way God has created us as people made in His likeness. OUR WORTH IS IN OUR DESIGN.

Suggested Reading

1. Schuller, Robert H. *Self-Esteem: The New Reformation*. Word Books, 1982.
2. Seamands, David A. *Freedom From the Performance Trap*. Victor Books, 1991.
3. Job 30:15; Psalm 36:2; 49:16-19; 62:9; Proverbs 20:27; Ecclesiastes chapters 1-12; Jeremiah 49:16a; Daniel 4:28-32; 5:26-28; Matthew 16:26; James 2:1-9.

The sense of being made in the divine image changes everything. It may even transfigure everything. The sense that God and man belong in one great bundle of life because God has given to man a certain likeness to Himself is one of the most transforming thoughts which can come to man. . . . Man's inner recovery requires a rediscovery and a reappropriation of his birthright. Man fully aware that he was made in the divine image can face his universe. There are other problems. . . . But this one matter settled, there is a sound basis for living.

Lynn H. Hough, *The Dignity of Man*[1]

Self-esteem is not a noisy conceit. It is a quiet sense of self-respect, a feeling of self-worth. When you have it deep inside, you're glad you're you. . . . You don't waste time and energy impressing others; you already know you have value.

Dorothy C. Briggs, *Your Child's Self-Esteem*[2]

It is high time that we declare all-out war on the destructive value system . . . which reserves self-worth and dignity for a select minority. . . . *Every child is entitled to hold up his head,* not in haughtiness and pride, but in confidence and security. This is the concept of human worth intended by our Creator. How foolish for us to doubt our value when He formed us in His own image!

Dr. James Dobson, *Hide or Seek*[3]

CHAPTER 3

Innate Self-Worth:
An Alternative to Earned Self-Worth

*I*magine with me for a moment one of those times in the evening when you tiptoe into your young child's room to see if they are okay and asleep. As you stand over your son's or daughter's crib and watch them quietly sleeping, you notice how their face looks so calm, peaceful, and angelic. They look so sweet, innocent, and lovable. As you gaze down upon that little bundle of humanity, no doubt you begin to experience an amazing assortment of feelings: love, warmth, pride, awe, tenderness, caring, and concern.

In those few moments of quietness, you don't see them as the "monster" that did all those things that drive you crazy. The yelling, crying, fighting, and misbehaving that took place throughout the day fade into the background. All hassles are set aside as you look at this sleeping form and see a little *person*. You feel a deep warm love for them simply because they are there.

Before leaving the room, you feel the strongest urge to pick them up, hold them in your arms, and kiss them softly on the cheek. But you don't. Why not? Because you don't want to wake them up and spoil the moment. You know that as soon as they open their eyes and mouth you will have to deal with their behavior (Doing) and you will lose the enjoyment of their Being. So you lean over, gently kiss them on the cheek, and quietly leave the room.

I know it is hard for some of you to feel that God really loves you when you have failed and made such a mess of things. We all think our mistakes, failures, sins, and shortcomings stand as witnesses against us that we don't deserve to be loved. We believe God must be fed-up with our bad attitudes and stupid choices, and that He wants nothing to do with us until we straighten out.

During times like these we need to look at the face of a sleeping child. Watching them in their simplest and purest human form, can remind us that this is how God sees us. *He came into our bedroom last night, looked down upon us while we were sleeping, and saw us as His child, created in His image, and He deeply loved us.* He saw us in our truest humanity—formed from dust, finite and fallen, but bearing His image in our very being—and He loved us for WHO WE ARE and not for what we have or have not done.

In the previous chapter we discussed how each of us have tried so hard to earn or prove our worth and importance by all the external ways we act (a works-oriented self-esteem). This chapter is going to focus on another way to establish a healthy sense of worth and value, one which is unrelated to anything we do. This worth is a *gift* given to us from God; it is built into the very ESSENCE of our human personality. Just like a sleeping child, our worth is innate and internal because it resides in the very nature of our BEING, our EXISTENCE, our PERSONHOOD, our HUMANNESS, our SELF-HOOD. This measure of our worth and importance remains constant and can never be earned or taken away.

Putting First Things First

This is not to say that doing well, accomplishing good things, behaving in ways that are right and moral, pleasing people and God, or looking attractive are not important. We all know they are. But it's relegating them to a *secondary position* as standards of measurement for personal worth, value and significance. Our *primary* measure for worth and importance is being a person, being a *human being*. This brings the scales of self-esteem back into balance. The following diagram illustrates this truth.

Many non-religious writers have affirmed the innate worth and dignity of human life in a clear and straightforward way. In their attempts to provide help for hurting people, they have done a fine job of pointing us in the right direction. They fall short, but they do move us toward the ultimate answer to what makes a human life precious and sacred. For example Nathaniel Branden writes:

> As a being who possesses the power of self consciousness—the power of contemplating his own life and activities—man experiences a profound need for a conceptual frame of reference from which to view himself, a need for a self-intelligibility which it is the task of psychology to provide.[4]

As humans, we are unique in our awareness of our existence. We are aware that we talk to ourselves about our place and importance in this life—

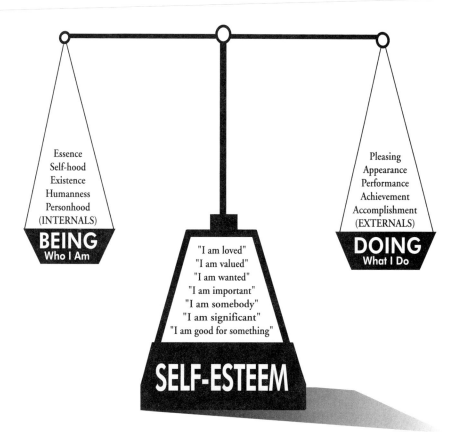

animals don't worry about such matters. Self-awareness activates in us a "profound" need to find a "conceptual frame of reference" from which to define human worth and value. But unlike Dr. Branden, I believe it is the task of theology, not psychology, to provide it. As we shall see in more detail later, the Christian perspective—that each person is made in the image of God—gives us a "frame of reference" that provides the ultimate answer to the problem of self-worth and self-intelligibility (understanding who I am and why I am living on this earth).

Balancing Being and Doing

Self-esteem is the combination of BEING and DOING and we cannot avoid it. But it is essential that we understand that it is our uniqueness as human beings that is the primary basis of human worth and value. Doing is secondary. We take a very important step in the right direction when we separate Being self-worth from Doing self-worth (Being ◄──────► Doing).

Self-esteem that is primarily resting on Doing is like standing on only one foot. We feel unstable, awkward, shaky and insecure. But when we see that our worth rests primarily in our Being, it's like standing on both feet—we feel solid, stable, balanced, and secure. "Being worth" remains a constant while "Doing worth" can fluctuate and vary because life is always changing.

Albert Ellis is a well-known psychologist and atheist. He clearly believes people have innate worth that is based on our uniqueness as human beings. He describes it this way:

> If there is an objectively definable concept of self-worth or intrinsic personal value it can only realistically be conceived as the individual's existence, being, aliveness, or becoming. . . . Other definitions of self-worth, such as the concept that it consists of mastery, or social acceptance, or the actual achievement of one's potential for being happy, seem to be illogical in that (a) they invariably refer to product rather than living process; (b) they are really concerned with one's extrinsic rather than intrinsic value; and (c) they lead to moralistic and self-defeating patterns of behavior on the part of those who believe in and follow them.[5]

Dr. Ellis points out the important need for having a standard for determining self-worth that is primarily derived from who we are. He affirmed that personal worth is innate and intrinsically linked to our being.

Taking the Next Step

It is the unique human qualities like reason, speech, self-determination, and self-consciousness that lead us to believe that our worth is directly related to our being a person, and specifically, a person made in the image of God. This connection is clearly made by the renowned philosopher, educator and author Mortimer J. Adler. Here's how he describes it in his fascinating little book, *How to Think about God.*

> Philosophical reflection can appraise all the scientific evidence and the facts of common experience that have a bearing on the special status of man in the order of nature. It can establish, beyond a reasonable doubt, the conclusion that man differs in kind from all other animals, by virtue of having intellectual powers and powers of action not possessed by them to any degree. It can explain why a human being, and nothing else on earth, is properly regarded as a person. To this extent, philosophy makes contact with the Western religious belief that man and man alone, is made in the image of God, who is also a person, not a thing.[6]

Wow! I hope you are as touched by the significance of this statement as I was when I first read it. It clearly brings together philosophy and Judeo-Christian thought regarding human worth. Believing in a personal God, Dr. Adler sees the important link between the *uniqueness of humankind* and the creative act of God in making us *in His image*.

Adler is not alone in seeing the importance of this relationship, Dr. Francis Schaeffer, a Christian theologian and philosopher and the founder of L'Abri in Switzerland, also brings this connection into clear focus. In his book *He Is There and He Is Not Silent*, he wrote:

> The dilemma of modern man is simple: he does not know why man has any meaning. He is lost. Man remains a zero. This is the damnation of our generation, the heart of modern man's problem. But if we begin with a personal beginning and this is the origin of all else, then the personal does have meaning, and man and his aspirations are not meaningless. Man's aspirations of the reality of personality are in line with what was originally there and what has always intrinsically been.[7]

When modern man began to believe that God did not exist and that the arrival of human life on earth was the result of chance and time, he lost the "frame of reference" that gave life ultimate value and meaning. When we believe that a personal God is there and that He created human beings in His image, then we restore the worth and meaning of human life for all of history. The link between human worth (the psychology of self-esteem) and the Judeo-Christian view of God as our Creator is reaffirmed again by Dr. Schaeffer in his book, *Genesis in Space and Time*:

> The Bible tells me who I am. . . . I do not need to be confused, therefore, between myself and animal life . . . Suddenly I have value, . . . I understand how it is that God can have fellowship with me and give me revelation of a propositional nature. Furthermore, I can see that all men are so differentiated from non-man, and I must look upon them as having great value . . . because of his origin. Thus the flow of history has tremendous implications for every aspect of our lives. I stand in the flow of history. I know my origin. . . . As I look at myself in the flow of space-time reality, I see my origin in Adam and in God's creating man in His own image.[8]

HERE IS HOPE! Here is the answer to WHY you and I, like the sleeping child mentioned earlier, have innate and intrinsic worth and value. The worth of every person around this world, is grounded in the Christian perspective that we are made in God's image.[9] The first record of this great truth is found in the book of Genesis when Moses wrote:

> Then God said, "Let us make man in our image, in our likeness." . . .
> So God created man in his own image, in the image of God he
> created him; male and female he created them... the Lord God
> formed the man from the dust of the ground and breathed into his
> nostrils the breath of life, and *man became a living being*.... God saw
> all that He had made and it was very good (Genesis 1:26-27, 2:7,
> 1:31, italics mine).

Because God exists and we are made in His image, **there is an unbroken line of intrinsic worth, value, goodness and identity that runs from each of us back to God.** Our quest for personal identity ("Who am I?") and personal esteem (What am I worth ?") has been answered! Our quest for a *reasonable* answer to the question of our origin and worth has been satisfied. The noted writer and statesman, William Jennings Bryan, described it this way in his book *In His Image*:

> A reasonable person searches for a reason and all reasons point to a
> God, all-wise, all-powerful, and all-loving. On no other theory can
> we account for what we see about us. It is impossible to conceive of
> the universe, illimitable in extent and seemingly measureless in
> time, as being the result of chance. The reign of law, universal and
> eternal, compels belief in a Law Giver. . . . It is shameful to spend
> the time that God has given for nobler use in vain attempts to
> exclude God from His own universe and to find in chance a substitute
> for God's power and wisdom and love.[10]

A heart warming story that supports this amazing truth can be found in Max Lacado's illustrated book, *You are Special*.[11] This is a must buy book. Briefly, the story goes like this:

In a village at the foot of a hill lived a group of small wooden people known as Wemmicks. All the Wemmicks had been carved by Eli, a woodworker who lived at the top of the hill. He personally made each wooden Wemmick different from the others.

Everyday, all day long the Wemmicks would go around town putting stickers on each other. Gold star stickers were given for being pretty or talented but gray dot stickers were put on those who were not.

Punchinello was one of those Wemmicks who got a lot of gray dots because he often goofed up or made mistakes. Eventually other Wemmicks started saying he was not a good wooden person. Gradually, Punchinello believed them, saying to himself, "I am not a good Wemmick." So he began to hang around other Wemmicks who had lots of gray dots.

Then one day he met Lucia. She did not have any dots or stars. Punchinello asked her why she didn't have any stickers. Her answer was to change his life.

She said she went up the hill everyday to see Eli, the woodcarver and she encouraged Punchinello to go see Eli himself. Doubting whether it would make any difference, Punchinello decided to visit Eli.

To his surprise he found Eli had been waiting to see him and Eli even knew his name! Punchinello also learned that Eli thought he was pretty special because be had made him.

Then Punchinello asked why the stickers didn't stick to Lucia. Eli answered, "Because she has decided that what I think [of her] is more important than what they think. . . . the more you trust my love, the less you care about their stickers."

Just before Punchinello left, Eli had one more point to make, "Remember, you are special because I made you. And I don't make mistakes."

When I first began to see the relationship between my worth and God created me in His image and likeness, I knew my life was never going to be the same. The changes came slowly, but they have been lasting. Let me explain how this happened.

Suggested Reading

1. Schaeffer, Francis A. *Genesis in Space and Time*. Intervarsity Press, 1972.
2. Hough, Lynn Harold. *The Dignity of Man*. Abingdon-Cokesbury Press, 1950.
3. Job 36:5; Psalm 33:6-9,13-15; 100:3-5; 145:8-9,13-14; Proverbs 22:1-2; Isaiah 64:8; 66:1-2; Acts 10:9-29; Galatians 6:3-5; Revelation 4:11.

Can I, looking back on my own life and history, truthfully describe it as an eager quest? Was it I who was all the time seeking an elusive Good, or was I the elusive one, artfully evading a Good that was seeking me? And if haply there has been a finding, is it I who have at last found Him whom I sought, or is it He who has found me? ... And shall the glory now be mine or His? Shall I sing of my achievement or of His gift?

John Baillie, *Invitation to Pilgrimage*[1]

People reach out today—in a complicated, changing, and uncertain world—for a sense of their own individual identity. But they don't want just any kind of identity; what they seek is an identity they can be proud of. They want to know who they are, *and they* want to feel a sense of respect for who they are.

Maxwell Maltz, *The Search for Self-Respect*[2]

People reach out today—in a complicated, changing, and uncertain world—for a sense of their own individual identity. But they don't want just any kind of identity; what they seek is an identity they can be proud of. They want to know who they are, *and they* want to feel a sense of respect for who they are.

Because man is made in the divine image the proper study of mankind is God. He looks with entire astonishment at the discovery that he must study God to find what he himself is like. There is no pride in this. Rather there is stark though glad humility. There is no self-worship. Rather there is awed and yet happy worship of the God who has given to man this amazing gift.

Lynn H. Hough, *The Dignity of Man*[3]

CHAPTER 4

My Choice
to Be an Imagebearer

"Larry, some of what you have said makes sense. But how did you find this perspective and how did this knowledge move from your head to your heart? How did it become real to you so you felt better about yourself?"

Having been asked these questions many times, I thought it might be helpful if I described how I first began to appreciate the significance of my being made in the likeness of God. This truth became real to me in two ways. First, I began to get a better philosophical understanding of what the Bible said about the worth of human life to God. Then *I gave myself permission to feel* how it applied to me personally. The second step came when I started learning how to be more accepting and loving to the person I once was that lived in the memories of my past.

It started in the fall of 1966. Several months earlier I had returned to Oregon from a fifteen-month hitchhiking trip around the world. I traveled through approximately twenty-five countries from Sweden to Portugal, to Israel, Iraq, and Kuwait, to New Zealand, Fiji, and Hawaii. I had lived all my life in the Pacific Northwest, mostly in Cascade Idaho, and I was unprepared for what was going to happen after my return from such an extensive trip. I had just begun working on a Master's degree in New Testament at Wheaton College when I went into a time of deep questioning. I felt depressed, cynical, lost, sarcastic, and alone. As a Christian, I also felt guilt for feeling this way.

This painful and confusing time was caused by re-entry culture shock and what I jokingly call my mid-life crisis (at age twenty-six). The way I had perceived the world before my trip no longer fit what I now knew. The diversity of values, beliefs, customs, religions, and struggles of each culture

I visited called into question my own beliefs and values. The old wine skins of my mind could no longer hold the new wine of my thoughts and experiences. The wine skins were ready to burst.

I began searching for a better way to understand my humanity and my Christian life in light of what I had learned about people around the world. To do this, I made a genuine effort to become more honest with myself and with God about my feelings, conflicts, fears, questions, and personal history.

Facing and Accepting Myself: The Good, the Bad, the Ugly

One important area I began to face with a new honesty was how I viewed myself. Slowly, I began to look at the feelings and opinions I held about myself and tried to understand how I came to picture myself in those ways. I knew the feeling of inferiority had played havoc in my life for years, but I had no idea when it started or in what ways I had tried to cope with it. By accepting my feelings rather than denying or fighting them, I became aware of a major mistake I had made. In the eighth grade I had compared myself to other kids and concluded, "I am not as good as they are," and my feeling of inferiority was born.

From a few specific things, I came to an inaccurate conclusion about myself as a person. It was true that I was not gifted in some areas like math and music. It was also true that I was struggling with a learning disability (probably dyslexia) that no one knew about in those days. In fact, by fourth grade, I had come to believe *I was a dummy*, and I gave up trying to succeed in school. This lasted until the last half of my senior year in high school. Both of these self-opinions were tragic errors in judgment, and the negative impact affected my life for years to come.

Eventually, it became clear I wasn't alone in making this mistake. By observation and from conversations with people around the world, I realized everyone was making this same mistake to some degree. All of us were constantly evaluating and being evaluated on the basis of the things we did. You were somebody by what you did, how much you earned, what you owned, or who you knew. The external proofs of status and importance in one culture meant very little in another.

Obviously, I had my list of external proofs that I was somebody: sports, girlfriends, college degrees, traveling, and "being a good Christian." I worked hard to feel like I was somebody, that I was a good person, but it never lasted. It was a constant struggle; I never felt secure. Returning from the world trip made it look even more hopeless. I could see through the emptiness of people trying to earn their importance. It was a game, a big joke because death mocked it all.

Gradually, I realized I needed a new way to look at myself, a new way to determine my worth and the worth of everyone I had met, a way that was separate and distinct from external criteria. Thinking about the various world views that might be comprehensive enough to fit me and four-and-a-half billion others, the idea of being made in God's image came to mind. The way this happened might sound a bit strange, but I have no doubt it was a gift from God.

One day while sitting in my room thinking about life, my world trip, and all that was happening, I began talking to God about it. My eyes were closed and I was half praying, half reflecting when a picture formed in my mind. Jesus and I were sitting in a love seat in space looking down at the world. We were talking about life and the things that happen between peoples and nations. Suddenly a desire rose in me to ask Jesus what He thought about me personally. Bracing myself against the left side of the love seat, I prepared myself for what I expected Jesus to say: "I love Larry, BUT—he is not reading the Bible enough, he thinks too much about sex, he is too selfish, etc, etc, etc." Instead, I heard: "I feel sad because Larry doesn't know who he is. He doesn't know he is made in God's image."

Surprised by this answer, I was startled back into reality. As I continued to think about what had just happened, deep in my heart I sensed there was something about this idea that could make a difference. That people were created in God's image was not a new idea to me. I had believed in it for years; but now I had been touched by it in my heart. The more I allowed myself to feel the significance of this notion of my being an Imagebearer of God to become a FELT-TRUTH, the more I noticed subtle changes taking place at the center of my being. I began to experience, ever so softly, the feelings of hope, personal worth, and a renewed purpose for my life. Instead of feeling ashamed about being human, I felt a growing sense of dignity in my humanity.

My feelings of inferiority began to slowly decline along with my feelings of depression and cynicism. I felt a gentle release from the pressure of having to strive so hard to prove myself and there was a widening sense of freedom to be a person in my own right. *It was okay to be an ordinary human being.* I also felt a growing sense of integrity and confidence about being human and Christian at the same time.

The changes came slowly but as I gave myself permission to experience the feelings that came from this single truth, my life began to be transformed. The Bible clearly teaches that God is love but now God's love for me became more reasonable and understandable. Now I knew *why* God loved me. I knew I would always be a sinner and would continue to deal with a sinful nature, but God loved me as a person first and then as a sinner. *I could trust* that kind of love.

This simple shift of perspective from Genesis 3 (the sinful fall of mankind) to Genesis 1 (our being created in God's image) changed everything! *It began to transform everything.* It helped me understand and appreciate the love Jesus Christ demonstrated for us when He willingly gave His life on the cross for our salvation. Until this time, it felt paradoxical (a feeling I never shared with anyone) to believe that Jesus would choose to die for a bunch of sinful people who mostly didn't care anyway.

Now I saw with new eyes that Jesus did not die for you and me just because we were sinners. He died for us because he saw us as people made in God's image. **Our sins were the cause, but not the reason He gave His life for us. The reason was He knew our worth.** He saw us as Imagebearers first and sinners second. Jesus didn't die for our sins—He died for us!

This change of perspective changed my whole outlook not only about my worth but also it helped me to see the worth in everyone I met. I began to see in a new way that human worth was given to all people as a gift from God and affirmed by the life and love of the Lord Jesus. Human life has meaning and worth, not by chance, but by God's design. Self esteem was by God's design.

Stepping Up onto the Growing Up Road

As I continued to grow and enjoy the feeling of an improving sense of worth and value, I wanted to begin to live as I was designed to live—as an Imagebearer relating to God and others in open, honest, healthy ways. At that time, to be fully committed to my growing up (as I called it), I made a covenant with myself and with Jesus that involved four major decisions.

1. I decided to end the day by reviewing all the day's events and then thank God for one positive thing I had *experienced* as being good, pleasant, positive, and life-giving. This was hard to do in those early days because my inner world was dark and my outlook on life negative. Over time I began to regain a healthier perspective because I looked for and became more aware of the positive and good aspects of life.

2. I decided I was going to accept ALL my feelings no matter what I had been taught. I didn't have to like them but I did need to identify and own them. I was admitting and accepting what I already knew was true. To act like they didn't exist was lying to myself.

3. I decided I was going to be in charge of my choices and quit being such a pleaser. My habit was to do almost anything for anybody to make them happy, even if it meant betraying myself and suffering for it. I had a terrible time saying no without feeling guilty. Now I was going to grow up and be in charge of my choices and choose life as best I could one day at a time.

4. Because I had been so private about my thoughts and feelings, I decided

to become more verbally open and transparent. No longer was I going to hide inside myself and let people think they knew me when I knew they didn't.

Unknowingly, I had just given myself permission to reclaim four of the natural human abilities that God has given to us as people made in His image. I knew these decisions were good because I began to experience life-giving changes in my daily life. It was really hard to do at first, but as each day, week, and month passed, I felt healthier, stronger, and more positive about life. My life has never been the same.

Learning to Accept the Kid I Was in the Past

As my sense of worth grew and became more secure, I knew I was not working alone. I had read in Isaiah 9:6 that Jesus was called the "Wonderful Counselor." Having never talked with anyone about my inner world, I tried to imagine what it would been like to talk to a counselor who could be trusted and who was caring, skilled, knowledgeable, and safe. Picturing Jesus that way, I started talking to Him about everything, even my darkest childhood secrets. I began to practice doing what King David encouraged us to do in one of his poems, "Trust in him [God] at all times, O People; pour out your heart before him, for God is our refuge" (Psalm 62:8).

Slowly, I opened up and started "pouring out my heart to Him" about a lot of personal things from my past. I talked to Him about my natural father who had left when I was about seven years old. We did not meet again until I was thirty-three. I talked to Him about my Dad and his struggle with alcohol and the fighting that went on in our home in those years before we became Christians. I talked to God about my sexuality, including the time I was molested as a kid. I opened up about how I became trapped in my secrets, not knowing what to do with the feelings of shame, fear, guilt, and distrust. I talked to Him about my learning problems as a boy and how it affected my image of myself as a student, even in graduate school.

And need I say more about my high school or college years? Learning how to accept and love the boy I was in the past was painful but freeing. Knowing that my worth came from being created in God's image gave me the *courage* to be honest with myself and with God. I also kept reminding myself of the statement King David made when he wrote: "Remember not the sins of my youth and my rebellious ways; according to your love remember me, for You are good, O Lord" (Psalm 25:7).

In quiet and supportive ways, God brought people, books and ideas into my life that encouraged my growth and healing. Some call it recovery; I called it "growing up". It was at this time I found the book, *The Transparent Self* by Sydney Jourard. What he wrote was exactly what I needed to encourage me to continue my growth. Someone also introduced me to the books written by Dr. Francis Schaeffer. Even though I was overwhelmed by so much information, the truth that we are made in God's image reinforced what I had experienced earlier in my prayers.

As I grew in my acceptance, love, and compassion for the person I once was, the scales of self-esteem continued to come back into balance. I could see more clearly that my worth could never be lost or taken from me by any of my past experiences. I may have lost my innocence, my self-esteem, my perspective, but I never stopped being made in God's image. I was loved and valued simply for the way God designed me—to be a person like He is a person. Nothing I had done or failed to do, nothing that had been done to me could take that away. Based on this perspective I began to love and accept the person I once was no matter what age I looked at in my past. I was learning how to love myself as God loved me—true biblical self love.

Total Commitment to Being an Imagebearer

Eventually, I concluded that it was the Judeo-Christian faith that revealed HOW we received the unique human qualities that set us apart from the rest of creation, and psychology showed me WHAT those unique attributes were. The diagram on the next page shows this new addition to the scale of self-esteem.

For the next several years I researched what it meant to be made in God's image. In time I came to believe there are eight gifts that God bestowed on us as bearers of His image that make us a person like He is a person. These eight gifts are the ability to feel (experience unique emotions), to choose (be self-determining), to think (use reason), to communicate (use of symbolic-conceptual language), and to create (exercise creativity). We are also gifted with moral awareness (a conscience), self-awareness (self-consciousness), and spiritual awareness (spirituality).

Over the years I have become convinced that the inner security and peace that come from experiencing our worth from being made in God's image is one of the most important truths we can learn in life. Even though Albert Ellis and I are worlds apart in our views of the origin of human life, we agree on the changes that come into a person's life once they become convinced that their worth is in their BEING, not in their DOING. He wrote:

> I find that once patients are convinced that they are worthy just by
> *being*, they stop feeling so anxious about accomplishment. They, then,
> no longer think that they must be perfectly achieving in what they do
> or don't do. This is true because their previous anxiety to achieve,
> to be loved, to set the world on fire, originated in the underlying
> feeling (belief) that "only in this way can I become worthwhile."[4]

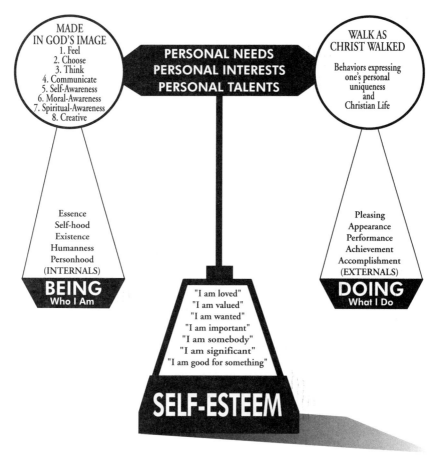

I Offer This Gift to You

For years you may have been searching for a way to feel better about yourself. I certainly did. I encourage you to give this perspective some serious thought. In making you in His image, God placed a worth on your life that can never be taken away by anyone or anything. Your life is sacred.

Whatever your background or experiences, however good or bad you have lived your life, you can learn to accept, forgive, and like yourself better because God loves you and cares about your well-being. Let's see how this perspective is given further proof in the Bible.

Suggested Reading

1. Seamands, David. *Healing of Memories*. Victor Books, 1986.
2. Schuller, Robert H. *Self-Love*. Hawthorn Books, 1969.
3. Psalm 16:11; 23:1-6; 24:1; 31:14-15; 33:13-15; 121:1-2; Isaiah 42:5.

The word "esteem" literally means to appreciate the worth of. Why do men stand in awe of the stars and the moon, the immensity of the sea, the beauty of a flower or a sunset, and at the same time downgrade themselves? Did not the same Creator make man? Is not man himself the most marvelous creation of all? This appreciation of your own worth is not egotism unless you assume that you made yourself and should take some of the credit.

Maxwell Maltz, *Psycho-Cybernetics*[1]

The loss of the assurance that man has been made in the divine image is one of the most tragic experiences which can come to man. There is no adequate compensation ... He is an orphan in the universe if he has lost the sense of the unique mark which God has made upon his life.

Lynn H. Hough, *The Dignity of Man*[2]

What is at stake in our civilization is whether man shall remain—or re-become—a sacred thing. Let us do what we can for our part to restore man to his dignity by showing how Christianity makes of man in all his entirety a mystery rooted in the Holy.

Jean Mouroux, *The Meaning of Man*[3]

CHAPTER 5

God, the
Master Designer

King David held a unique place in Hebrew history (1040-970 B.C.). As a shepherd boy who became the second king of Israel, he had a feeling for life that was unmatched by his peers. His openness for a personal relationship with God as Creator earned him the title, "man after God's own heart" (1 Samuel 13:4). I believe David held this title more for his views of God and mankind than because of his daily conduct.

As a shepherd boy, he spent countless hours sitting alone. He studied the wonders of natural life around him during the day or gazing wistfully at the star-filled sky at night, a silvery-white moon hanging in space. They were a display of the power and splendor of God's creative handiwork (Psalm 19:1). Psalm 8 also reflects some of the wonder and awe he felt when he saw himself against the vast backdrop of space. The beauty of nature touched him deeply: emotionally, intellectually, and spiritually. No one can fully appreciate David's feelings when he wrote, "O Lord, our Lord how majestic is your name in all the earth! You have set your glory above the heavens. From the lips of children and infants you have ordained praise . . . " (Psalm 8:1-2).

Once while reflecting on the wonders of creation, he became philosophical and asked some of the heart-felt questions we have all asked at one time or another: "Who am I?" "Why am I here?" "What's the meaning of all this?" "Why would God care for human beings?" Sensing his own insignificance when compared to the great expanse of the heavens, he wondered what there was about humankind that would attract the personal attention of the Creator.

When I consider your heavens, the work of your fingers, the moon and the stars, which you have set in place, what is man that you are mindful of him, and the son of man that you care for him? (Psalm 8:3-4).

David wrote many psalms reflecting the sovereignty, wonder and glory of God. That's why his answer to these questions has great relevance for us today. It affirms the unique and significant place people hold in God's creation because of how we were created: "You [God] made him [us] a little lower than the heavenly beings and crowned him [us] with glory and honor" (Psalm 8:5).

Crowned with Glory and Honor

What an affirming picture David had of the origin of man in contrast to what many people would have us believe since the publication of the *Origin of the Species* by Charles Darwin in 1859. David went back to his view of creation as the foundation for human dignity and worth. He knew why God cared for us. God cares because He designed the human being in a special way and by doing so bestowed on us glory and honor. We are a part of God's great universe yet distinct from it. In this way, God could show His creative design in how He made man and by that design bring glory to Himself and worth to us. Being unique from other creatures, we are the special objects of God's personal love. Our ability to have a personal relationship with God gives us a special place in creation. We belong here! We are wanted and valued! Like David, understanding and experiencing this truth can fill us with a sense of worship. "Oh Lord, our Lord, how majestic is your name in all the earth" (Psalm 8:9).

A Panoramic View of Life from Outer Space

This psalm is special to me because it records the experience of a person being awe-struck by the boundlessness of the heavens, and yet seeing with *spiritual eyes* the significance God places on human life. Using only his imagination, David projected himself into space, looked back at the earth, and grasped some of the wonder of it all. He saw that even in the context of an awe-inspiring universe mankind stands in distinct contrast to the rest of what God has made. We were designed for nobility and worth.

More than three thousand years later, we have been privileged to see our world from outer space through the lens of a television camera aboard a spacecraft. Astronauts have seen the earth the size of a basketball or even a marble; yet, a few days earlier, they were involved in the daily activities of life in their own homes and neighborhoods.

This phenomenon of experiencing two kinds of reality about human existence had a transforming impact on the lives of most of the American astronauts. Colonel James Irwin, who flew on the 1971 Apollo 15 moon-landing mission, described how this experience affected him in his book *To Rule the Night*.

> As we reached out in a physical way to the heavens, we were moved spiritually. As we flew into space we had a new sense of ourselves, of the earth, and of the nearness of God. We were outside of ordinary reality; *I sensed the beginning of some sort of deep change taking place inside of me.* Looking back at that spaceship we call earth, I was touched by a desire to convince man that he has a unique place to live, that he is a unique creature, and that he must learn to live with his neighbors (italics mine).[4]

While looking back at earth, the orderliness of the universe, the six billion people who inhabit this planet, and the uniqueness of the human being, what explanation would satisfy the questions: "What is it all here for?" "Could all this just have happened by chance or is there a Divine Being behind the universe?" "Does human life have ultimate meaning or are we just cosmic accidents?" "What gives my life personal meaning and direction?" "By what rules do I live my life in my relationships with others?"

There are only two explanations for the origin of human life and we have to decide which one to take to heart and follow. One explanation says, "It all happened by chance. There is no God and we are only the product of cosmic chance" (what Schaeffer calls the impersonal plus time plus chance). The other answer says, "Life came by design. God is there and we were created in His image and likeness. This makes human life intentional, purposeful, valued and sacred."

Both explanations require us to exercise our faith by choosing which one we will trust to build our lives upon—but their impact on our lives are worlds apart.

I hope that both reason and faith will lead us to believe in the conclusions David expressed in Psalm 8 and what James Irwin described upon his return from his moon flight. Observing creation and human life from that distant panorama, we can not help but feel humbled, yet honored that God values, loves, and cares for what He has made. In his book, *Does God Exist*, the distinguished Catholic theologian, Hans Küng, expressed it this way:

> This earth of ours is a speck of dust in comparison with the totality of the Milky Way, which includes some hundred billion individual stars, one of them being the sun. . . . The more, then, I reflect on the amazing conclusions of astrophysics and, again, like human beings from time immemorial, look up into the clear night sky, am I not to

wonder what it all means, where it all comes from? To answer, "Out of nothing," is no explanation. Reason cannot be satisfied with that. The only serious alternative . . . is that *the whole stems from that first creative cause of causes, which we call God and indeed the Creator God.* . . . Believing in the Creator of the world means affirming in enlightened trust that the world and man do not remain inexplicable in their ultimate source, that the world and man are not pointlessly hurled from nothing into nothing, but that in their totality they are meaningful and valuable.[5]

Hans Küng is right. Human life, your life, my life has meaning, value and purpose. This becomes even more personal when we think of God, not just as a Creator, but as our Heavenly Father. It is this view of God that Jesus emphasized most in his teachings. Paster Robert Schuller expressed it this way:

A high sense of self-worth based on the Fatherhood of God gives us a deep foundation for a faith and philosophy that can build hope for human dignity! . . . we are children of God. The tragedy is that too many human beings have never discovered their divine heritage . . .[6]

An example of discovering one's heritage on a human level was experienced by my wife Gail in 1996. She had almost no contact with her Grandparents so she had little interest in her family history. We were on vacation in Cascade, Idaho when she remembered that her Great Grandfather had homesteaded somewhere in the area in the 1890's.

Gail's relatives had immigrated to the United States in the 1860's from North Wales to work in the slate quarries in Vermont. Her Great Grandfather Humphrey Humphreys then came west with the Lathrop wagon train and settled on a homestead in Valley County near Cascade. He married and raised thirteen children on one hundred and sixty acres of farm and timber land. So we decided to find the family homestead. As we researched the records at the title company and talked to the "old timers" in the area, we located the farm – an open field at the foot of a mountain range. We were thrilled to find it.

I encouraged Gail to walk onto the property by herself so she could experience what it was like to walk where her Great Grandfather and Grandfather had walked. I watched her quietly walk on to the land and shortly she came back crying softly. Standing on the land where her ancestors had lived caused her to suddenly feel a deep, personal connection to her blood heritage. She felt she belonged here because Great Grandpa Humphreys had "made a place for me".

As we talked we realized how sad it is that God, our divine ancestor, had created a place for us on this beautiful earth, that we belong here, that we are his children, that he crowned us with honor and glory, and yet so few of us have ever felt the deep connection we have to our divine heritage. Two years later Gail and I traveled to Wales to make an even deeper connection to her family history. Maybe this is what the Psalmest wants us to know when he wrote:

> Know that the Lord is God. It is he who made us, and we are his; we are his people, the sheep of his pasture . . . For the Lord is good and his love endures forever; his faithfulness continues through all generations (Psalm 100:3,5).

God has bestowed on us dignity and worth simply because of our origin, our divine roots. This is why we can affirm what the United States Constitution defends: "All men are created equal" . . . created equal in worth because every human being on earth is created in God's image. Every member of the human family has a divine heritage that gives them worth and identity as a human being. As we shall see in the next chapter, our worth is bestowed on us at conception.

Suggested Reading

1. McDowell, Josh. *His Image My Image*. Here's Life Publishers, 1984.
2. Dr. James Dobson, *Hide or Seek: How to Build Self-Esteem in Your Child*. Revised Edition, Fleming H. Revell Company, 1994.
3. Nehemiah 9:6; Psalm 24:1; 95:6-7; Proverbs 14:31; Jeremiah 10:12; Zephaniah 3:17; Zechariah 12:1.

Ever since men have suppressed God they have lost the concept of personhood. . . . He no longer understands himself and he lives in confusion. . . . The Bible portrays man as the masterpiece of God and his unhappiness as the consequence of the misuse of this masterpiece.

Paul Tournier,
The Whole Person in a Broken World[1]

By "person" we mean to convey the idea that man is a being with the power of self-conscious decision, a being with intelligence, emotions, and will. We are saying that he is morally free. We are saying that he is sacred. In making man in his own image, God made him a person, a being with . . . the power to say I AM—I am a *self*.

Earl Martin, *Toward Understanding God*[2]

O man, scorn not that which is admirable in you! You are a poor thing in your own eyes, but I would teach you that in reality you are a great thing! . . . Realize what you are! Consider your royal dignity! The heavens have not been made in God's image as you have, nor the moon, nor the sun, nor anything to be seen in creation. . . . Behold, of all that exists there is nothing that can contain your greatness."

Gregory of Nyssa, *4th Century A.D.*[3]

CHAPTER 6

The Human Being:
A Marvel of Creative Design

On March 9, 1979, I had an experience I'll never forget. On that day my first and only child was born. I had the privilege of seeing my son born even though it was a caesarean birth. As I saw the doctor lift the baby from the womb I thought, "So this is the one I have felt kicking in the night. This is God's newborn Imagebearer." Kent James Day was typed on the birth certificate and a new person was introduced into this world.

Even though I never saw the physical development of Kent during pregnancy, modern technology has allowed us to see special documentaries on the growth and development of the human fetus. We have been allowed to enter the secret chamber of the womb to witness the wonder of how a single egg and sperm become a person. It is nothing short of awesome!

What is sad is that we can feel such a sense of pride, wonder, and awe at the birth of our children but feel that our birth was no big deal, maybe it was even a big mistake. When we begin to feel the same sense of wonder about our birth, our newborn life, as we do about our child or any child, we will began to experience the healing in the message expressed by David in Psalm 139.

Fearfully and Wonderfully Made

In the last chapter we saw how David was impressed with the beauty and wonder of nature. Now we will see how he also stood in awe of the marvelous way a baby develops in its mother's womb. David's sense of personal worth was deeply affirmed by seeing the connection between God as Creator and the development of himself as a new born human being. He wrote:

For you created my inmost being; you knit me together in my mother's womb. I praise you because I am fearfully and wonderfully made; your works are wonderful, I know that full well. (Psalm 139:13-14, italics mine).

An outpouring of praise is the natural response of our heart when we realize how unique and precious we were as a baby both in body and being. When we look at a newborn, we are touched by how dainty their physical features are and we stand in awe of this miniature person. Yet, hidden inside their body is something even more awesome—their being, their personality, the essence of their humanness. When we can see with spiritual eyes and feel in our heart the wonder of the design of our being, praise and worship of the Designer is the natural response. Worship of God is deepened when we come to a new appreciation of our worth. We are bestowing honor on the Person who designed us in His image.

But it is difficult for genuine thankfulness, gratitude, and appreciation to come from a heart that is filled with pictures of a person who feels they are no good, unwanted, or a nobody, or who feels they do not deserve to exist. One of my clients summarized it so clearly when she said, "I really felt like I didn't deserve to be alive—like somehow I should apologize and say, 'I am sorry for my existence.' "

People and circumstances can make us feel that our existence is some kind of mistake or accident. In contrast, David gives us a simple, clear, personal testimony of the positive effect a healthy view of God and a proper view of our design and birth can have on our core sense of worth and identity.

Human life is sacred (your life is sacred) and nowhere is it more easily demonstrated and experienced than when we look into the face of a newborn. Just as a child bears witness to the existence of his parents, our being made in God's image bears witness to the personhood of God. It can also reassure us of God's desire to have a relationship with us in positive, healthy, and life-giving ways. This is how Dr. Schaeffer affirmed the significance of these connections:

The universe speaks of God as a person. **When God made man in his own image, he stated something more fully about himself than he has in any other part of the whole scope of the universe.** Angels would also speak of this, but the Bible's emphasis is on man, and it is man that we all know. In the midst of that which is, there is something personal—man. And this gives evidence of the personality of the great Creator of the whole. If God had stopped his creation with the machine or the plant or the animal, there would have been no such testimony. But by making man in his own image, the triune

God who communicates and who loves prior to the creation of all else had created something that reflects his personality, his communication and his love [bold mine].[4]

It may be hard to fully grasp the implications of what Dr. Schaeffer is saying. Imagine for a moment the significance this places on our lives when we were conceived and born as newly arrived bearers of God's Image. *Our being born a person, a human being, displayed something more fully about God than did anything else in the world.* Our unique qualities of personality point to God our Creator.

Lee Strobel did a great job supporting this perspective in his recent book, *The Case for a Creator.* This award winning journalist and former atheist writes about the compelling evidence for an intelligent designer found in the fields of cosmology, physics, astronomy, biochemistry, biology and DNA research, and in human consciousness (what I call in this book, self-awareness). When we add to self-awareness the other seven attributes of feeling, choosing, thinking, communication, moral awareness, spiritual awareness and creativity, we see what Strobel calls, "the evidence of God's fingerprint" in our unique human design. He wrote,

> Amazingly, many scientists and philosophers are now concluding that the laws of physics and chemistry cannot explain the experience of consciousness in human beings. . . . They cite its very existence as strong evidence . . . in favor of a creator who imbued humankind in his image.[5]

Insight into the divine origin of our worth can bring deep personal and spiritual healing and meaning to our lives. It can touch the core of our sense of identity with a healing affirmation that can transform our negative self-opinions into positive ones.

To experience what David wrote, we need to begin to daily remind ourselves of the phrase, "I am fearfully and wonderfully made in the likeness of God." We need to say it *out loud* and with a little more meaning each day. We shouldn't be surprised if a lot of "ya buts" cross our mind that try to block this truth from getting into our heart; that's pretty normal. For years we have carried inside these deeply felt negative self-opinions and we have told ourselves about them "a thousand times."

It would be natural to discredit any new information that would be different from what we have always believed about ourselves. We are used to feeling negative about ourselves but by being open to experiencing new feelings, we can gradually accept this new view as applying to us personally. As this truth moves from our head to our heart, we begin to experience feelings like awe, wonder, joy, relief, gratefulness, sadness, and tears. This is the link between worship and self-esteem—"I praise you God because I am fearfully and wonderfully made" (Psalm 139:14).

The more we appreciate the significance of our design the more thankful we feel to God for the gift of His image. We respond naturally by wanting to praise God personally and publically for His love. His love is unconditional and our worth is innate and unconditional. Neither can be earned or taken away; they can only be appreciated and enjoyed.

Once this happens we will feel a desire to affirm the worth and value of those around us. It is easier to give to others what we have come to appreciate for ourselves. The implications of accepting God's estimate of our worth are beyond comprehension. It will have a positive impact on our marriages, families, churches, schools, and communities.

God Cares about the Daily Affairs of Our Lives

Once this connection is experienced we are in a position to know why God continues to care about the daily affairs of our lives. This is the second great truth of Psalm 139. David was aware that God knew every detail of his life—his feelings, thoughts, motives, and behaviors. God was intimately acquainted with all his ways from the best of the best to the worst of the worst. What touched David was the awareness that God still truly cared for him. This is how he wrote about it:

> O Lord, you have searched me and you know me. You know when I sit and when I rise; you perceive my thoughts from afar. You discern my going out and my lying down; you are familiar with all my ways. . . . Where can I go from your Spirit? Where can I flee from your presence? If I go up to the heavens, you are there; if I make my bed in the depths, you are there. If I rise on the wings of the dawn, if I settle on the far side of the sea, even there your hand will guide me, your right hand will hold me fast. . . . How precious to me are your thoughts, O God! How vast is the sum of them! Were I to count them, they would outnumber the grains of sand. When I awake, I am still with you (Psalm 139:1-3,7-10,17-18).

What a contrast to the experiences of many people today who believe that God does not exist or who have, by choice or by default, relegated God to such a minor role that He is irrelevant in their outlook on life. If God does not exist or does not care, then the importance of a human life can only be determined by oneself or by society. In his book *Kingdoms in Conflict*, Charles Colson shows what the logical conclusions are for such a position.

The death of God ultimately spells the death of what it means to be truly human. For if worth is not God-given, it must be established by man. And atheistic philosophies, such as the Soviet system, treat man as an object whose value is determined solely by his usefulness to society. . . . Christianity can never be utilitarian; it holds every human being as precious because human beings are created in the image of God.[5]

Our lives are significant because we are Imagebearers of God. We are not just highly sophisticated animals who die and become expensive worm food! People intuitively know this. But where atheistic philosophies (Nietzche, Sarte), atheistic governmental systems (China), or atheistic psychologies (Freud, Ellis) have left a great spiritual void in both individual lives and in societies, certain tenets of the New Age Movement are now trying to fill.[6] Some people are convinced that New Age teaching is the true path of enlightenment, love, and peace. Emphasis on the beliefs that we are god, that we are part of one big cosmic spiritualness, is now competing with atheistic humanism and Christianity for the hearts and minds of people.

Sadly, the philosophy behind the New Age Movement is as empty in content as is atheism. Any belief system that interprets the word "God" to mean a metaphor rather than a person is ultimately letting its believers down. Life is not just spiritual self-stimulation.

The message David proclaimed in Psalm 139 has both content and experience. God exists—a sovereign, creative, caring, personal God—and we are fearfully and wonderfully designed in His image. These are ultimate truths on which to build one's sense of worth and identity. We can experience the feelings of personal worth and security knowing that God cares for and values what He has made. This has all been made clear to us because of Jesus and what He accomplished on the cross on our behalf.

Appreciating that we are fearfully and wonderfully made does not mean we will not fail. As we shall see in the next chapter, the same person who gave us Psalm 139 also made some wrong and sinful choices. One choice even led to the murder of another human being.

Suggested Reading

1. Brand, Dr. Paul, and Philip Yancey. *Fearfully and Wonderfully Made.* Zondervan Publishing House, 1980. Also: *In His Image.* Zondervan Publishing House, 1984.
2. Strobel, Lee. *The Case For a Creator.* Zondervan Publishing House, 2004.
3. Deuteronomy 32:6; Job 12:10; Psalm 119:73, 76-77; Isaiah 46:4; Malachi 2:10a.

It is dangerous to make man see too clearly his equality with the brutes without showing him his greatness. It is also dangerous to make him see his greatness too clearly, apart from his vileness. It is still more dangerous to leave him in ignorance of both. . . . Let man now know his value. Let him love himself, for there is in him a nature capable of good; but let him not for this reason love the vileness which is in him.

Blaise Pascal, *Pascal's Pensées*[1]

Every man thus created, whether he is a sinner . . . or in human eyes a saint, has a dignity in our eyes because of the personal being that God has given to him. Having given this dignity of personal being to man, God also values it . . .

David Cairns, *The Image of God in Man*[2]

The feeling of being important to Christ and to each other was intended to be the normal experience of our lives. . . . Christians who believe we should negate self . . . fail to stress that humankind also has great worth to God. . . . We are fallen sinners, yet we still were created in God's image . . . which gives all humankind intrinsic worth.

Josh McDowell, *Building Your Self-Image*[3]

CHAPTER 7

God Sees People
as Worth Forgiving

*H*e sat slumped in the chair, fighting back the tears as he told me what he had done. Slowly, he revealed how he had gotten sexually involved in a relationship he knew was wrong. For years, he had bottled up his feelings, but the pressure had become too great. Now words and tears poured from his heart like water from an overfilled cup.

His pain was greater than that of the average person because he was married and in full-time Christian work. In his opinion, he was the worst hypocrite alive. His self-esteem was gone and the guilt he felt had drained the joy from his life. He wondered if he would ever be freed from the pain of self-hate that ruled his life. All his prayers for forgiveness failed to ease the burden he felt making him feel even more guilty, confused, and hopeless.

Being an ordinary, fallible human being, he had failed in a way he never believed possible. In the past he had always felt self-righteous and spiritually superior to others who had failed or "done bad things." Now the consequences of his choices were devastating to his feelings about God, his feelings about himself, and his outlook for his Christian life and ministry.

Gradually, he finished his story and I felt I had been allowed into the secret world of his heart. At that vulnerable moment he needed to be treated with the respect to which he was entitled as a person made in God's image. I needed to respond to him as I imagined Jesus would have done—with compassion, acceptance, honesty, grace, and truth. He knew he was a sinner. What he needed was to be reassured that *God saw him as a person worth forgiving.*

As ordinary human beings, we all have things we wish we could erase from our memory. We did things or things were done to us that have kept our spirits in bondage to the feelings of anger, rage, fear, guilt, and shame. Which one of these words touch the memory of our past that's hidden in the secret chambers of our hearts: stealing, incest, embezzlement, murder, rape, tax evasion, adultery, insurance fraud, abortion, molestation, beatings, lying, promiscuity, abandonment, pornography, same sex encounters, sex with animals, cheating, divorce?

Psychological and spiritual restoration and healing from memories like these is possible if we could accomplish three things. First, we need to expand and improve our impressions of God. For most of us, our concept of God is too small or inaccurate. The awfulness of our situation or the seriousness of our failure becomes bigger than our sense of who God is.

Second, in the darkest times in our lives, we are in a position to come to a new and deeper appreciation for what Jesus Christ accomplished on our behalf. Jesus' ministry as Savior and High Priest was meant for these kinds of situations. We can personally experience the healing effect of Jesus' love and forgiveness when we face our situation honestly, knowing He affirmed His love for us at the cross.

Third, we need to deal with the self-esteem "stuff"—the old self-pictures that return from our childhood memories when we got into trouble for doing bad things. Our worth and our sinfulness become so entangled we feel they are one. It's natural to feel the guilt and shame of our sinfulness and lose perspective about our worth. We see ourselves as an awful sinner but we can't see we are also an Imagebearer.

It is important to learn to separate these issues—our worth from our sins (worth ◄———► sins). We need to understand that deep down inside, underneath it all, there is something significant about us that is totally separate from being sinful, fallen, and in need of forgiveness. Dr. Schaeffer had an interesting way of describing this difference. He wrote:

> Man's sin causes all these separations between man and God, man and himself, man and man, and man and nature. The simple fact is that in wanting to be what man as a creature could not be, man lost what he could be. . . . But there is one thing which he did not lose, and that is his mannishness, his being a human being. Man still stands in the image of God—twisted, broken, abnormal, but still the image-bearer of God. Man did not stop being human. . . . In the Bible's teaching man is fallen but significant.[4]

Which Picture Do You See?

There is an interesting picture of a lady that can help us grasp the importance of separating our worth (our significance) from our sinfulness (our fallenness). I use it to illustrate many different things, but one of the most important areas in which I use it is to help people improve their understanding of their sense of worth and significance.

Look at the picture for a few moments. When you think you see the lady, note her age and appearance and then continue reading.

Which lady did you see, the old woman who looks tired and grumpy or the young, pretty one who seems to be dressed in high fashion? Yes, there are two images in this one picture and I want you to be able to see both. If you saw the old woman first, then you know she has a big nose and hooked chin. Her mouth seems partially open and she has sad eyes that are looking down. She is wearing a fur shawl and a feather comes out of her hair.

The other image is a young, pretty lady, also wearing the fur shawl and a choker necklace. She is looking back over her right shoulder and has a pretty chin and long eyelashes. Have you seen them both yet? If you haven't it may help to know that the young girl's necklace is the old lady's mouth, and the nose of the old lady is the chin of the pretty girl.

What the picture illustrates is when our mind forms a conclusion as to what we see, it can be difficult to see another alternative. We have to develop a conscious strategy to try to get the images to flip so we can see the second picture. When it finally does reverse and we see the second image, we *physically feel the shift* of perspective that happens inside us. It may flip back to the first image quite easily but with practice and familiarity, we can move back and forth between the two images with ease.

The same is true about understanding our worth. This picture illustrates how easy it is for us to see ourselves as a sinner (the old lady). We are familiar with seeing ourselves as a sinful, bad, evil, carnal person and we have many Bible verses to support it. And the fact is, it's true.

But it's also important to note and that we are also Imagebearers (the young lady). Knowledge of our sinfulness without a knowledge of our nobility leads to self-hate. A knowledge of our nobility without a knowledge of our sinfulness leads to arrogance and pride. We are both the pretty lady and the old lady; we are both noble (Genesis 1) and sinful (Genesis 3). I have been emphasizing the worth and importance of human life, not to discredit or to minimize the truthfulness of our sinfulness, but to try to bring a better sense of balance between the two. Like the picture of the two ladies, I want us to see and accept both our beauty as Imagebearers and our ugliness as sinners.

Let's Put Things Into Perspective

To help us put this into perspective, Let me draw our attention to two people—Adolf Hitler and Mother Teresa. Both were created in God's image but their personal lives impacted our world from opposite ends of the continuum.

Hitler used his human abilities (feeling, thinking, choosing, etc.) to bring about the most hideous human atrocities imaginable. He brought darkness, death, and destruction to this world in an unprecedented fashion.

In contrast, Mother Teresa uses her human abilities to bring food, medicine, and shelter to those she calls "the poorest of the poor." She and her helpers work among the sick, forgotten, homeless, rejects of the rejects bringing love, life, and light where only death and darkness seemed to reign.

Any of us could become like them because our ability to choose makes it possible to do both great evil or great good. Some of us do more evil than good; while others of us do more good than evil. Because this is true, everyone is in need of God's love, mercy, and forgiveness. It is imperative that we separate human worth from human sinfulness and self-worth from salvation. We will talk about this in greater detail later in the book.

Good People Make Bad Choices

Why are these distinctions important? Because I want to make it clear that FORGIVENESS ONLY MAKES SENSE IF WE ARE WORTH FORGIVING. People do not forgive someone if they cannot see their worth or value; we cannot forgive ourselves if we can't see our worth and value. But when we see the good in them—the good in us—we can forgive.

This doesn't mean that a person's wrong actions are to be minimized or excused away. Things they have done that are illegal or morally wrong need to be confronted and punished. If their crimes are bad enough they may have to be removed from normal society for life.

Seeing the good in someone is seeing them as made in God's image—and what God made is good (Genesis 1:31). Thousands of people can give testimony to how their lives were changed for the better because someone *saw the good in them*. No matter how bad they had been, someone treated them with love and respect and it made a difference. Someone believed in them.

Believe in the God Who Sees the Good in You: David's Story

As we have seen, having personal worth and value does not mean we will automatically do the right things. David was a good man, and yet, he didn't always choose to do what was right. As the King of Israel, he could have married any single woman he wanted for a wife; but when he saw Bathsheba, a beautiful woman who was already married, he wanted her. So he set in motion a chain of events that eventually led him to commit adultery with Bathsheba. He also had her husband, Uriah, intentionally killed in battle so he could have his wife.

When Nathan, a prophet of God, confronted David with the wrong he had done, David's conscience was stricken and his heart broke in remorse (2 Samuel 12:13). David wrote a moving personal account of his experience in Psalm 51 and Psalm 103. He talked about God, sin, and human sinfulness hundreds of years before Christ was born. He did not have the teachings of the New Testament to help him; yet what David wrote is as true today as it was almost three thousand years ago.

David was aware of how people are born with a nature and the freedom to do wrong. Even more significantly, he demonstrated how psychological and spiritual healing and restoration occurs when a person is honest with themselves and with God. David wrote:

> Have mercy on me, O God, according to your unfailing love; according to your great compassion blot out my transgressions. Wash away all my iniquity and cleanse me from my sin. For I know my transgressions, and my sin is always before me. Against you, you only, have I sinned and done what is evil in your sight, so that you are proved right when you speak and justified when you judge. Surely I was sinful at birth, sinful from the time my mother conceived me. Surely you desire truth in the inner parts; you teach me wisdom in the inmost place. Cleanse me with hyssop, and I will be clean; wash me, and I will be whiter than snow. . . . Create in me a pure heart, O God, and renew a steadfast spirit within me. . . . Restore to me the joy of your salvation and grant me a willing spirit, to sustain me. Then I will teach transgressors your ways, and sinners will turn back to you (Psalm 51:1-7,10,12-13).

For David, forgiveness and healing began with a proper view of God. God was a God of "unfailing love," a God of "great compassion," a God who is "right . . . and justified when he judges," a God who responds to a broken heart of repentance by forgiving and gradually restoring the joy of life to those who come to Him honestly and openly. The God David believed in is a God who loves and who believes in people and sees the good in them (who sees His image in them). He is one who responds affirmingly to the broken hearted (Psalm 51:17).

A broken and humbled heart is not a heart filled with self-condemnation and self-hate; it is heart filled with sorrow, remorse, regret, and hope. Sorrow because a great wrong had been committed and people were hurt. Hope because God is a God who cleanses from sin, restores the joy of salvation, and creates a new heart in those who face their failures and wrongs with honesty and openness. Hope because God is a God who values us and desires a relationship with the people He created in His image. **We are forgiven not because we deserve it but because we are worth it.**

Forgiveness means: "Thank you, God, for not holding my sins against me." (*see* Mark 11:25; Acts 7:60; 2 Timothy 4:16.) When *personal worth* is separated from *personal sinfulness forgiveness makes spiritual and psychological sense.*

David reaffirmed these truths again in Psalm 103. He reminds us what God is like and then who we are as people He created. As we have seen in Psalm 139, a proper understanding of these two truths is directly linked to the feelings of worship and thankfulness that come from knowing we have been forgiven. He wrote:

> Praise the Lord, O my soul; *all my inmost being*, praise his holy name. Praise the Lord, O my soul, and forget not all his benefits— who *forgives* all your sins and *heals* all your diseases, who *redeems* your life from the pit and *crowns* you with love and compassion. . . . The Lord is compassionate and gracious, slow to anger, abounding in love. . . . He does not treat us as our sins deserve or repay us according to our iniquities. For as high as the heavens are above the earth, so great is his love for those who fear him; as far as the east is from the west, so far has he removed our transgressions from us. As a father has compassion on his children, so the Lord has compassion on those who fear him; for he knows how we are formed, he remembers that we are dust (Psalm 103:1-5,8,10-14, italics mine).

David found comfort in remembering who God is: compassionate, gracious, forgiving, and great in His loving kindness. David also found comfort in the knowledge that God remembers that we were made from dust. God knows we are not perfect. We are both finite and fallen.

The Christian view of life builds on these great truths. It affirms our worth as human beings inspite of our sinfulness. The Apostle Paul wrote, "God demonstrated his own love for us in this: while we were still sinners, Christ died for us" (Romans 5:8). **The cross of Jesus is the greatest affirmation of our worth we could ever hope to find.**

Anyone, anytime, anywhere under any circumstance can accept God's love and forgiveness because it is reasonable, possible, necessary, and desirable to do so. God wants a relationship with us and sees us as worth forgiving because we are made in His image. Like David, when we come to God by faith we can experience feelings of forgiveness, healing, cleansing, and peace. We can feel a sense of joy, hope, and thankfulness return because of the affirmation that God sees the good in us. He sees our worth. These changes may come gradually but they will be life-transforming.

Suggested Readings

1. Gillquist, Peter. *Love Is Now*. Zondervan Publishing House, 1970.
2. McDowell, Josh. *Building Your Self-Image*. Tyndale House Publishers, 1984.
3. Psalm 25:7; 51:17; 86:5; 130:3-5; Micah 7:18-19; Ephesians 1:7; Colossians 1:13-14.

True atheists do not, I presume, feel disappointed in God. They expect nothing and receive nothing. But those who commit their lives to God, no matter what, instinctively expect something in return. Are those expectations wrong?

Philip Yancey, *Disappointment with God* [1]

I had grown up with an image of God as an all-wise, all-powerful parent figure who would treat us as our earthly parents did, or even better. . . . Then came that day in the hospital when the doctor told us about Aaron and explained what progeria meant. It contradicted everything I had been taught. I could only repeat over and over again in my mind, "This can't be happening. It is not how the world is supposed to work."

Harold S. Kushner,
When Bad Things Happen to Good People [2]

When Christianity says that God loves man, it means that God *loves* man. . . . The problem of reconciling human suffering with the existence of a God who loves, is only insoluble so long as we attach a trivial meaning to the word "love," and look on things as if man were the centre of them. Man is not the centre. God does not exist for the sake of man.

C. S. Lewis, *The Problem of Pain* [3]

CHAPTER 8

I've Done Everything Right,
So Why Am I Suffering?

Anthropology has shown that every culture until modern times has had a creation story as part of its religion. A creative being or beings were involved in some way in the arrival of human life on this earth. Because we are human we are conscious of our existence and thus we are conscious of our mortality. This awareness of our existence and death creates a unique problem for us: How do we explain and deal with human suffering and death? How do we resolve the paradox between our uniqueness and worth as human beings and the inevitable ending of each human life? We experience life for a few short years and then what? In his pulitzer prize winning book *The Denial of Death*, Ernest Becker gave us a succinct picture of this problem.

> Man is literally split in two: he has an awareness of his own splendid uniqueness in that he sticks out of nature with a towering majesty, and yet he goes back into the ground a few feet in order blindly and dumbly to rot and disappear forever. It is a terrifying dilemma to be in and to have to live with.[4]

Any view of human life that begins with chance as our origin reduces life to a fleeting journey going nowhere only to end by chance at the foot of a cold granite tombstone. Human worth and human relationships find temporary meaning but the burdens of life can become unbearable under the weight of tragedy. Human hardship and suffering are the result of fate, and when death comes, there is nothing. No wonder Becker calls it a "terrifying dilemma."

If we believe that a Creator exists, we are not necessarily protected from feeling that life is some kind of cruel joke if tragedy should shatter our world. In his discussion of Kierkegaard's torment over human majesty and human mortality, Dr. Becker again gives us a most graphic picture.

> What does it mean to be a self-conscious animal? The idea is ludicrous, if it is not monstrous. It means to know that one is food for worms. This is the terror: to have emerged from nothing, to have a name, consciousness of self, deep inner feelings, an excruciating inner yearning for life and self-expression—and with all this yet to die. It seems like a hoax, which is why one type of cultural man rebels openly against the idea of God. What kind of deity would create such complex and fancy worm food?[5]

Being human means we can relate to a Creator and to each other in a deeply personal way. This is why sickness, disease, hardships, or tragedy can be so devastating. Its impact sends powerful shockwaves into our deepest beliefs about God, our worth, and our relationships with others. This is especially true if we have really tried to be a good person and are still hit hard with some kind of hardship or tragedy. It's worse if, for some reason, we feel we deserve it.

Recovering from hardship or tragedy is possible when we regain a truer and healthier concept of God and when we regain a healthier perspective of who we are and why we are here. Self-worth and the worth of others are intrinsically connected to our divine origin. We are more than just expensive worm food; we are made in God's image. Two examples of people who learned this and recovered from the trauma of their suffering were Job and Joni. Let's look at Job first.

Life Is Not Fair—But God Is Good[6]

The life of Job has become one of my favorite stories. It never used to be because I hated my problems and everyone else's. I did everything I could to ignore them. But the story of Job is so human. It records the effect tragedy and suffering has on a person's life as it impacts their concept of God and their self-concept. Through it all, Job found some answers that transformed his life. They may be helpful to us today.

Briefly, the story begins by describing Job as a righteous man who desired to do what was right. He loved God and did what God wanted. He loved his family and prayed for them daily that God would forgive them for any wrongs they may have done.

Suddenly, Job's children were killed, his possessions were stolen, and he lost his health. At first, Job tried to keep his faith intact but eventually his pain broke through and he began to speak. He felt he had been treated unfairly, that his anguish was unjustified because he had not done anything wrong. He had been *doing* everything he felt he was supposed to do. So when tragedy came, the shock waves went to the center of his being and undermined his beliefs about himself and God.

In his own defense, Job refers to his belief that God was the originator of human life. Now, in his pain, Job wanted to know whether God was trying to destroy what He created: "Your hands shaped me and made me. Will you now turn and destroy me? Remember that you molded me like clay. Will you now turn me to dust again?" (Job 10:8-9).

Later in his discourse, Job argued that the reason he had treated his slaves with honor and respect was because he believed he would be held accountable to God as their Creator.

> If I have denied justice to my menservants and maidservants when they had a grievance against me, what will I do when God confronts me? What will I answer when called to account? Did not He who made me in the womb make them? Did not the same One form us both within our mothers? (Job 31:13-15).

Job's conduct toward others was directly influenced by his knowledge that God was the creator of human life. This fact was the basis for Job's respect for others; and he had, to the best of his ability, done everything he believed was right and moral. So why was he suffering? Job thought that if he could stand before God and plead his case, he could defend his position.

Stop and Consider the Wonders of God

In contrast, Job's three friends tried to convince him that his tragedy and suffering were the result of his hidden sins. They kept saying, "People don't suffer unless they deserve it." When their efforts failed, a young man named Elihu encouraged Job to stop and consider God's wondrous works of wisdom as displayed in creation. (Job 37:14) Nature would demonstrate something about the person and character of the Creator.

Elihu's counsel moved Job toward a new awareness of God; and this prepared the way for God to interact with Job personally and directly. Job was to experience God in a more comprehensive and truthful way than he had ever experienced before. The amazing thing about this first encounter was that God both *affirmed* Job as a person and yet *confronted* him with his ignorance.

> Then the Lord answered Job out of the whirlwind and said, "Who is this that darkens counsel by words without knowledge? Now *gird up your loins like a man*, and I will ask you, and you instruct Me! Where were you when I laid the foundation of the earth!". . . (Job 38:1-4, NASB, italics mine).

God treated Job with respect by first saying to him, "Gird up your loins like a man." Repeatedly, Job had asked for a personal audience with God so he could present his case. Now God took him at his word and honored Job's request, respecting him as a person who wanted an honest exchange. Langes commentary said this about Job's request:

> It is not repelled as impious. God meets the appeal, and evidently treats it with respect. . . . It is as though, in comparison with other men, the Almighty declared him a worthy antagonist . . . [7]

God never mocks, belittles, humiliates or puts down a person who wants an honest encounter with Him. On one hand, nothing is more affirming of one's value and importance than being given the opportunity to engage another in a healthy relationship. But on the other hand, Job was going to discover that God was bigger than he had ever imagined. Job would never be the same.

For the next three chapters (39-41) God elevates and expands Job's conception of the universe and of Himself as Creator. What a mixed blessing Job was going to experience as God laid out in panorama the wonders of the universe as witnesses to His wisdom and power. In the light of his new-found knowledge about God and His sovereign role in the universe, Job's arguments, which had been rooted in too small of a world view, no longer made sense.

And what was Job's response? He was humbled (not humiliated), silenced and transformed! He felt insignificant when compared to God and all His creation. A clearer and more comprehensive picture of God and His relationship to His creation began to change Job deep in his inner being. King David and astronaut James Irwin had experienced a similar awakening and transformation. Job's views of God, the world, human suffering, and his self-concept underwent a similar modification.

> Then Job answered the Lord and said, "Behold I am insignificant; what can I reply to Thee? I lay my hand on my mouth. Once I have spoken, and I will not answer; even twice, and I will add no more" (Job 40:3-5, NASB).

For a second time, God affirms and confronts Job by telling him to gird up his loins like a man (stand up like a human being) and answer some further questions about life. Once again, Job is faced with the inadequacy of his own wisdom and power in understanding the ways of God and the ways of the world; and again the results were both humbling and healing. Confronted with his ignorance, Job admits that he is wrong in his attitude toward God, and he apologizes (repents).

Then Job replied to the Lord: 'I know that you can do all things; no plan of yours can be thwarted . . . Surely I spoke of things I did not understand, things too wonderful for me to know. . . . My ears had heard of you but now my eyes have seen you. Therefore I despise myself and repent in dust and ashes' (Job 42:1-6).

Job saw God and human life from God's perspective and it changed Job forever. When Job said that he despised himself, he did not mean that he thought he was a no-good, good-for-nothing human being. It meant he felt ashamed and remorseful for thinking about God in such inaccurate ways. Repentance is born of remorse. Self-hate never promotes repentance; rather it triggers the desire for self-destruction. Repentance allowed Job to grow, change, and be healed of his misconceptions and pain. He was free to worship God anew because God dealt with him as a person who possessed the abilities to think, feel, and choose.

God would not have challenged an animal to do what he desired of Job. God esteemed Job and engaged him in a relationship because God loved Job as his Imagebearer. Ernest Becker gives us a clear picture of Kierkegaard's conclusion of why the anxiety over our mortality is answered by acquiring a healthier God concept and a healthier self concept.

One goes through it all to arrive at faith, the faith that one's very creatureliness has some meaning to a Creator; that despite one's true insignificance, weakness, death, one's existence has meaning in some ultimate sense because it exists within an eternal and infinite scheme of things—brought about and maintained to some kind of design. . . . His life thereby acquires ultimate value in place of merely social and cultural, historical value. He links his secret inner self, his authentic talent, his deepest feelings of uniqueness, his inner yearning for absolute significance, to the very ground of creation. . . .[8]

From Job to the present day, God continues to be there for us. The anxiety and despair that comes from tragedies can be transformed into hope and victory. Let's listen to another person who knows because of what happened to her.

A Modern Day Job—The Story of Joni

It was a hot July day in 1967 when Joni Eareckson (now Todda) ran across the sand toward the cool, inviting water of Chesapeake Bay. Like all fun-loving teenagers, she was bubbling over with the excitement and anticipation as she dove into the water. Instantly, her head struck a hidden sandbar and her life was never to be the same. Upon impact she felt something like an electric shock combined with a vibration sensation go through her body. She felt no pain but was unable to move. Unknown to her, at that moment she had broken her neck and was now a quadriplegic. All her dreams, plans, and activities would drastically change.

At first Joni's optimism sustained her through the early medical tests. But when the doctor told Joni and her mother that her injuries were permanent, she said that the word "permanent" slammed into her consciousness like a bullet. The shockwaves of reality reverberated to the very core of her being. Depression, total loss of self-esteem, and fear of a bleak future forced her into facing two fundamental questions about life: Does God exist? Why do people exist? She wrote:

> I had absolutely no idea of how I could find purpose or meaning in just existing day after day—waking, eating, watching TV, sleeping.
>
> Why on earth should a person be forced to live out such a dreary existence? How I prayed for some accident or miracle to kill me. The mental and spiritual anguish was as unbearable as the physical torture.
>
> But once again, there was no way for me to commit suicide. This frustration was also unbearable. I was despondent, but I was also angry because of my helplessness. How I wished for strength and control enough in my fingers to do something, anything, *to end my life*. Tears of rage, fear, and frustration only added to my despondency. . . .
>
> I prayed desperately: "God I have just two choices: either You exist or You don't. If You don't exist, then I don't see any logical reason for living. If people who believe are only going through motions that mean nothing, I want to know. Why should we go on fooling ourselves? Life is absurd most of the time. And it seems man's only end is despair. What can I do, Lord? I want to believe, but I have nothing to hang on to."[9]

Being stripped of all physical mobility put Joni into a unique place in life. She could do nothing to physically help herself. During her darkest hours when she wanted to die, when she thought of killing herself, she realized she was totally helpless even to do that. But she also gained an important insight. This is how she described it:

> I was angry that my life had been reduced to the basics of eating, breathing, and sleeping—day in and day out. But what I discovered was that the rest of the human race was in the same boat. Their lives revolved around the same meaningless cycle—except with them, it wasn't as obvious. Peripheral things distracted them from the fact that they were caught on the same treadmill. Their jobs, schools,

families, and recreation occupied them enough so they never consciously recognized that their lives were the same as mine—eating, breathing, sleeping. . . . My life was reduced to absolute basics. So now what? *What am I to do with my life?* I wondered. *I have no body, but I am still someone.* I had to find meaning, purpose, and direction, not just some measure of temporary satisfaction.[10]

Slowly, Joni became aware of the truth that *God was interested in her as a person* in spite of her physical condition. Through reading (the Bible, C. S. Lewis, and Francis Schaeffer) and conversations with a Christian friend, she began to learn that she was created in the image of God. She began to feel that God still had a purpose for her life and she was going to discover it. She wrote:

> It was true. God knew that I had hands and feet and arms and legs that did not work. He knew what I looked like. And none of these things really mattered. What counted was that *I was His workmanship, created in His image. And He wasn't finished with me* (Ephesians 2:10, italics mine).

> In the days that followed, I thanked Him for "me"—whatever I was in terms of mind, spirit, personality—and even body. I thanked Him for the way I looked and for what I could and could not do. As I did, the doctrine of His sovereignty helped everything fall into place, like a jigsaw puzzle.

> Not only was there purpose to my life at this point, but there was an iceberg of potential as well—10 percent above the surface, 90 percent below. It was an exciting thought—an entire new area of my life and personality not even developed yet![11]

Joni had been developing one of her Imagebearing qualities—her ability to be creative. Art therapy began as a part of her overall rehabilitation but later the results of her efforts were to become nationally known. First, she learned how to hold a pencil in her mouth and draw lines and circles. After many hours of practice she was able to make letters and write notes to her family. This sense of accomplishment gave her a more positive outlook on life. Gradually she began drawing pictures and I can still remember seeing her pictures at the Christian book store. She writes:

> My drawing, still self-expression in style and simple in approach, was more of a therapy than I had anticipated. As a reflection of my new mood, I began to sign "PTL" on my drawings—for "praise the Lord"—an expression of my belief that God cares for me. It was a simple expression, giving Him the glory for His direct help in restoring this one aspect of my individuality.[12]

God forbid that any of us should ever have to experience the tragedies of Job or Joni! But it is clear from their stories that hardships, tragedies, and diseases impact both our God-concept and our self-concept. We have also seen how people's lives change for the better when they begin to feel like there is someone who cares for them and stands by them in the hard times, who believe they are worth it.

One of the best examples of this profound truth is found in the life story of Christopher Reeve. Reeve's was a good athlete, and accomplished actor and welcomed all over the world as Superman of Hollywood Fame. Yet I remember the day I heard the news that Reeve had suffered a tragic horse riding accident. It was Memorial Day 1995 when on the third jump of a riding competition, he was thrown head first from his horse. His neck was broken at the first and second vertebrae leaving him unable to move or breath. Miraculously, he survived but I remember thinking, "How could Superman be a quadriplegic and be as helpless as a baby?"

This is how he described his dilemma and the life changing impact of a statement his wife Dana said to him at a most vulnerable moment in his life.

> Dana came into the room. She stood beside me, and made eye contact. I mouthed my first lucid words to her. "Maybe we should let me go." Dana started crying. She said, "I am only going to say this once: I will support whatever you want to do, because this is your life, and your decision. But I want you to know that I'll be with you for the long haul, no matter what." Then she added the words that saved my life. "You're still you. And I love you."[13]

Can you imagine what it would be like to have God look at you or me and say, "you're still you, made in my likeness. And I love you."

I firmly believe we will never be free from the slavery of performance based self-esteem until we see more clearly the healing truth that *our worth rests in who God is and who we are as people made in His likeness*. If we don't experience these truths, we will feel a continual, sometimes driven, need to keep trying to prove that we are important, desirable, loveable—a somebody. We will suffer repeated feelings of inferiority, insecurity, jealousy, anxiety, or despair. Hardships, tragedies, and physical losses can make the burden become even more unbearable! On the other hand, Joni's life bears witness to the relationship between our healing, our being made in God's image, our self-esteem, and our creativity.

If you are going through an unusually hard time right now, I would encourage you to be open with God about your thoughts and innermost feelings. Be honest with God; pour out your heart before Him, even as Job and Joni did. Then consider the wondrous works of God, *especially the uniqueness of how you are fearfully and wonderfully made in the image of God.* Ask God to meet you personally and help you change your outlook on life.

Suggested Reading

1. Eareckson, Joni. *Joni*. Minneapolis: World Wide Publications, 1976.
2. Yancey, Philip. *Disappointment with God*. New York: Harper Collins Publishers, 1988.
3. Psalm 34:18; 46:1-3; 116:1-6; 147:3-6a; Daniel 3:16-18; Romans 5:3-5; 8:28-29; 2 Corinthians 1:3-4; James 1:2-5.

Man was made in the Father's image . . . Looking heavenward man can find inspiration in his lineage; looking about him he is impelled to kindness by a sense of kinship which binds him to his brother.

William Jennings Bryan, *In His Image*[1]

The healthy self-concept which Christ taught, then, involves neither haughtiness and pride nor inferiority and worthlessness. It is one of humble reverence for God and every member of His human family. We are to see our fellowman as neither better nor worse than ourselves; rather, we are to love them *as* ourselves, and that prescription puts the entire matter of self-worth into its proper perspective.

Dr. James Dobson, *Hide or Seek*[2]

What then does a man possess of which a sheep knows nothing? . . . The answer is seen in that free and intelligent action which we have already confronted when we considered man as made in the divine image. Man can think and plan and act. . . . He is capable of intellectual and moral and spiritual fellowship. . . . Everything in the teaching and the work of Jesus is based upon an awareness of these distinctions.

Lynn H. Hough, *The Dignity of Man*[3]

CHAPTER 9

Jesus Reaffirms the Worth
of Human Life

People have been fascinated with the life and teachings of Jesus Christ for two thousand years. There have been and still are debates over whether He was the divine incarnation of God or a highly esteemed prophet of God, an ideal model of a good and moral human being or an example of a fully self-actualized person. But whatever a person thinks, there is one thing that can't be denied—*Jesus Christ placed great worth and value on human life.*

This truth runs through everything Jesus taught and did. The four Gospels record the amazing story of this remarkable person and they tell how his whole life demonstrated the respect and care He felt for those around him; how He encouraged their faith in God and in a way to live that was good—morally and spiritually.

If Jesus taught these things and was only human, they would still be exactly what we need to hear again today. Because Jesus is called "Immanuel," meaning, "God with us" (Matthew 1:23), we have even more of a reason to accept what He taught about the worth and value of a human being. Since Jesus is the incarnation of God, we have a reconfirmation of the worth of human life reinforcing what was shown earlier in the Old Testament.

One incident in which Jesus affirms human worth occurred when he was preparing his disciples for their ministry. Jesus told them a simple story about a sparrow.

God Attends the Memorial Service for a Sparrow

As a kid can you remember holding a memorial service for a dead bird? I can still picture the scene when several of us kids conducted a graveside service for a dead blue bird. We gently laid his bright blue body in a freshly dug hole and covered it ever so carefully, as if trying not to hurt it. We put a simple cross on its grave and one of us said a prayer returning the bird back to God. I was not a Christian at the time and my concept of God was quite simple; but I do remember thinking that God must have felt sad about the dead bird because it was so pretty.

Many years later while traveling in the Mediterranean countries, I rediscovered the connection between God, my importance to God and a sparrow. I found that in those countries they still use sparrows for both food (which I ate on one occasion in Portugal) or as song birds.

When traveling in Israel, I read the Bible stories while at the locations where they happened. On one occasion, I read the story in which Jesus sends out the twelve disciples for the first time to preach about the kingdom of heaven (Matthew 10).

Before leaving, Jesus prepared them for the hardships they were to experience in their work. He knew they would be successful but He also knew they would be mocked, ridiculed, rejected, arrested, even physically beaten. This kind of treatment can be devastating on one's sense of esteem, so He prepared them for it. He encouraged them not to worry (v. 19) and not to be afraid (v. 26) and then affirmed their personal worth and value to God as illustrated in the story of the common sparrow.

> Are not two sparrows sold for a penny? Yet not one of them will fall to the ground apart from the will of your Father. And even the very hairs of your head are all numbered. So don't be afraid; *you are worth more than many sparrows* (Matthew 10:29-31, italics mine).

Jesus knew that hardships in life are more successfully handled if one's sense of worth is secure. It still hurts to be rejected, that's normal, but it does not have to be devastating. He knew that we can be more successful in overcoming the feelings of insecurity, anxiety, worry, fear, and rejection when our worth is primarily determined by how God values us rather than being dependent on human approval and acceptance.

Several years later when facing my own feelings of inferiority, I reread this story. I remembered sitting on that hill in Israel and I imagined listening to Jesus telling this story. Only this time it was different. A story that had been only in black and white (head knowledge) turned to color (became a heart-felt belief). I realized that if God attends the memorial service of a sparrow, how much more valuable to God are you and I who are made in His image!

Self-Esteem and Religious Legalism

How we love to elevate the importance and status of people based on their public adherence and conformity to religious behaviors and customs (legalism). Often the value of living up to religious expectations is placed higher than the value of a person's life.

I wonder how many people have been snubbed, ignored, rejected, abandoned, condemned, or gossiped about because they have failed to live up to the religious standards expected of them by a particular group. In our religious circles we often treat people less warmly when they don't dress right, talk right, think right, or act right. We often think less of people who find themselves in a difficult period in their lives such as an unmarried pregnant teenage girl, a couple going through a divorce, or an adolescent or adult going through a time of rebellion.

This practice was also common in Jesus' day. One such occasion happened when Jesus was confronted by some religious people looking for a way to condemn him for breaking the Sabbath. He had just entered the synagogue when they asked him, "Is it lawful to heal on the Sabbath?" Among those waiting to hear Jesus' answer was a man with a crippled hand.

The answer Jesus gave affirmed the worth he placed on a human being. His answer included both a question and an affirmation statement. First the question:

> He said to them, "If any of you has a sheep and it falls into a pit on the Sabbath, will you not take hold of it and lift it out?" (Matthew 12:11).

This is a rhetorical question. Everyone knows what the answer is: "Yes, of course we would lift it out. Do you expect us to leave a valuable sheep in that condition overnight and possibly find it dead or stolen by morning?"

Jesus, knowing there was no other reasonable answer than yes, then affirms the worth of a person over conformity to religious legalism. He said, *"How much more valuable is a man than a sheep!* Therefore it is lawful to do good on the Sabbath" (Matthew 12:12, italics mine). Then to back up his words with action, even at the risk of being condemned or rejected by some of those present, he healed the crippled man's hand.

If I had been among those watching and listening, I would have liked to talk to Jesus afterward and ask him, "Jesus, why do you think a person is more valuable than a sheep?" I firmly believe his answer would have been,

"Human beings are more valuable than animals because in the beginning God created them, male and female, in His image."

I am confident this would have been Jesus' response because this was the answer Jesus gave to another group of people (the Pharisees) who were again trying to find a reason to condemn Him. This time they asked Him about His views on divorce. Before Jesus answered their question, He first took them back in time to the origin of human life and the beginning of the institution of marriage.

> "Haven't you read," he replied, "that at the beginning the Creator 'made them male and female,' and said, 'For this reason a man will leave his father and mother and be united to his wife, and the two will become one flesh'?" (Matthew 19:4-5).

Jesus intentionally went back to Genesis 1:26-27 and 2:24 to give His perspective (world view) behind His answer before He addressed the issue of divorce. His answer gives us a glimpse into what Jesus thought about the origin and worth of human life and the sanctity of marriage. In his book *The Christian View of Man*, H. D. McDonald wrote:

> The fundamental basis for the Christian view of man is the value which Jesus Christ placed on human nature . . . This is the first and most important truth that can be deduced from Christ's statements about and treatment of man. Each and every man is, *coram deo*, a creature of infinite worth. Jesus saw beyond the externals of life, the distinctions of class, the disparities of conditions and the shame of corruption, to the priceless value of human life itself. It was through Jesus Christ that this estimate of man first found revolutionizing expression in human history. Herein indeed lies one of the most distinctive contributions of Christianity to civilization.[4]

His commitment to His views and His willingness to do His Father's will eventually cost Him His life. He taught, "Greater love has no one than this, that he lay down his life for his friends" (John 15:13). At another time, Jesus said He "did not come to be served but to serve, and to give his life as a ransom for many" (Matthew 20:28).

The Cross on which he died became the greatest symbol ever of the affirmation of our worth as human beings. Jesus' willingness to endure its pain and humiliation came out of His love and compassion for all human kind, even the worst of us. In his book *The Dignity of Man*, Lynn Hough expressed it this way:

If we hold the tenets of classical Christianity the cross becomes the greatest of all the tributes to human dignity. . . . And as we contemplate the corpus of massive convictions which constitute this ancient and living faith we stand amazed at the dignity which it confers upon mankind. Unhesitatingly Christianity asserts that man was worth the costly act of the incarnation and still more costly act of the cross. The death of the Son of God upon the cross for man is the final expression of the evaluation which God Himself gives to humanity. The cross was a divine act of unthinkable agony. And in God's mind and heart man was worth the cross. No wonder the cross lifts up men's heads when it is the divine seal upon human dignity.[5]

If you have had the opportunity to see the movie, *The Passion of the Christ* by Mel Gibson, you have witnessed how the "cross was a divine act of unthinkable agony". Jesus Christ endured the cross to make a clear statement to you and me that he sees our worth and value and he died for us because he saw us as worth it. He was there at creation and knows we are made in the image and likeness of the Creator.

Jesus once told a parable about a pearl buyer to illustrate this point. Jesus said:

"The kingdom of heaven is like a merchant looking for fine pearls. When he found one of great value, he went away and sold everything he had and bought it." (Matthew 13:45)

Jesus, like the merchant, paid the price of his life to purchase you and me because **he saw you and me as a pearl of great value to him.** Jesus never confused a person's worth with a person being a sinner. We shall see this more clearly in the next chapter on Jesus' teaching about the lost coin, lost sheep, and lost son.

Suggested Reading

1. Lucado, Max. *No Wonder They Call Him the Savior.* Multnomah Press, 1986.
2. Tozer, A. W. *Knowledge of the Holy.* Harper and Row Publishers, 1961.
3. Matthew 6:25-26; Romans 8:38-39; Ephesians 3:14-19.

Another question in the dilemma of man is man's nobility. Perhaps you do not like the word "nobility," but whatever word you choose, there is something great about man. . . . Evangelicals have made a horrible mistake by often equating the fact that man is lost and under God's judgment with the idea that man is nothing—a zero. This is not what the Bible says. There is something great about man . . . It is the Bible which explains *why* man is great.

Francis Schaeffer,
He Is There and He Is Not Silent[1]

At the very moment when we assert the dignity of man we are reasserting the goodness of God. . . . It is that which lies at the heart of the revelation of God in Jesus Christ. . . . Man's dignity is secure because it is according to the divine nature to give him precisely that dignity. A self which is made for good and which can return to good after wandering in ways of evil is the only sort of self the God we see in the face of Jesus Christ could be responsible for creating.

Lynn H. Hough, *The Dignity of Man*[2]

We are children of God. The tragedy is that too many human beings have never discovered their divine heritage, so they live like animals. . . . The Fatherhood of God . . . lays the firm foundation for a solid spiritual self-esteem.

Robert Schuller,
Self-Esteem: The New Reformation[3]

CHAPTER 10

Being Lost Does Not Mean Being Worthless

When I was a junior in high school I lost a valuable ring. It belonged to my mother but had been promised to me when I was old enough to take care of it. One day I decided to get used to wearing it, so I put it on and went out to play catch with some friends. My parents were not home, and you guessed it; I lost the ring. When I realized it was missing, a cold wave of fear swept through me. Desperately, we searched every inch of the yard but it was nowhere to be found.

I had been a Christian for only a couple of years, but I remembered being taught that if I prayed and asked anything in Jesus name, God would do it. Whether I was right or wrong in my application, I figured this was one of those times when I could put my education to use. Closing my eyes, I prayed as sincerely as I knew how. After finishing, I opened my eyes to begin the search and to my great surprise, the ring was right between my feet.

I can't describe how relieved I felt as I picked it up and returned it to the jewelry box. I also felt quite surprised that God had answered my prayer; and so quickly. On future occasions I have not gotten the same result because I had to learn that prayer is not magic. But on that day my faith in God grew a little.

Over the years I have wondered about that experience because I don't know if my prayer helped quiet my emotions so I could see the ring, or if God brought the ring from somewhere across the yard and placed it between my feet. The second possibility sounds more like a real miracle, but it doesn't matter because I learned two lessons from that experience: God can choose to answer prayers in line with our desire and, the ring did not become worthless just because it was lost.

Years later, it is this second lesson that was to become the most important when it comes to understanding a Christian view of self-worth. We need to learn what Jesus already understood—to separate worth from sinfulness; to separate being lost from being worthless. This is what Jesus taught in his stories in Luke 15 about the lost sheep, lost coin, and lost son.

Parables of the Lost and Found

Common experience tells us that if we lose something and it isn't important to us, we don't spend much time looking for it. But the greater the value we place on something, the more pain and loss we feel if it becomes lost and the greater the effort we put into trying to find it.

Jesus used simple, life-like stories similar to my lost ring to teach the profound truth of the great worth and value God places on our lives. The occasion Jesus used to teach this truth was at a meeting where tax collectors and sinners (the "bad" people of society) were gathered around Jesus to hear him teach. In the crowd were also some religious people (Pharisees and teachers of the law) who saw themselves as being better than others. Jesus overheard them say among themselves, "This man welcomes sinners and eats with them" (Luke 15:2).

Because they devalued the importance of some people there, Jesus wanted to make a clear statement about how God loved and valued all people despite outward appearances. Jesus also wanted people to know there was great rejoicing in heaven when a person returns to God in faith. He told three parables to demonstrate the effort people, as well as God, put into searching for something important that has been lost. He also described how excited and happy they became when it was found. The first parable was about a lost sheep. Jesus said:

> Suppose one of you has a hundred sheep and loses one of them. Does he not leave the ninety-nine in the open country and go after the lost sheep until he finds it? And when he finds it, he joyfully puts it on his shoulders and goes home. Then he calls his friends and neighbors together and says, 'Rejoice with me, I have found my lost sheep.' I tell you that in the same way there is more rejoicing in heaven over one sinner who repents than over ninety-nine righteous persons who do not need to repent (Luke 15:4-7).

Because most of us have never been shepherds, it may be hard to identify with the experience of losing a sheep. But you probably can recall losing a favorite pet like a cat or dog. Remember the fear, and desperation you felt as you walked around the neighborhood whistling and calling its name? You looked everywhere, talked to everyone and imagined everything from the worst to the best. Why all this fuss for just a pet? Because you loved it and placed great value on it. It was important to you; and you felt great relief and happiness when you found it.

This is what Jesus was trying to get people to realize about how God feels toward us. God loves us and has placed great value on our lives. We are important to God because He is our Creator, our heavenly Father, and we are His Imagebearers.

The parable of the woman who lost one of her ten silver coins brings this same truth into focus (Luke 15:8-10). But in my estimation, the parable of the lost son is one of the most significant affirmations of our worth to God that can be found in the Bible. This story is uniquely different from the other two because free will is involved.

A son, who was deeply loved by his father, wanted to leave home, so he asked for his portion of the inheritance. I imagine they spent hours discussing the matter, but in the end the father, respecting his son's free will, honored his request.

After receiving his part of the inheritance, the young man left his father and family, traveled to another part of the country, and "squandered his wealth on wild living" (Luke 15:13). The father loses his son to a way of life that went against everything good his father wanted for him. Eventually, the consequences of his choices and the circumstances of life brought the young man to the end of his rope. He hit the bottom of the barrel. Feeling the cumulative effect of his bad choices, he took a good, hard look at his life. Realizing there was a better way, he decided to do something about it. This is how Jesus told it:

> When he came to his senses, he said, "How many of my father's hired men have food to spare, and here I am starving to death! I will set out and go back to my father and say to him: Father, I have sinned against heaven and against you. I am no longer worthy to be called your son; make me like one of your hired men." So he got up and went to his father (Luke 15:17-20).

There are many things we could discuss about the son's return home but I only want to emphasize a few. (1) He realized what a terrible condition he had gotten himself into; (2) he realized that the solution was found in reestablishing a relationship with his father; (3) he felt he wasn't worthy to be a son if he returned home, so he would offer himself to be a hired hand; (4) he made a *decision toward life* by getting up and heading home.

The amazing part of this parable was how Jesus portrayed the boy's father. In the father, Jesus tells us important things we need to know about our heavenly Father.

> But while he [the son] was still a long way off, his father saw him and was filled with compassion for him; he ran to his son, threw his arms around him and kissed him. The son said to him, "Father, I have sinned against heaven and against you. I am no longer worthy to be called your son."

> But the father said to his servants, "Quick! Bring the best robe and put it on him. Put a ring on his finger and sandals on his feet. Bring the fattened calf and kill it. Let's have a feast and celebrate. For this son of mine was dead and is alive again; he was lost and is found." So they began to celebrate (Luke 15:20-24).

Even though his son came home feeling like a failure and feeling unworthy of anything that once represented his original status as a son, his father restored him to full sonship! Why? *Because his father had never lost sight of the fact that he was still his son and he knew what his son meant to him!* So he responded to a broken and repentant son with compassion and love by clothing him, feeding him, and placing a ring of sonship on his finger. He restored his son to the status that had originally been his by birth.

Like King David earlier and this young man here, Jesus made it very clear that our heavenly Father sincerely loves us because He knows our origin—He made us in His image. No matter how bad we have been, or what other people think of us, or even how we may hate ourselves because of all the rotten things we have done, God is love and we are loved! We are important to God. Yes, we are sinners and we need God's forgiveness but we never lost our worth because it is ours by design.

We may have lost our perspective of who we are as bearers of God's image because we decided to walk away from God. Our lives may be a mess and we may feel like the worst sinner alive; but whenever we realize our condition, we can decide to return to God because of what Jesus has done for us. We can experience His love, compassion, and forgiveness. We can be reunited with God and our relationship restored with Him the way it originally was intended to be. This is what the Bible calls salvation and there will be a celebration in heaven because that which was lost is now found; that which went astray has returned.

Whether we are a Christian or not, Jesus taught that God places a high value on our lives and when we begin to grasp a sense of what Jesus meant in these three parables, it changes our lives.

Humbled Yet Proud to Be Human and Christian

We have looked at several Bible passages to help deepen our appreciation of our worth given to us by God as a gift. It is an intrinsic worth that is never lost and never varies because it rests in our being made in God's image. We have shown that we are not just cosmic accidents trying to make the best of a few short years before dying and becoming expensive worm food.

We have presented the logic and rationale behind the idea that **Our worth is in our design.** The degree to which we have lost sight of our divine origin and the significance that puts on our lives is the degree to which we suffer the needless consequences of trying to acquire our sense of worth and self-esteem from temporal and external sources.

A renewed perspective on who God is, who we are, and what Christ accomplished on the cross on our behalf can provide us with a more secure sense of self-worth and the freedom necessary to grow toward wholeness— psychologically and spiritually. These three truths provide a solid foundation on which to build our lives; a solid rock to which we can anchor our souls in a world of drifting currents and changing tides; a refuge for safety when the storms of life batter us on our journey to becoming the person God designed us to be.

How to become fully who we are as Imagebearers of God is the focus of the rest of this book. To become happier, healthier people we need practical skills to help us become fully human and fully alive. We need to *reclaim* and give ourselves *permission* to develop our unique human abilities to feel, to choose, to think, to communicate, to be self-aware, morally-aware, spiritually-aware, and creative. The remainder of the book is going to devote two chapters each to these eight attributes. The first will be the **permission** chapter, encouraging you to accept that attribute as personally yours. The second will be the practical **how to** chapters that provides the skills necessary for your personal growth and change. The more we grow by using these image-bearing gifts the more we become whole persons.

Since our worth is secure in being made in God's image and our salvation is secure because we are in Christ, we are free to learn to accept ourselves and to grow and change in all eight areas of our lives.

On the diagram on the next page, place a mark on the percentage level you presently feel you are at for each human ability. As you read, learn and grow you can come back to this diagram and mark your progress.

Becoming a Whole Person Designed after God's Likeness	
Unique Human Quality	Growth Potential
	10% 20% 30% 40% 50% 60% 70% 80% 90% 100%
Ability to Feel (feeling)	
Ability to Choose (self-determination)	
Ability to Think (reason)	
Ability to Communicate (use of verbal-symbolic language)	
Ability to be Self-Aware (self-consciousness)	
Ability to be Morally Aware (moral-consciousness)	
Ability to be Spiritually Aware (God-consciousness)	
Ability to Create (creativity)	

Now, let's continue the journey of discovery of our worth and identity as a person made in the image of God. May you begin to become all that God designed you to be.

Suggested Reading

1. Yancey, Philip. *The Jesus I Never Knew*, Zondervan, 1995.
2. Tozer, A. W. *The Pursuit of God.* Christian Publications, Inc., 1958.
3. Matthew 7:7-12; 23:37; 1 John 4:9-10,18.

PART II

And in God's Image

"Then too I was ignorant of what in us is the principle of our existence and what is meant by the words of Scripture 'after the image of God'— as to that I was entirely ignorant. . . .

In particular I discovered that the phrase 'Man, created by Thee, after Thine own image' was not understood by your spiritual children, whom you have made to be born again by grace. . . .

Being ignorant, then, of how this image of yours could subsist, I ought to have knocked at the door and asked in what sense the doctrine was to be believed. . . ."

The Confessions of St. Augustine
(354-430 A.D.)

The art of being is the art of knowing ourselves, of accepting and existing in harmony with ourselves, and of living out, in action, the highest possibilities of our nature. It includes three basic concepts: self-awareness, self-acceptance, and self-assertion. . . . Self-awareness begins with learning to be more conscious of our feelings and emotions.

Nathaniel Branden, *Honoring the Self* [1]

The way we handle our feelings helps us toward true humanity or keeps us from it. . . . God made us in his image, but he understands and accepts us marred and scarred. He understands and accepts our human framework of his image. . . . In accepting ourselves as God made us, we find feelings a part of our life; and because God gave them to us, they are of worth.

Joan Jacobs, *Feelings!* [2]

Feelings can be described and explained in simple and direct ways. There is nothing mystical or magical about them. . . . Not to be aware of one's feelings, not to understand them or know how to use or express them is worse than being blind, deaf, or paralyzed.

David Viscott, *The Language of Feelings* [3]

CHAPTER 11

Feelings:
Welcome to the Human Race

PERMISSION

Years ago a kind and sensitive Christian woman came for counseling. Three years earlier Donna and her husband, the natural parents of three children, had adopted two little Korean girls. Both parents felt God's leading to make a home for them, and they waited anxiously for the day when they could pick them up at the airport.

But something unexpected was about to go wrong. As soon as the two girls stepped off the plane, the older girl developed an instant dislike for Donna—"even before the first words were spoken." For the next three years Donna tried her best to overcome this and be the mother she wanted to be and felt she should be; but nothing worked.

Her emotional world became cluttered with negative feelings, along with the growing burden of guilt she carried for feeling the way she did. She prayed daily, but nothing changed. Then she tried to deny and repress her feelings, only to find they persisted. The building tension and anger made things worsen to the point it began to have a negative affect on her marriage and her relationships with her other children.

The counsel and advice she received from her husband and well-intentioned Christian friends only added to her sense of failure. She felt she *should* be able to love the girl; after all, she was a Christian and God could love the girl through her. Besides, God gave these two girls to them; she *had* to make it work. To fail was unthinkable; but the unthinkable was slowly becoming reality. Things continued to deteriorate until she decided to seek professional help.

In our first session it became clear that Donna was doing the very best she knew how, but she had received an inadequate education on how to understand her feeling life. Her feelings about her situation had become so entangled with her feelings about herself that her decision-making ability had become paralyzed. Seeing no way out left her feeling desperate, trapped, confused, and angry. Worst of all, her faith in God was being seriously shaken as her prayers remained unanswered. Why was God allowing this to happen? Didn't He care?

Beginning with our first sessions, we started working on a reeducation program on how to accept, understand, and work with her feelings. She needed be reassured that God created her in His image to be a feeling person and that it was *okay* for her to accept all her feelings—the ones she liked as well as the ones she didn't like. This started releasing her from an emotional prison that just a few weeks earlier had seemed inescapable.

We also worked together on helping her learn that what she felt about the girl was a totally separate issue from what she felt about herself. Her self-esteem "stuff" had to be separated from her life-situation "stuff." Pulling these two issues apart emotionally was difficult, but it was important that she recognize the crucial distinction between them in order to be able to work on improving each. Then from a position of freedom and restored self-acceptance, she could work with her feelings about the adoption that had gone wrong.

Gradually, positive changes began to happen. Knowing that it was okay to be a feeling person began to alleviate the guilt, self-condemnation, and sense of spiritual failure she had known for so long. Lifting this burden gave her the energy and freedom to begin understanding her feelings about the child and to look for positive solutions in dealing responsibly with the situation.

Feeling Free to Feel

Like Donna, most of us have struggled at times with what to do with our feelings. There has been a great deal of misunderstanding about the part feelings play in the Christian life. There are those who say we should not rely on our feelings because they will lead us astray; they are not to be trusted. Others teach that only certain kinds of feelings are acceptable; the rest are bad, sinful, or unchristian. Still others insist that feelings are the last things to be taken seriously, asserting that facts are what are important and feelings need to be relegated to a minor role.

In contrast, there are people who say, "If it feels good, do it!" They give the impression that feelings are great and their free-spirited life style looks attractive. But their abuse of this notion has made us gun-shy and blind to seeing the healthy side of feelings.

Common experience has taught us that our feelings are a constant companion of daily life. Whether or not we like them, whether or not we accept them, whether or not we even want them, we know that we can't stop experiencing them. At times we may have been successful at denying, repressing, ignoring, or rejecting a lot of feelings—but we have never been able to free ourselves of them. Why is this so? Because our ability to feel is inherent in our nature. It is a God given part of what makes us human.

Feelings Make Us Human

Can you imagine what we would be like if a surgeon could perform a "feeling-anectomy" on us? What if we had a small appendage like a "feeling appendix" that, if removed could turn us into nonfeeling humans? We would be like Spock on "Star Trek," having no capacity to understand or empathize with people who experience common human emotions. Our personalities would lack warmth, affection, and emotional color.

None of us can do that. But many of us do learn how to *tune out* or *numb out* our feelings, and in time, we find we are out of touch with ourselves and with our world. To be unaware of our experiences is to lose contact with one of our most important human attributes. It is to diminish a true sense of what it means to be a person—a person made in the likeness of God.

Here are some examples of statements that encourage us to deny, distrust, or discredit our feelings. Eventually, this leads us to the problems of not knowing who we are, what we feel, or what to do with our feelings when we can no longer deny them.

- "How can you feel that way? That's terrible!"
- "You don't really feel like that; you just think you do!"
- "If you were a good Christian you wouldn't feel like that!"
- "That's stupid to feel that way; There's no reason for it."
- "How can you possibly feel like that when you have so much going for you? Aren't you being self-centered?"
- "I hate feeling like this so I am not going to think about it!"
- "I am not supposed to feel this way; something must be wrong with me."
- "I don't want to feel any more because feelings are too confusing and too painful."
- "You shouldn't feel that way—it's not nice!"
- "You can't call yourself a Christian and feel like that!"

Other sentences like these are constantly running through our minds. All of them work against our natural ability to feel. Joan Jacobs, a minister's wife, had a nice way of saying it in her book *Feelings*:

> Feelings are integral to our humanity, but for many Christians being human is less than attractive. In our striving to work up to the mountaintop, to what we should become, our feelings remind us to our dismay, that we are human. We haven't arrived. To admit our humanity, and the feelings and frailties that go with it, seems to deny our Christianity.[4]

Because feelings are an intrinsic part of being a person, learning how to accept, understand, and work with our feelings allows us to learn how to be human. It is not a sign of becoming unchristian, unspiritual, losing control, being emotionally weak, being nonrational, or, as some would say, "being a sissy." Instead, it is becoming a Christian person who is real, human, and healthy.

It is true, as some will argue, that animals have feelings, but the capacity, range, and meaning of human emotions is unmatched by any other creature on earth. In his book *The Language of Feelings*, David Viscott described it this way:

> Not to feel is not to be alive. More than anything else feelings make us human. Feelings make us all kindred. . . . When we lose touch with our feelings, we lose touch with one of our most human qualities. . . . Without an awareness of what our feelings mean, there is no real awareness of life.[5]

This part of God's image in us has suffered greatly because of misguided teachings, distorted ideas, and defensive reactions to the proper place feelings have in the Christian life. But the God-given ability to feel is still ours; and with the support of a few helpful perspectives, we can RECLAIM and own this part of our specialness. We can give ourselves PERMISSION to grow each day to become feeling human beings who are also Christians. Let's look at some ideas that can encourage us to take this step.

A Divine Origin for Our Ability to Feel

Psychological theories and scientific research about human emotions and feelings are by necessity based on a person's world view. Research can show the motivational and perceptual value of feelings as well as the developmental sequences of human emotional growth, but they may not always begin with some explanation for the origin of human life.[6]

If we start from the view that God does not exist, then the uniqueness of our emotional nature is the result of a cosmic accident. Chance is the mother of human life and human feeling, but chance cares nothing about its offspring. While the possession of feelings may have great temporal value and meaning for daily life, our feeling life can have no lasting meaning. The existential atheist Jean-Paul Sartre represents this view in his book *Existentialism and Human Emotions*:

> Man is nothing else but what he makes of himself. . . . Man is condemned to be free. Condemned . . . because once thrown into the world, he is responsible for everything he does. . . . Man being condemned to be free carries the weight of the whole world on his shoulders; he is responsible for the world and for himself as a way of being.[7]

Being "thrown into the world" by chance and knowing that we cannot escape its realities or the reality of our death creates what Sartre calls the "feeling of existential despair." Despair can kill one's motivation to live when hardships and tragedies turn life into a cruel joke. If our feeling ability is to have both temporal and eternal value, we need to begin with a divine origin of life. This divine Being must be big enough to account for the whole of life including human personality, human emotionality, and choice.

The personal-infinite God of the Judeo-Christian faith is that Creator. God—being a person with a feeling nature—by design created us in His image to be feeling beings. A divine origin affirms the beauty and worth of our feeling nature. Feelings take on greater significance and meaning when they are seen to encompass our highest personal and spiritual aspirations.

God is the reference point for the fullest meaning of our feeling nature and how it is to function in an integrated, mature, healthy personality. We have permission to be a feeling person because God designed us that way when He created us in His image.

God Is a Feeling God

A thoughtful reading of the Bible will easily show that God is a feeling God. This really became clear to me when I decided to read the Book of Deuteronomy as if it was the first time I was going to learn something about God. I pictured myself stranded on a deserted island, walking on the beach and finding a waterproof container. Inside was a book written by Moses for the people of Israel. While reading the book I was struck by the fact that God was a feeling God experiencing a wide range of feelings (some of which I had been taught "good Christians" were not supposed to feel). A few of the feelings mentioned were anger (1:34), compassion (4:31), jealousy (5:9), loving kindness (5:10), love (7:8), wrath (9:7), affection (10:15), mercy (13:17), hate (16:22), delight (28:63), and care (32:10).

God feels and He created us with the ability to feel. If we numb out or act out our feelings we diminish our true humanness and harm our relationship with God, with ourselves and with others. By giving ourselves permission to accept our feelings we affirm the gift God has given us. Then we can learn to work with our feelings in a responsible way and become healthier, happier Christian human beings.

Jesus Is a Feeling Person

If we read the New Testament Gospels and record all the feelings Jesus experienced, we would find that He was no stranger to feelings. Summarized below are a few of these events to give us a glimpse into this side of his personality.

He Felt:	Situation:
Compassion	for the people who were like sheep without a shepherd (Matthew 9:36).
Distressed	in the Garden of Gethsemane before His arrest (Matthew 26:37).
Forsaken	while being crucified on the cross (Matthew 27:46).
Anger and Grief	at the hardness of people's hearts when He healed a man's withered hand on the Sabbath (Mark 3:5).
Wonder	at the unbelief of people (Mark 6:6).
Indignation	when the disciples tried to keep children away from Him (Mark 10:14).
Love	for the man who asked how to inherit eternal life (Mark 10:21).
Sorrow	in Gethsemane knowing that His death by crucifixion was not far away (Mark 14:34).
Tears	for the city of Jerusalem (Luke 19:41). and at the death of Lazarus (John 11:35).
Deeply Moved (angered)	at the evilness of the death of His friend Lazarus (John 11:36).

These are just a few examples of the feelings Jesus experienced as he encountered the realities of life—rejections, human needs, poverty, death, sickness, oppression, prejudice, and friendships. Jesus, as the incarnation of God, "fashioned in the likeness of man" (Philippians 2:7), was a feeling person just like you and me. The Presbyterian professor and theologian B. B. Warfield said this about the feeling life of Jesus:

Nothing is lacking to make the impression strong that we have before us in Jesus a human being like ourselves. . . . Jesus appears before us in the light of the play of his emotions as a distinct human being, with his own individuality. . . .[8]

Jesus is not shocked or offended by the humanness of our feelings. The writer of Hebrews tells us that Jesus is a high priest who can empathize with our feelings, so we can come to Him with confidence and talk to Him in our times of need (Hebrews 4:14-16).

The example of Jesus' life can be an encouragement for us to be like the person we admire, love, and follow. The apostle Paul taught that God is working in us to transform us into the image of Christ (2 Corinthians 3:17-18) and one aspect of becoming like Christ is to become a feeling person even as He was. In this way we can develop a Christ-like heart that values human life, that values the needs for moral standards and moral respect toward one another and that can be empathetic with the failures, needs, and losses that are common to human life. We can also *really enjoy* life.

Misunderstandings about Feelings

Another important step toward being willing to give ourselves permission to experience our feelings and emotions is to question some of the misunderstandings we have about them. They discourage us from becoming feeling people because the acceptance of these misunderstandings creates their own set of feelings: fear, guilt, self-doubt, and uncertainty. Then we react to these secondary feelings and become distracted and confused about how to deal with the primary ones.

Myth 1—*If we feel something, it's always a fact (the truth)*. This misunderstanding assumes that if we feel a feeling strong enough, long enough, or deep enough, then what we feel must be the truth. I first recognized this myth when I began to face my own feelings of inferiority. For years I had assumed that because I felt inferior, I was in fact inferior. As a young teenager I had no idea how to cope with this painful feeling except to try to be the best at something I did. This didn't solve my problem; in fact, it got worse after I became a Christian. There were a lot of religious things I could now compare myself to and feel inferior about spiritually.

This began to change when I started accepting my feelings as being an important part of who I was as a human being. Then I started looking at what they were trying to tell me. I learned that what they told me may not be the truth. By separating the feeling half of the sentence from the fact half, I could evaluate whether my feelings were telling me the truth or telling me a lie.

A realistic examination of the statement, "I feel inferior; therefore I am inferior," revealed that my feeling inferior did not prove I was inferior any more than feeling like a monkey would prove I was a monkey. It was true that I was inferior to others *in some ways* such as wealth, education, talents, or family pedigree, but it was a lie to believe my life was less important or valuable than another person's.

It is important for all of us to learn to separate the feeling half of a statement from the fact half (feeling ◄————► fact). All feelings prove is that we know how to feel! They say nothing about whether they are telling us the truth.

The way we find out if what we feel and what we have concluded based on our feelings are both true is by taking an honest, truthful, realistic look, at the facts. By accepting our feelings, we are free to look at the facts and learn if we are dealing with a lie or the truth.

This is especially important when dealing with self-esteem feelings like feeling inferior, unloved, worthless, or unwanted. Often, we have failed to separate these deeply felt feelings from the facts and we have suffered the death-producing consequences of thinking this way. From the list of examples below, see if any sound familiar to you:

- I feel unloved . . . therefore I am unloved.
- I feel like a nobody . . . therefore I am a nobody.
- I feel worthless . . . therefore I am worthless.
- I feel unwanted . . . therefore I am unwanted.
- I feel like a big nuisance . . . therefore I am a nuisance.
- I feel like a nothing . . . therefore I am nothing.
- I feel like a failure . . . therefore I am a failure.
- I feel insignificant . . . therefore I am insignificant.
- I feel unimportant . . . therefore I am unimportant.
- I feel I am defective . . . therefore I am a defect.

There may be other feelings not listed that are uniquely your own. If you have not separated the "I feel" from the "therefore I am," you may be suffering the painful effects of believing lies about yourself.

By separating our feelings from the message of our feelings, we can begin to examine where we went wrong in our conclusions. Then by looking honestly at truth, especially biblical truth, we can correct the mistakes in our thinking that have kept us believing in the lies, distortions, and misconceptions we hold about ourselves.

Jesus promised that when we know the truth, the truth will set us free (John 8:32). He was talking about the truth he was teaching and I call this capital *T* truth. I know that little *t* truth, the truth about our personal lives, can also set us free. The truth about our worth is that we are Imagebearers of God. Then we may be someone who also has failed at times, who happens to be unloved by some people, who happens to be a nuisance on occasions, who happens to be unimportant and unwanted by some families or organizations, who happens to have committed some criminal acts. These are little *t* truths of life, but have nothing to do with our worth.

To help bring this point home, I'll ask you the question I ask my clients: "A hundred years from now, will these people's opinion of you have any bearing on your worth as a person?" Obviously, the answer is no. We'll all be dead. The opinion that counts is Jesus' opinion, and we have seen how God loves what he has "fearfully and wonderfully made" in His image.

Just as lies have their set of feelings, truth has its own set of feelings. When we begin to accept the feelings created by truth we begin to break the bondage of thinking like this. Little *t* truth sets free but capital *T* Truth sets absolutely free.

Myth 2—*If I feel something, I will do something bad.* Many of us are afraid of our feelings because we believe they might cause us to act in bad, sinful, or unchristian ways. We see them as scary or dangerous, so we try to deny their existence. As one lady said so clearly, "I don't want to feel certain feelings because I am afraid of what the results might be. I am afraid my feelings might take me over." She was trapped in myth 2. After all, isn't anger just one letter short of d-anger?

Two of the most "dangerous" feelings people struggle with are anger and sexual desire. When we were young and impressionable, anger and sexual feelings were often scary and confusing. They created painful difficulties for us privately and in our relationships with others. Impulsiveness, immaturity, deep inner pain, or the lack of knowledge or skills prompted us to do things that left us feeling guilty and ashamed. In our attempt to control our feelings, we started believing that if we could stop feeling them we could avoid doing something bad or sinful again.

By making feeling and behaving one issue, we became trapped in our thinking. Here are some examples:

- If I feel angry . . . I'll do something bad.
- If I feel proud of myself . . . I'll act self-centered.
- If I feel sexually aroused . . . I'll do something immoral.
- If I feel I want something nice for myself . . . I'll become selfish and greedy.
- If I feel jealous . . . I'll be mean to someone.
- If I feel bitter . . . I'll act nasty and hateful.
- If I feel human . . . I'll do "worldly" things.

Just as feeling and truth are two separate issues, we also need to recognize that how we feel and how we choose to act are two separate issues (feel ◄————► act). In the past, feeling and acting may have been so entangled that we may have failed to clearly separate them—to see them as separate and distinct parts of our Imagebearing. Real freedom comes when we learn we can choose to act in line with our feelings or we can act in an opposite direction depending on what our sense of judgment tells us is the most life-giving choice. For example, we may feel like taking a nap and we decide to take one; we may feel like stealing something but choose not to do it; we may feel like being dishonest in a business deal but decide to act honestly; we may not feel like mowing the lawn but decide to do it anyway to avoid a bigger problem later.

The important thing to remember is that feelings don't make us do anything! They may urge, prompt, push, encourage, or tempt us to do something but we can feel without doing. Feelings want to move us and we can see this in the fact that the same Latin root word meaning "to move" is also found in the words emotion, motivation, motive, and motion.

Feelings may guide our decisions but it's the use of our ability to choose that decide what we will do or not do. Willard Gaylin makes this important distinction in his book *Feelings: Our Vital Signs*:

> Feelings are the fine instruments which shape decision-making in an animal cursed and blessed with intelligence, and the freedom which is its corollary. They are signals directing us toward goodness, safety, pleasure, and group survival. . . . Feelings, therefore, particularly the complex and subtle range of feelings in human beings, are testament to our capacity for choice and learning. . . . Because we are intelligent creatures—meaning that we are freed from instinctive and patterned behavior to a degree unparalleled in the animal kingdom—we are capable of, and dependent on, using rational choice to decide our future. Feelings become guides to that choice.[9]

The ability to feel and the ability to choose how we will act or think are two distinct facets of being made in God's image. To feel is to be human; to choose to act and think in life-giving ways is to be mature, to be Christ-like. To know this is to free us to become a feeling person.

Myth 3—*If I experience certain feelings, I am a bad person*. This misunderstanding about feelings assumes that nice people feel nice feelings and bad people feel bad ones. Almost every person I've counseled, especially Christians, have reported feeling guilty for experiencing feelings which their family, culture or church has labeled bad, sinful or worldly. Statements like,

"How can you feel that way and claim to be a Christian?" or "You shouldn't feel like that—don't you know what the Bible says about that?" implies that only bad people or unspiritual Christians experience certain feelings such as resentment, depression, discouragement, jealousy, worry, hate. Here are a few familiar statements illustrating myth 3:

- I feel guilty because . . . I still feel resentful.
- I feel guilty because . . . I am tired of being a parent.
- I feel I am bad because . . . I feel sexually aroused by someone other than my spouse.
- I feel guilty because . . . I want to do something nice for myself.
- I feel I am bad because . . . I am fed up with people using me because I can't say no.
- I feel guilty because . . . I still don't feel forgiven by God when I know I should.
- I feel guilty because . . . I felt relieved when they died.

To presume that a person, whether Christian or not, is immune to the normal feelings common to all humans is a mistake. The truth is, we are human beings and we will experience the normal range of feelings common to humanity.

Being a Christian can help us work with our feelings more effectively; but if we feel guilty or that we're a bad person because of our feelings, we will find ourselves divided against ourselves. We will try to deny, reject, or repress the unacceptable feelings and by doing so diminish our ability to find a workable solution for our situation. We will spend more time and energy trying to cope with superficial feelings, rather than with the important ones we need to face. We will be struggling with self-worth issues instead of accepting the realities of life and learning how to deal with them from a Christian perspective.

Nathaniel Brander had a clever way of describing this struggle in his book, *The Disowned Self*:

> One of the tragedies of human development [and I would add, of becoming like Christ] is that many of a person's most self-destructive acts are prompted by a blind, misguided . . . attempt to protect his sense of . . . self-esteem. . . . When a person represses certain of his emotions because they threaten his sense of control or conflict with his notion of "strength" or "maturity" or "sophistication", he disowns part of himself . . . Do such attempts succeed? They do not. Self-esteem cannot be built on a foundation of self-alienation. The consequences of such attempts is the sabotaging of one's ability to enjoy life.[10]

I suspect that many Christians are unhappy and not enjoying life, because they do not understand the gift of being made to be a feeling person as God designed them to be. The three myths mentioned earlier could explain why they "disown" this part of themselves and find themselves divided against themselves. *They become their own worst enemy.* I know this was true for me as a Christian. So I chose to change. Was it easy to change my attitudes and thinking habits about feelings? No! At first it was confusing, scary and difficult. I had built a whole system of safe guards around my feelings so I could protect myself from *experiencing* life. Some of these safe guards helped me cope and survive my past. But now, I found they restricted and handicapped my present desire to become a healthy feeling person. Giving myself permission to accept all my feelings, at my own pace, meant I had to believe there were better, healthier ways to deal with them. I committed to accepting all my experiences in life so I could learn to be an open, honest, real person. The journey to change was well worth it.

As I learned to be more aware of the full range of my feelings and accepted them unconditionally, the more free I was to think of options to better my life. Then I started making the choices necessary to make it happen. Feeling, thinking and choosing began to work together to make my life be as I believe God intended it to be. Brandon described it this way:

> Man is not merely a thinking machine; he is also a being who feels, who experiences emotions; and he is also a being who acts . . . his effective functioning as an organism, the fulfillment and enjoyment of his life, depends on the successful *integration* of thought, feeling and action.[11]

Challenging the three myths about feelings is one way to liberate ourselves from the imprisonment of feeling guilty for feeling. Responsible handling of our feelings begins when we realize the power we have as choice-makers to think and act differently in dealing with life. Choice-making is an effective way to manage our feelings. We will discuss this in detail in chapters 13 and 14, but first we need to know it's okay to be a feeling person. Our ability to feel is a gift—the gift of being created in God's image.

Giving ourselves permission to become the feeling person we were designed to be is one of the keys to becoming alive, real, and colorful as a person. It is one of the keys to living a healthy Christian life. It is not easy at first to remind ourselves that it's okay to experience our feelings. We are used to denying or fighting them. But when we give ourselves permission to acknowledge and accept them, we are in a position to start working with them in positive and life-giving ways. We can make better decisions when we know how we feel. Feelings do not have to control us. We can control them.

In the next chapter we will learn some of the perspectives and skills necessary to help us be more willing to experience our feelings. We will also learn how to work with our feelings more effectively in daily life.

Suggested Reading

1. Viscott, David. *The Language of Feelings.* Pocket Books, 1976.
2. Jacobs, Joan. *Feelings! Where They Come From And How To Handle Them.* Tyndale House Publishers, Inc. 1976.
3. Genesis 43:30; Job 3:25; Psalm 17:10; 73:21-26; 119:73,76; 143:4; Proverbs 14:10,13; 15:13; 28:14; Matthew 26:75; Luke 24:36-43; 2 Corinthians 1:8-9; 2:4; Philippians 1:7.

Emotions affect the whole person and each emotion affects the person differently. . . . Changes in emotions can alter the appearance of our world from bright and cheerful to dark and gloomy, our thinking from creative to morbid, and our actions from awkward and inappropriate to skillful and effective.

Carroll E. Izard, *Human Emotions* [1]

To live truthfully is to live true to feelings. . . . Of course everyone or almost everyone already believes he can feel. In fact, everyone does feel, but most people's feelings are hidden or mixed up. . . . People come into the world speaking the language of feeling but are forced to learn the language of defending and holding in.

Joseph Hart (and others), *Going Sane* [2]

So where do feelings fit into the life of a Christian? . . . We make progress in the process of being all God intended for us when our feelings, an integral part of humanity, become acceptable to us as well. The love of God doesn't change because we've begun to discover what we're like inside. Because God loves us we can be free to care for ourselves, to admit honestly how we feel. . . . Our feelings are important to our Christian growth.

Joan Jacobs, *Feelings!* [3]

CHAPTER 12

Trust Your Feelings:
You Can't Afford Not To

HOW TO

*T*he movie *Back to the Future,* was a smash hit when it was first released. Part of its appeal was the fantasy of entering a time machine that could transport us back to the 1950s. There have been many fictional variations of time-machines designed by eccentric inventors, but none matched the super high-tech Delorean used by Michael J. Fox.

Imagine for a moment that we just entered such a machine. We're transported back to 1996, the year the summer Olympic games are being held in Atlanta, Georgia. As part of the Olympic year celebration, the Olympic torch was lit on Mt. Olympus in Greece, flown to the east coast of the United States, and then carried across the country by thousands of runners, finally arriving at the Olympic site for the opening of the games.

Imagine that you are living in a town or city where the Olympic torch is passing through. One day you receive a telephone call from the person in charge of organizing the runners to carry the torch through your area. He invites you to be a part of this grand occasion by asking if you would be willing to carry the torch for a certain section of the route. You ask a few questions and then you agree to do it. You thank him for the opportunity, say goodbye, and you hang up. What feelings do you think you would experience in those next few moments? (Pause for a moment before continuing.)

No doubt you would experience an assortment of feelings ranging from shock, disbelief, suspicion (It must be a joke), uncertainty, and curiosity (Why Me?) to feeling excited, challenged, honored, motivated (I'd better get into shape), and privileged. It would feel awesome to be a part of something that big, that significant, that special.

I also would feel a sense of panic as I imagined myself being the only runner in the entire United States to fall during my run, with a headline shouting my mishap across the national wire services: "Runner Falls and Snuffs Out Olympic Torch."

My family and I did see the Olympic torch when it passed through Portland, Oregon. Just seeing it moved me to tears. I love sports and the torch represented what the summer Olympics were all about—the best athletes in the world competing to honor their country and themselves by doing their best and hoping it is good enough to win a gold metal. But there are two lessons I want to draw from this story. The first deals with self-worth and the second with accepting, understanding and working with our feelings.

Torch-bearer—Image-bearer

Some of the most moving stories on TV were the interviews with people who actually carried the Olympic torch. They were deeply touched by the experience and described how honored they felt. They represented a cross-section of society in respect to age, race, gender, and physical ability, but everyone's faces revealed a deeply felt sense of joy and pride for their part in the event.

But I was also saddened when I thought how we can feel such a sense of pride, honor, and pleasure for being an Olympic torch-bearer and yet feel nothing about being God's image-bearer. Being chosen by God to carry His image is the highest honor God has bestowed on us. Truly, we are fearfully and wonderfully made; we have been crowned with honor and glory! This is not changed by skin color, nationality, gender, handicaps, education, age, wealth, sins, or crimes.

Like those who carried the Olympic torch, I pray that each of us will realize the significance of being an Imagebearer of God and begin to feel, deep in our hearts, the honor, worth, esteem, and sense of identity this single truth can bring. Being open to God and to **experiencing the truth** of our being made in God's image can transform our lives. Part of that transformation comes in learning how to accept and work with our feelings. Let's look at some of the ways we can learn how to do this.

Looking at Feelings like Colors of the Color-Spectrum

Feelings are like crayons. They come in an assortment of colors. When we make a commitment to ourselves and to God to become more of a feeling person, the idea of equating feelings with colors may be helpful. That we already connect feeling to color can easily be illustrated by statements we make. For example, we call jealousy "the green monster" and we have heard the expression, "I am green with envy."

Anger and related feelings such as frustration, irritation, exasperation, resentment, bitterness, cynicism and hate are all associated with shades of the color red as in, "I was so mad I saw red."

Red is also associated with romantic feelings such as love (red roses, red hearts) or sexual feelings such as passion, desire, or sensuality. We talk about the "red light district" and the "Scarlet A," both associated with human sexuality.

We use color to describe the feeling of being down or in the dumps by saying, "I feel blue today." If we have been unhappy and discouraged for a period of time, we feel some shade of gray. If we are depressed, it "feels" black or dark blue. Black has long been associated with depression, death, mourning, and grief.

People coming out of a depression notice color returning to their inner life. The hues they notice include soft green, yellow, orange, soft pink, and white. These represent the return of positive feelings such as hope, fun, relief, joy, peace, freedom, pleasure, happiness, enjoyment, love, and gratitude. They are feelings of returning life and are revealed by statements such as, "I feel as if I have been living in this big, dark cloud and finally the sun is starting to shine again," or "I am beginning to see the light at the end of this dark tunnel."

We can't force every feeling into a color, but thinking of them as colors can encourage us to become more accepting of our feelings. Just as the beauty of the natural world around us would be drastically affected if any colors were eliminated, so does the rejection or acceptance of feelings in our inner world make life either colorless and drab or colorful and meaningful.

The more we accept the different colors of the feeling spectrum— whether bright-colored feelings such as excitement, happiness, anger, and fear, or pastel-colored feelings such as contentment, thankfulness and hope—the more colorful we become as a person. Have you noticed how much more colorful clothing, skiing outfits, vans, and business offices have become since the cultural changes of the 1960s and 70s when feelings and colors were given more acceptance? By experiencing a wider range of feelings, the quality of our lives becomes richer and fuller—we become more fully human and fully alive.

The same is true in our relationships with one another. The more open we are to experiencing feelings in our daily relationships, the more we can connect and deal with ourselves and those around us. We may think some feelings are "ugly colors," but these are an important part of the whole of life. It may not always be easy but learning to view feelings as colors helps us to grow emotionally.

I Know What I Feel, I Just Can't Seem to Find a Word for It

Another important step toward becoming a healthier feeling person is learning how to label our feelings accurately. We don't take the time (or we have not learned how) to find the right labels for our feelings. Dr. Gaylin noted this problem:

> When we leave the more basic and primitive emotions and enter into the range of more subtle, more specifically and exclusively human emotions, of shame, embarrassment, guilt, pride and so forth, we find how confused people are in the labeling of even their own feelings.[4]

Generally, the more intense, bright, or familiar feelings are not hard to label—such as excited, thrilled, happy, hurt, mad, jealous, or anxious—and we talk about them more frequently. There are, however, a lot of what I call "pastel-colored feelings" that are softer, gentler, and quieter. They are not spoken about much, but may in fact be the more important ones. The brighter-colored feelings often cover up or distract us from noticing these softer feelings. For example, anger can often hide feelings such as relief, shyness, helpfulness, vulnerability, disappointment, or sadness. We talk about our anger but say nothing about the other feelings. In this case, anger becomes what I call a "bedspread feeling" because it covers up other feelings. A feeling list can be found in the back of the book. It's not meant to be complete, but to provide a starting point for improving your ability to name your feelings. Reading this list through several times can help you develop the vocabulary and the skill to identify and label your feelings more accurately.

You'll notice a sentence at the top of the feeling list: "I feel (have felt) . . . when . . ." Using it can help you identify where you have experienced a specific feeling but may not have labeled it with that word. A completed sentence might read like this, "I feel accepted when someone gives me a big hug." You can also use it to answer questions like, "Is this feeling a familiar feeling I have felt before or is this a new experience I am having now."

Many benefits come from practicing the skill of accurately labeling feelings. One benefit is an improved sense of self-acceptance. *Our feelings are part of us and to accept our feelings is to accept ourselves. It authenticates the real person we are.* It also improves our ability to communicate our feelings to others by being able to speak more clearly about what we are experiencing. There is something freeing about being truthful with ourselves about our feelings. Being able to name them helps us own them.

Feelings Are like Grapes: They Come in Clusters

When I first began working on accepting all my feelings, I was surprised to learn that I experienced several feelings at the same time about a single situation. Some feelings were brighter, more intense or bigger in percentage than others; but there were always two or more feelings present in every situation. The question, "How do you feel about that?" misled me to believe I was supposed to have only one feeling; so when I felt several feelings simultaneously, it confused me. The question could be more accurately asked, "What are your feelings about that?"

Robert Plutchik observed this in a research project that dealt with the physiological changes mental patients experienced during psychiatric interviews. The research team had a hard time drawing conclusions. In his book *The Emotions*, he wrote:

> As I thought about this, it seemed to me that the major difficulty was our inability to evaluate the patient's emotions. Of particular importance was the fact that their emotions were always mixed, and difficult to specify or unravel. This observation suggested a possible parallel between mixed emotions and mixed colors. We notice, for instance, that certain hues such as red and green or yellow and blue are complementary or opposite. This is also true of emotions: joy and sorrow, love and hate, acceptance and rejection.[5]

Knowing that it's normal to experience mixed feelings frees us from this confusion. Learning how to accept this cluster of feelings sometimes means accepting two seemingly contradictory feelings at the same time— excitement and dread, happiness and disappointment, joy and anger, trust and distrust, relief and regret, excitement and fear. The statement, "I want to and I don't want to," is an example of the mixed feelings we can experience in response to the same reality.

Another example of experiencing mixed feelings occurred when the two women went to the tomb of Jesus and found it empty. An angel told the women that Jesus had risen from the dead and that they would find Him in Galilee. Matthew wrote:

> "So the women hurried away from the tomb, *afraid yet filled with joy*, and ran to tell his disciples" (Matthew 28:8, italics mine).

Feelings of relief, sorrow, and regret often accompany the death of someone we love who is finally released from their suffering brought on by aging, a disease, or an accident. *Each feeling goes to its own personal place in our heart.* We feel relieved because the person we love is no longer in pain; we feel sorrow because we no longer have them with us; we may feel regret because we didn't do or say some things before they died.

Knowing that it is okay, healthy, human, and Christian to accept mixed feelings is an important key to being a whole person.

Welcome Feelings as Friends: They Bring Us Important Information

Psychological and spiritual growth begins when we accept our feelings and see them as friends who are telling us important information about life. Dr. Viscott wrote:

> The language of feelings is the means by which we relate with ourselves, and if we cannot communicate with ourselves we simply cannot communicate with others. . . . Reality can't be comprehended without taking into account feelings.[6]

Feelings communicate. They tell us something important about our values, beliefs, attitudes, expectations, needs, choices, interpretations, demands, behaviors, and past experiences. They keep us informed about what is going on physically, mentally, socially, and spiritually. They tell us about life in both our inner and outer worlds at any given time.

To understand what our feelings are trying to convey, we need to accept them and follow them back to their connection to our inner world. We do this by asking, "What are my feelings trying to tell me about my beliefs, my self-esteem, my lifestyle, my choices, my view of God, and so forth?" We need to pause long enough to hear the information our feelings are sending. Failure to do so can be costly.

Feelings are like indicator lights on the panel of our car. They tell us how things are functioning. Imagine we're driving to an appointment when suddenly the oil light comes on. Running late, we decide to ignore it, convincing ourselves that it came on by mistake. A few miles later we hear the second message but this time it's coming from the motor—the soft sound of "click, click, click."

Again, we decide to ignore it because we don't have time to stop and check under the hood. A little further and we get a third, more dramatic, message as the motor starts to rattle and bang. Finally, it freezes up, stops running and the car comes to a halt. Many of us run our lives in the same way. Certain feelings try to give us important information about what's going on, but we ignore them. After all, we have been taught not to trust our feelings because they could lie to us or lead us astray. Besides, the pace of modern life doesn't allow us the time needed to pay adequate attention to their message. So we keep on "driving."

A sense of being unhappy or tired may be the first warning, signaling a need to rest, to take a vacation, to change our perspectives, to reorganize our values and priorities, or to negotiate some other changes. But we keep pushing on until the second set of signals tell us we are in more serious trouble. We may be mildly depressed, unable to sleep, overly sensitive, irritable, experiencing periodic panic attacks, or feeling uptight like a spring about to come uncoiled.

Still we continue to ignore these messages. We don't know what else to do but "keep going." Besides, we were taught that it's better to "burn out for God than to rust out." Eventually, we realize we have ignored our feelings too long to take care of the problem, and the consequences may be a nervous breakdown, feelings of suicidal depression, or a personal tragedy like the breakup of a home or the loss of a job.

Accepting and understanding our feelings are the only ways we can find out what they are trying to tell us. Then we can decide what we need to do if we want to improve things. We may not like some of our feelings at times, but the more we learn from them and the more we discover their importance to our well-being, the more valuable they become in helping us become happy and mature Christian human beings. We no longer have to be afraid of them or intimidated by their presence in our daily experiences. We can learn to work with our feelings rather than work against them. We don't have to be victimized by them; they can become our friends.

Feelings Can Be Located Physically

If we took the feeling list and physically located where each feeling is experienced, we would learn they can be found in four general areas. A few examples can help us see this.

• *Head and Neck:* We can feel dizzy, confused, pressured, dense, thick-headed, dazed or dumb. We can feel open-minded or clear-headed or that "our head is in a fog." Our throat can tighten under the strain of anger, fear, sadness, or panic.

• *Chest, Back, and Shoulders:* Joy, peace, love, warmth, sadness, and sorrow are examples of feelings of the heart. We can feel "like a ton of weight has been lifted from our back" or that there are "tight bands around our chest" that restrict breathing.

• *Stomach:* We get butterflies in our stomach (nervous, fear). Anger, loneliness, or insecurity may be described as "having a knot in the pit of our stomach."

• *Loins and Legs:* Fear and sexual feelings are located here. Shock, fright, or terror can "buckle our knees," or create the sensation of wanting to run or go to the bathroom.

Some of the most life-giving feelings we can experience are feelings of the heart. We can know our Christian life is on the right track when the feelings of love, joy, peace, patience, kindness, goodness, faithfulness, gentleness, and self-control (Galatians 5:22-23) are experienced more frequently in our heart than in our head.

Feelings Are Never Buried Dead: They Are Buried Alive

It has surprised people to learn that feelings they thought were gone, dead, and buried were actually still very much alive. This is because feelings are never buried dead; they are always buried alive. To prove this we simply need to allow ourselves to think back for a few moments about a situation from the past. We will soon discover that the feelings we thought were gone forever slowly return. If the feelings are positive and we like reexperiencing them, we are likely to let the thoughts remain; but if the feelings are negative and painful, we try to force the thoughts from our mind.

Feelings have energy, and when they are buried their energy goes someplace. It often shows up disguised as a spastic colon, ulcerated colitis, a stomach ulcer, hives, constipation, or a migraine headache. Not knowing how to *think through and feel through* a memory to a healthy resolution, we remain intimidated by the memory and imprisoned in our crazy-games, unable to cope with the feelings that return.

I define a crazy-game as any method we use to try to avoid feelings we don't like or to create feelings we want both of which bring *death-producing consequences* to us and to those around us. Generally it is a *reaction* to a life situation, for example, there are good people who try to please everyone and are constantly finding themselves hurt, used, and overextended. Pleasing becomes a crazy-game. When we use alcohol or drugs, to cope with negative feelings such as boredom, shame, guilt, depression, anger, or fear by trying to create feelings of relief, pleasure, fun, or self-confidence, then alcohol and drug use become a crazy-game. One man tried to stuff his feelings deep inside till he learned that this didn't work. He said it was like swallowing a gold fish but it later turned out to be a piranha.

Sex becomes a crazy-game when used as a way to cope with feeling lonely, unwanted, or unloved or as an attempt to build one's ego. Some Christians go to church and become involved in all kinds of activities in an attempt to feel spiritual and avoid feelings of pain, guilt, or fear; church-going becomes a crazy-game. Adults still trying to earn the approval, love, and acceptance of a parent, but find it impossible to achieve and are left feeling hurt, resentful, and depressed, are playing crazy-games.

Emotional liberation is possible when we learn how to accept our feelings and learn new *life-giving ways* of working with them. This is more easily done when we experience the freedom, courage, and strength that is ours that comes from knowing our worth is secure in being made in God's image. We are free to be honest with ourselves and to learn a new way of life because we are assured of God's love for us.

Feelings in Four Dimensions

Having said what I did about buried feelings and their relationship to the past, it is very important that we know that we *do not* need to go back and relive our feelings about our past—not right at first! Many of us have come from serious dysfunctional backgrounds and we would stop our growth right now if it meant having to recall and reexperience a lot of feelings from our past.

What is important to know if we are to become a healthier feeling person is that we can learn how to accept our feelings one day at a time and improve our ability to work with them successfully on a daily basis. As each day passes we will become more comfortable with a wider range of feelings and learn the skills necessary to handle them effectively. Gradually, we will develop the confidence needed to deal with specific past, memory-based feelings. We work on it when we decide we are ready. In becoming more aware of and accepting of our present feelings, it is helpful to know that feelings can be viewed on a continuum from positive (pleasant) to negative (unpleasant) on one dimension and from uncomfortable to comfortable on another. The following diagram illustrates this.

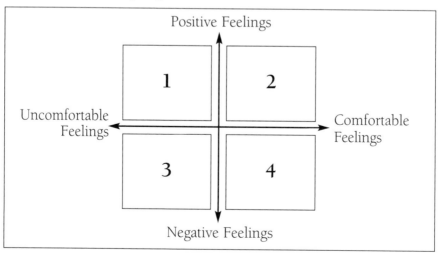

A fascinating thing about our attitude toward feelings is that many of our most positive feelings are also the most uncomfortable ones for us to accept. Positive feelings such as feeling loved, proud of ourselves, important, forgiven, successful, free, and happy can be very uncomfortable for many of us to experience (quadrant 1).

Can you remember when someone gave you a genuine compliment and it got into your heart and it felt really good? Do you remember how another part of you felt embarrassed, unworthy, shy, silly, distrustful, or afraid and you reacted (crazy-game) to the compliment by diminishing or shutting down the good feelings the compliment was intended to produce? We can do this by saying things silently to ourselves such as, "If they really knew me they wouldn't have said what they did," or "They are just being nice, they really don't mean it." Some of us remember the Bible verse, "Pride comes before destruction" (Proverbs 16:18) and this scares us into shutting down the compliment.

We can also push the compliment away by saying out loud, "Oh, that was nothing," or "I could have done better if I'd had more time." Christians often turn good feelings away by saying, "God deserves all the credit," and while I am all for God being honored, I also want people to learn to feel the life-giving benefit compliments are designed to bestow.

God has always condemned a "fat head," but He has never condemned a "fat heart;" and most of us have hearts that are so shriveled we can't even accept an honest compliment. Like a dried sponge dropped into warm, soapy water, we need to "soak in" all the good feelings the compliment meant to give. In this way we can truly honor God and honestly enjoy the rewards of our efforts. A heart filled with gratitude and thankfulness to God for feeling alive is true humility.

While we use all kinds of crazy-games to stop ourselves from experiencing positive feelings, we are more than willing to experience negative ones such as unhappiness, guilt, depression, loneliness, ugliness, or uselessness. Why? Because they have become comfortable feelings for us. By comfortable I don't mean we like them! It's just that they have been around for so long we have become used to them. Like an old pair of shoes, they have become a part of us and we would be lost without them. They have become negative-comfortable feelings (quadrant 4). By giving little time and attention to experiencing our positive feelings, our inner feeling world gets out of balance.

When we reverse this process by *consciously soaking in our positive experiences*, we begin to nurture and strengthen our inner being. We need to practice feeling feelings. Positive feelings such as love, compassion, joy, gratitude, enjoyment, contentment, freedom, self-respect, self-liking, or belonging are feelings we need to learn to enjoy experiencing. I call these feelings "life-giving feelings." They come as a result of healthy thinking and good choice-making. Our goal is to learn how to accept and work with *all* our feelings—whether positive, negative, uncomfortable, or comfortable.

Two Ways to Control Feelings: Reactive v. Proactive

It can be scary and threatening to start allowing ourselves to be more open to experiencing our feelings when we have spent a lifetime trying to deal with them in the best ways we knew how.

Sometimes we used methods that were good, healthy, and life-giving. At other times we really blew it because we started doing things that were wrong, unhealthy, and death-producing. We were trying to control our feelings from a defensive position.

Controlling feelings defensively means *reacting* to feelings and trying to stop or change our experience of them by rejecting them, denying them, rationalizing them away, blaming them on others, projecting them onto others, or burying them under sex, alcohol, drugs, work, television, religion, or the misuse of Bible verses. We have used hundreds of crazy-games to control our feelings, but it keeps us on the defensive and in bondage. Even if we have acted out our feelings in hostile, aggressive, and destructive ways, we are still using crazy-games to keep feelings in check and under control. Underneath all that toughness is a tender heart; it simply was better to be tough and mean than to feel like a child again and be hurt.

A friend once told me, "Larry, feelings have never killed anybody. It is what people do to try to stop feelings that kills them." He also said that suicide was the ultimate crazy-game because in the person's attempt to stop their feelings, they win by losing.

What we need are life-giving ways to work with our feelings that are positive, purposeful, intentional, proactive, and Christian. We need ways to manage our feelings that allow us to be aware of them, but also provide handles for dealing with them in healthy, self-respecting, and self-controlled ways.

The two most effective methods for managing feelings successfully are the exercise of our ability to choose (self- determination) and our ability to think (reason). To work with our feelings through good choice-making and sound reasoning is to experience being fully human and truly Christian. Like two hands on a steering wheel of a moving car, we can control our feelings and move in directions we know are more life-giving. This means we take a proactive attitude toward our feelings and work with them in an assertive and positive way.

The principle involved here can be seen in the simple examples of how we attend to our physical needs. If we feel thirsty, we get a drink; if we feel hungry, we eat; if we feel the need to go to the bathroom, we go. Can you imagine what would happen if we decided to not go to the bathroom for the rest of the month because we didn't have time—and besides, it's boring doing the same thing over and over and over again? The idea is ridiculous. Yet we make this kind of mistake when it comes to other areas of our life. Life would be so much better if we would learn how to take care of ourselves psychologically, emotionally, socially, and spiritually in the same way we take care of our biological needs.

Learning to be aware of and accepting of our feelings can help us make better choices and improve the quality of our lives. Dr. Viscott said it so clearly when he wrote:

> When a person assumes responsibility for his feelings, he also assumes responsibility for his world. Understanding feelings is the key to mastery of ourselves, finding true independence. . . . While this idea implies that each of us is on his own, it also means that there's much that each of us can do to set straight the disjointed pieces of his life and bring them into harmony. Indeed, I suspect if each person accepted the responsibility for putting his own emotional world in order, the larger world might also become more real, harmonious, and even peaceful.[7]

This is one of the greatest lessons we can learn in life: *We have the power to choose life, to choose life-giving ways to work with our feelings.* I believe Jesus' whole life demonstrated this capability and is part of what made him such a remarkable person.

While each of us may be on our own, we are not alone! God, having created us in His image, will help us learn to live as he designed us to live. God is more interested in our well-being than we will ever be and He wants to help us learn effective ways to live our Christian life. The apostle James stated it this way:

> If any of you lacks wisdom, he should ask God, who gives generously to all without finding fault, and it will be given him (James 1:5).

Talking with God is an important part of our healing and growth process. He designed our being so He knows how we function and what we need. When we combine His help with our abilities—to feel, choose, and think—we can develop the skills necessary to work with life more effectively. The following diagram illustrates how we can work responsibly with our feelings by the exercise of our abilities to choose and think.

To use this chart successfully, first write out a brief paragraph summarizing the situation that makes you unhappy. Second, identify and label the set (cluster) of feelings you don't like related specifically to that situation. By doing a "feeling inventory" you can *accurately identify* your feelings and have a more honest sense of what it is you're dealing with.

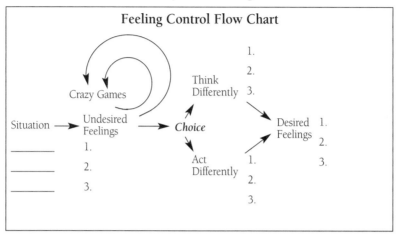

This is an important step in the successful use of the flow chart. It takes a while to learn how to be relaxed in the presence of some of our feelings. If you don't take time, you are more likely to fight your feelings and react to them in crazy-game ways. This will not work and you'll recycle back into the situation, solving nothing.

Once you become comfortable with your feelings—meaning they don't intimidate or manipulate you into overreacting—you are able to learn from them the important information they are trying to convey. The progress you make in accepting your feelings will help you move to the third step, which is finding ways to solve your problem.

Now you can go to step three and use the two proactive techniques of choosing to think differently or choosing to act differently to bring about a healthy feeling change. The positive use of your ability to choose will give you a *sense of self-control* over your feelings rather than your feelings controlling you. Developing a deep appreciation for your choice-making ability is the key that moves you from unhappiness to happiness, from pain to healing, from bondage to freedom, from self-hate to self-caring, from resignation to gratitude, from defeat to victory, from depression to joy. This is the evidence of a successful movement from step three to step four.

Choosing is the bridge we cross when we want to move from the side of unwanted feelings to the side of desired feelings—from death-producing feelings, to life-giving feelings. To decide to start the trek across the bridge by choosing life is not easy but it's worth it! The next two chapters will develop this idea in depth. But let me say here that God has given us two amazing gifts in the ability to choose and the ability to think. Both are ours to use in making life better for ourselves and for others around us.

As Christians, many of us know a lot of biblical truth in our head, but we lack the experienced affirmation in our hearts to confirm it. This is because we have not seen the positive value of accepting feelings as an important part of Christian life. The evangelical Christian's reaction to existentialism, neo-orthodoxy, liberal theology, or emotional pentecostalism has been to back away from feelings in favor of an intellectualized theology. The meaningful Christian life is one that accepts both content and experience. I call it "Experienced theology". I experience the truths of Scripture.

There is a great potential for healing, growth, change, recovery, and restoration when we begin to appreciate how God's image is revealed in our ability to feel, choose, and think. We have discussed ideas and perspectives to help us value our feelings and to see some of the positive ways we can work with them to bring color and richness into our daily life. Let's look at the gift of choice-making and see what exciting things lay in store for us there.

Suggested Reading

1. Gaylin, Willard. *Feelings: Our Vital Signs.*, Ballantine Books, 1979.
2. Powell, John. *The Secret Of Staying in Love.* Argus Communications, 1974.
3. 1 Samuel 30:4; Psalm 55:1-2,4-5; 94:19; 119:28,70; Proverbs 17:22; Ezekiel 36:26; Luke 2:33,47-48; 24:32,52; Romans 9:1-2; 15:13; 2 Corinthians 1:3-4; 7:6; Philippians 2:26-28; 4:11-13; 1 Thessalonians 4:13-14,18.

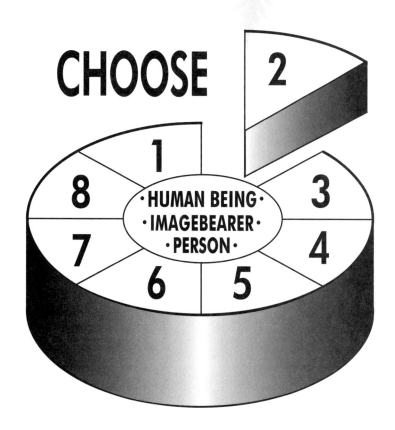

CHOOSE

1
2
3
4
5
6
7
8

· HUMAN BEING ·
· IMAGEBEARER ·
· PERSON ·

Man's dignity is seen with a certain authentic finality when it is seen that he is the master of that free choice which determines destiny. . . . All the achievements of man have been based upon his ability to do one thing when he might have done another. . . . **Individual character is the crystallization of free choices into permanence.** Free men choosing are the most significant phenomena of human life (bold mine).

Lynn H. Hough, *The Dignity of Man*[1]

Of all the wondrous powers with which God has endowed man, his will—the power of determining what he does, and so what he is—is the most wonderful. This is indeed the deepest trait of the divine image. God gave man to a very large extent the power of deciding and making himself. The mind, with all its wondrous capacities; the soul, with all its wealth of feeling; the spirit, man's moral and religious nature— all these have been given that he might be able to exercise that royal prerogative he has from God to will, so fashioning his own being and destiny for eternity.

Andrew Murray,
How to Raise Your Children for Christ[2]

Man has free choice, or otherwise counsels, exhortations, commands, prohibitions, rewards and punishments would be in vain.

St. Thomas Aquinas, *Treatise on Man*[3]

CHAPTER 13

Man: The Choice-maker

PERMISSION

Dr. Viktor Frankl, a European psychiatrist, has developed one of the most positive schools of psychological thought of our time. But it was not always so. For three years he suffered brutal Nazi attempts to dehumanize him in the concentration camps of Auschwitz and Dachau. He experienced the unthinkable atrocities that only human beings can inflict on each other.

After his arrest he was stripped of everything—literally stripped to his skin—and subjected to horrifying pain, suffering, brutality, starvation, filth, disease, and physical labor. The smell of death hung over everything, like an early morning smog. In his book *Man's Search for Meaning*, he described what happened.

> It can be readily understood that such a state of strain, coupled with the constant necessity of concentrating on the task of staying alive, forced the prisoner's inner life down to a primitive level. . . . With the majority of the prisoners . . . [this] led to a total disregard of anything not serving that purpose, and explained the prisoner's complete lack of sentiment. . . . The majority of prisoners suffered from a kind of inferiority complex. We all had once been or had fancied ourselves to be "somebody." Now we were treated like complete nonentities. . . . Without consciously thinking about it, the average prisoner felt himself utterly degraded.[4]

But there were prisoners whose lives demonstrated compassion in the midst of hate, life in the midst of death, beauty in the midst of ugliness. Their spiritual lives deepened; their love for the beauty of art and nature increased, and their appreciation for the truth "that love is the ultimate and the highest goal to which a man can aspire" became absolute.

In 1965, I spent a summer working on a kibbutz in Israel. Some of my co-workers survived these camps, their tattooed identification numbers still clearly visible on their forearms. Once during a meal I asked two men about what happened to them and how it affected their faith in God. One man described how his faith in God and his belief in certain truths found in the Bible were deepened beyond description. It gave him an inner strength to endure and not surrender to the ever-present enemy of despair.

The other man explained why he had become an atheist. He could not believe a God could exist who would not do something about the atrocities he witnessed. Deep inside I remember thinking, I wonder what made one man's faith go one way and the other go the opposite? Years later, while reading Dr. Frankl's book, I found part of my answer. It came down to a single word—CHOICE. Dr. Frankl wrote:

> We who lived in the concentration camps can remember the men who walked through the huts comforting others, giving away their last piece of bread. They may have been few in number, but they offered sufficient proof that everything can be taken from a man but one thing: the last of the human freedoms—*to choose one's attitude in any given set of circumstances, to choose one's own way.*
>
> And there were always choices to make. Every day, every hour, offered the opportunity to make a *decision*, a decision which determined whether you would or would not submit to those powers which threatened to rob you of your very self, your inner freedom. . . . Even though conditions such as lack of sleep, insufficient food and various mental stresses may suggest that the inmates were bound to react in certain ways, in the final analysis it becomes clear that the sort of person the prisoner became was the result of an *inner decision*, and not the result of camp influences alone. Fundamentally, therefore, any man can, even under such circumstances, decide what shall become of him—mentally and spiritually. *He may retain his human dignity even in a concentration camp* (italics mine).[5]

There it was—the innate ability to be a choice-maker. The two men, cited above, representing us all, demonstrated one of mankind's most unique human attributes, the ability to choose—to choose one's own attitude in the midst of any circumstance.

Why Don't I Feel like I'm a Choice-Maker?

We were born to choose; we cannot escape it. It is part of what makes us human and gives us innate worth. If a surgeon could perform a "choice-anectomy" we would be reduced to a robot, doing only what we were told to do. Void of any sense of free will, we would become human puppets dancing to the will of an outside puppeteer. Controlled by others we would become only a shadow of what a true human being is; we would be robbed of one of the important characteristics of what it means to be truly human.

So when did most of us lose our connection with our power to choose—to be in charge of our decisions? By looking back over our life we can identify certain times when we gave away or had taken away our sense of being a choice-maker. A few examples of what others have said may make this plain.

- "I was a junior in high school when I realized my parents accepted me and approved of my decisions only when I did what they wanted me to do."
- "I gave it up when I got married."
- "In order to be liked, I did everything possible to please other people, to the total disregard of my feelings and needs."
- "I never had it! It has always been that way as far back as I can remember."
- "It seemed like I needed to give up my freedom when I was taught I had to surrender totally to God's will and be dependent on Him."
- "I have always been under somebody's thumb. Before I die I wish I could have just one time in my life when I felt like I could do just what I wanted to do."
- "I gave it to my parents when I was a child but I took it back when I was a teenager. I was accused then of being stubborn and rebellious."
- "As a child and even as an adult, at times I took it only to feel so guilty I would then give it back. It keeps going back and forth."
- "After I became a Christian, I wanted to please God and to do His will for my life. To do this I felt I no longer was free to do what I wanted. I was supposed to obey God and do what He wanted."
- "It was taken from me when the abuse started. I had to become passive and compliant if I wanted to survive."

These statements show some of the ways we lose our sense of being in charge of our choices. Bad experiences, dysfunctional family backgrounds, wrong instructions, poor theology, distorted perspectives, or harmful encounters with people shape us into becoming reactive people, trying to survive our circumstances rather than being proactive people choosing life.

The statements show the tension we feel between having the freedom to be self-directing, independent and grown-up, as opposed to being controlled, dependent, and feeling like a child in an adult body—a child trying to win approval or avoiding punishment.

Some people become strong-willed and rebellious to prove that "no one is ever going to tell me what to do!" They don't realize they are just as out of control as the compliant person. They fight anyone or anything they think is trying to control them.

Two things can help us develop a healthy perspective about our decision-making ability. First, we need a renewed appreciation for the truth that God created us in His image to be choice-makers and it's okay for us to reclaim what God created us to be. Then we can give ourselves permission to grow and develop our ability to choose. Second, we need some practical ideas on how to become better decision-makers. Some of us have not done a very good job at choosing life but we can learn how.

By What Name Shall We Call It?

Psychology has done extensive research on the positive relationship between mental health and a person's ability to choose. Many terms are used to describe this unique human attribute such as free will, volition, autonomy, self-determination, assertiveness, inner locus of control, choosing, decision making, self-regulation, independence, and self-control. Each term, if reduced to its common denominator, describes a single, unique feature of our personhood.

We choose and we were designed to choose. We may not know why we do what we do, but we know we are in possession of a remarkable gift. Nathaniel Branden calls it "Volitional Consciousness" and sees it as an attribute that makes us different from animals. Our daily survival rests on two uniquely human qualities—reason and choice.

> The relation of man's reason to his survival is the first of two basic principles of man's nature which are indispensable to an understanding of his psychology and behavior. The second is that the exercise of his rational faculty, unlike an animal's use of his senses, is not automatic—that the decision to think is not biologically "programmed" in man—that to think is an act of choice.[6]

Animals possess the basic instincts necessary to help them move toward survival. But human beings, unlike animals, use both reasoning and choice to develop a unique form of living. Our lives go far beyond just biological survival; we can provide for our emotional, social, and spiritual well being.

Our freedom to feel or not feel, to think or not think, to be moral or not moral are connected to our ability to choose. Like Dr. Branden, Victor Frankl includes choosing in his definition of human.

> Man cannot avoid decisions. Reality inescapably forces man to decide . . . man is ultimately self-determining. What he becomes— within the limits of endowment and environment—he has made himself. In the living laboratories of the concentration camps we watched comrades behaving like swine while others behaved like saints. Man has both these potentialities within himself. Which one he actualizes depends on decision, not on conditions. It is time that this *decision quality of human existence* be included in our definition of man (italics mine).[7]

We are BEINGS who have the ability to choose life or death, happiness or unhappiness, joy or despair. We can choose to be kind or cruel, compassionate or hateful, caring or cold, moral or immoral.

Wayne Dyer is another well-known person whose lectures and writings have encouraged thousands of people to see the possibilities in the power of choice. His book *Your Erroneous Zones*, is one of the most helpful books available on choosing life. Two central themes run throughout his book. He wrote:

> The first involves your ability to make choices about your own emotions. Begin to examine your life in the light of choices you have made or failed to make. This puts all responsibility for what you are and how you feel on you. Becoming happier and more effective will mean becoming more aware of the choices that are available to you. YOU ARE THE SUM TOTAL OF YOUR CHOICES. . . .

> The second theme that will be emphasized . . . is that of taking charge of your present moments. . . . There is only one moment in which you can experience anything, and that is now, yet a great deal of time is thrown away by dwelling on past or future experiences. Turning your now into total fulfillment is the touchstone of effective living, and virtually all self-defeating behaviors (erroneous zones) are efforts at living in a moment other than the current one.[8]

The ability to choose, combined with taking charge of the present moment, are two powerful psychological and spiritual healing truths. Psychiatrist Dr. William Glasser understood the healing power in choice-making when he developed his theory called "Reality Therapy." In his book *Control Theory*, he contends that we behave irresponsibly because we will not accept and work with the reality of the world around us when we make decisions.[9]

While these writers stress the importance of our ability to choose in helping us become a healthy person, they say nothing about the origin of our choice-making ability. If asked, they could give only one of two answers: we came into possession of this amazing human ability either by chance or by design.

We Were Designed to Be Choice-Makers

Great significance and meaning can be given to this special faculty when we believe it has been given to us by our Creator, who is a choice-maker. Human beings did not become self-determining as a result of a cosmic accident; it is not the result of mere chance. Instead, it is the mark of God's image in each of us.

Choice-making is our birthright and the Judeo-Christian view of man explains *how* we acquired this unique gift, while psychology tells us *why* it is an important part of a healthy personality (mentally and spiritually).

Many people do not give God credit for the way He designed the human being as a choice-maker. But for those who can, a deepening appreciation for our power to choose can make us thankful to God for the wonder of His creative design.

We will find that it is in the freedom to choose that we find the nobility of man. In his book *The King of the Earth*, Erich Sauer clearly affirmed that God gave us free will in order to bring glory to Himself and to honor us. It is a gift He bestowed only on human beings.

> Where there is no freedom everything is slavery, even all the apparently "good." *Only on a foundation of freedom can there be true dignity and nobility of man.* That is why God wanted to crown the ranks of His creatures with a *being* capable of becoming conscious of the difference between good and evil and of *choosing* the good. In so doing He wished to show man the highest form of kindness. He wished to render supreme victory possible to him, to grant him the noblest joy, to adorn him with the most glorious crown (italics mine).[10]

Our being created in the image of God is an expression of God's divine love. He has bestowed on us the highest form of honor by giving us the privilege of being in charge of our choices. He knew that in that freedom He risked the possibility we would choose evil over good, death over life, unhappiness over happiness.

Parents can understand this perspective because as our children grow, we give them more and more freedom to be in charge of their choices, even at the risk of them making bad decisions. Only in this way can they grow up and become mature, independent, responsible adults.

A Fresh Look at Adam and Eve

Many Christians confuse our innate ability to choose with being rebellious. Ideas like "total obedience to God," "total submission," "totally surrendering to God," or being "totally dependent on God" build an impression that being compliant and passive is being spiritual. As a new Christian, I was taught that the sinful fall of Adam and Eve was the result of their rebellion against God. Gradually, I began to feel my making wrong choices meant that being in charge of making choices was somehow wrong.

The fact that Adam and Eve made a wrong choice does not discredit the wonder of their God-given ability to make choices. Neither does it diminish the freedom that accompanies the right to exercise that ability. To be in charge of one's choosing is a completely separate issue from the kind of choices one makes (freedom to choose ◄————► kind of choices made). We need to separate these two issues—pull them apart emotionally—if we are to recapture the wonder, awe, and power of being a choice-maker.

In the Genesis story, God honored mankind by creating Adam and Eve in His image as self-determining beings (Genesis 2ff). When God set limits (boundaries) regarding the tree of the knowledge of good and evil, He did not say, "You CAN'T eat from the tree . . ." because it would have been counter to the way God created the human personality. What God said was, "You MUST NOT eat. . . ." There is an important difference between "you cannot" and "you must not," the difference being that "must not" is a directive, whereas "cannot" focuses on lack of ability.

For example, if I said to you, "You cannot go across the street," you would probably hear, "He doesn't think I can do it. He thinks I'm helpless," and you would feel an urge to get up and cross the street just to prove you could. On the other hand, if I said, "You must not go across the street," it assumes you're not helpless, you do have the ability but you're being asked to choose not to. *Voluntary obedience* or *voluntary submission* is life-giving because it honors free will; but forced or coerced submission leads to apathy, depression, or rebellion (hidden or open).

When God commanded that Adam and Eve "must not eat of the tree," He did not question, remove, or invalidate their innate ability to be in charge of their choices—to be choice-making beings. The Bible says that when Eve was tempted she was deceived about her concept of God and whether the consequences would really happen. She chose death. Adam followed suit (and only God knows why). But in the act of choosing—not in the kind of choice made—they demonstrated their nobility as Imagebearers. Erich Sauer described it this way:

If He (God) were not to allow ethical creatures the possibility of exercising their free choice, they would no longer be ethical person-alities. They would be mere passive toys of His sovereignty, mere creatures governed by instinct, in reality nothing more than more highly gifted and more complexly controlled animals.

There could be no more talk of a nobility of man. . . . The holy nature of God could never have glorified itself, and with this the chief object in the creation of man would have been missed. But precisely because this object is of necessity grounded in God Himself as holy love, we must say: *God's own nature requires that He should of His own free will limit Himself so as to leave room for the unhindered self-determination of His ethical creature* (italics mine).[11]

What an affirmation of our nobility as human beings and what a positive support for our permission to be choice-makers! Is there anything that can affirm the worth and nobility of a person or a nation more than being free to choose—to choose life? And what tragedy and loss we suffer when we choose death, when we choose sin. Nevertheless, the worst derelict slumped over in the corner of a doorway, empty wine bottle lying beside him, has innate worth and value—not because of the kind of choices he is making, but simply because he is a human being—made in the likeness of God.

What is true for an individual is also true for a nation. Democracy is built on the principle of freedom of choice. Peoples and nations want the right of self-determination and no country likes to be occupied and under the control of another. The fall of communism in Eastern Europe gives testimony to the human desire to be free. Democracy as a political philosophy honors freedom of choice better than any other governmental system. The Declaration of Independence clearly affirms this in the line:

We hold these truths to be self-evident, that all men are created equal; that they are endowed by their Creator with certain unalienable rights; that among these are life, liberty and the pursuit of happiness. That to secure these rights, governments are instituted among men, deriving their just powers *from the consent of the governed* . . . (italics mine).

To feel in charge of one's choices is empowering and life-changing. It is also true that to feel the loss of one's freedom to choose causes a person to feel victimized and powerless. This leads to all kinds of physical, emotional, and spiritual problems.

We have looked at what people have said supporting our need to be decision-makers. Let's see how the Bible encourages us to be what God designed us to be.

Choose Life

Moses was one of Israel's greatest leaders. He led the Hebrews out of Egypt and through the Red Sea after more than three hundred years of national enslavement. It was through Moses God gave the Ten Commandments at Mt. Sinai and led the nation through the wilderness to the edge of her new homeland. Now Israel was camped on the east side of the Jordan River, preparing to enter the land God had promised to her forefathers.

Nearing the end of his life, Moses brought the people together and reviewed the teachings God had given them. He concluded his talk with one of the most powerful statements in the Bible.

> Now what I am commanding you today is not too difficult for you or beyond your reach. . . . This day I call heaven and earth as witness against you that I have set before you life and death, blessings and curses. Now CHOOSE LIFE, so that you and your children may live and that you may love the Lord your God, listen to his voice, and hold fast to him. For the Lord is your life . . . (Deuteronomy 30:11,19, caps mine).

The union of these two words—**choose life**—is the key to physical, social, mental, and spiritual health and happiness. The ability to choose is imbedded in the very being of every newborn child. From the moment of birth until the moment of death our lives are a witness to the kind of choices we have made or failed to make.

Choosing life means exercising self-determination in the direction that brings life-giving results. It is choosing the beliefs, values, perspectives, attitudes, morals, and actions that bring happiness, health, love, strength, aliveness, realness, freedom, and self-respect. It is choosing to treat others the way we would like them to treat us. Choosing life is being truthful, trustworthy, moral, kind, strong. Spiritually, choosing life is choosing to have a relationship with Jesus Christ that is personal, real, and alive.

God never intended for us to lose our birth right, our freedom to be in charge of our choices. It is a mark of His image in each one of us. What God wants is what Moses wanted his people to do: to choose life, not death; choose health, not sickness; choose good, not evil; choose hope and happiness, not despair; choose love, not hate.

Choose Whom You Will Serve

After Moses's death, Joshua took charge and led the people into battle to take possession of the promised land. Near the end of his life, Joshua also assembled the people for a concluding speech. He reviewed their history, summarized their victories, then presented them with a choice. They were to choose what god they were going to worship and serve.

> Now fear the Lord and serve him with all faithfulness. Throw away the gods your forefathers worshiped beyond the River and in Egypt, and serve the Lord. But if serving the Lord seems undesirable to you, then *choose for yourself this day whom you will serve* . . . But as for me and my household, we will serve the Lord (Joshua 24:14-15, italics mine).

Humans are spiritual beings and one of the most important decisions we make in life is how to be in a relationship with God. What kind of God is big enough to account for life and to command our highest admiration, respect, and worship? What kind of God is big enough to encourage our willing cooperation so that we choose life, not death? The God of all creation, the God of the Judeo-Christian faith is that God. We will look at this subject in greater detail in chapters 23 and 24. What's important here is that our ability to choose finds a special expression in the development of our faith in God.

Choose Your World View

As a young man, Elihu sat quietly listening to the debate between Job and his three friends concerning the cause of Job's suffering. Their arguments revealed their views of God, sin, suffering, life, and mankind. The more Elihu listened, the more angry he became. Finally, he spoke up and challenged them with his perspectives.

> Hear my words, you wise men; listen to me, you men of learning. For the ear tests words as the tongue tastes food. Let us discern for ourselves what is right; let us learn together what is good (Job 34:1-4).

A moment of decision is always encountered when an alternative perspective is given. Elihu recognized that ultimately the choice of how to understand the world was Job's. He revealed this when he said, "You must decide, not I" (Job 34:33). And what were some of the things Elihu challenged Job to consider? Let's look at a few.

- It is unthinkable that God would do wrong, that the Almighty would pervert justice (34:12).
- God is might, but does not despise men (36:5).
- God is exalted in his power. Who is a teacher like him? (36:22).
- How great is God—beyond our understanding (36:26).
- Stop and consider God's wonders (37:14).

We all must choose our view of the world. As we live out our beliefs and values, we experience the consequences of our choice. A world view too small to explain and give meaning to life both psychologically and spiritually is a world view that ultimately will fail us.

Job learned this painful truth when he discovered that his views of life were inadequate to cope with the reality of tragedy. Whatever view of life we choose, it needs to be big enough to include the wonders of the universe, the uniqueness and worth of human life as well as deal with human evil and human tragedies. The Judeo-Christian view of life meets this need. Elihu is right! The choice is always ours.

Choose What Is Better

Mary and Martha were friends of Jesus. Once when he was passing through their village, Martha opened her home to him as her guest. She became busy with the work of getting things ready while Mary was sitting, listening to Jesus talk. Martha became upset and said to Jesus, "Lord, don't you care that my sister has left me to do the work by myself? Tell her to help me!" (Luke 10:40). Jesus' answer was quite revealing.

"Martha, Martha," the Lord answered, "you are worried and upset about many things, but only one thing is needed. *Mary has chosen what is better*, and it will not be taken away from her" (Luke 10:41, italics mine).

Choosing life is choosing what is better. Jesus affirmed Mary in her decision to choose the better way. Many of us would have felt guilty not being busy and we would have been like Martha—busy but unhappy, resentful, and hurt. If Martha felt good about what she was doing, she too would have been choosing life.

Take Up Your Cross And Follow Me

Jesus was the preeminent choice-maker. At a place called Gethsemane He faced the most significant decision of His life—His impending crucifixion. Those of you who have seen the movie *The Passion of The Christ* know what this looked like. Earlier, He had enjoyed what must have been the high point of His earthly life. He had taken Peter, James, and John up to a mountain to pray, and while He was praying "the appearance of his face changed, and his clothes became as bright as a flash of lightning." Moses and Elijah both appeared and talked with Jesus about His coming departure to Jerusalem.

While Peter was talking to Jesus about what they had witnessed, a cloud surrounded them and the disciples became afraid. Then a voice spoke saying, "This is my Son, whom I have chosen; listen to him" (Luke 9:35).

A day or so later when Jesus knew that His time had come, the text says; "Jesus resolutely set out for Jerusalem" (Luke 9:51). He knew full well what lay ahead—His rejection, suffering, death, and final triumph in His resurrection. He stood alone in understanding the divine fulfillment of the Passover Sacrifice, in which He would die for the sins of mankind. He tried to prepare His disciples for what was to happen, but they "did not understand any of this" (Luke 18:31-34).

Could He have chosen to avoid the whole thing by escaping to Arabia? Yes, but it would have been a profound self-betrayal with eternal consequences—for Himself and for all humankind. Self-betrayal is always a death-producing choice.

It would have been just as empty if He allowed Himself to be crucified because He was unable to choose to do otherwise. There would be no honor, integrity, or salvation in His death if He had been merely a compliant victim of circumstances. It would have been a weak act rather then an act of strength and character. But Jesus said, "No one takes it from me, but I lay it down of my own accord" (John 10:18). When faced with the option of choosing life or choosing death, He chose life.

But how could His decision to die on a cross be choosing life? It may seem like a contradiction, but the answer is found in the big picture. Jesus was a choice-maker, not a pleaser, not a morally programmed martyr. He chose the cross, not because it was a nice thing to do, not to prove what a wonderful person He was. He chose the cross because He came to do the will of His Father—it was the right thing to do. He chose it because He knew the joy that would be His once the suffering and shame was over. The writer of Hebrews gives us insight into this.

> Let us fix our eyes on Jesus, the author and perfector of our faith, who for the joy set before him endured the cross, scorning its shame, and sat down at the right hand of the throne of God (Hebrews 12:2).

Jesus wanted to experience the joy that was waiting before Him, but a cross stood in the way. To take possession of that joy He had to go through the agony and pain. What would Jesus accomplish that would be important enough for Him to choose to be crucified? Here are a few ideas:

- Jesus demonstrated his great love for us when he died in our place for our sins. "Greater love has no one than this, that one lay down his life for his friend" (John 15:13).
- God would reconcile the world to himself through Jesus' death (2 Corinthians 5:19).

- Death and the fear of death would be defeated (1 Corinthians 15:54-57).
- Satan and his works would be destroyed (1 John 3:8, Hebrews 2:14-15).
- Through Jesus, God would cancel the debt of sin held against us by nailing it to the cross (Colossians 2:13-15).
- Jesus would return to the glory He had with God before the world began (John 17:5).
- Jesus would be seated at the right hand of God making intercession for us (Romans 8:34).

Wow! What an accomplishment! No wonder Jesus kept His eyes on the joy that was set before Him and chose life, even though He had to die on a cross to achieve it.

For years I was confused and scared by what Jesus meant when He told his followers, "If anyone would come after me, he must deny himself and take up his cross daily and follow me" (Luke 9:23). I thought this meant we were supposed to deprive ourselves of everything in life that was not considered spiritually necessary. Generally this meant not having too much fun, not owning too many material things, not doing any worldly things (as defined by my home church), not being too earthly minded, etc. Now I have come to believe these are not the issue.

I think Jesus was encouraging us to be choice-makers, even as He was a choice-maker. He wanted us to choose life. **Anytime we choose life there will be a cross in the way.** It will always cost us something to choose to do or think what is good, right, healthy, and life-giving for ourselves and others—but the benefits are worth it. Like Jesus, if we want to experience the benefits set before us, we must go through the cross to get there. If we want to get a college degree, we need to decide to put up with the hardships and discipline it takes to earn it. If we want to lose weight and we are offered a piece of cake, we need to say to ourselves and others, "I would really like a piece, but my decision is no, thank you." Learning how to say no to oneself is practicing self-denial. Self-denial is not denial of self. If we don't have a self, we can't practice healthy self-denial.[12]

Self-Determination Is Not Stubbornness

All of us have met strong-willed people and we know how difficult they can be at times. We may have been accused of being stubborn or rebellious ourselves when, in fact, we were just holding firm to a belief or course of action we knew was right for us. Determination is a wonderful thing if it is directed toward life-giving results.

In the 1984 Olympics in Los Angeles the women's marathon was about to be completed. The TV cameras were focused on the entrance into the coliseum, when in staggered a young Swiss runner. She seemed half conscious and was weaving from side to side. Still she was determined to finish the race. It was a pathetic scene, a world-class athlete staggering down the track like a wounded deer. But every time officials move toward her to help, she leaned away, brushing them aside with her hands, trying to get them to leave her alone.

The depth of her determination to finish the race may never be understood by most of us. To have been stopped short of her goal might have caused more damage to her spirit than if she were allowed to finish and then receive medical aid. She did finish, collapsing in a heap just past the finish line. A day or two later, I saw her shining eyes and smiling face on an interview program with other Olympic athletes.

To be determined evokes a feeling similar to that of being stubborn or angry but it's different. It's more quiet, solid, and peaceful. It's not will power, because will power almost always fades in the presence of negative feelings or temptations.

Determination is more settled and directed because it reflects the quiet resolve of the heart to stay on course, despite the cross one must bear. Jesus showed this in the Garden of Gethsemane when He prayed three times that if possible, the cross could be avoided. But it was not possible, and He chose to fulfill His Father's will (Matthew 26:36-46).

The happy person is one who is in charge of making one's own decisions as an Imagebearer of God and who makes choices for life. The apostle Paul said it this way: "If you have a clear conviction, apply it to yourself in the sight of God. Happy is the man who can make his decision with a clear conscience" (Romans 14:22, New English Bible).

How are we to know whether a person is being stubborn and rebellious or whether they are exercising self-determination based on conviction? In some cases, only time and God will be the judge. We can thank God for John Wycliffe whose determination and faith in God's help went against great opposition to fulfill his heartfelt vision to produce the first English translation of the Bible. Eventually, he was martyred for his convictions.

Can I Be Both Independent and Dependent at the Same Time?

Many Christians suffer from a conflict between being told to depend on God at one moment and then told to be independent as an adult the next. Double messages are continually being given by Christian friends and leaders. On one hand we are told, "Use your head," "Be responsible," and "Make up your mind and do it;" and on the other we are told, "Don't lean on your own understanding," "Depend totally on God," and "Be careful that you're not being selfish and self-centered." Christians who have a sensitive conscience, or who have a poor sense of worth and who desire to please God, can become paralyzed in their ability to choose. They become caught in a double bind. I personally suffered from this for years. Often the pressure and unhappiness I felt undermined the joy of my Christian experience. Not wanting to appear "unspiritual" I remained silent, trapped in my private agony. But my world trip and the changes that took place in my view of life forced me to deal honestly with this pain.

Another person who suffered from this dilemma was Garry Friesen when he had to decide which college to attend. He prayed fervently that God would show him His will, but no definite leading was given. He eventually made his decision, but the experience left him perplexed. He wrote:

> Why had it been so hard for me to find God's will when I so sincerely sought for it? And why, after I had made the decision, did I lack the certainty that the decision I had made was the correct one? . . . It was at that point that I began my pilgrimage to seek the reason for my difficulty in finding God's will for that particular decision."[13]

Eventually his search led him to write a most interesting and helpful book on this subject of Christians making decisions. His book *Decision Making and the Will of God,* helps Christians understand what the Bible says about God's will as it pertains to decision making.

Healing begins when we realize that it is not an either/or issue—either dependent or independent. It is both/and. We are both independent and dependent. God created us with the ability to choose and we honor God as our Creator when we own and exercise our choice-making ability. We were designed to grow up—to become independent human beings in charge of and responsible for our decisions. God doesn't control us and He has never wanted to. He would be working at cross-purposes with the way He designed us. He wants us to exercise SELF-control in His direction, in harmony with His will.

But we are dependent on God in that we need to consult with someone who really knows what life's about so that we can make good decisions. Who better to talk to than the Person who created life and knows how it works? Who better to talk to than a loving heavenly Father, a knowledgeable and trustworthy Consultant, or the "Wonderful Counselor" spoken of by Isaiah the prophet? As the horse goes before the cart, our need to be in charge of our choices goes before what kind of choices we make. Once this distinction is appreciated, we discover we can be both a human being and a Christian, We can be both independent and dependent. No one can take the ultimate weight of decision-making off our shoulders. But the more we know about how things really are, the lighter the burden will be.

Pig Pens in Our Lives

Our choices will not always be good, right, or healthy. It is human to choose to think and act in ways that are not life- giving. In an earlier chapter we read about the parable of the young man who decided to leave home (Luke 15:11-13). He asked for his portion of the inheritance and then left for a distant country. In time, through a series of bad choices, he spent everything he had in wild living. When a famine came, he had to work for a man who needed someone to feed pigs in the field. The young man became so hungry he wanted to eat the pods that were being fed to the pigs, but "no one gave him anything." As the effects of his choices bore down on him, he began to come to his senses and *decided* to go back to his father and make amends (v. 17-20).

By any standard, his poor choices had messed up his life. And yet it was by the exercise of this same ability, he began his return home. As readily as his father had respected his son's choice to leave, he equally respected his son's choice to return. Consequences of choices taught him lessons about life that instruction had failed to do. He learned from his choices and used them to make new and better ones.

As I took an honest look at myself, I began to see this same principle in operation in my life. Good choices produced life-giving benefits and poor choices produced death-producing results. So one of the most important decisions I ever made and still practice to this day is this: "I am going to eliminate out of my life all my own self-created pain!" Everyday I practiced making choices that were life giving and not pain producing. This book represents how I studied, learned, practiced and grew is my ability to eliminate the pig pens in my life.

Our choices do not determine our worth. God loves us in the same manner as the father loved his returning son. Fortunately, God trusts in the instructional value of consequences, so when the stench of the pig pens in our lives becomes bad enough, we can wake up and come to our senses and say, "This stinks! I am tired of being like this and I am going to do something about it." Some people call it "hitting bottom" or "coming to the end of the line," but what ever we call it, it is waking up to the need to change and then choosing a better way to live. The exercise of our choice-making ability determines whether our lives are filled with pig pens or flower gardens.

Being able to choose is an amazing gift that God has bestowed on us. It's nice to know that life can change for the better whenever we make up our minds to decide to change.

Reclaiming our permission to be in charge of our choices is both psychologically and spiritually healthy. Realizing that God created us in His image to be self-determining can bring deep, inner healing as we begin to exercise our freedom to be the person God designed us to be. Once we have given ourselves permission to be a choice-maker, we can move forward in learning how to do it more successfully. The next chapter will help us with this step.

Suggested Reading

1. Frankl, Viktor. *Man's Search for Meaning.* Pocket Books, 1963.
2. Dyer, Dr. Wayne. *Your Erroneous Zones.* Avon Books, 1976.
3. Exodus 35:21; 1 Kings 18:21; 1 Chronicles 29:17; Psalm 119:30; Proverbs 21:16; 29:11; Isaiah 7:15; Mark 1:40-42; John 6:15; 2 Corinthians 9:7; Titus 1:8, 2:2,5,6; Philemon 14; 1 Peter 4:3, 5:2.

To live is to choose. It is through the making of successive and resolute choices that man traces out his life. Becoming adult is the whole programme. . . . The negation of life is to act against one's better judgment through weakness, because one does not dare to take the responsibility for one's decisions.

Paul Tournier, *The Meaning of Persons* [1]

When I got tired of hurting, I started making choices. Big choices. They meant risks and a change of lifestyle, but I knew that if I didn't, I would live in the pain forever. The early choices were the most difficult, because I had made so few real choices in my life. So many choices were made FOR me that just learning HOW to make a significant choice was a hurdle. In making my life-changing decisions, I learned the process of choice making, a gift I cherish in my lifestyle today.

Sharon Wegscheider-Cruse,
The Miracle of Recovery [2]

Authentic freedom is an exceptional sign of the divine image within man. . . . Man's dignity demands that he act according to a knowing and free choice. Such a choice is personally motivated and prompted from within. It does not result from blind internal impulses or from mere external pressures.

Walter M. Abbott, S. J.,
The Documents of Vatican II [3]

CHAPTER 14

Self-Determination: The Doorway to Freedom

HOW TO

*O*nce upon a time there were two frogs who lived on a dairy farm. They were best of friends and their lives were filled with fun and adventure. One day while playfully jumping around the barn, they mistakenly hopped into a bucket of cream. For several minutes they swam around desperately trying to escape. Gradually, they both began to tire until finally one frog said, "It's hopeless! There's no way we can get out. I can't take it any more!" So he stopped kicking and sank to the bottom of the bucket.

But the second frog was determined to find a way out. He was convinced that there must be some way to spare his life, so he kept on swimming. Suddenly, under his hind feet, he felt something solid and with all his strength he leaped. He barely cleared the edge of the bucket and landed safely on the floor, completely exhausted. His persistent kicking had turned the cream to butter and a lump of butter provided a way of escape. Overjoyed with his new-found freedom, he went on to live a happy and productive life.

All of us have problems and hardships we wish we could overcome, but we become tired, discouraged, and frustrated. We do the best we know how, but things don't seem to improve. When we try a few things and they don't work, we feel like giving up and sinking to the bottom of despair and self-pity. This is known as victim thinking.

Like the second frog, we need to be determined and persistent to find answers and solutions that can make life better. God has created life in such a way that miracles do happen. God wants the best for us and He will help us learn better ways to work with our problems more effectively. If we are open, patient, and connected to our ability to be in charge of our choices, we can learn how to be better choice-makers. Let's look at some of the ways we can do this.

The Art of Being a Kind and Strong Person

In 1970 one of the first books ever written on assertiveness was published. When Robert Alberti and Michael Emmons wrote *Your Perfect Right,*[4] I am sure they never dreamed it would sell over a million copies. Over the past forty years dozens of books have been written and thousands of classes have been taken on assertive living. Yet there still remains a lot of confusion about the place of assertiveness in the Christian life. Teachings on meekness, self-denial, and dying to self seem to fly in the face of assertiveness. Let's see if we can clear some of this up.

Human beings basically function in life from one of three life styles. This means that the majority of our attitudes, beliefs, and actions would best fit into one of three categories—passive (non-assertive), aggressive, or assertive.

The first group of people develop what I call the *"Kind But Weak"* life style. These people try hard to be nice all the time. They want to please everybody and have everybody like them. They'll do most anything to avoid conflict and confrontation. If things go bad, they feel it's their fault and they try to fix it. They avoid doing or saying anything that would appear to be mean, selfish, or self-centered. In trying so hard to be nice they become weak. They bottle up a lot of negative feelings only to experience periodic outbursts when they blow up like a volcano. Then they feel really guilty for being so mean and un-Christian and they will do anything to make up for it.

Kind but weak people often feel as if life is running them, that they are being picked on and abused. They see themselves as victims, but when they do try to stand up for themselves, they see themselves as being mean and selfish. This creates feelings of fear and guilt, so they return to being kind— but remain weak. They feel guilty when they say "no," so they give an avalanche of excuses or apologies to justify why they "can't" do something.

Worrying about what others will think, they become pleasers. They blame themselves (and sometimes others) when things go wrong, but feel powerless to make any changes. In trying to appear pleasant and helpful, they often feel trapped and used. This leads to feelings of anger, resentment, hurt, and depression. Often they work even harder to please, hoping that someday, somehow, things will change. But in time they realize it hasn't worked. Having focused so much on pleasing others, they discover they don't know who they are anymore. They don't know what they want, need, or feel.

Two problems lie at the core of this lifestyle. The kind but weak person is trying to gain a sense of worth from the approval of others. They have also lost connection with the power of being in charge of their choices because they have allowed their decisions to be controlled by others. Many of you recovering from co-dependency know what this feels like. Love is a choice, not an addiction.[5]

A second group of people develop what I call the *"Strong But Angry"* lifestyle. They are verbal, aggressive, and know exactly what they want. They are skilled at manipulating and controlling others, getting them to believe or do what they want. They always think they are right and blame others (never themselves) when things go wrong. They don't seem to care what other people think or feel, so they often try to dominate the situation. Saying no is easy for them, because everything must gain their approval. They display little genuine concern for how others feel and lack genuine human warmth and caring. They tend to be judgmental and critical, making them uncomfortable to be around. They defend their own right to choose but do not know how to give the same privilege to others, especially if the other person's choices affect them.

Two problems lie at the core of this lifestyle. The strong but angry person gets their self-esteem from power and control. Inside they are weak and scared, but they find protection and power in their aggressiveness. No one is ever going to hurt them, control them or use them again—ever!

To let go of power and control and become more kind and cooperative is to feel weak. This is scary, so they return to being strong but angry. This points out their other problem—their strength comes from anger. Take their anger away and they would feel vulnerable and helpless, like the passive people they control and dominate. Their strength is not strength of character but strength of overcompensation.

These two lifestyles have been described briefly to contrast their characteristics. In reality, people function somewhere along a continuum between an extremely passive life-style to a very aggressive and dominating one. For years I tried to find some place on this continuum where I could function, but I never could seem to find it. I couldn't continue being a pleaser, but I didn't want to be mean and aggressive either.

What I really wanted was to be both a *"Kind And Strong Person"*. Gradually, I realized that this was a third alternative life-style I could choose to live. It was based on the belief that God wants us to be in charge of our choices as Imagebearers and that we can begin at any time to become a healthy, assertive Christian. It may feel strange at first but in time we will awaken to its life-giving benefits. We can grow into being a kind and strong person. The diagram on the following page illustrates the difference.

Kind and strong people are those who have a good sense of self-worth. They also see the worth in others. A Christian view of self-esteem attaches worth to our being made in the image of God. This worth is stable and secure because it rests on the truth of who we are as Imagebearers rather than on what we do. This gives a person inner strength to accept and be themselves and to accept others for who they are. These people are open and accepting of both their own feelings and the feelings of others. They are as committed to their own well-being as they are for the well-being of others.

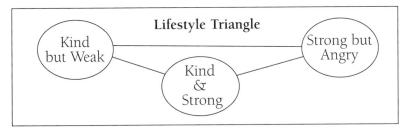

Lifestyle Triangle

Kind but Weak — Kind & Strong — Strong but Angry

Kind and strong people have accepted and experienced the joy in their ability to be a self-determining person. This gives them an inner strength that comes from having a clearer grasp of what it means to be in charge of their choices—to be assertive. They also accept the right of others to be in charge of their decisions.

Kind and strong people also direct their choices toward life-giving results—both present and eternal. They learn how to choose life more successfully each day so that they and others experience the benefits. Personal convictions based on Christian values, combined with the power to choose, make them strong and kind. The well-known Christian songwriter and singer Gloria Gaither talked about a Christian's approach to decision making in her book *Decisions*:

> I am concerned about decision making because I believe our choices do matter, not just for today or the present moment, but forever. . . . I believe that Jesus Christ came to show us God's value system more clearly, so that we could learn how to make new kinds of choices— choices with "eternity" in them. The more we learn to live with a "forever" view, the more we are released from the stranglehold of pessimism and materialism.[6]

Learning the art of being kind and strong—being assertive—is learning how to be like Christ. It is learning how to choose for one's self how to act or think in a way that is life-giving and Christian. It is more than just standing up for yourself; it is standing up for life the way God designed it to be. As we learn to live this way, we will feel strong, healthy, clean, uncluttered. We feel a sense of self-control and self-respect—and that feels good.

It takes time to learn how to become a kind and strong person, but it can be done one choice at a time, one day at a time. It is best to begin with the simplest choices first. One woman chose to return to a gas station to pick up a coupon she had forgotten for her purchase. Her kind but weak self would have said, "Oh well, it's no big deal," and she would have dropped it. But her new self chose to return to ask for her coupon. This was an important step toward becoming kind and strong. It was making a growth choice. We need to begin with little things to build our confidence. Eventually we will be able to handle the big things.

To live life the way we choose, we need to be willing to be a bit disturbing to those who want to control us. When we stand true to our convictions and discuss them with others, we risk offending them. The Pharisees were offended when Jesus described how their blind loyalty to man's traditions nullified the Word of God (Matthew 15:5-12). The people in his hometown "took offense at him" because they knew him as the carpenter's son and they couldn't understand where he acquired his wisdom or his power to do miracles (Matthew 13:53-58). Some of Jesus' disciples were offended by what he taught about himself and many of them "turned back and no longer followed him" (John 6:60-66).

Whenever we choose life, we risk someone not liking what we do or say. We have to accept the fact that they might get upset but it is a risk we need to take if we are to grow and become the person God designed us to be. Dr. Bruno Bettelheim gives a good description of what we are talking about in his book *The Informed Heart*. Having survived both Dachau and Buchenwald, two German concentration camps, he knows the importance of the connection between freedom and decision making. He wrote:

> I hope by now it is clear that the concept of autonomy used here has little to do with what is sometimes called "rugged individualism," . . . or noisy self assertion. It has to do with man's *inner ability to govern himself*, and with a conscientious search for meaning despite the realization that, as far as we know, there is no purpose to one's life. It is a concept that does not imply a revolt against authority *que* authority, but rather a *quiet acting out of inner conviction*, not out of convenience or resentment, or because of external persuasion or controls (italics mine).[7]

Even though I completely disagree with his view that there is no meaning to one's life, Bettelheim is right on the mark with his description of being kind and strong. Owning our inner ability to govern our choices, combined with inner convictions that are biblical and life-oriented, describes the life of a kind and strong person. It is being Christ-like.

As human beings we all bear God's image in our personhood. When we become a Christian we can also bear Christ's image in our character. Paul wrote about this in his letter to the Corinthian people in Greece. "Where the Spirit of the Lord is, there is freedom. And we, who with unveiled faces all reflect the Lord's glory, are being transformed into his likeness with ever-increasing glory, which comes from the Lord, who is the Spirit" (2 Corinthians 3:18).

The Spirit of God is working in every Christian to transform us to be like Christ in both our inner character and outer conduct. This is a process of growth and change, and choice making plays a vital part in it. It takes time, but it is part of what helps us become emotionally mature Christians.

Jesus lived true to who He was and to what He knew was good and right. When we are kind and strong like Him, we will live true to who we are and what we know is good and right for us. Our courage to choose life is part of what it means to grow up and be like Christ. To choose life is an act of faith. We can be thoughtful and kind to others, but we also need to be in charge of our decisions.

To do this, it's helpful to have a set of assertiveness skills to use when necessary. In his book *When I Say No, I Feel Guilty*, Manuel Smith is most helpful in giving us several assertive tools we can use when we are trying to be kind and strong or when we are trying to deal with the painful effects of criticism. These skills are Broken Record, Self-Disclosure, Fogging, Negative Assertion, and Negative Inquiry.[8] He gives examples of dialogues for each of these skills so that we can see how they work in real life. Anyone wanting to be both kind and strong needs to learn how to use them when necessary. In this way we can show real love for ourselves and for others. It is what Paul called, "speaking the truth in love." It is learning how to say what we mean—letting our yes mean yes, and our no mean no. Unconditional love for someone does not mean we betray ourselves to try to prove to them we love them. It means respecting ourselves and them enough to choose to remain true to our convictions while at the same time loving them. We do not have to ruin our life just to prove our love for someone.

Self-Control Is Saying "I Choose"

The Bible clearly shows that one of the marks of a healthy Christian life is self-control. Peter wrote that faith, goodness, knowledge, self-control, perseverance, godliness, kindness, and love are qualities that make us effective and productive in our walk with Christ (2 Peter 1:5-8). Paul also included self-control as part of the fruit of the Holy Spirit along with love, joy, peace, patience, kindness, goodness, faithfulness, and gentleness (Galatians 5:22).

Self means having a sense of being a person and control means being in charge of one's choices. All the books on assertiveness, taking charge of our lives or doing the will of God are built on the premise that human beings are unique in being aware of their ability to choose. Innate in our design is the need for self-control. We pay a great price when we forget this and let others make our decisions for us. Living a passive or an aggressive life-style is to betray one of our unique qualities that makes us a person and not a puppet or a dictator.

Trusting God does not mean He makes our choices for us. It means we trust God for the information and perspectives necessary for us to make good choices. Self-control is saying, "I want to do this, but I choose not to." It is also saying, "I don't want to do it, but it's necessary and I'm willing to do it."

Self-control does not mean controlling others. Proverbs 29:11 says, "A wise man keeps himself under control." A wise person is also one who realizes he is not responsible for controlling everything and everyone else. Jesus practiced self-control but he was not in the habit of controlling others. He taught, confronted, and encouraged people and then He let go and honored their freedom to decide. I think this is the meaning behind his phrase, "Let those who have ears to hear, let them hear" (Matthew 11:15).

The Pioneer Family

It is natural to feel apprehensive about taking charge of one's life. It is hard work and takes effort, dedication, and a commitment to act in a self-directing manner—but the results are worth it. People who are beginning to learn how to be better choice-makers have found encouragement in thinking of themselves as being like the early pioneers. Many pioneer families moved onto a new homestead that was covered with trees. To clear an area where they could live, the trees had to be removed one by one, one day at a time, until finally the land was cleared. It was hard work, but when they finished, they had a good feeling of accomplishment as well as having a place they could call home.

This is similar to what we do in our inner world when we begin to practice choosing life. Daily, as we make a conscious effort to practice being in charge of our choices, we can systematically remove the clutter from our lives: the resentments, guilt, fears, and worries. We can also start building a life that we enjoy. People unaccustomed to feeling in charge of their decisions—about what to think, what to believe, or how to act—can learn to do so one choice at a time. Each day as we widen our area of self-control, we will find we become stronger, happier, and more fulfilled Christian human beings. We have more "room to live" and more room to be ourselves. It is not without its risks and setbacks but its worth it.

Give Your Wanter a Chance to Grow

One of the best ways to begin exercising our ability to choose is to begin doing things we want to do rather than *just* what we have to do or should do. Self-control is feeling free to makes choices that are in line with our needs, wants, desires, and interests. Wanting comes naturally to children. They are open and straight-forward in telling us what they want and when they want it. This is both refreshing and frustrating, yet so important. Their wants may not always be right or appropriate but they are expressed. We know where they are coming from. Soon they learn the lesson, "You can't always have what you want just because you want it!"

Sadly, many of us have over-learned this lesson. Gradually our "wanter" began closing down. Feelings of frustration, disappointment, and guilt caused us to slowly lose connection with our inner self. Life settles into a poor imitation of what it was designed to be. People have described it this way:

- "Life circumstances were harsh and we did not have the time or money to do the things we wanted. We did what had to be done."
- "People made me feel that what I wanted and liked were dumb and stupid. So I tried to quit thinking about it."
- "My Mom (Dad or Spouse) was so self-centered that the things I wanted were completely ignored or put down."
- "I had such a strong need to please others I ignored what I wanted in order to get them to like me and accept me."
- "Broken promises discouraged me to the point that I quit asking for what I wanted."
- "People had so much control over me, there was no room for what I wanted or liked."
- "I was always afraid if I did what I wanted, I would start doing things that were sinful or wrong and I would miss God's perfect will for my life."

These comments reveal how fear and guilt can make   us become timid about life. We feel trapped, stifled, and unmotivated to fulfill our desires and dreams. Our child-like naturalness and spontaneity about life becomes restrained or repressed. One night after a self-esteem class, a woman went home and told her husband about the excitement she felt about learning how to give her "wanter" a chance to grow. His response was, "You have to remember, my 'wantas' are your 'gottas'!" Fortunately, he was kidding, but his statement reflects the way people have had their wants and desires squashed.

One of the best ways we can show real love for ourself is to give ourselves permission to fulfill our wants and desires. We can also show love to our spouse, children, and friends by helping them fulfill their wants and desires. The national Make A Wish Foundation is a good example of people helping people make heartfelt dreams come true. Three ideas can help us begin to move in a positive direction. First, we need to know that God is in partnership with us. God is happy when we are happy. David wrote:

> Trust in the Lord and do good. . . . Delight yourself in the Lord and he will give you the desires of your heart. (Psalm 37:3-4).

The statement, "He will give you the desires of your heart" can be interpreted two ways: God will place desires in our heart so when we respond to them He helps us fulfill them; or these are the desires that come from our unique background and personality and God will work with us to help them come true. I think both views are true. The main idea is that God will help us.

Solomon gives us another strong voice of encouragement: "Hope deferred makes the heart sick, but a longing fulfilled is a tree of life. . . . A longing fulfilled is sweet to the soul" (Proverbs 13:12,19). To awaken to our needs and wants can create feelings of fear and uncertainty, but when we begin to fulfill them it becomes life-giving and healing to the soul. In the years I have been a counselor, I have found that 80 to 90 percent of what people want and desire is good, healthy, right, and natural.

Second, we need to make a "wanter" list. We can write down all the things that come to mind of the things we want: places to go, things to eat, projects to complete, people to meet, events to attend, books to read, habits to change, sins to overcome, and goals to accomplish. Making a list and working to fulfill it helps us feel alive again—like we are accomplishing something.

Third, when we begin to do this, it's best to start with the easy ones first. These are safe, easily accomplished, and within our grasp of faith. Our freedom to choose allows us to say yes or no to ourselves depending on the factors that need to be considered such as time, money, other people, or prior commitments. In 1989 we took a trip to Kenya, Africa, because we wanted to see the African animals before modern life impacted them even more. It took a year to save the money, but it was a trip our family will never forget!

People often feel selfish when they first begin to fulfill their desires. Others have reported feeling self-indulgent, self-centered, and guilty. But they also felt happy, free, excited, and alive. One lady reported, "I am proving to myself I can do a lot of things I would never have considered doing." She was overcoming a lot of fears that kept her life passive. Another woman once said, "I have done the two things I have always wanted most, have children and a home. Now what do I do with the rest of my life?" She was twenty-eight years old! As we talked, she revealed that for years she had been interested in cake decorating but felt guilty doing something she really enjoyed that was not focused on her home or her children. This soon changed for the better.

Did you know that truly selfish people are not aware they are being selfish? They feel life is supposed to come their way and when it doesn't, they get angry. They are used to getting what they want, or at least fighting for it. The people who feel they are being selfish are in most cases not being selfish at all. They are too sensitive about being selfish to be selfish. They misjudge any effort given to meeting their desires and needs as being bad. They feel guilty—but it is a false guilt.

One lady spent her whole life living for her husband and kids, only to become seriously depressed. She said, "I don't know who I am anymore. I don't even know what I need or want." At the end of a session, I suggested she buy her favorite magazine, go home, and fill the tub with a hot bubble bath and just soak in the warmth and enjoyment for a half an hour. She burst into tears and said, "Larry, I can't do that. I'd feel so guilty!"

Time and practice will help us find the balance between caring for others and caring for ourselves. One evening in my self-esteem classes we talked about how to do this. A week later one of the women in the class told a touching story about her decision to give her "wanter" a chance to grow. It illustrates how small a desire (a longing) may be, yet how life- changing its fulfillment can become.

The Story of the Little Yellow Rubber Duck

Edie was born in Idaho in 1921 and grew up missing the chance to have her own rubber duck. As a little girl she desperately wanted one, but because of the death of her mother, she was placed in an orphanage in Boise, Idaho. Time slipped away and then she was "too old" to have one. She was now in her fifties and her childhood desire had been completely forgotten.

A day or two after the class, she was walking down an aisle in a store when she walked past a shelf loaded with little yellow rubber ducks. Instantly, her mind flashed back to the class and the encouragement everyone had been given to fulfill just one longing of their heart, no matter how small it was. She remembered her childhood desire to have her own rubber duck, but now she was *really* too old. But she turned around, walked past the shelf a second time. An argument started inside her that went something like this: "This is something I have always wanted ever since I was a kid! I think I'll get one for myself." "Well, that's really stupid! Someone your age doesn't need a rubber duck. They're for kids, not adults." "But it's such a little thing and it doesn't even cost that much. And I've always wanted one." "Don't be ridiculous! You don't need it. Besides, what will people think if they find out you bought one at your age?"

On the fourth trip past the shelf she made her decision and bought herself a duck. Part of her felt guilty and another part of her felt silly and happy. But every time she took a bath, her yellow rubber duck joined her in the tub. Seeing   it bobbing up and down beside her made her feel a warm sense of joy and pleasure. Soloman was right, choices of the heart are sweet to the soul!

The duck cost only a dollar or two, but she received thousands of dollars worth of therapy just having it in the tub bobbing up and down with her. The most meaningful part of this story is that she is my mother and when I went to her home the duck was always sitting on the edge of the tub. This small, life-giving choice was a first step toward more significant changes that were to take place in her life in the years that followed.

Exercising our ability to choose in life-giving directions is the key to change. Doing a few little things on our "wanter list" can be the beginning of some exciting changes in the way we live. We can begin to create a new past—a new history.

Creating a New Past

Choices can only be made in the present. We are where we are today because of the decisions we made in the past. We will go where we want to go in the future only by the choices we make today. *If we are in charge of the choices we make today, we can create a new past and shape a new future.* William Jennings Bryan once wrote, "Destiny is not a matter of chance, it is a matter of choice; it is not a thing to be waited for, it is a thing to be achieved."

Many of us have said, "I can't change. I've always been this way. That's just me." But one of the most important things we can learn about choosing is that we can always change if we make a decision to do so. We may not know how to change; we may not have the desire to change; we may even believe we can't change. But we are created in God's image and choice-making is a fundamental part of our personhood. Certainly, we are free to continue making the same old choices we always have, and in doing so we'll continue to add more months and years to our same old past.

But when we begin to make new and better choices one day at a time, day after day, we gradually begin to create a new past. As the weeks and months of a new past accumulate, we slowly change and become more like the person we would like to be. Life also changes and becomes more positive. Even though we can't change our old past, we can redeem it and be making peace with it. Then we can learn from it the lessons needed to make better choices today. Our past can make our present have a richness and fullness to it that would otherwise be missing. (We will talk about this more in chapters 19 and 20).

By choosing life each day we can also work with our future. By setting goals and then working each day to achieve them, we can arrive at the destination we chose months, even years earlier. In time we are not the same person we were when we first began. We have changed one choice at a time. Abraham Maslow described the connection between creating a new past and choice-making this way:

> Let us think of life as a process of choices, one after another. At each point there is a progression choice and a regression choice. There may be a movement toward defense, toward safety, toward being afraid; but over on the other side, there is the growth choice. To make the growth choice instead of the fear choice a dozen times a day is to move a dozen times a day toward self-actualization.[9]

Self-actualization means becoming the person God designed us to be. Developing each one of our abilities (like intelligence, choice-making, self-awareness, and communication) is becoming a person. We are also becoming more like Christ. Maslow's quote could read this way as well with just the changing of three words, "to make a growth choice instead of a fear choice a dozen times a day is to move a dozen times a day towards *becoming like Christ.*"

The power of choice-making is never more alive than when we choose to change and create a new past. The following diagram illustrates this idea.

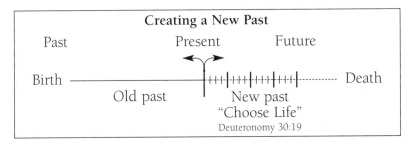

A decision to do one thing is also a decision not to do something else. When we create a new past it means that we are letting go of the choices that created the old past. This can be both relieving and sad because we get used to making decisions that are not good for us. It does require a conscious effort to change and grow which not everyone is willing to do.

When we ask God to help us change and nothing happens, we may need to take a more honest look at ourselves. We could be praying for a magical solution so we don't have to work at making new choices.

For example, in his book, *Direct Decision Therapy*, Dr. Harold Greenwald believed that behind many of our present day problems are decisions we made in the past. We remain loyal to these decisions today even when the consequences are hurting us now.[10] He calls these decisions "life decisions" because they shape our lives from that point forward.

The well known T.V. talk show host and author Dr. Phil McGrow calls them our "critical choices". In his book, *Self-Matters*, he said that by reflecting on your personal history, you should be able "to identify a handful of critical choices, choices you've made that have shaped the remainder of your life . . . those decisions can teach you much about who and how you have become who you are."[11]

I can remember when I first identified one of these life shaping choices in my past. It took place in the eighth grade when I tried to "do something" to overcome my painful feelings of inferiority. I decided to become the best basketball player and the best kisser in the eighth grade class – and I went to work on both. At that moment, my sense of "being somebody" became attached to athletics and girls.

If we understand the context in which such decisions are made, we will discover that we made the best decision we knew how under the circumstances. Now we need to review these past decisions and make new ones that are undated, healthier and more life-giving.

Every decision we make has a payoff. If we take an honest look at our choices, we can discover the thinking behind them and the payoff we gained. Then we can make new decisions that will begin to create our new past.

Wishing we could change is different from a decision to change. If we only wish but continue to make the same old choices, we add more years to our same old past. But the moment we begin making new and life-giving decisions, we begin creating our new past. This is a slow process and sometimes is not understood as one of God's most loving ways of healing.

Dramatic Change v. Gradual Change

Many of us have not seen the value of gradual change because of the importance we put on dramatic change. It is seen as a more significant demonstration of God's power to heal or change us. Dramatic changes happens suddenly. One moment we are one way, the next moment we are different. All of us desire dramatic change when we are struggling with bad habits, negative feelings, or painful experiences. We want the instant cure that brings quick relief.

People who experience dramatic changes are more likely to be given a chance to tell their story at church because it has a special appeal—more like God performed a "real" miracle. People are impressed—but when it doesn't happen to us, it's disillusioning. If dramatic change has happened for you, thank God for it! But we also need to be open to the dignity and value of gradual change.

Gradual change is the more normally experienced form of change, just as physical healing is a slow process. Its value lies in the fact that we have a better sense of how it's happening. We are aware of the new choices we make in how to think and act differently that produce the desired results. We are familiar with the ground we have covered and the pace we have taken to accomplish what we had done. We are more aware of how God worked with us in quiet and subtle ways to encourage us in our growth.

In my office I have a little ceramic snail, turtle, and frog sitting on a stand to represent how we progress in our "growing up" process. Some people are snails, changing very slowly. Other people are turtles. They plod along slowly and steadily, making changes more quickly than a snail. Others still are frogs, sitting and thinking for a long time and then they make a big leap of growth.

Choices are the stuff that changes are made of. It is a blessing from God that our growth can be gradual. Our inner world has time to *adjust* (to assimilate and integrate) to the new past we are building. It allows us time to learn and use our knowledge and skills to deal with life more effectively. By enjoying the rewards of our work, we are encouraged to continue our efforts. As Christians we will come to know what the apostle Peter was saying when he wrote: "His divine power has given us everything we need for life and godliness through our knowledge of him who called us by his own glory and goodness" (2 Peter 1:3). We no longer need to feel guilty or apologetic for being like a snail, a turtle, or a frog.

The Freedom to Fail

We will go through a period of transition when we decide to create a new past. What we are doing is new and unfamiliar, so it's natural to feel awkward, scared, and uncertain at first. But gradually it feels better. It's like learning to drive a stick-shift car for the first time. There are so many things to remember, so many things to do and we often goof. We kill the engine or hop it down the road for several yards. But with practice, things begin to come together.

When we first begin to change, it can feel like things are getting worse rather than better, but in time things begin to smooth out.

We are not always successful at staying on course. Taking charge of our choices can result in both successes and failures. We need to know we have the freedom to fail or we will remain stuck. Many books have been written on how to succeed, but few address how to develop a healthy view of failure. In his book *The Freedom to Fail*, G. Don Gilmore presents a way of looking at failure that frees us from its paralyzing grip on our lives.

> Nowhere is our unreality and lack of freedom more obvious than when we face the problem of failure. . . . The freedom to fail, like the matter of being a real person, always proceeds on the assumption that God has an eternal purpose for a person's life. . . . The freedom to fail as a live option is authored by God for our growth and development in the world. . . .The really free person in God's grace is free to succeed or fail in the world because he is assured that the victory of his life is already accomplished in the death and resurrection of Jesus Christ.[12]

With our worth secure in our being made in God's image and our salvation secure because of our being in Christ, we are free to change, grow, and create a new past even if we fail and goof up along the way. We are free to learn from our failures (past, present, and future) and improve on our ability to choose life. A woman once said to me, "From all of my worst mistakes, I have learned the most." To be a choice-maker is to be a risk-taker. Self-determination and faith belong together if we are to be the person God created us to be. We cannot side-step choosing if we want to create a new past that is fulfilling and meaningful.

The Freedom to Find Options

When we accept our freedom to choose, we also awaken our ability to see options. Life becomes a rut, a repetitious merry-go-round, a treadmill of meaningless activity when we are powerless to see alternatives. Reactions become the norm, and unhealthy habit patterns and addictions become our prison. A man once said to me, "Life is an adversary and I am in constant combat!" He described the outcome of someone unable to identify options. But this is not how God designed us to be. In his book *Somewhat Less than God*, Leonard Verduin affirms the freedom we have in being option-makers.

> In the Christian perspective man is a creature of option. . . . The Genesis story is not so much interested in telling us *how man came to*

be as to inform us as to *what man is*, a creature made in God's image and therefore capable of choosing and able to steer his ship. The next thing the Bible wants us to know is that man steered badly by a bad exercise of option. The rest of the Book informs us of the posing of a new option, a new chance, for "decision determines destiny."[13]

Verduin refers to the new choice of restoring one's relationship with God through faith in Jesus Christ. We can also take this same principle and apply it to new options and new beginnings we can choose every day. Becoming wise choice-makers means being creative in our thinking. It is learning the art of expanding our view of the alternatives available to us. Options will help us become aware of the difference between living and merely existing.

The use of an illustration on the following page of an old elevator floor indicator can help us discover our options in how to think or act differently. Each floor represents a different option. By drawing this picture we can begin to write in the various options we can think of about something we want to change. We need to relax so that we can be creative in coming up with possible choices. It's easy to write in the two extreme options (one and six) because they come naturally to mind. They usually represent our reactions to the situation rather than thoughtful choices. By continuing to think of other positive solutions we can fill in the other numbers with life-giving choices. Eventually we can settle on the best option and that becomes our final choice. This is choosing life at its best.

Taking the time to look for options can change our lives dramatically. Life is life, with both its good and bad aspects, but we can have a powerful impact on life by how we choose to deal with it. This is God's gift to us—the power of choice-making. There is truth to the statement, "Life is what we make it."

Teeth Marks on the Toilet Seat

Several years ago while cleaning the bathroom, a shudder went through me as I discovered three distinct sets of teeth marks on the toilet seat. My son was about three or four years old then, and any parent with kids that age finds these kinds of surprises. "What was he thinking?"

As I wondered why he did it, I realized he had become quite creative in solving a problem he was facing. Our toilet seat was padded and didn't stay up, so when he had to go potty, he concluded, he needed three hands: one for his pants, one for the seat, and I am sure you've figured out the rest. Obviously, I talked to him about it and he changed his behavior; but I thought how typical this was of how we make many of our choices. Sometimes we make wrong or unhealthy choices because we don't know

OPTION 1 _____

OPTION 2 _____

OPTION 3 _____

OPTION 4 _____

OPTION 5 _____

OPTION 6 _____

any better. Like my son, we need to be informed so we can stop thinking or acting in ways that are not good for us or for those around us.

Other times we know we are making wrong or poor choices but we keep making them anyway. They have taken on some meaning or reward (payoff), and we don't want to let it go even if it means hurting ourselves. We're angry or scared or we are trying to prove something. Perhaps we don't care any more and to change our choices would mean we need to change our attitude. Soloman describes what happens to a person who disregards or minimizes the consequences of the wrong choices.

The evil deeds of a wicked man ensnare him, the cords of his sin hold him fast. He will die for lack of discipline, led astray by his own folly. (Proverbs 5:22-23)

We cease to be victims of life when we feel the empowerment of being in charge of our choices. A great book that can help us stop being a victim and become a stronger and healthier person is *Boundaries* by Dr. Henry Cloud and Dr. John Townsend. They define boundaries as "the personal property lines that define who you are and who you are not." Here is how they describe it,

> The concept of boundaries comes from the very nature of God. God defines himself as a distinct, separate being, and he is responsible for himself. He defines and takes responsibility for his personality by telling us what he thinks, feels, plans, allows, will not allow, likes, and dislikes. . . . In the same way he gave us his 'likeness' (Genesis 1:26), he gave us personal responsibility within limits. . . . We need to develop boundaries like God's.[14]

As Imagebearers we can choose to change the way we act and feel at any time. Another exciting area where our ability to choose finds its special expression is in how we choose to think. We'll talk about this next.

Suggested Reading

1. Cloud, Henry and Townsend, John. *Boundries.* Zondervan, 1992.
2. Smith, Manuel. *When I Say No, I Feel Guilty.* Bantam Book, 1975.
3. Deuteronomy 7:6-7; 10:14-15; Psalm 17:3; 20:4; Proverbs 8:10; 19:3; 25:28; Matthew 27:1; 2 Corinthians 2:1; Galatians 6:7-10; 1 Peter 1:13; 5:2-3.

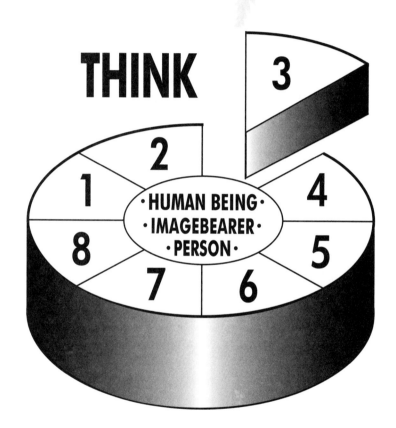

THINK

3

2

1

4

8

5

7

6

·HUMAN BEING·
·IMAGEBEARER·
·PERSON·

Man is but a reed, the most feeble thing in nature; but he is a thinking reed. The entire universe need not arm itself to crush him. A vapour, a drop of water suffices to kill him. But, if the universe were to crush him, man would still be more noble than that which killed him, because he knows that he dies and the advantage which the universe has over him; the universe knows nothing of this.

Blaise Pascal, *Pascal's Pensees* [1]

———— ✦ ————

By means of his mind, his reason, man is able to create culture and civilization; this is his *humanitas*—that which distinguishes him from all other living creatures. . . . Man alone has science, . . . he alone has art, . . . he alone has religion. . . . Man alone has speech.

Emil Brunner, *Man in Revolt* [2]

———— ✦ ————

It is the fact that man is made in the rational and moral image of God which gives him, in a universe of selfless things, the value of an end in himself; which leads God to set value on him, and even in his sin to desire, and take infinite pains for, his recovery. . . . What is true generally of the infinite value of man in God's sight is true particularly of man's capacity for a *divine sonship*. Man, in the Christian Gospel, is called to a relation of sonship to God.

James Orr, *God's Image in Man* [3]

CHAPTER 15

Reason and the Nobility of Man

PERMISSION

School had just opened and LaVerne sat quietly in her first grade class. In school for the first time, her little eyes drank in everything that was going on around her. She lived in the country on a farm and she was not used to having so many people around her. At home, she would play alone for hours, but now her world had just grown larger. She felt scared, unsure of herself, and shy. But she also felt excited because this was the beginning of school—this was a time to learn.

Things were going well until the teacher told the kids to get out a piece of paper and print their name on it. LaVerne had no idea how to print her name. At home, no one had taken the time to teach her the alphabet. She was totally lost. So she did the only thing that came to mind—she copied the name of the girl next to her as her own.

Suddenly, she became aware of the teacher standing over her. Pointing her finger at the name on the paper, the teacher accused LaVerne of cheating. Being accused of cheating in front of the whole class was to shape her self-opinion for the rest of her life. She said, "I could feel all the kids staring at me. I was a cheater. I was so dumb I couldn't even spell my name. I never did like school after that. It was like I had written across my forehead, 'I am dumb, I am a cheat.' To this day, I am sensitive to being accused."

LaVerne never went to college even though her Dad encouraged her. "I never thought I was smart enough to go to college and I would be wasting Dad's money. Beside, I had a good job after high school and I planned to get married and have kids."

Many of us could tell a similar story about how we began to see ourselves as being unintelligent, dumb, or stupid. Something happened that began to shape our self-picture that we were not very smart. Many of us are still standing in the shadows of our childhood memories. We never really learned how to think. We lost our appreciation for our mind—for our ability to think.

In my office, a man once made the comment, "Larry, I haven't done much thinking this week because I just don't like to think."

Who hasn't felt the same way? Thinking about our life is not easy. It can even be painful. Still, our ability to think is one of our most effective tools for dealing with life. It is one of the distinctive characteristics of our humanity. It is a mark of our nobility as creatures made in the image of God. We need to reclaim this gift as ours. We need to give ourselves permission to develop and use our mind to deal with life more effectively.

The Ability to Think Makes Us Human

Mankind is unique in our possessing the ability to reason. This fact had been recognized and affirmed by both nonChristian and Christian writers for centuries. Men like Plato, Aristotle, Augustine, Aquinas, Descartes, Pascal, Locke, Kant, and Hegel all saw the ability to reason as the sole possession of man. In his book *The Difference of Man and the Difference It Makes*, Mortimer Adler wrote:

> With the one exception of Rousseau, for whom the difference between man and brute lies solely in man's free will, all the others attribute man's difference to the fact that man alone among living things has the power of reason, intellect, thought, or understanding —manifested in the distinctively human activities of logical discourse, lawmaking, artistic production, scientific investigation, philosophical argument, the handling of general or abstract ideas, and so on.[4]

Many modern writers in the field of psychology have also affirmed the specialness of our thinking ability. In his book *The Psychology of Self-Esteem*, Nathaniel Branden points to it as one of the characteristics that makes human beings distinct from animals. This ability gives humans an identity and dignity unique to our species. This is how he expressed it:

> Man's defining attribute, which distinguishes him from all other living species, is his ability to reason. This means: to extend the range of his awareness beyond the perceptual concretes immediately confronting him, to abstract, to integrate, to grasp principles—to apprehend reality on a conceptual level of consciousness. . . . Man

is a rational being . . . The capacity to reason—to perform explicit conceptual integrations, guided by logic—is unique to man.[5]

Brandon made another important observation when he separated our ability to think (Being) from our successful use of this ability (Doing). He wrote:

> To define man as a rational animal is not to imply that he is an animal who invariably functions rationally, but rather to identify the fact that . . . the attribute that essentially differentiates him from other animals, is his ability to reason . . . The hallmark of that ability is his power of propositional speech.[6]

It is important for our personal growth that we make a clear separation between our ability to think from how well we use this skill (Ability◄———►Use of Ability). These are two separate issues. This will help us reclaim our ability to think because it is a gift to us from God.

We also need to know that our ability to think is a separate issue from the content of our thinking (Ability◄———►Content). What we think about can be either good or bad, healthy or unhealthy, but that is separate from the fact that we are thinking beings. This was one of Descartes' great insights. He wrote:

> *I think, therefore I am.* . . . From this I knew that I was a substance whose whole essence or nature consists entirely in thinking. . . . I am therefore a thinking thing, that is to say, a mind, an understanding or reason—terms the significance of which has hitherto been unknown to me.[7]

Many of us need to know its significance and that it's okay for us to start using our minds again. It is right and healthy that we reclaim and give ourselves permission to develop our intelligence. It is part of what makes us truly human. We don't need to stay trapped in the memories of our childhood. We no longer need to see ourselves as being dumb or stupid. We have a mind and we can learn to use it.

Our Ability to Think Is a Gift from God

What is the origin of our ability to reason? How did the human species acquire this unique faculty? As we have pointed out before, we only have two answers. We came into possession of this special endowment by chance or by design.

A Christian view of life says that we acquired this special ability by design. God bestowed it upon us as part of what it means to be made in His likeness. Mortimer Adler has pointed out that "only the Christian philosophers . . . speak of man as being created in God's image."[8] Then he adds this affirming note to the origin of our reasoning ability.

> Man's intellect (i.e., his power of conceptual thought) is the immaterial component in his constitution that makes him a person, requires his special creation, gives him the hope of immortality, and endows him with freedom of choice.[9]

Our thinking ability is a unique component of our personhood given to us by our Creator. It is what makes us a person.

Blaise Pascal was a French scientific genius and religious philosopher during the seventeenth century. He wrote some masterpieces of religious philosophy, including his book *Pensées*. Pascal saw our ability to think as evidence of the creative handiwork of God. It is a faculty given to us by design and is a mark of our nobility. He wrote:

> Man is obviously made to think. It is his whole dignity and his whole merit; and his whole duty is to think as he ought. Now, the order of thought is to begin with self, and with its Author. . . . Thought constitutes the greatness of man. . . . All our dignity consists, then, of thought. . . . Let us endeavor, then, to think well; this is the principle of morality![10]

Pascal also made the important distinctions between our (a) ability to think, (b) the way we use that ability, and (c) the content of our thinking. We were designed to think as part of being made in the image of God; but the exercise of our rational faculty is something we have to choose to do. It is not automatic.

We also have to make decisions about what goes into the content of our thinking. The information that pours into our minds comes from a million sources. It is our privilege, even our responsibility, to choose to "think well"—to think positive, healthy, and moral—to think Christian.

Many of us have lost our appreciation for our ability to use our mind. Our identity and worth became connected to how successful we were in using our intelligence and we have lost the joy of knowing that we still have a mind.

In my self-esteem seminars I ask the question, "In school, how many of you can remember feeling like you were a dummy?" A self-conscious laughter will fill the room, but a lot of hands will be raised. Then I ask, "How many of you still believe that you are dummies?" An amazing number of hands will rise again. When given the chance, some painful stories have been told.

Most of us have sold ourselves short by believing that intellectually we just don't have what it takes. We can't imagine that we could learn how to successfully use our mind to improve the quality of our lives.

We can reclaim this gift as personally ours and begin using it in life-giving ways. First, let's see if we can recall when we lost our belief in our ability to think.

The Mind Is a Terrible Thing to Waste

Our mind—the ability to learn and to reason through things—is one of God's special gifts to us. So where did we lose our belief in ourselves and in our ability to think? When did we begin to feel that somehow we were just not as smart as other people? When did we lose our confidence in our own ability to use our mind—to have a mind of our own? When did we start letting other people do our thinking for us?

When I asked myself these questions, I realized for the first time how my learning problems affected my picture of myself. Today, I probably would be diagnosed as dyslexic, but back in my elementary school days I was told I day-dreamed too much.

My problems began in first grade when I had trouble learning the basics. In second or third grade, I can remember walking up to the board to spell or do a math problem, my mind going totally blank with fear. The longer I stood there, the more anxious I became. Hearing the kids giggling behind only made me feel more self-conscious. Finally, I would be told to return to my desk. While I felt relieved, I also felt humiliated.

Suffering the embarrassment and shame of not being able to perform like the other kids, I became convinced it was because I was dumb. By the time I reached fourth grade, I felt so discouraged and disheartened, I decided to quit trying. (Dummies can't do it anyway, so why try?) Any teacher who had me as their student was working with a kid who had quit—his heart was not in it.

It was not until the second semester of my senior year in high school that I changed this decision and put my heart back into trying to do well in school. Now I have four college degrees and people call me Dr. Day, but I still can't spell very well and I have difficulty reading out loud. Now you are reading my book. And what does this prove? It shows what we can do if we begin to believe in ourselves—believe in the way God designed us to be.

Over the years, I have heard many interesting and sad stories about how people lost or gave away their right to develop their mind. Some people never learned how to think for themselves because they were always told what to think. Others had it taken away by people who wanted to control their mind to make them be a certain way. Some of them lost confidence in their ability to develop their mind because of things that happened to them.

But a lot of us lost it because of hurtful things people said to us. See if you recognize any of the following:

- "You haven't got the brains God gave a crowbar!"
- "Use your head, you idiot!"
- "You're so dumb! I can't believe you did that!"
- "You think you're so d— smart don't you? Well, you don't know s—!"
- "You haven't got a brain in your head!"
- "If brains were dynamite, you wouldn't have enough to blow your nose."
- "You numb skull!" "You scatter brain!" "You air head!"
- "What did you do, leave your brains on the shelf?"
- "If you were only half as smart as your brother/sister you might amount to something."
- "Who do you think you are? Einstein?"
- "Use your head for something more than a hat rack."
- "You haven't got the brains of a billy goat!"
- "What were you thinking of, you dummy!"
- "Anybody with a half a brain should have known better!"
- "You thought s—-! You just do what you're told!"

There are lots of reasons why we fail to learn how to think for ourselves. These statements point to a few. When we add to them things like learning problems, the need to please, the need to survive a dysfunctional family, or to survive an oppressive religious or political system, we can see how we would forget we are entitled to have a mind of our own.

When we lose confidence in our right or our ability to think, we begin to let others think for us. How could anyone believe they have a right to think or even trust their own ability to think after such a prolonged indoctrination about their lack of brains? Someone has to be in charge of your mind. It may as well be you.

To Think or Not to Think—That Is the Decision

How many times have we heard the phrase, "Stop and think it through"? We are thinking beings whether we like it or not. It's designed in our personhood. But being choice-makers, we have the power to decide whether we are going to think or not think. We are in charge of whether we will use our mind to improve life or to harm it. In her novel *Atlas Shrugged*, the out spoken atheist Ayn Rand stated it this way:

Man's mind is his basic tool of survival. Life is given to him, survival is not. . . . To remain alive, he must think. But to think is an act of choice. . . . Reason does not work automatically; thinking is not a mechanical process; . . . Man has been called a rational being, but rationality is a matter of choice . . . Man has to be man—by choice; he has to hold his life as a value—by choice; he has to learn to sustain it—by choice; he has to discover the values it requires and practice his virtues—by choice.[11]

Our ability to consciously use our mind to improve our lives is one of the most important truths we can learn about ourselves.

Most of us will think *about* our problems until they drive us nuts; but few of us learn how to think *through* our problems and use our mind to make our lives better. When we decide to learn how to do this, life gets exciting. It's fun to be human.

Our rational faculty is one of the factors that defines us as being human. We may fail to become fully human but we cannot cease being human. In his book *Being Human . . . Becoming Human*, Helmut Thielicke described it this way:

Human existence, as we have seen, means that humanity is the only form of being that has to know and comprehend itself, that has thus to act in responsibility to its destiny. This is what distinguishes human being from animal being. . . . We are not puppets directed from outside but *by creation are endowed with gifts that make us centers of action* and thus expose us to the risk of *winning our own identity, as the Creator intended, or failing to achieve it.*

We are rational beings. . . . We are not at the mercy of deterministic evolution but with the help of reason can choose among the available possibilities and thus plan our future.[12]

When we realize that our ability to think can be a useful tool to help us live more effectively, we discover one of the wonders of our being—of being made in the likeness of God. Then it is up to us to decide whether we are going to choose to think; think truthfully or untruthfully, think positively or negatively, think realistically or unrealistically, think rationally or irrationally, think optimistically or pessimistically, think as a Christian or think as a nonChristian.

The Ability to Think Is Our Birthright

Learning how to use our minds is an exciting adventure! It begins the moment we decide to reclaim our birthright to be what God created us to be —a thinking being. God designed it to be that way because its use is essential to our ability to grow and mature physically, emotionally, and spiritually.

God affirmed our design when He appealed to our ability to reason as a way to understand our relationship with Him. God wanted the people of Israel to see with their minds what God wanted to do about forgiving them for making wrong choices. The prophet Isaiah wrote:

Come now, *let us reason together*, says the Lord. Though your sins are like scarlet, they shall be as white as snow; though they are red as crimson, they shall be like wool (Isaiah 1:9, italics mine).

Israel's moral and spiritual life had deteriorated to the point that God sent Isaiah to confront them. They had turned away from God and wanted to follow and worship the idols and gods of the nations around them. They were also treating each other in wrong and harmful ways. God wanted them to stop and think about what they were doing. He wanted them to follow His ideas to their logical conclusions as a way for them to see the folly of worshiping gods that were too small, of turning to gods who were unable to forgive, unable to love. This is how God described the way people were using their minds in facing their ways.

They know nothing, they understand nothing; their eyes are plastered over so they cannot see, and their *minds closed* so they cannot understand. *No one stops to think*, no one has the knowledge or understanding to say, . . . "Shall I bow down to a block of wood?" (Isaiah 44:19 italics mine).

God wanted them to open their minds so they could see with new eyes the bigger picture of life. He wanted them to come to know and understand Him as the Creator of all life and to see the importance of a personal relationship with Him. Love and forgiveness were found in Him. God said:

This is what the Lord says—your Redeemer, who formed you in the womb: I am the Lord, who has made all things, who alone stretched out the heavens, who spread out the earth by myself, . . . It is I who made the earth and created mankind upon it. . . . Turn to me and be saved, all you ends of the earth; for I am God, and there is no other. . . . I, even I, am he who blots out your transgressions, for my own sake, and remember your sins no more. . . . I am he who will sustain you. I have made you and I will carry you; I will sustain you and I will rescue you (Isaiah 44:24, 45:12, 43:25, 46:4).

God can ask human beings "to stop and think" because He designed us in His image to think. But God put us in charge of our mind. We decide whether we will be open- or closed-minded. Life begins when we choose to be open-minded. An open mind can lead to an open heart.

We need to give ourselves permission to use our thinking ability to help us grow into mature Christian human beings. We can encourage each other to develop our minds in healthy, life-giving ways as people who can be proud that we are made in God's image. We can be proud to be human. Christians need to know they are free to develop and use their minds. The apostle Peter wrote: "Be clear-minded and self-controlled." (1 Peter 4:7). The apostle Paul placed a high value on the healthy development of our mind. In his letter to the Corinthian church he wrote:

> When I was a child, I talked like a child, I thought like a child, I reasoned like a child. When I became a man, I put childish ways behind me. . . . Brothers, stop thinking like children. In regard to evil be infants, but in your thinking be adults (1 Corinthians 13:11, 14:20).

Growing up and learning how to use our mind as mature adults is both human and Christian. It is a mark of our nobility. When I see my son using his mind to think through a situation in order to make a good decision, it makes me feel proud of him as his Dad. I believe God feels proud of us when He sees us learning how to use our mind the way He designed it to work. This is why it is so important that we reclaim this gift as ours and then give ourselves permission to develop it. Learning how to use our mind is the subject of the next chapter.

Suggested Reading

1. Ellis, Albert. *A New Guide to Rational Living.* Wilshire Book Company, 1975.
2. Collins, Gary. *Your Magnificent Mind: The Fasciniating Ways It Works for You.* Baker Book House, 1985.
3. 1 Chronicles 28:9; Job 12:3; 38:36; Psalm 13:2; 55:2; Proverbs 9:10,12; 13:20; Isaiah 26:3; 32:3-4; Jeremiah 17:10; Matthew 9:4; 22:37; Romans 1:21,28; 14:13; 1 Peter 4:7.

Dear friends, this is now my second letter to you. I have written both of them as reminders to *stimulate you to wholesome thinking.* I want you to recall the words spoken in the past by the holy prophets and the command given by our Lord and Savior through your apostles.

The apostle Peter, 2 Peter 3:1-2 (italics mine). [1]

———— ❧❧ ————

The possibility thinkers perceptively probe every problem, proposal, and opportunity to discover the positive aspects present in almost every human situation. . . . They have trained themselves to look for possibilities in all areas of life.

Robert Schuller,

Moving Ahead with Possibility Thinking [2]

———— ❧❧ ————

Rationally and realistically organizing and disciplining his or her thinking a human can live the most self-fulfilling, creative, and emotionally satisfying life. . . . [But] Let's face it, humans have trouble thinking straight . . . Can we, then, call humans truly rational animals? Yes, we can. And no, we can't. They have the most incredibly mixed-up *combination* of common sense and uncommon senselessness you ever did see.

Albert Ellis,

A New Guide to Rational Thinking [3]

~ᴗᴠᴗ~

Who, Me?
Think for Myself?

HOW TO

What would you have done to survive years of captivity in a North Vietnamese POW camp? How would you have used your mind to survive years of being held hostage by Lebanese terrorists? Survivors have told us some amazing stories about how they used their minds in creative ways to stay sane and alive. The situation demanded it of them.

Most of us have not enjoyed what a powerful tool our ability to think can be in helping us deal with life more effectively. We merely do what we can to adjust or adapt to our circumstances, and we miss out on the exciting difference it makes when we consciously use our mind to think in creative and life-giving ways.

Reclaiming and giving ourselves permission to use our ability to think is the first step to understanding what an amazing ability we humans are blessed with. The next step is to see how we can exercise and develop the use of our mind for creative, rational living. Learning how to use our mind to develop reasonable and healthy ways to live is learning how to be the person God designed us to be.

For example, years ago I read an amazing story about how one of our soldiers survived years of captivity in a Vietnamese prisoner of war camp. My memory of the details has faded but the main impact of the story remains. The story goes like this.

An American solder (let's call him Steve) was captured, put into a prison camp, and tortured. His captors wanted to get as much information from him as possible. They also wanted to break his spirit so he would become a typical inmate. As the months of confinement and suffering dragged on, their tactics began to take a toll. Steve started questioning whether his country still remembered him. He wondered if the American public still stood by him because of the propaganda he was being fed by his captors.

Gradually, his health and his spirit began to fail. The enemies of depression and despair—even insanity—were becoming unwelcome cellmates.

Then it happened. One day while standing in the prison yard, Steve was looking through the wire and bamboo fence at one of the North Vietnamese guards. As he thought about this Communist soldier, an amazing thing transpired. Steve mentally stepped back from his situation and started to reflect on the big picture of what was going on. Looking at the truth, he saw his situation with new eyes.

He suddenly realized that while it was true that he was physically the prisoner of war, he was in fact the free man! The Communist soldier was the real prisoner. While he might be standing outside the prison wall, thinking he was free, he was, in fact, a mental prisoner of Communist ideologies.

As an American, Steve knew what freedom meant—free to speak, free to worship as he chose, free to vote his conscience. The Communist soldier had to conform to the Party line or suffer the consequences. Seeing this vision transformed Steve's mental outlook on life. To use an earlier illustration, it was like seeing the picture of the pretty lady for the first time after only being able to see the old woman. Now he felt free in his spirit. He felt hopeful, encouraged, and strengthened. He knew the truth and the truth had set him free! He had been transformed by the renewing of his mind.

Gradually, Steve began to encourage his fellow prisoners. As the years passed, he became one of the most important leaders in the camp at helping other prisoners to keep their morale high.

After the war, when the POWs were released and returned to the United States, Steve was given special recognition for his work among his fellow prisoners. Many of them said they would not have survived had it not been for him. His life—his perspectives, ideas, and words—encouraged, supported, and helped them through a horrible time.

The human mind is amazing. Its potential for helping or hurting ourselves can boggle the mind. Let's look at some of the ways we can learn how to use our ability to think to help us create the kind of life that is alive, healthy, and productive—the way God intended it to be.

The Importance of Positive/Optimistic Thinking

Earlier, we made an important distinction between our ability to think and the content of our thinking (ability ◀────▶ content). One way we can use our mind in a life-giving way is to see the importance of developing positive, healthy, and optimistic thinking habits.

By an internal law of the soul, we become what we think. In 1952, Dr. Norman Vincent Peale wrote *The Power of Positive Thinking*. It has sold millions of copies. It touched a deep need in the human spirit, providing perspectives and encouragement to people who were looking for help in how to live life more successfully. He wrote it to demonstrate how faith in oneself, combined with faith in sound mental health principles and spiritual truths as found in the Christian faith, can transform a person's life.

Learning the art of positive thinking helped people move from defeat to victory, from depression to joy, from failure to accomplishment.

Dr. Peale did not refer to the idea that we are made in God's image, but if we apply this view to what he says about self-confidence, we can see how it fits.

> Believe in yourself! Have faith in your abilities! Without a humble but reasonable confidence in your own powers you cannot be successful or happy. But with sound self confidence you can succeed. A sense of inferiority and inadequacy interferes with the attainment of your hopes, but self-confidence leads to self-realization and successful achievement. . . . You can develop creative faith in yourself —faith that is justified.[3]

To see ourselves as made in God's likeness gives us a reasonable and sound basis to believe in ourselves. We can see the significance of our life, and yet, be humble because our worth is a gift from God. It is not something we earned; it was bestowed on us. Because of this, we are free to use our ability to think to approach life with a positive frame of mind. Faith and prayer become important contributors in developing positive thinking habits. Dr. Peale spoke of it this way:

> One of the important functions of prayer is as a stimulus to creative ideas. . . . God our Creator has laid up within our minds and personalities all the potential powers and ability we need for constructive living. It remains for us to tap and develop these powers.[4]

As human beings, God has given us everything we need for a good life. Almost two thousand years earlier this same message was given to us by the apostle Peter. He connected it to the Judeo-Christian way of life. He wrote:

> Grace and peace be yours in abundance through the knowledge of God and of Jesus our Lord. *His divine power has given us everything*

we need for life and godliness through our knowledge of him who called us by his own glory and goodness.

For this very reason, make every effort to add to your faith goodness . . . knowledge . . . self control . . . perseverance . . . godliness . . . brotherly kindness . . . [and] love. For if you possess these qualities in increasing measure they will keep you from being ineffective and unproductive in your knowledge of our Lord Jesus Christ (2 Peter 1:2-3, 5-8, italics mine).

We make a big step toward life when we begin to use our abilities—like choosing (self-control) and thinking—in positive ways. Positive thinking isn't just brainwashing ourselves with phrases like, "Every day, in every way I am getting better and better." It is deeper and more exciting than that. It's seeing with new eyes the possibilities we have for using our mind to help us experience life in healthy ways.

The healing power in positive thinking has been missed by so many of us because we have developed such unhealthy thinking habits. The content and pattern of our thinking has become negative or pessimistic. We may justify our negative ways of thinking because of what has happened to us, but the day we decide to change this is the day we begin building a new past.

We can change our thinking habits because these habits were learned— we were not born with them. For over twenty-five years Dr. Martin Seligman has studied the difference between optimists and pessimists. In his book *Learned Optimism*, Dr. Seligman presents some of the latest research on the ways people learn their thinking habits. He wrote:

Habits of thinking need not be forever. One of the most significant findings in psychology in the last twenty years is that individuals can choose the way they think. . . . Unlike many personal qualities, basic pessimism is not fixed and unchangeable. You can learn a set of skills that free you from the tyranny of pessimism and allow you to use optimism when you choose.[5]

So what makes one person become an optimist and another a pessimist? It develops from the way we learn to think and talk to ourselves about why bad things happen to us in life. It is intimately connected with our self-esteem. This is how Dr. Seligman explains it.

Your habitual way of explaining bad events . . . is more than just words you mouth when you fail. *It is a habit of thought learned in childhood and adolescence.* . . . [It] stems directly from your view of your place in the world—*whether you think you are valuable and deserving, or worthless and hopeless.* . . . Learned helplessness is the giving-up reaction, the quitting response that follows from the belief that whatever you do doesn't matter. . . . Your way of explaining events to yourself determines how helpless you can become, or how energized, when you encounter the everyday setbacks as well as momentous defeats (italics mine). [6]

A person who learns to be optimistic in their heart will experience life more abundantly. They will be more open, alive, adventurous, and engaged in healthy risk taking. They will develop a more positive mind-set about life—about both the good and the bad things that happen. They will feel more content in life. They will not see themselves as victims.

The Christian view of life says that we have God's banner of love over our lives. The importance of healthy thinking was clearly emphasized by the apostle Paul in his letter to the Philippians.

Do not be anxious about anything, but in everything, by prayer and petition, with thanksgiving, present your requests to God. And the peace of God, which transcends all understanding, will guard your hearts and your minds in Christ Jesus. Finally, brothers, whatever is *true*, whatever is **noble**, whatever is **right**, whatever is **pure**, whatever is *lovely*, whatever is **admirable**—if anything is **excellent** or **praiseworthy** —think about such things (Philippians 4:6-8, bold italics mine).

All human beings have the ability to think because we are created in God's image. But developing the mental habit of thinking in positive, optimistic ways is learned. Once we realize this, we are free to make a conscious effort to practice learning new healthy thinking habits. Doing so will have a beneficial impact on the quality of our life. Choosing to think in life-giving ways can bring about amazing changes. Optimistic thinking is life-giving thinking.

The Importance of Rational Thinking

Another way we can enjoy the use of our ability to think is to learn how to think realistically and rationally. Just because we think doesn't guarantee we will always think rationally. In fact, a lot of our feelings and reactions are caused by the irrational beliefs and expectations we hold. We blame our feelings and reactions on the circumstances outside of us when, in fact, the problem can also be found inside of us—in our irrational way of thinking and interpreting.

While the situation may be the external stimulus, our feelings about it are the product of our internal beliefs and what we say to ourselves about those beliefs. The often-used quote by Epictetus, the famous first-century stoic, helps capture this idea: "Men are disturbed not by things, but by the views which they take of them."

Suppose you and ten of your friends went out to dinner one evening. After a fun time together, you all leave the restaurant to go to your cars, only to discover that every car has two flat tires. How would you react? What would your feelings be and what would you do? Would everyone's reaction be just like yours?

If circumstances produce feelings, then everyone would experience the same feelings. The problem is the same. But we know that people's feelings and reactions would vary widely. Why? Because each person will think differently about the situation and talk to themselves differently about it— they will interpret it differently.

Seeing the flat tires triggers their beliefs about how they think life is supposed to be. If reality does not conform to their beliefs or expectations, then what they tell themselves about the situation produces strong feelings. If their beliefs are irrational or unrealistic, they will experience a different set of feelings from those produced by rational or realistic thinking.

Our thinking produces our feelings. This is one of the most exciting facts about being human that we can learn. It helps us see how we can develop better self-control over our feelings by changing our thinking habits and self-talk. In his book *A New Guide to Rational Living*, Dr. Albert Ellis describes this process in detail. As a Rational-Emotive therapist, he developed a simple formula for understanding how thoughts and feelings are connected. He teaches people how to understand what he calls the ABCs of our emotional life. A is the activating event, B is our beliefs, and C is the emotional and behavioral consequences. I have added D to represent the desired feelings and actions we would like to create. The diagram below visually represents this.

Generally, when something happens, like getting a flat tire, we think that it is the situation that has caused our feelings and is responsible for our reactions (A=C). While the flat tire may be the stimulus (A), it is our beliefs

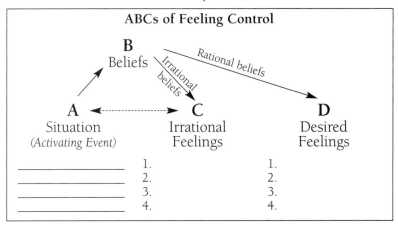

and what we say to ourselves because of those beliefs (B) that creates the kind and intensity of feelings we experience (C or D).

If what we think and say to ourselves is irrational, unrealistic, or untruthful, we would experience such feelings as shock, anger, impatience, irritation, suspicion, and high frustration (C). In reaction we might blame our spouse, kick the car, yell at those around us, or stomp around, acting like an idiot. Or we might get depressed, sit down and cry, feel guilty, feel sorry for ourselves, and ask, "Why me? What did I do to deserve this?"

If what we think and say to ourselves is more reasonable and realistic, we would experience feelings such as surprise, frustration, disappointment, confusion, humor, and helplessness (D)—but they would not be as intense or heavy. We might say to ourselves, "Well, what do I do now?" (D) and we would begin to **think** of ways to solve the problem. Our minds would become activated to think of possible solutions rather than merely ponder the problems. We would start thinking through the problem rather then just thinking about it. Just thinking about problems can drive us nuts; but thinking it through to a solution is fun, exciting, and rewarding. This distinction is very important if we want to learn how to work with our feelings more effectively. It will improve, heal and change our lives for the better the moment we begin to consciously work at it. And it IS work! But it's worth it!

The Healing Power of Self-Talk

A healthy way we can work with our feelings, thoughts, and actions is to become more aware of how we talk to ourselves. What we tell ourselves has a powerful effect on our lives. It is constantly at work but most of us have not recognized its potential for making our lives miserable or happy.

Dr. David Stoop, a Christian psychologist, has written a most helpful book titled *Self Talk*.[7] According to him, we talk out loud at the rate of 150 to 200 words a minute. But research suggests that we talk to ourselves at about the rate of 1300 words per minute.

Our conversation with ourself is in word by word sentences, but most of it is in mental pictures and images, like a slide show. Our thought-life puts blocks of ideas or pictures together that form part of our self-conversation.

From the moment we awake in the morning until we drift asleep at night, we carry on a nonstop conversation with ourselves. Even while you're reading these words, you're talking to yourself. You may be talking to yourself about what you're reading, about an idea triggered by your reading, or about something totally unrelated to this book. But you're talking to yourself about something. Are you aware of it, right now?

Becoming aware of this uniquely human skill is the first step to being able to accept it. Then we can use it as a powerful tool to help ourselves develop a healthier sense of self-worth and self-acceptance. We can talk to ourselves about our thoughts and beliefs, our feelings, and our choices. We can use it to develop a healthy sense of self-control that works for our well-being rather than against it.

We can change our moods, attitudes, and feelings by recognizing what kinds of sentences we are telling ourselves, and then changing these sentences. Dr. Albert Ellis was one of the first psychologists to bring this to our attention. It is central to the theory of Rational-Emotive Therapy. In the first edition of his book *A Guide to Rational Living*, he points out the important connection between self-talk and the control of our feelings.

> For permanent and deep-seated emotional changes to be effected, thinking changes, or drastic modifications of the individual's philosophy of life, appear to us to be necessary in most instances. . . . Sustained emotion, in particular, normally stems from sustained thought. And since adult human beings usually think in terms of internalized phrases and sentences, or self-talk, they sustain their emotions by talking to themselves or by telling themselves certain kinds of sentences.

> In general, negative emotions, such as feelings of depression, anxiety, anger, and guilt are intensified and sustained by such self-propagandizing sentences as "This is awful!" "I can't stand that!" And positive emotions, such as love, joy, and elation, are intensified and sustained by sentences such as "This is fine!" or "I like that!" *Because this is so, human emotions can often be radically controlled or changed by determining precisely the kind of sentences lying behind them and then by changing these sentences.* (italics mine)[8]

Clear, healthy, truthful thinking and self-talk lead to positive, healthy, life-giving feelings. To change our feelings from ones we don't like to ones we do, we need to *listen to ourselves* so we can identify the internalized sentences we keep telling ourselves that are unrealistic, unhealthy, untrue, and then work at changing these sentences.

Acceptance v. Resignation—Letting Go v. Giving Up

Many of us have learned to think and talk to ourselves in ways that resist accepting reality. We like to blame, complain, or deny. Often we fight reality rather than learning how to work with it. This keeps us stuck in victim thinking. Fighting reality is what I call our "Don Quixote Complex."

In 1605 Meguel de Cervantes of Spain published a novel about a Spanish landowner who wanted to be like the knights of old. He took the name Don Quixote of La Mancha, dressed up in his knights armor, and then set out to be a hero. He saw windmills as giant enemies and he attacked them whenever found. He charged into the windmills with great courage and passion, but this tall, thin "hero" is always knocked to the ground on impact. But did he give up? Certainly not. He just got up, dusted himself off, got back on his scrawny horse Rocinante and rode off to eventually attack another windmill—repeating the cycle again.

We are acting like Don Quixote when we *fight* reality rather than *work with* reality. We attack "our windmills" with great passion and courage, but reality knocks us down. Learning how to *accept and work with reality* is learning how to live life more successfully. There is a big difference in our thinking and self-talk between accepting something and just resigning ourself to it. Resignation leads to feelings of depression, defeat, and despair. Acceptance leads to feelings of relief, sorrow, freedom, and peace. Our feelings will tell us which one is the thoughts of our heart. We can trust our experience. Our energy, courage, and determination can still be used, but now it is being used in a life-giving way.

There is also a big difference between giving up and letting go. In our heart if we have "given up," we will feel defeated, depressed, resentful, cynical, and hopeless. We still feel trapped or stuck. But if we "let go," we will feel relieved, sad, free, settled, and still hopeful. We will feel like we can still work to improve or change things because we are not fighting ourselves or fighting reality.

Learning how to think differently and how to talk to ourselves differently are the keys to working with our feeling life in healthy ways. The renewing of our mind may be a necessary part of this process.

Be Transformed by the Renewing of Your Mind

Renewing the mind can transform our personality and life. Learning how to see things from new perspectives can free us to be the person God created us to be. The apostle Paul spoke of this principle when he was telling people about the Christian way. He wrote about it on two separate occasions. He related it to the transforming effect the truth of knowing Jesus Christ can have on a person. But the principle is true for being both human and Christian. He wrote:

> Do not conform any longer to the pattern of the world, but be transformed by the renewing of your mind. Then you will be able to test and approve what God's will is—his good, pleasing and perfect will (Romans 12:2).

You were taught, with regard to your former way of life, to put off your old self, which is being corrupted by its deceitful desires; *to be made new in the attitude of your minds*; and to put on the new self, created to be like God in true righteousness and holiness (Ephesians 4:22-24, italics mine).

Dr. Robert Schuller once wrote: "TRANSFORMED THINKING transforms everything."[9] Transformed thinking will transform our feelings—especially our feelings about our worth and identity. Feelings do not come over us like the flu or like bad weather. They are created by our thoughts, beliefs, ideas, expectations, and ways of interpreting. Our feelings can be modified and changed by changing the thought patterns behind them. To learn this skill is to learn the art of self-control!

It is freeing, exciting, and empowering to discover that we don't have to be victims of our feelings. We are in charge of our feelings. We can change them by choosing to change the way we look at life—by the renewing of our mind. The healing power in positive, healthy, and realistic thinking from a Christian view of life could benefit us more than we ever imagine. It may require a drastic change in our philosophy of life or it may be as simple as changing a single word in a self-talk sentence. Let me explain.

Learn How to Identify the Trigger Words

As a general rule, our feelings reflect the way we think.[10] We create or sustain our feelings by our own self-talk. If our feelings are self-caused (or self-sustained), then we need to recognize that to a great extent we are doing it to ourselves.

There are certain words that trigger heavier negative feelings. When we talk to ourselves using words such as "have to," "should," "must," "terrible," "horrible," and "awful," we self-create feelings such as anxiety, guilt, fear, anger, insecurity, and depression. Several years ago, Dr. Ellis coined a word to identify this process. The word was must-urbation. Just like masturbation is a physical self-stimulation activity that creates sexual feelings, must-urbation is a mental self-stimulation activity that creates psychological feelings.

If we want to change our feelings from death-producing ones to life-giving ones, we need to work at eliminating the use of these trigger words in our self-talk. Words like "should," "have to," and "terrible" are black and white; they are absolutes. Most of the time they are irrational words because they leave no room for reality—for real life. Yes, we probably need a few have tos, shoulds, and terribles. But as a general rule, it's to our benefit to eliminate as many of these words from our self-talk as possible. "I have to," can be changed to, "It's right for me to." "That's terrible," can be changed to, "That's wrong," or "That's really sad." Changing these words in our thinking really does make a difference in how we experience life.

Years ago I made a sticker which condensed some of the main trigger words we use in our self-talk (see the diagram below). I wanted people to observe themselves to see how often they used these words—to see how they made life either miserable or pleasant.

Help Stamp Out Must-Urbation	
Death *(make a choice)*	Life
must	want to
should	like to
have to	willing to
supposed to	would be right to
obligated to	would be helpful to
expected to	would be beneficial to
it's terrible	it's unfortunate
it's horrible	it's inconvenient
it's awful	it's sad

Whenever they experience strong negative feelings, I wanted them to look for the trigger words creating those feelings. We will find them embedded in our self-talk sentences. Then I wanted them to make a conscious choice to change those words from the death side to those on the life side, and by doing so, experience how they could be in charge of how they felt.

Using the words found on the death side impacts us physically. We will feel uptight, tense, pressured, nervous, desperate, panicky, trapped, etc.

When we use the words on the life side, our bodies experience a positive benefit. We will feel relieved, more calm, more free, more relaxed, less pressured, less tense, less up-tight, less nervous. We will feel a sense of self-control. Going back to the example of the flat tire, which sentence feels more life-giving to you, "It's terrible to have a flat tire just after eating a nice meal!" or "It's unfortunate to have a flat tire just after eating a nice meal"?

We can tell when we have been successful at stopping our must-urbating— our catastrophizing—because our feelings will tell us so. Physically, we can feel a shift take place that tells us we have been successful at changing our trigger words and improved our sense of well-being. We are learning to become our own best friend. This is a powerful way to use our ability to think. I believe it is the way God intended for it to be used.

Imagination: Its Potential for Life or Death

Our imagination is a marvelous part of our ability to think. It plays a far more significant role in our lives than most of us realize. Our imagination can build the most beautiful cathedrals and it can destroy our sense of being a valued and loved human being. An imagination that has lost connection with reality or with truth (especially biblical truth) is an imagination that will create feelings we cannot long endure.

This happens because the feeling part of us doesn't know the difference between a vivid imagination and reality. It simply responds to thoughts, images, and pictures as if they are real just as it was designed to.

A way to illustrate this is to talk about what I call the "domino complex." This occurs when something happens and our imagination goes from one bad thing, to the next, to the next, to the worst-case scenario. We imagine the worst and get all bummed out, but our feelings were mostly caused by our imagination. You know what I'm talking about if your child or spouse was an hour or two late getting home some night (without calling home).

Or imagine that you're visiting with one of your friends at your home. It is a hot, humid day and you decide to make some fresh lemonade. Your friend follows you into the kitchen to help squeeze some fresh lemons. After cutting one in half, you invite your friend to join you in eating part of it while you continue making the juice. You begin chewing and sucking on the lemon.

Is your mouth watering or puckering up as you pictured yourself biting into a lemon? We know that it's all in our imagination. But the feeling part of us is responding to our imagination, and we are experiencing what Maxwell Maltz calls a "synthetic experience." This famous plastic surgeon wrote about this in his excellent book *Psycho-cybernetics*. This is what he said.

> Experimental and clinical psychologists have proved beyond a shadow of a doubt that the human nervous system cannot tell the difference between an "actual" experience and an experience imagined vividly and in detail. . . . this type of "synthetic" experience has been used in very practical ways to improve skill in dart throwing . . . [in] shooting basketball goals . . . in public speaking . . . [in] overcoming fear of the dentist . . . [and to] develop self confidence.[11]

A major portion of our sense of self-esteem, along with many aspects of life in general, is linked to our imagination. We imagine what people are going to say; we imagine what people are going to think; we imagine what might happen, and the feeling part of us responds to our imagination. I am a mountain climber, and I was talking to a woman today about rappelling over the edge of a cliff with ropes and carabiners. She imagined herself doing the same and it created visible signs of fear on her face.

Spiritually, many of us have an active imagination about what we think God thinks of us. If we think He is angry or disgusted with us, we will suffer the negative feelings this picture creates. The feeling part of us will not know if He is really angry or if this is our imagination. It simply responds.

Knowing what the truth is—knowing what reality is—will be crucial if we want to develop an honest sense of our self-worth and an honest relationship with God. Dr. Maltz affirmed the important connection between self-esteem and our concept of God. He saw God as a Loving Creator—our heavenly Father.

> The aim of self-image psychology is not to create a fictitious self which is all-powerful, arrogant, egoistic, all-important. Such an image is as inappropriate and unrealistic as the inferior image of self. Our aim is to find the "real self," and to bring our mental image of ourselves more in line with "the objects they represent." . . . How can you know the truth about yourself? How can you make a true evaluation? It seems to me that here psychology must turn to religion. The Scriptures tell us that God created man "a little lower than the angels" and "gave him dominion"; that God created man in his own image. If we really believe in an all-wise, all-powerful, all-loving Creator, then we are in a position to draw some logical conclusions about that which He has created—Man. . . . If we take the premise that God is a loving Creator and has the same interests in his Creation that an earthly father has in his children, then . . . what brings more glory, pride, and satisfaction to a father then seeing his off-spring do well, succeed and express to the full their abilities and talents?[12]

Deep-down many of us do not like the person we are. We see ourselves as bad, unlovable, or inferior. The Bible says as we think in our heart, so are we (Proverbs 23:7 K.J.V.). If we looked at the imaginations of our heart, we would find that we still carry negative childhood pictures about ourselves. Our present feelings about ourselves are emotional responses to those past pictures—but these pictures may not be accurate. They represent the conclusions we made about our worth based on works (doing) rather than worth based on birth (being).

To change our feelings, about ourselves we need to change our imaginations. We need to bring our thinking into line with the truth—the truth that we are made in God's image, the truth that Jesus loves us. We need to tell ourselves the truth until we finally take it to heart.[13]

This is what Dr. Maltz so clearly pointed out when he said that psychology needed to turn to the Judeo-Christian view of life to find the right picture for the origin of human life that gives worth and meaning to our being.

The apostle Paul also saw the value of our mind (our ability to think) as a tool to move from old, death-producing thinking to new, life-giving thinking. He wrote:

> We demolish arguments and every pretension that sets itself up against the knowledge of God, and we take captive every thought to make it obedient to Christ (2 Corinthians 10:5).

Bringing our imagination into line with the truth of our being made in the image of God is seeing our worth the way Jesus sees it. It is letting our imagination become captivated by the vision of who we are as Imagebearers of God. We can respond to God's love for us because it is reasonable. It can be trusted because He sees us as worth it. This truth can move from our head to our heart—from merely an intellectual idea to an experienced idea.

To enjoy a sense of self-worth based on truth is to experience life the way God, our heavenly Father, intended it to be. What would bring more glory, pride, and satisfaction to God the Father than seeing those who are designed in His image, and those who have been redeemed in Christ doing well—succeeding and expressing their interests, talents, and abilities in exciting and life-fulfilling ways?

What is true about our worth and identity is also true about most things in our lives. It is our imagination that interferes with our daily choices to develop our interests and talents. We are afraid of so many things, and most of our fear is produced by our imagination. Our lives can change for the better the moment we decide to take control of our imagination. We need to bring it into line with truth or reality and then make the kind of choices that are the most life-giving at that moment. This is being like Christ in the best sense of the word.

Making a conscious effort to work with our imagination in healthy ways is learning how to work with our feelings in a positive way. We learn how to control them rather than letting them control us.

The Truth Shall Set Us Free

God designed the human mind and heart to respond in a positive way to truth. Truth inspires its own set of feelings just as lies do. We know that sometimes the truth hurts, but most of us would rather know the truth than to be told lies. There is something clean, solid, and trustworthy in truth.

Another way we can use our ability to think is to see how important it is to think the truth rather than to think lies or half lies. I had to work with this when it came to accepting my childhood.

My natural father was partially Dutch and my dad partially Swedish. As a boy I saw more prestige, power, and glory in thinking of myself as a rugged Viking than some boy wearing a funny hat and wooden shoes with his finger stuck in a dike. It was hard for me to let go of my fantasy and accept the truth of my natural heritage. But the truth set me free—free to talk honestly about my early childhood, my father, my ancestral roots; free to enjoy and appreciate the Dutch culture and their contributions to mankind just as I did with the Scandinavian culture.

Thinking the truth, telling ourselves the truth, and speaking the truth are all important if we want to be emotionally and spiritually healthy. If our feelings are products of our thinking, then it is crucial that the content of our thinking contains truth, both little *t* truth (the truth about ourselves and life in general), and capital *T* truth (truth from God as found in Scripture).

When our thinking and self-talk includes Judeo-Christian truth, our emotional life can take on a whole new dimension. I know that Christians have not always been the best examples of what healthy human beings were designed to be. But we Christians are human beings too, subject to the laws of gravity, laws of nature, and laws of mental health like all human beings. If we violate the laws God designed in our humanness, we will suffer the consequences even as a nonbeliever would. God's truth can bring healing when it is embraced by faith. A couple of examples will help us see this.

Jeremiah was a prophet to the people of Israel at the time the Babylonian army destroyed the city of Jerusalem. The army sacked the temple of God and took a great number of people into captivity. The book of Lamentations expresses the pain and anguish Jeremiah felt over this great loss. The tragedy he witnessed caused him to feel a deep sense of grief. He felt isolated, shut out, rejected, and persecuted. Jeremiah blamed God for his misery and pain. He blamed God for his feelings. This is how he expressed it over 2,500 years ago.

> I am the man who has seen affliction by the rod of his wrath. He has driven me away and made me walk in darkness rather than light; indeed, he has turned his hand against me again and again, all day long. . . . He has walled me in so I cannot escape; he has weighed me down with chains. Even when I call out or cry for help, he shuts out my prayers. . . . Like a bear lying in wait, like a lion in hiding, he dragged me from the path and mangled me and left me without help (Lamentations 3:1-3, 7-8, 10-11).

Jeremiah poured out his heart and revealed his deepest thoughts and feelings about his circumstances. Then he revealed the pain of seeing his final hopes trampled under the pounding hooves of a conquering army.

> So I say, "My splendor is gone and all that I had hoped from the Lord."
> I remember my affliction and my wandering, the bitterness and the gall. I well remember them, and my soul is downcast within me (Lament. 3:18-20).

In today's terms, Jeremiah was depressed. His mind was filled with the reality of the devastation (small *t* truth) and his feelings reflected that reality. But there was a greater reality beyond the present circumstances that would bring hope in the midst of pain. In both his thinking and in his self-talk, the truth (capital *T* truth) of who God is and what God can do provided feelings of hope and comfort. It helped begin to heal the wounds of the heart. This is what he wrote:

> Yet *this I call to mind* and therefore I have hope: Because of the Lord's great love we are not consumed, for his compassions never fail. They are new every morning; great is your faithfulness. *I say to myself*, "The Lord is my portion; therefore I will wait for him." The Lord is good to those whose hope is in him, in the one who seeks him; it is good to wait quietly for the salvation of the Lord (Lament. 3:21-24, italics mine).

Can you imagine what Jeremiah would have felt if he thought God did not exist? Or imagine how he would have felt if he thought of God as vindictive, without compassion, or concern for the well-being of mankind? But he saw God as loving, compassionate, and faithful and this brought hope and healing. Truth does make a difference! Truth does heal!

The other example is that of King Solomon. He wrote one of my favorite books in the Bible: Ecclesiastes. In it he confronts the reality of his own death, which sours his feelings about life. He had spent a life-time building his fame and fortune, only to have it collapse into meaninglessness in the light of his tomb stone. Over and over we see evidence of his self-talk by such phrases as, "I thought to myself" (1:16), "I thought in my heart" (2:1). Here is how he expressed it.

> Yet when I surveyed all that my hands had done and what I had toiled to achieve, everything was meaningless, a chasing after the wind; . . .
> The wise man has eyes in his head, while the fool walks in the darkness; but *I came to realize* that the same fate overtakes them both. Then *I thought in my heart*, "the fate of the fool will overtake me also. What then do I gain by being wise?" *I said in my heart*, "This too is meaningless."

. . . Like the fool, the wise man too must die! So I hated life, . . . *So my heart began to despair* over all my toilsome labor under the sun (2:11,14-15,16-17, 3:20, italics mine).

It's hard not to feel what Solomon is saying if you have ever been there. Whose heart wouldn't despair if life became meaningless in the light of one's own death? Hardship and the awareness of one's own mortality can make the heart become cynical. Despair, anger, and depression all reflect the pessimistic mind-set that has taken over one's thinking. There needs to be something we can call to mind that will touch the heart and restore hope and meaning to life.

I made a fascinating discovery in my Bible reading when I read the book of Ecclesiastes and then read the book of Philippians a few days later. I would encourage you to do the same. Note the stark contrast between the feelings and beliefs of King Solomon and those of the apostle Paul. Solomon lived nine hundred years before Christ. He did not know of him. Paul did, and this made a big difference when Paul was facing his own death. This is how he expressed it in a letter from a Roman jail to the people of Philippi.

Now I want you to know, brothers, that what has happened to me has really served to advance the gospel. As a result, it has become clear throughout the whole palace guard and to everyone else that I am in chains for Christ. . . . I eagerly expect and hope that I will in no way be ashamed, but will have sufficient courage so that now as always Christ will be exalted in my body, whether by life or by death. *For to me, to live is Christ and to die is gain.* If I am to go on living in the body, this will mean fruitful labor for me. *Yet what shall I choose? I do not know! I am torn between the two: I desire to depart and be with Christ,* which is better by far. . . . I consider everything a loss compared to the surpassing greatness of knowing Christ Jesus my Lord, . . . *All of us who are mature should take such a view of things.* (Philippians 1:12-13,20-23; 3:8-9,15, italics mine).

Can you sense how Paul's experience of knowing the person of Jesus Christ set him free from despair and pessimism? Opening our heart to a relationship with Jesus is not just a religious thing to do. It is a human thing to do. Knowing Him is knowing a person that can be with us in any situation, under any condition. This is why true Christianity is not a religion. It is a relationship with a person—the Christ of *Christian*ity.

Knowing and thinking about truth creates the feelings truth was intended to produce. When we meditate on biblical truth, it can move from just head knowledge to heartfelt knowledge. It can change from black and white into color.

Like a feather floating down from the sky and coming to rest on the ground, truth needs to float down from our mind until it rests in our heart and becomes **felt-truth**. It is then that we learn the importance of thinking about truth. It is then that we learn how truth can set us free.

Jesus gave us this promise when he said, "If you hold to my teaching, you are really my disciples. Then you will know the truth, and the truth will set you free" (John 8:31-32). Little *t* truth sets free; capital *T* truth sets absolutely free. When we use our ability to think on the truth, our feelings will respond as they were designed to do. Experiencing biblical truth is one of the most life-giving things we could ever hope to encounter.

In summary, God gave us a wonderful gift when He created us in His image to be rational beings. Our ability to think is one of our most important attributes in helping us live a successful and healthy life. God never wanted us to lose sight of our freedom to use our mind in dealing with life more effectively. As Christians, we can develop a deeper appreciation for this unique gift because we know it comes from God. We will become even more excited and thankful for this ability when we start using our mind in more life-giving ways.

Reclaim this gift as yours. Then give yourself permission to develop your thinking skills to become the person God designed you to be! Then you will discover what it feels like to be a healthy human being and a happy Christian.

Suggested Reading

1. Burns, David D. *Feeling Good: The New Mood Therapy*. Penguin Books, 1980.
2. Stoop, David. *Self-Talk: Key to Personal Growth*. Fleming H. Revell, 1982.
3. Esther 6:6; Psalm 1:2; 19:14; 48:9; Proverbs 2:10,11; Isaiah 55:8-9; Daniel 12:3; Matthew 16:23; Luke 24:45; 1 Corinthians 1:18-25; 2 Corinthians 4:4; 11:3; Ephesians 4:17-19; Hebrews 3:1.

COMMUNICATE

Nature does nothing in vain; and man alone among the animals has speech. . . . Voice indeed indicates the painful or pleasant, and hence is present in other animals. . . . But speech serves to reveal the advantageous and the harmful, and hence also the just and the unjust. For it is peculiar to man as compared to the other animals that he alone has a perception of good and bad and just and unjust. . . .

Aristotle, Politics [1]

Other classical *differentiae* of man besides that of being the only reasoning animal . . . [is] He has . . . been called "the laughing animal," and language is assuredly a capital distinction between man and brute. . . . *He has a deliberate intention to apply a sign to everything.* The linguistic impulse is with him generalized and systematic.

William James, *The Principles of Psychology* [2]

Secular anthropologists say that somehow or other, they do not know why, man is the verbalizer. . . . The Christian position says, "I can tell you why: God is a personal-infinite God." There has always been communication, before the creation of all else, in the Trinity. And God has made man in his own image, and part of making man in his own image is that man is the verbalizer.

Francis Schaeffer,
He Is There and He Is Not Silent [3]

CHAPTER *17*

The Miracle
of Human Language

PERMISSION

W hen I would put my young son to bed in the evening, often he would say to me, "Daddy, talk to me." In the past these words would have paralyzed me. For most of my life I had learned to keep my feelings and thoughts to myself. I had learned well the three rules of survival: don't talk, don't feel, don't trust. So when I did speak up, it was guarded, calculated and selective. I knew I was giving a false impression of who I was—what I felt, thought, or believed—but I couldn't make myself do it any differently. I was too scared of what might happen!

For years, many of us have known we needed to communicate better with others. We have felt guilty, sad, even angry at ourselves because we couldn't seem to "get the words out," but basically we haven't changed. Sometimes our relationships with our friends, our spouse, or our children were at a breaking point, yet we remained silent, afraid, and unable to speak openly and honestly. When we finally got mad enough we might speak up but it was mostly complaining, accusing, or blaming. Then we would retreat back into silence.

In contrast, others of us have chattered away like magpies but have said little about what was really going on inside. Some ideas and feelings were expressed but became lost in the verbiage. When we got mad, we had no problem giving people "a piece of our mind" but the verbal damage done left little to work with. We felt powerful but deep inside we felt bad.

Common experience teaches that if our relationships are to be healthy and meaningful, we need to communicate effectively. So why don't we? I believe there are two major reasons. First, sometime in the past (usually during our childhood or teen years) we learned how to "be quiet." *We gradually gave away our permission to be a verbal person.* In some cases we even came to believe we didn't have a right to speak. Second, many of us are not sure how to communicate without causing problems. We are doing the best we know how but we are afraid of hurting someone's feelings. We're afraid we'll get in trouble by making them mad. Fear keeps us silent.

Over time this creates the lack of a fundamental belief about ourselves that entitles us to be a verbal person. Either by what others have said, or because of bad experiences, or simply by default, we learned to be careful about what we said. We hid within ourselves and by doing so we hid our true self from others, sometimes even from ourselves. It may have been okay to say some things as long as they were nice, polite, clean, Christian, or met someone else's approval. But gradually we lost our natural childlike openness to be genuine, honest, real, and at times embarrassingly candid—but human. Here are a few examples of statements that may have influenced us to become verbally inhibited.

- "Why don't you be quiet! You don't know what you are talking about!"
- "Children are to be seen, not heard."
- "Don't say anything if you can't say something nice."
- "No, you can't talk! You don't have anything worth saying."
- "You shouldn't say that. That's awful!"
- "How can you say that! You're a Christian."
- "Don't you ever talk to anyone that way again."
- "You don't have the right to talk to me that way."
- "Go ahead, open your mouth and show us how dumb you are."
- "Don't you ever stop talking? You're driving me nuts!"

Statements like these are not the only reasons why we became less verbal as we grew older. We also did things that made us feel guilty or ashamed—like stealing, lying, or something sexual—and we went silent with fear: fear of punishment, fear of disapproval or rejection, fear of what others would think of us.

There were other times when we really did try to talk about something but we were ignored, brushed aside, or not taken seriously. We became discouraged and decided not to try anymore. We figured it wouldn't do any good anyway. And who can ever forget those times when we said something that really embarrassed us and took months, even years to get over?

Things I Wish I Had Never Said

Mary remembered one such incident. She and her family had just returned to live in the United States after spending her first fifteen years in Mexico. Entering her senior year of high school as a fifteen-year-old, she knew very little about the American culture: its music, customs, manners, or language. She spoke English but her native language with its rich color and meaning was Spanish.

In the first weeks of school she felt socially awkward and out-of-place, at times even overwhelmed with all the differences. She had never been exposed to some of the words and slang the kids used in school. One day she noticed the "F— word" that had been carved on her desk. Not knowing what it meant and wanting to learn about her "new culture," she (in total innocence) raised her hand in class and asked what it meant.

The words had barely left her lips when she was plunged into feelings of total humiliation and embarrassment by the laughter and the scene it created in the classroom. She said, "I became a mouse and it took me years to get over that one experience."

Verbal Language—The Distinctive Mark of Being Human

For whatever reasons, all of us have been affected by past experiences that have caused us to lose our appreciation for being a verbal person. But change, growth, and freedom begin the moment we accept verbal expression as a fundamental right of human beings because it is an innate part of our Being. Even the United States Bill of Rights affirms this privilege—the right to free speech.

The ability to speak is a unique characteristic of human life. Mortimer Adler has done a scholarly work on the uniqueness of man in his book *The Difference of Man and the Difference It Makes*. He saw human speech as the pivotal act that distinguishes human kind from all other creatures. He wrote:

> Let me repeat: among scientists who consider the matter, there is unanimous agreement that man and man alone uses verbal symbols and has a propositional language and syntactically structured speech. . . . Common experience also provides evidence to this fact, evidence so clear that common-sense opinion . . . has long held speech to be probably the most distinctive mark of man. . . . man is the only talking, the only naming, declaring or questioning, affirming or denying, the only arguing, agreeing or disagreeing, the only discursive, animal.[4]

If common experience bears witness to the uniqueness of human speech, then watching a child's language skills develop is one of the greatest wonders on earth. King David must have sensed this when he wrote:

> "O Lord, our Lord, how majestic is your name in all the earth! You have set your glory above the heavens. From the lips of children and infants you have ordained praise . . ." (Psalm 8:1-2).

Language development in a child points to the One who designed it and brings glory to His name, even by those who do not know of its origin. It's fascinating to see how week by week their ability to talk continually emerges, going far beyond the general cooing, cries, and squeals of infancy. As the linguistic part of the brain matures, children begin connecting specific words to certain objects and then verbalizing it. It seems like they can go to bed at night to awaken in the morning with new words somehow added to their growing vocabulary. Eventually, these words form simple sentences and a verbal person emerges.

Often I stood in awe of this unique human gift as I watched my child grow in his verbal ability. Few parents ever forget the first time "we thought" we heard our child say "Ma Ma" or "Da Da" and we became an identified person. Gradually they learn how to make themselves known by talking about their feelings, wants, and ideas. And who could ever forget the period when it seemed like every time they spoke it was a question, "Daddy, why this . . . ?" "Mommy, why that . . . ?" "Teacher, why does . . . ?"

At times I would think, *It doesn't matter how long they work with a chimpanzee or how many signs it can learn in sign language, it will NEVER be able to develop the ability to communicate the way humans do. It will never learn to speak, read, and write in symbolic language.* In his discussion on the uniqueness of man, the eminent Julian Huxley made this distinction clear.

> The first and most obviously unique characteristic of man is his capacity for conceptual thought; if you prefer objective terms, you will say his employment of true speech. . . . True speech involves the use of verbal signs for objects, not merely for feelings. Plenty of animals can express the fact that they are hungry; but none except man can ask for an egg or a banana.[5]

Speech—God's Gift by Design

When we accept the fundamental belief that we possess a distinctively human faculty such as the ability to verbalize, it once again prompts us to ask the question of how did humankind acquire this "obviously unique characteristic?"

As we have pointed out earlier, the choices as to the origin of speech are two: human speech was acquired by chance or by design. Aristotle said it was "nature" that endowed man with the gift of speech. Secular anthropologists and psychologists say that "somehow or other" man is a talking being. In his fascinating book *The Miracle of Language*, linguist Charlton Laird reported:

> In short we know nothing about how language started, and we have

not even the materials from which we might hope to find out. Logically, of course, there must have been a time when some primordial creature . . . opened his carnivorous jaws and said, "Bup," or "Ickey," and his bored wife . . . or his worst enemy in the next cave, or somebody, understood him, and language was born.[6]

If the ability to communicate is by chance, we can still accept that this ability is unique and needs to be developed and matured because it is a basic part of our Being. Everyone working in education, mental health and human relations knows that good communication is the key to growth, healing, and the development of better cooperation between people and nations. There is great value and meaning to improving our ability to communicate. It is good and right that we grow and improve in our communication skills.

When we believe that this ability is ours by Design the eternal and spiritual value for becoming more of a verbal person is affirmed as well. Speech is a gift from God, and you and I are entitled to be verbal. It is not a cosmic accident that human beings talk. It is because God specifically and on purpose made us this way. Language is another of God's unique gifts given to us as human beings made in His image. He did this so He could communicate with us and we with Him. We could also communicate with ourselves (self-talk) and with each other. Here's how Francis Schaeffer expressed it.

When God made man in his own image, he . . . created something that reflects his personality, his communication and his love. Man can be communicated to by God, because, unlike non-man, man has been made in the image of God. Man is a verbalizing being, and God can communicate to man in verbalizations. Man thinks in propositions, and God can communicate to man propositionally in verbalized form.[7]

Human beings are verbal beings because God used language to bear witness to His personal existence. Schaeffer goes so far to say that every time a person communicates with another "whether he knows it or not, even if he is the greatest blasphemer that ever lived or the atheist swearing at God . . . even when he says, 'There is no God'—he bears testimony to what God is."[8]

When people talk, they also bear witness to their own personhood as well. Even though human languages differ, all people share in common the ability to use verbal-symbolic language. In this way we can exchange ideas, share feelings and experiences, and work more cooperatively together for the betterment of life. To the degree this gift is exercised, we become healthier psychologically and spiritually as a Christian, as a human being, and as a society.

We Authenticate Our Personhood When We Communicate

With improved communication comes an improved sense of self-acceptance. Why? Because when we begin to communicate more effectively, we begin to live the way God designed us to live.

In the past we may have had a difficult time communicating honestly and accurately and we found our relationships with others "all mixed up." We became silent when we should have spoken. We yelled, screamed, and verbally attacked when we really needed to listen and ask questions to improve our understanding.

Confusion, defensiveness, misunderstanding, and overreacting have characterized our relationships. This directly contributes to our unhappiness and the unhappiness of others.

A client once told me that as a little girl she was always talking until one day someone yelled at her, "Don't you ever shut up?" She said, "The pain and embarrassment only deepened my resolve that when I grew up no one was ever going to tell me to shut up again!" For years she held true to her decision to the distress of husband and friends. Recently she made a new and healthier decision. Now, her words are much closer to representing the real person she is—they authenticate her real self, not her crazy-game self. She is also learning to be a better listener.

Things change for the better when we accept that God created us to be communicating human beings. Sydney Jourard spent years researching the subject of self-disclosure, and he presents some very helpful ideas in his book *The Transparent Self*. He has an interesting challenge to put before us.

> A choice that confronts every one at every moment is this: Shall we permit our fellows to know us as we now are, or shall we remain enigmas, wishing to be seen as persons we are not? This choice has always been available, but throughout history we have chosen to conceal our authentic being behind masks. . . . We camouflage our true being before others to protect ourselves. . . . Man, perhaps alone of all living forms, is capable of being one thing and seeming from his actions and talk to be something else. Not even animals and insects and fishes which Nature expertly camouflages can do this "seeming" at will; they do it by reflex.[9]

When we don't communicate, we feel disconnected, hidden, unknown, and unseen. But when we begin to represent ourselves more accurately through improved verbal and listening skills, we feel more like a real person. Our true self begins to emerge and we become more visible. We find we don't feel as alone, hidden, isolated, or disconnected because we have been our true selves with others. We have not mislead them by living what Dr. Jourard calls "a cosmetic life of pretense." We can trust ourselves when we know we have been honest with ourselves and *appropriately* transparent with others. If they like us and treat us respectfully, we can begin to trust them more because we know they are responding to the real person we are.

Self-Disclosure: A Key to a Healthier You

Improvement in our ability to communicate is the evidence of a growing and healthy personality. It is becoming the kind of person God created us to be. Reclaiming and restoring the gift of being a communicative person will have positive results. Dr. Jourard had an interesting way of putting it.

> When I say that self-disclosure is a means by which one achieves personality health, I mean it is not until I am my real self and I act my real self that my real self is in a position to grow. *One's self grows from the consequence of being.* People's selves stop growing when they repress them. This growth-arrest in the self is what helps to account for the surprising paradox of finding an infant inside the skin of someone who is playing the role of an adult (italics mine).[10]

Personality growth and health are intrinsically designed in our very being. This is why secular psychologists have been successful in helping people when they encourage growth in the important areas of our personality —feeling, choosing, thinking, and now communicating. But they fail to adequately explain the origin of the innate need to communicate and they fail to see why becoming a verbal person has both social and spiritual value.

Sadly, on the other side, there are Christians who would have us believe if we just obeyed God and forgot all this "stuff" about self, everything would be better. They have helped people come to some understanding of God and Christianity, but they do not have an adequate explanation for the growth process of the healthy personality.

Because human language finds its origin in God the Judeo-Christian view of life gives a big YES to our becoming the verbal persons we were created to be. We authenticate our worth and identity when we choose to accept and exercise our ability to be a communicative person. We also authenticate the worth and value of another person when we truly respect their need to be a verbal being. Faith, courage, and determination are necessary if we want to learn how to become effective communicators.

Self-Worth and Healthy Communication

A spiritual respect for the worth of a person is the foundation upon which all healthy communication is built. Two thousand years ago the apostle James made it quite clear why we need to verbally treat each other with respect and dignity. The reason for this is grounded in our being made in God's likeness. The relationship between communication and respect for one another is clearly demonstrated in his letter.

> All kinds of animals, birds, reptiles and creatures of the sea are being tamed and have been tamed by man, but no man can tame the tongue. It is a restless evil, full of deadly poison. With the tongue we praise our Lord and Father, and with it we curse men, *who have been made in God's likeness.* Out of the same mouth come praise and cursing. My brothers, this should not be (James 3:7-10, italics mine).

It is normal and inevitable to experience differences or conflicts in our relationships with others. When this happens our mouth can become our greatest liability or our greatest asset. If we get defensive and try to protect our shaky self-image, or we let our feelings trigger us into reacting, we can play all kinds of crazy games–belittling, accusing, withdrawing, gossiping, criticizing, controlling and a legion of others. In their book, *Do I Have to Give Up Me to Be Loved By You?* Dr. and Dr. Paul describe it this way:

> Many people grew up in homes where conflict meant fights that left each person wounded or out for revenge. Witnessing the anger, hurtful battles or the coldness, tension, and distance created by such arguments after led to the conclusion that conflicts are too painful and must be avoided.[11]

The Paul's then do a fine job of explaining how people take one of two pathways to handle conflicts in their relationships—the path of the intent to protect or the path of the intent to learn. The diagram on the next page illustrates the process the Pauls used to help people change. Which path one takes makes a world of difference on the health and quality of that relationship. Like James, I believe all respectful communication finds its spiritual, psychological, and social reference point in our being made in God's likeness.

When we extend to each other the rights and privileges of being a verbal person, we promote life and health to both our humanity and our Christianity. To the degree we are not able to communicate with each other (or our communication is abusive and disrespectful), we promote distance, distrust, and unhealthy consequences in our relationships with God and others. Friendships, marriages, families, and church life are all affected when people practice poor communication habits.

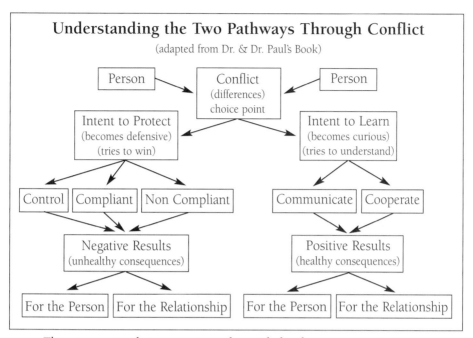

Understanding the Two Pathways Through Conflict
(adapted from Dr. & Dr. Paul's Book)

The perspective that we are innately entitled to be a communicative person as Imagebearers of God needs to touch each of us deep in our hearts. We need to give ourselves permission to be the communicative being God designed us to be. This can free us to be more willing to learn how to talk, to listen, and to understand. All the effort, risks, and struggles we go through to become better communicators will prove worthwhile. We can begin to step out from behind the memories of our past and become the verbal person we want to be and need to be.

We will also begin to extend to others the same privileges and permissions as fellow Imagebearers of God. We will be more likely to listen to them, to want to understand and think things through with them in solving conflicts and problems. We will want to know them in a more truthful way rather than remaining a mystery to each other.

Becoming a better communicator is exciting and life-giving. Let's look at some of the ways we can learn how to improve our ability to be a communicative person.

Suggested Reading

1. Jourard, Sidney. *The Transparent Self*. D. Van Nostrand Company, 1971.
2. Powell, John. *Why Am I Afraid to Tell You Who I Am?*. Argus Communications, 1969.
3. Exodus 4:10-11a; 33:11; Job 7:11; 9:33-35; Psalm 15:1-2; 34:12-14; 45:1; 64:3; 94:9a; Proverbs 18:7,21a; 26:24; Matthew 12:34b; Acts 18:9; James 1:19.

Man is the being to whom God speaks, with whom he thus enters into a personal relationship. After having created the whole inorganic world, and all the plants and animals —a world blindly and impersonally subject to him— God created man in his image; that is to say, a personal being, a partner in dialogue, a being to whom he might speak and who could answer, to whom he gave liberty, and whose liberty, refusals and silences he respects, but whose replies he also awaits.

Paul Tournier, *The Meaning of Persons* [1]

Man . . . is a creature endowed with the power of speech. . . . And he is for that reason speech-related to all other human beings. . . . His relationship to his Maker is likewise speech-related, so that the very idea of personal relationship between the two is dependent upon communication between them.

Leonard Verduim, *Somewhat Less Than God* [2]

Moses said to the Lord, "O Lord, I have never been eloquent, neither in the past nor since you have spoken to your servant. I am slow of speech and tongue." The Lord said to him, "Who gave man his mouth? . . . Is it not I, the Lord? Now go; I will help you speak and will teach you what to say. . . ."

Exodus 4:10-12

CHAPTER 18

The Joy in Becoming a Verbal Artist

HOW TO

Do any of these statements sound familiar? Maybe you have even said them yourself. I know I have.

"Just a minute. You haven't let me finish my sentence yet!"

"Why won't you shut up and listen to me?"

"That's not what I said! Don't put words in my mouth."

"Why won't you talk to me?"

"You never listen to what I have to say, so stop interrupting me!"

"We haven't talked for so long I feel like we don't know each other any more."

"It doesn't do any good to try to talk to you because you never listen anyway; just forget it!"

Statements like these often express the frustration we feel when we are not able to communicate effectively. Something is not working right and it makes us feel angry, helpless, and confused.

"What can I do differently that I haven't already tried?" we wonder. We know that good communication is vital if our relationships are to be alive, intimate, and lasting. Without it we become lonely, isolated, and disconnected from others and from God.

People who communicate well do three things: (1) they exchange information, (2) they clarify anything that is confusing or not understood, and (3) they work toward greater cooperation in making life healthier and happier for everyone concerned. This is accomplished best when the person TALKING speaks openly, honestly, and clearly; and when the person LISTENING hears things accurately and correctly.[3] If there is a breakdown on either side, the quality of communication suffers. Using the following diagram, let's look at the role of the Speaker first to learn how to improve our communication skills.

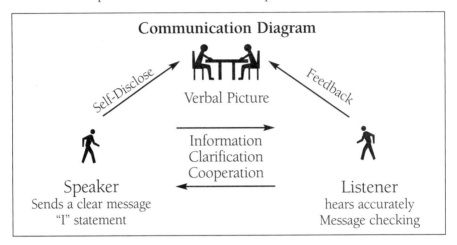

Communication Diagram

Self-Disclose   Verbal Picture   Feedback

Information
Clarification
Cooperation

Speaker
Sends a clear message
"I" statement

Listener
hears accurately
Message checking

Sending Clear Verbal Messages

Verbal communication or talking takes place when we use words to inform others about our feelings, thoughts, beliefs, questions, expectations, wants, needs, desires, or experiences. Simply put, it's the way we give information to someone. We can use other words or phrases in place of "talking" to represent what it means to be a verbal person: expressing ourselves, being self-disclosing, being self-revealing, being open, or being transparent. It can also mean sharing, filling someone in, confessing, or bringing someone up-to-date.

To be heard accurately, information needs to be sent in a clear and understandable way. If the person speaking sends vague or unclear messages, the person listening is going to have a hard time understanding what is being said. Trying to figure out what someone is saying can be frustrating and time consuming. So why do we send unclear messages? Why do we say things "in a round-about way?" Look at the following list and see if you can identify any that describe you.

- We don't want to make someone upset.
- We want to avoid a conflict or a fight.
- We don't want to hurt someone's feelings.
- We want to test people first to see how they react.
- We are afraid of rejection, criticism, or punishment.
- We don't want to be held responsible for what we say.
- We are unsure of what we feel, think, want, or believe.
- We don't have the time or energy to do it better.

- We are mad so we refuse to talk sense.
- We feel too insecure to be specific.
- We don't trust the other person.
- We are not assertive enough to say what we want to say.
- We say what we think the other person wants to hear.
- We just don't care anymore so we don't try.
- We lack the necessary skills to speak more clearly.

If we can identify the reasons why we don't speak clearly, we can correct it and become a better speaker. Learning the following skills can also help us become more confident in talking to others.

Skill 1—We need to learn to remind ourselves that being made in God's image entitles us to be a verbal person. All of us become verbally shy when we begin to speak from the heart. We need to tell ourselves that it's okay to talk because it's an innate part of our nature. It is something God gave us. Self-coaching is reminding ourselves that it's all right and necessary for us to speak clearly about our ideas, feelings, and needs. That's being human. That's being Christian. We don't have to be obnoxious, loud, or overbearing; we can be "kind and strong," firmly committed to being what God designed us to be—a verbalizing Being.

Skill 2—We need to learn to be clear with ourselves about ourselves. We are going to have difficulty speaking clearly to others if we are out of focus with ourselves. For example, have you ever said, "I don't know what I think; so stop bugging me!" or "I know what I want to say, but I just can't seem to find the words to say it"? This happens when things are not clear in our own mind. Clear thinking and labeling our feelings accurately are important antecedents to being able to express ourselves openly and clearly. We need to practice identifying what we feel, think, want, need, or believe and then speak about it clearly to others.

Skill 3—We need to learn to use "I" statements when talking to others, especially when we are dealing with an emotionally sensitive subject. As children, many of us grew up under the tyranny of "you" messages. We heard statements like, "What are you kids doing in there?" or "You're so stupid! You never do what your told!" or "You're so selfish! You don't care about anybody but yourself." These "you" messages came across as blaming, condemning, or controlling statements. They are shaming statements and shaped our self-image.

The endless flow of "you messages" over time creates in us an automatic defense reaction. We become defensive even before we think. Hearing someone say, "You always, . . ." or "You never, . . ." creates feelings of fear or guilt and we'll automatically react by either taking the blame or we'll counterattack with our own "you messages." Triggering people's automatic reaction system decreases the effectiveness of good, clear message sending.

The best ways to avoid this unnecessary "clutter" is to communicate with "I" statements. We do this by speaking in first person singular "I" and "my": "I feel, . . ." "I need to know, . . ." "I don't understand, . . ." "My position on that is. . . ." Learning to say what we want to say using "I" statements can bring about amazing results.

I first learned this skill by accident during that painful time in my life in 1967. I wanted to become more open and transparent as a person but I wanted to do it in a way that would not sound condemning or preachy. I wanted to talk in a way that would help others feel less defensive about what I said and yet allowed me to be open and clear in my communication. When I thought of saying things in "I" form, it was like being let out of a verbal box. I no longer had to remain hidden inside myself.

At first, it was hard to use "I" statements because my church had taught me to think of the word "I" as being bad. In a nutshell the lesson was: "It's bad to focus on yourself. Look at the word 'sIn' and 'prIde'. The letter 'I' is in both. The biggest problem in the world today is an 'I' problem." Being a new Christian, this made me feel that thinking of myself and saying "I" was sinful or bad.

But as I continued practicing my new found skill, I was amazed to see the positive effect it had in cleaning up one of my communication difficulties. Later, while reading the Gospels, I noticed that Jesus used "I" statements when he wanted to be clear: "I thirst," "I am the Light of the World," or "I am the Good Shepherd." This encouraged me to continue my efforts at improving my ability to speak more clearly and honestly.

To learn this skill, practice saying *out loud* sentences about how you feel, what you think, or what you want, leaving out every "you" or "your" in the sentence. Try this in both imagined and real conversations. For example, if you go to a bakery instead of saying, "Do you have any fresh chocolate doughnuts today?" say instead, "I would like to buy a dozen chocolate doughnuts. Are there any available?" Instead of saying to your kids—who have just messed up the front room—"Will you kids pick up your toys! You've made a big mess, so clean it up!" try saying, "I want the toys picked up in the next couple of minutes because I want the front room to look nice again."

This will feel awkward at first but the positive results will encourage you to continue your efforts. Practice it long enough and it becomes a natural part of your life. Obviously, you don't have to use it every time you talk, but it is a great tool to have available to send a clearer message.

Skill 4—We need to learn to take the hidden expectations out of our "I" messages. In healthy communication, we take hidden expectation or demand out of our nonverbal and verbal messages when we state clearly what we want or need or expect. There will be times when we just want to let people know how we feel about something without wanting anything changed; but frequently we express our feelings as a way to get someone to DO something we want. For example, "I am tired of staying home every weekend," really means, "I am tired of staying home every weekend, and it's YOUR responsibility to come up with something for us to do!"

A better way to make the expectation clear would be, "I am tired of staying home every weekend and I would like for us to sit down this evening for a few minutes and talk about some things we can do on weekends. Will you do that with me?" The feelings are expressed, the wants and desires are made clear, the hidden expectations are out in the open, and cooperation is encouraged.

Skill 5—We need to learn to picture ourselves as verbal artists. All of us have stood before a painting and admired or questioned the work of the artist. With the use of paint, canvas, and brush the artists paint their impressions for all to see. In a sense, we are verbal artists using words to paint pictures for others to see. Think of colors as feelings; thoughts and expectations as form and patterns; and behaviors as the actions of life.

To help others know and understand us, we need to paint verbal pictures about what is known to us but hidden from them. We do this by being expressive, colorful, and clear in the verbal pictures we paint. Gary Smalley and John Trent have done a great job describing this skill in their book, *The Language of Love.*[4] They call it painting "emotional word pictures," and just as in painting, practicing one's verbal artistry makes one a better speaker.

Skill 6—We need to learn to give people the necessary room to experience our verbal portrait. Many of us, trying to get our message across, sometimes dump our words on people. It's like throwing the paint of our feelings and thoughts *at* them rather then presenting a picture *before* them. When we allow them the space necessary to experience our picture, they can decide how they want to respond. It is the responsibility of the speaker to paint a clear picture and then give the listener the room to receive and process the message their way.

If they don't understand and that becomes known, we can give them additional information or clarify things that might bring understanding and cooperation. But there are going to be times when no matter how hard we try, no matter what approach we take, no matter how much time we put into it, someone is still not going to understand. I remember one woman in counseling, bursting with frustration and anger toward her husband, yelling, "I just don't understand why he doesn't understand me!" It is not our job to *make* people understand us. Our job as the speaker is to make the message as clear as we can until we are satisfied that we have done so and then we need to let go. We need to give time and God's Spirit a chance to help bring understanding.

Skill 7—We need to learn that our choices can communicate when words may fail. There is some comfort and satisfaction in knowing we have done our reasonable best to make ourselves clear even if understanding or cooperation was not accomplished. At that point we may have to go ahead and make some choices, hoping that the understanding will come later. Jesus demonstrated this with His disciples when He first began telling them about His coming crucifixion. He informed them that He was going to Jerusalem; He was going to suffer and be mistreated by others; He was going to die and after three days He was going to be resurrected to life (Mark 8:31-33). Jesus "spoke plainly about this" but Peter didn't understand and began to rebuke Jesus saying, "This shall never happen to you" (Matthew 16:22). The disciples didn't understand Jesus even though he spoke about it several times, but Jesus continued to move toward Jerusalem. In time, his choices and God's Spirit opened His disciples' understanding.

Skill 8—We need to learn how to speak in a salt and pepper tone of voice. It is not uncommon for most of us to raise our voices if we feel angry, frustrated, hurt, or scared. We all give excuses and justifications for why we yell (or whine) but the truth is, yelling is usually counter productive. It makes others feel scared or resentful. Some are intimidated into conformity, while others silently or vocally become more stubborn and resistant.

Yelling can make us feel powerful, but most yellers don't like being that way. Some have said, "I don't like being a screaming maniac, but what else can I do? They just won't listen to me or do what I tell 'em if I don't yell." Sometimes yelling can inspire people or help get a point across, but if emotions are running high or tempers are hot, we need to use a skill that helps us speak with more confidence and control. King Solomon expressed it this way, "A gentle answer turns away wrath, but a harsh word stirs up anger" (Proverbs 15:1).

Learning how to talk to a person in a salt and pepper tone of voice means using a tone of voice similar to the one when asking for the salt and pepper at meal time, but said with more meaning and importance. We don't scream, "Pass the salt and pepper please!" Nor do we whine for it. We ask for it in a straight forward, matter-of-fact way. It also helps to lower our voice into our chest when we talk rather than speaking from our throat. This makes the sound of our voice have more depth and strength. Learning these skills helps us be more successful in communicating our message.

Skill 9—We need to learn how to separate our need to communicate clearly from our hope for the desired results. Just because we tell someone something clearly and meaningfully does not guarantee they will cooperate with us. This means we are bound to experience feelings of sorrow and disappointment at times. The trick is to do this without becoming indifferent or resentful.

Healthy sorrow and disappointment come as a result of accepting that (1) things can't always be the way we want it to be, (2) we can't always have what we want, (3) we won't always have someone's cooperation even if it is reasonable and right, and (4) someone won't always live the way we think they should, no matter how right we are in what we have told them.

If we don't separate speaking clearly from desired results, we will either withdraw, say nothing and feel like a martyr (be passive) or we will become aggressive and try to force our views or ways on others. Accepting sorrow and disappointment as a normal part of life is more easily accomplished if: (1) our self-worth is not in question, (2) we can accept the realities of life in a realistic and healthy way, and (3) we feel free to choose other life-giving options in place of the one we desired. Jesus was called the "Man of Sorrows" and I am sure some of the sorrow came from accepting the fact that people still rejected Him and His message even though He knew what He said was good, right, and true.

He Who Has Ears to Hear, Let Him Hear

Up to this point we have been looking at what characterizes being a good message sender (Speaker). Now we need to turn our attention to what makes a good Receiver (a good Listener). Listening is the other half of the communication connection. Listening is also one of the most effective ways of telling someone that they are valued and important. It shows we are interested in them and are willing to take the time to hear them.[5]

It is a fact of life that no matter how clear someone has been in their presentation, if we don't hear them accurately, miscommunication takes place. This can cause misunderstanding or conflict to occur, and our freedom to cooperate becomes restricted. Here are some of the reasons we may be poor Listeners:

- We get mad or are already mad at the person.
- We are distracted or preoccupied.
- We are too set in our own opinions.
- We are afraid we will be influenced in some negative way.

- We are too busy and don't have time to listen.
- We have too many personal problems.
- We hear only what we want to hear.
- We are bored with what is being said.
- We listen with a judgmental ear.
- We don't understand the language spoken.
- We jump to conclusions too fast.
- We don't like the person talking to us.
- We feel too insecure to listen to the person.
- We filter what is said through our own prejudices.
- We don't trust the person talking to us.
- We didn't learn the basic skills of good listening.

My son described his not listening as "shutting my ears, not with my fingers but with my mind." To be a good listener we need to be willing to open our ears and learn the skills necessary to listen more effectively. Knowing we have learned poor listening habits can be liberating because it means we can unlearn them and develop new ones—if we choose to do so. It takes time to develop better listening habits, but the benefits are worth it. Here are some skills we can learn to become better listeners.

Skill 1—We need to learn to remind ourselves (self-talk) that the person speaking is a person made in God's image and therefore has a right to speak and to be heard. A good listener is someone who makes the other person feel like they are entitled to talk. There is something freeing and life-giving when we affirm the person's right to speak by being open and willing to listen. Voltaire best captures this thought when he said, "I may disagree with what you say, but I will defend to the death your right to say it." A good listener takes this position because it affirms the importance of dialogue.

Skill 2—We need to learn how to quiet down our inner world. For many of us our inner world is so noisy we can't hear what people are saying. Our own inner pain, self-belittlement, pent up frustration or constant negative self-talk makes it hard to accurately listen to people. We are screaming on the inside while appearing to be listening on the outside.

There have been times when my clients have come to a session bubbling over with a new idea they learned somewhere. They didn't realize that a few weeks earlier I had discussed the same thing with them—but they didn't "hear it." With the passing of time, their inner world quieted down enough to be able to hear what was being said. We become better listeners when we have learned to listen to and manage our own feelings.

Skill 3—We need to learn to listen with our feelings. In learning to be a good listener there are certain feelings we need to learn to trust, such as feeling confused, feeling unsure about what was said, or feeling that something is not making sense. On the positive side, we can learn to trust the feeling that something has been accomplished, resolved, or cleared up.

Learning how to monitor these feelings helps us know whether we have received the message accurately. If we don't pay attention to these feelings, we'll probably accept whatever is said without being sure we are on the same wave length. Awareness of these feelings improves our ability to listen.

Skill 4—We need to learn the art of message-checking. In learning to trust our feelings, there will be times when we sense we don't understand or we'll feel the need to make sure we heard them correctly. Misunderstanding someone and yet responding as if we understood, creates a lot of unnecessary clutter in our relationship. The TV program "Three's Company" was famous for creating scenes where people misunderstood each other. They provided us with hours of laughter and entertainment—but in real life it's not so funny and can lead to pain and unhappiness.

We use many words to describe the process of making sure we hear someone accurately. It has been called paraphrasing, active listening, reality checking, giving feedback, reflective listening, and message-checking. All of them have us repeat back (in some fashion) what a person has said to make sure we have heard them accurately. By saying, "Is this what you mean, . . ." or "See if I have heard you correctly, . . ." and then summarizing their message, we can assure them, as well as ourselves, that we have heard them accurately. Any need for more information or clarification can be handled long before additional problems occur.

Skill 5—We need to learn the "bite your tongue" technique. Usually when something has been said that creates in us a strong surge of feelings or ideas we feel a need to interrupt. We may want to defend ourselves or argue over some point, so we're tempted to not let others finish what they want to say. At that moment, if we placed the tip of our tongue between our front teeth and bite down hard enough to prevent it from slipping, we would be amazed at how our listening ability improves. Biting the tip of our tongue (which we can do unknown to them) allows us the time to hear them out; then we can respond as a good listener.

Skill 6—We need to learn to listen with the intent to look for solutions. Obviously, there are going to be times when we have a conflict or disagreement with someone. I remember when I used to think that a perfect marriage or a perfect friendship was one that did not experience any conflicts or differences. When we learn to substitute the word "healthy" for "perfect," we can accept that differences and conflicts will always happen but we can use our skills and abilities to work things out. We can work for solutions that produce feelings of resolve, relief, and harmony. This builds a healthy relationship rather than a perfect one.

Listening with the intent to understand and to work toward resolution is life-producing. It is saying, "I am going to listen as carefully as I can until I feel I've understood you so that we can work together for our mutual happiness." Both speaking clearly and listening accurately are fundamental to developing good problem-solving skills.

Skill 7—We need to learn how to respect the other person's speaking space. Back in the 1950s the Hula-Hoop was the rage among young people and most everyone took their turn. A single individual was in charge of making the hoop work and was given the necessary room to show their skill. The same principle is true for being a good listener.

To do this we picture the other person standing inside a space about the size of a Hula-Hoop. Inside that area they are an Imagebearer with all the rights and privileges that come with that position, including the freedom of speech. By honoring a person's speaking space and letting them have a voice in the affairs of life, we become better listeners. We can use this same picture to honor all our imagebearing abilities—feeling, choosing, creating—and it can help us be better speakers and listeners when used as a communication skill.

Skill 8—We need to learn to be curious about people. Have you ever noticed how curious people tend to listen better? Watch any child. When they are curious or interested they listen, ask questions, and listen some more. Curious people learn.

Sometimes familiarity, stubbornness, or defensiveness can stifle our curiosity and rob us of important information. If we are to be good listeners, we need to reawaken our sense of curiosity. We need to hold our reactions at bay and ask more questions to gain a clearer understanding of where a person is coming from. A better quality relationship results from being interested and curious about the person we are listening to.

Being Transparent with God: The Art of Therapeutic Prayer

One area where healthy communication is immensely important is in our relationship with God. He is continually inviting us to join Him in a dialogue because He values an open, trusting, relationship with us as people made in His image. God continually speaks to us through many avenues: nature, other people, the Bible, and especially through Jesus Christ and the Holy Spirit. God wants us to be open to listening to Him.

He also wants us to be open to talking to Him. Sometimes our hearts have become so "closed down" and tight we can't even let out the feelings and emotions that make us feel so dead inside. Praying from the heart loosens up and softens our heart and allows us to come back to life. Our heart may be full of tears, so we need to give ourselves permission to cry the tears out. As water softens hard soil, tears soften a hard heart. Tears from the heart are healing. David knew this and wrote about it in one of his psalms.

> Trust in him [God] at all times, O people;
> pour out your heart to him
> for God is our refuge (Psalm 62:8).

Pouring out our heart to God is what I call therapeutic prayer. It is being honest with ourselves and with God in open conversation about anything and everything—no longer hiding our feelings, desires, fears, past experiences, hurts, doubts, questions, or wrongs from ourselves or from God. It is best to pray out loud so we can hear our own words and validate that what we are saying to God is from the heart. This helps us be more specific and honest in our conversation with God. Heart-felt prayer feels authentic, genuine, and solid. Our heart knows when we have spoken the truth.

This kind of prayer demonstrates a new level of our faith and trust in God that He will not violate our integrity as a person nor will He punish us for our honesty. We sometimes forget that He already knows everything about us anyway. If He wanted to "get us," He could have done it a long time ago. So our openness with God in prayer is for our sake and for the sake of our relationship with Him.

This brings a new freedom in our relationship with God. It allows us the freedom to decide how we want to deal with life, because we have laid our heart open before Him. God is also given the freedom to work in our lives because we have been open and personal in asking for His help. Prayer gives God the moral right to enter into our experience. Since God has given us freedom of will, it is when we pray that He is morally free to work out His will in our experience. This kind of prayer rests on the belief that *God wants the best for us and that He will work on our behalf to make life good*. Here are a few examples of people in the Bible who poured out their hearts to God to ask for help in their personal circumstances.

Job	My face is red with weeping, deep shadows ring my eyes; . . . My intercessor is my friend as my eyes pour out tears to God (Job 16:16,20).
Hannah	. . . I am a woman who is deeply troubled. I have not been drinking wine or beer; I was pouring out my soul to the Lord . . . I have been praying here out of my great anguish and grief (I Samuel 1:15-16).
Jeremiah	My eyes fail from weeping, I am in torment within, my heart is poured out on the ground because my people are destroyed

. . . Arise, cry out in the night . . . pour out your heart like water in the presence of the Lord (Lamentations 2:11,19).

David   O Lord, hear my prayer, listen to my cry for mercy; in your faithfulness and righteousness come to my relief. . . . My spirit grows faint within me; my heart within me is dismayed . . . Let the morning bring me word of your unfailing love, for I have put my trust in you. Show me the way I should go, for to you I lift up my soul . . . Teach me to do your will, for you are my God; may your good Spirit lead me on level ground (Psalm 143:1,4,8,10).

Communicating with people is often time limited, but God is always available (24-7-365). This means we can talk with God anytime, anywhere, under any circumstances about anything—it is being transparent with God. I know from experience that this can result in great inner healing as well as healing in our personal relationship with God and with others. When our heart is liberated, our tongue is freed.

In summary, it is freeing to know that we were designed to be communicative beings, and that Jesus Christ redeemed us so that we could live as we were designed to live. Not only will we feel better as a person but we can also build healthier and happier relationship with God and others. As human beings, God has given us all the necessary attributes to speak and to listen—but He has put us in charge of developing these skills. We will have to overcome some fears and some bad habits, but it can be done if we choose to do it. Developing both the attitudes and the communication skills to be all that God designed us to be is both psychologically and spiritually healthy.

Suggested Reading

1. Paul, Jordan and Margaret Paul. *Do I Have To Give Up Me To Be Loved By You.* CompCare, 1983.
2. Smalley, Gary and John Trent. *The Language of Love.* Focus on the Family, 1988.
3. 1 Samuel 1:15; Job 32:18-20; 33:3; Psalm 142:2-3a; Proverbs 10:19; 11:12; 12:15; 15:1-4, 31; 18:13; 31:8-9; Mark 1:35; John 16:29; 2 Corinthians 6:7a.

BECOME
SELF-AWARE

5

4

3

· HUMAN BEING ·
· IMAGEBEARER ·
· PERSON ·

6

2

7

1

8

We found resemblance to God, first of all, in the fact that man, like his Maker, is a *personal, self-conscious* being. In this one fact he stands apart from, and above, all orders of the inferior creation. . . . He can turn his mind back in reflection on himself; can apprehend himself; can speak of himself as "I." This consciousness of self is an attribute of personality which constitutes a difference . . . between the human and the merely animal.

James Orr, *God's Image in Man* [1]

~~~

We are all endowed with freedom of choice: to remain static and do nothing with our lives; or to make something . . . of ourselves. . . . We must rise to that challenge! We can do it, because we have in our power a priceless tool—the ability to understand ourselves.

David Abrahamsen,
The Road to Emotional Maturity [2]

~~~

Self-awareness, reason, and imagination have disrupted the 'harmony' which characterizes animal existence. Their emergence has made man into an anomaly, into the freak of the universe. He is part of nature, subject to her physical laws and unable to change them, yet he transcends the rest of nature. He is set apart while being a part. . . . Man is the only animal for whom his own existence is a problem which he has to solve and from which he cannot escape.

Eric Fromm, *Psychoanalysis and Religion* [3]

CHAPTER *19*

———⟶⟵———

Humankind:
The Self-Conscious Species

PERMISSION

"*K*now thyself" was Socrates' favorite advice to the young students of ancient Athens. He could say this because human beings are unique as self-conscious beings. Deep in our design we are endowed with the distinct ability to be aware of ourselves. We are conscious of our own existence and of our daily experiences in life. We are also aware that we talk to ourselves about our life.

The great historian Arnold Toynbee spoke at a Japanese university on the subject of surviving our modern times. During his lecture he made a most important statement—that self-awareness is a "specifically human" faculty. In his book *Surviving the Future*, he stated:

> I have said that we should live in order to love, and I do think that love should be the first call on every human being. . . . Man seems to be unique among living creatures on this planet in having consciousness and reason, and therefore having the power of making deliberate choices, and we need to use these specifically human faculties in order to direct our love right.[4]

Toynbee is not alone in seeing the uniqueness of our ability to be self-aware. In his book *The Psychology of Self-Esteem*, Nathaniel Branden affirmed that this characteristic of our humanness makes us separate and distinct from animals. It confers on us a "unique stature." He stated:

> One of the most important consequences of man's possession of a conceptual faculty is his power of self-awareness. No other animal is capable of monitoring and reflecting on its own mental operations,

of critically evaluating its own mental activities, of deciding that a given process of mental activity is irrational or illogical . . . and of altering its subsequent mental operations accordingly. . . . No other animal is aware of its own mortality. . . . No other animal has the ability—and the responsibility—to weigh its actions in terms of the long-range consequences for its own life . . . [or] to think and plan in terms of a life span. . . . No other animal faces such questions as: Who am I? How should I seek to live? By what principles should I be guided in my actions? What goals ought I to pursue? What is to be the meaning of my life? What should I seek to make of my own person?[5]

These are not the only areas in which we experience the touch of self-awareness. We also sense it when we ask such questions as: What are my feelings? What do I want? What do I need? What are my impressions? What is my experience? What do I think? What is my opinion? What does my intuition tell me? How do I understand this situation?

Self-Awareness Is Not Self-Centeredness

Questions like these can only originate from creatures that possess the ability to reflect inwardly, are conscious they are doing so, and then can connect to the right answers as they become aware of them. This ability to reflect on one's self is what we call "self-awareness" or "self-consciousness." William James expressed it this way:

Another of the great capacities in which man has been said to differ fundamentally from the animal is that of possessing self-consciousness or reflective knowledge of himself as a thinker.[6]

Self-awareness is a unique human faculty and it brings great depth and richness to our life. It is an ability that gives us innate worth and dignity by design. But the misuse of this ability can also lead us to build a false sense of self-esteem. Here is how it happens.

Self-Awareness and the Formation of Self-Esteem

Self-awareness has tremendous implications for understanding our need for self-esteem. Dr. Karen Horney has written a fascinating book about how we develop an idealized image of ourselves as a compensation for becoming alienated from our true self. In her book *Neurosis and Human Growth*, she wrote:

The individual alienated from himself needs . . . something that will give him a hold, a feeling of identity. This could make him meaningful to himself and, despite all the weakness in his structure, give him a feeling of power and significance. . . . Each person builds up his personal idealized image from the materials of his own special experience, his earlier fantasies, his particular needs, and also his given faculties. . . . The idealized image becomes an idealized self. And this idealized self becomes more real to him than his real self. . . . The change is in the core of his being, in his feeling about himself.[7]

Dr. Horney described this drive to make the idealized self become reality as "the search for glory." I would call it "the search for worth." Robert McGee calls it "the Search for Significance".[8] In any case, it becomes a search that can imprison the soul. Our real self, our true self, is the "alive, unique, personal center of ourselves; the only part that can, and wants to grow."[9] But it gets pushed aside so that our time, energy and attention are invested in building and maintaining our idealized self, our false self. I believe this is what the Bible is referring to when it condemns pride. It is a false pride because it is a pride built on internalized fantasy rather than internal truth. It is pride in a fake self.

Most of us may not be aware of when and how we began to build our idealized self-image. But in time we will feel the hollowness in it. We will feel the clutter, contradictions, and pain it creates because it has been built primarily on external measures of worth. Why will we sense this? Because we are self-aware beings and we talk to ourselves about our worth. This is how Dr. Horney describes it.

With all his strenuous efforts towards perfection and with all his belief in perfection attained, the neurotic does not gain what he most desperately needs: self-confidence and self-respect. Even though godlike in his imagination, he still lacks the earthly self-confidence of a simple shepherd. The great positions to which he may rise, the fame he may acquire, will render him arrogant but will not bring him inner security. He still feels at bottom unwanted, is easily hurt, and needs incessant confirmation of his value.[10]

Self-awareness makes self-esteem and the meaning of life problems only humans experience. Animals are not aware of such issues. They do not talk to themselves about their worth. Human beings do. If a doctor could perform a "self-awareness-anectomy," we would be free from such concerns. But we humans do the next best thing—we shut it down the best we can.

Self-Awareness Gives Us Innate Worth

But there is a better way. It is learning how to value and appreciate our ability to be self-aware as part of our original design. It is one of the unique qualities of our Being that gives us innate significance and worth. Then we are free to grow and develop our abilities in line with our true and real self.

Self-awareness points to the value and meaning of faith in a personal God who is the primary source for believing we are valued. Arnold Toynbee points us in the right direction when he spoke about human consciousness and the meaning of life. This is how he expressed it:

> When a human being wakes to consciousness as a child, he finds that he has been planted in a universe which is a mystery to him, and that he has been placed in this universe without ever being consulted, or even having been asked for his permission. In the immediate sense, he was planted in the universe by his parents, but who planted his parents and their predecessors there? *This is a mystery which goes back to the nature of the reality behind the universe.* Why are we here? What are we here for? . . . He soon learns that, besides having been born perforce, he is going to have to die perforce sooner or later. Of course, non-human living creatures face the same situation, but they are not aware of it as we are. Our human awareness of it is disturbing; and this disturbance stimulates our curiosity. . . . Religion is an attempt to discover how to reconcile ourselves to the formidable facts of life and death (italics mine).[11]

As human beings self-awareness creates in us a need to believe in some view of life that gives meaning to our existence. We need to find a conceptual frame of reference from which to view our existence so we can know if life is good or bad, a blessing or a curse. A healthy life in all its facets is dependent upon a person working well with their sense of self-awareness.

As we have noted about other unique human abilities, our possession of this unique faculty does raise the question of its origin. How did we acquire this "specifically human" faculty? Was it by chance or by design? Are we "the freak of the universe as Eric Fromm stated or are we fearfully and wonderfully made in the likeness of our Creator?

Self-Awareness Is by Design

God is a self-aware being. If we possess self-awareness by design—as part of our being created in the image of God—then eternity opens up to us. Self-awareness and spiritual awareness find their reference point in a Divine Being who designed us in such a way as to be aware of Him and aware of ourselves. We can know God and we can know ourselves. In the *Institutes of the Christian Religion*, John Calvin saw the connection between the knowledge of God and the knowledge of ourselves. He wrote:

> True and substantial wisdom principally consists of two parts, the knowledge of God, and the knowledge of ourselves. But, while

these two branches of knowledge are so intimately connected, which of them precedes and produces the other, is not easy to discover. . . . For as God, at the beginning, formed us after his own image . . . that the design of our being endued with reason and intelligence . . . [we] may aspire to the mark set before us of a blessed immortality.[12]

Self-knowledge comes not only from what the Bible says about us—as being both an Imagebearer and a sinner—but it also comes as a result of self-observation. Learning how to pay attention to oneself, to "tune into" oneself is another way to learning about ourselves. But we will never desire to do this—we will never have the courage to do so—unless we see the honor and the benefits this gift brings. Then we can give ourselves permission to reclaim what God bestowed on us as part of His original design. We can see the value in working with our self-awareness as a gift to help us grow and mature.

Where Did We Lose Our Permission to Be Self-Aware?

It is such an awesome thing to see young children begin to mature in their awareness of themselves. As a baby, they have no sense of separateness from their parents. But as the mind matures there comes a time when the child becomes aware of its separate existence—of their sense of self. We can observe some indicators of their budding sense of self-awareness when they get little looks on their faces of self-consciousness, when suddenly they become shy as they realize they are being watched, or when they begin to want to do things for themselves and say, "No, I do it."

Self-awareness continues to develop and becomes a permanent part of what makes us human—part of the essence of our being. But, for more reasons than we have time to present, we gradually lose connection with seeing self-awareness as a positive, life-giving part of our personality. In fact, many of us wish we could somehow eliminate our awareness of ourselves because it causes us so much difficulty.

We push things out of our awareness that cause us to feel bad—to feel pain, anger, shame etc. We try to shut down our awareness of our feelings, our needs, our thoughts, our wants, our memories so that we can cope. We can be quite successful at "tuning ourselves out" but we pay a price for it. Everything that goes into our subconscious still remains a part of us. But we are not aware of how it has shaped our personality and how it still influences the way we live today.

Being Self-Aware Helps Us Be Other-Aware

We are aware of ourselves and we know it. When we see this special ability as part of our being made in God's image, we can reclaim it and give ourselves permission to develop it. We can learn how to use it in positive and life-giving ways to develop a healthy Christian life.

As we have pointed out about other human attributes, the ability to be self-aware (Being) is a separate issue from how successfully we use this ability (Doing). When we begin to separate the gift of our sense of self-awareness from the specific application and use of our awareness (gift ◄————► use), we can begin to reclaim its wonder and importance in our life.

Not only can we learn of its importance in the development of our personal lives, but we can also see how it helps us improve our connections with others. Self-awareness helps us become other-aware. Gordon Allport delivered a series of lectures at Yale University. His book *Becoming*, was based on those talks. Here is what he said about the importance of self-awareness.

> The outlines of the needed psychology of becoming can be discovered by looking within ourselves; for it is knowledge of our own uniqueness that supplies the first, and probably the best, hints for acquiring orderly knowledge of others. . . .
>
> When we ask ourselves about our own course of growth such problems as the following come to mind: the nature of our inborn dispositions, the impress of culture and environment upon us, our emerging self-consciousness, our conscience, our gradually evolving style of expression, our experiences of choice and freedom, our handling of conflicts and anxieties, and finally the formation of our maturer values, interests, and aims.[13]

These questions can be asked because we humans have the unique ability to be introspective—to look into ourselves and think about how we became the person we are today. We are able to do personal soul-searching and ponder the course of our life. We can step back and take a good, hard look at ourselves and learn about what makes us tick. The apostle Paul spoke about this when he talked about our gifts and talents. He wrote:

> For by the grace given to me I say to every one of you: Do not think of yourself more highly than you ought, but rather think of yourself with sober judgment, in accordance with the measure of faith God has given you (Romans 12:3).

We can decide how we want to change and become someone better, someone we can like and respect, someone we can be proud of in the healthy sense of the term. Animals know nothing of this process. They do not reflect on their lives. They do not ask themselves questions about their lives because they are not self-aware. They are not made in the image of God.

Present Day Awareness v. Awareness of Our Past

In working with our ability to be self-aware, we need to separate being aware of ourselves in the present from the awareness of ourselves from our past (present awareness ◄———► past awareness). Both are important, but it is easier to start becoming more aware of what we think, feel, or need in the present than to try to understand our past, especially if our past contains a lot of bad memories and pain. The more unhealthy, dysfunctional, and abusive our past, the more we have wanted to keep it blocked out; so starting with the present is a good place to begin.

We can do this by asking ourselves questions such as: "What are my feelings right now?" "What am I experiencing right now?" "What do I need to do right now to take better care of myself?" "What do I need to say now to communicate in a more healthy way?" Questions like these help sharpen our ability to be more *present aware* of ourselves and to make *present choices* that are more life-giving. Abraham Maslow described the connection between self-awareness and choice-making this way:

> Let us think of life as a process of choices, one after another. . . . To make the growth choice instead of the fear choice a dozen times a day is to move a dozen times a day toward self-actualization. . . . A human being is not a tabula rosa, not a lump of clay or Plasticine. He is something which is already there. . . . There is a self. . . . A person who does each of these little things each time a choice point comes will find that they add up to better choices about what is constitutionally right for him. . . . One cannot choose wisely for a life unless he dares to listen to himself, his own self, at each moment in life, and to say calmly, "No, I don't like such and such."[14]

Self-actualization means becoming the person—the Imagebearer—God designed us to be. Developing each one of our Imagebearing abilities (like intelligence, choice-making, self-awareness, and communication) is becoming a person.

Daily personal growth and development are dependent on self-awareness and self-acceptance. In his book *Creativity and Conformity*, Clark Moustakas affirmed the importance of self-awareness as a component of growth and healing. He stated it this way:

> The first requirement for the growth of the individual self is the person remain in touch with his own perceptions. . . . Only the person can

fully know what he sees, what he hears, and what he feels to be fundamentally true. To the extent that he respects the authenticity of his own experience, he will be open to new levels of learning, to new pathways of relatedness to others, and to genuine respect for all life.[15]

By giving ourselves permission to be more aware of life day by day and specifically to be more self-aware, we will grow in our ability to accept ourselves and to be in charge of taking care of ourselves. As we become stronger emotionally and spiritually, our confidence will build and we will be more ready and willing to begin dealing with our past.

Making Peace with Our Past

Learning to make peace with our past can be one of the most interesting and rewarding adventures we can embark on.[16] It can also be one of the most painful. This is why its important to develop some perspectives and skills in the present to help us when we seek to understand our past.

This was the approach I took when I first began accepting and developing my appreciation for the gift of self-awareness. My new approach was to be aware and honest with myself, by accepting my present experiences. Then I worked with my present feelings with healthy thinking and healthy choice-making. As my confidence and self-acceptance grew, then I looked at my past and was able to start to accept and understand it. I gave myself permission to **feel my memories** about anything and everything, good or bad, including memories of my birth father, my experiences and the questions I had about be molested, about my home life with Mom and Dad, and about the poor choices I had made that only I knew about. It took time and I went at my own pace but it was the beginning of the healing of my memories.

The highly respected pastor and counselor, David Seamands, wrote about the importance of the healing of past memories. In his book *Healing for Damaged Emotions*, he described it this way:

> In the rings of our thoughts and emotions, the record is there; the memories are recorded, and all are alive. And they directly and deeply affect our concepts, our feelings, our relationships. They affect the way we look at life and God, at others and ourselves. We preachers have often given people the mistaken idea that the new birth and being "filled with the Spirit" are going to automatically take care of these emotional hangups. But this just isn't true. A great crisis experience of Jesus Christ, as important and eternally valuable as this is, is not a shortcut to emotional health. It is not a quickie cure for personality problems. It is necessary that we understand this, first of all, so that we can compassionately live with ourselves

and allow the Holy Spirit to work with special healing in our own hurts and confusions. We also need to understand this in order to not judge other people too harshly . . . salvation does not give instant emotional health . . .[17]

Accepting the present and then reflecting on the past is a process we can use over and over again as a way to develop our self-awareness. By accepting our present awareness of ourself and of our experiences, we can learn to accept our past with more compassion. A visual example that has helped me have the courage to accept my past is a simple filmstrip. I imagine every frame on the film recorded all of my life experiences from birth to the present. The extent to which I accept each and every frame on the filmstrip is the degree to which I make peace with my past. By using this approach we can learn how to integrate our past with our present and become a more mature, healthy, whole person. Learning how to accept and integrate our past self-awareness with our present awareness is the subject of our next chapter.

Suggested Reading

1. Seamands, David. *Healing For Damaged Emotions*. Victor Books, Wheaton, Illinois, 1981.
2. O'Connor, Elizabeth. *Our Many Selves*. Harper and Row, 1971.
3. Genesis 18:12-15; Deuteronomy 8:17-18; Psalm 4:3-4; 44:20-21; 51:6; Proverbs 16:9; 20:5; Mark 2:6-8.

Man is a dignity seeker—not a status seeker. He makes a terrible mistake if he thinks that status will insure self-worth. . . . You are on the road to emotional, mental and spiritual health when you discover that what you really want more than anything else in life is . . . to be able to know and appreciate yourself.

Robert Schuller, *Self-Love*[1]

"The childhood shows the man, as morning shows the day," said Milton, in *Paradise Regained*. . . . Unfortunately, . . . [we] tend to minimize our childhood feelings and experiences. . . . For us to admit this idea as true may mean our having to acknowledge that we have failed to grow up. . . . [as] historians examine the past to understand present events, so must we look into our childhood to understand ourselves as we are today.

David Abrahamsen,
The Road to Emotional Maturity[2]

I have unveiled my inmost self even as Thou hast seen it, O Eternal Being. Gather round me the countless host of my fellow-men; let them hear my confessions, lament for my unworthiness, and blush for my imperfections. Then let each of them in turn reveal, with the same frankness, the secrets of his heart at the foot of the Throne, and say, if he dare, "I was better than that man!"

Jean Jacques Rousseau,
The Confessions of Jean Jacques Rousseau[3]

CHAPTER 20

Self-Awareness:
A Key to Healing and Growth

HOW TO

*E*verybody liked Shirley—except her husband. No matter how hard she tried to please him, she was never good enough. She was constantly criticized and put down. Outside her home, she was accepted and well-thought of. Her neighbors and friends at church encouraged her and complimented her for her kind and giving spirit, but this had little effect on helping her like herself.

She told how she had always felt she was a bad person, that something was wrong with her. To make up for this, she had done everything she could to be nice and to get people to like her. It worked in most of her relationships but she never felt secure. Her husband's attitude toward her reinforced her deepest feelings of insecurity and dislike for herself.

As we talked, we tried to understand how such a negative self-opinion was formed. I asked her if the sentence "I am a bad person" felt like the most true one. She said no, but that it was close. I encouraged her to find a more accurate word that would give her a truer sense of her self-opinion. Then she could begin to change it.

When we met again, she reported that she had just gone through one of the worst, and yet, one of the best weeks she had experienced for a long time. She realized that her major self-opinion sentence was "I am wicked!" Then she told how this picture had formed.

As a little girl and later as a preteen, she had two sexual encounters that shaped her self-picture deeply and permanently. She felt traumatized both times. Telling no one, she tried to figure out on her own why this had happened. She thought it had to be something about her, and she eventually reached the conclusion, "I am wicked." Her conclusion was a lie, but her childhood reasoning made sense if we looked at it from her point of view.

She had been raised in the Catholic church all her life and she held the Virgin Mary in highest regard. Sexual purity was very important! When Shirley was sexually "corrupted" by these two experiences, in her mind compared to the Virgin Mary, she thought of herself as being evil and wicked. She spent the rest of her life trying to overcome this negative self-picture by being the nicest person you could hope to meet.

She would never have understood any of these connections if she had not made a conscious effort to put the puzzle together about her past. Self-understanding grows when we take the time to reflect back on our lives and piece together the puzzle of our life. We can see how things happened and how they shaped our sense of self-worth and identity. Our lives make sense when we put the pieces of the puzzle together of our growing up years. We were designed with the ability to be self-aware, to be introspective because we are made in the likeness of God.

25¢—Pieces Missing

Garage sales are popular where we live and my family enjoys going to them. Frequently, we find puzzles for sale and we have bought a few. If you went with us on one of these jaunts, would you buy a puzzle that had a price sticker on it that read, "25¢ pieces missing?" I seriously doubt it. Buying it doesn't feel right, knowing it's incomplete.

Our life is like a puzzle. It is a big picture made up of all kinds of smaller pictures and interlocking pieces. We have within us all the pieces of our life puzzle. Self-understanding improves when we begin to put the pieces together in order to see the whole picture.

Most of us sense our lack of self-understanding and this won't change unless we work on our life puzzle. We are aware there are pieces missing when we make statements like:

- "I remember things about my past, but I have no idea where they fit in."
- "My life is puzzling to me."
- "I don't understand why I feel this way. I just do."
- "My life doesn't make sense to me."
- "I don't understand myself; I am a mystery to myself."
- "I don't know why I do what I do! That's just me!"
- "I want to know how the pieces of my life fit together."

We will begin to understand and make sense of our life when we start putting our life puzzle together. Our life puzzle is made up of many parts: our feelings, thoughts, attitudes, beliefs, choices, dreams, fantasies, values, interpretations, desires, goals, and experiences. These represent the truths of our life whether we are looking at our past or trying to understand ourselves in the present.

We put our life puzzle together in much the same way we put together any puzzle. We start by turning the pieces right side up so we can see colors and designs. Putting the pieces right side up about our life is being honest with ourselves and about the truths of our life. King David said God desires that we be truthful about our inner world (Psalm 51:6).

The next step is to find the edge pieces and connect them until we have the border completed. While we're doing this, we begin to separate different colors and designs into separate piles. As we put these smaller piles together, they form partial pictures of what the whole puzzle will look like. Eventually, we will see where they fit in. As the pieces come together, the main picture becomes clearer, and eventually the puzzle is completed.

Even though we never complete our life puzzle, we can make tremendous progress in understanding ourselves when we start seeing the connections between our thoughts, feelings, and choices that are the truths of our lives. By putting the pieces together we can see how they interconnect and the picture will become clearer as to how we became who we are. We will better understand what make us tick.

Some parts in our life puzzle may be pretty ugly, and we would like nothing more than to throw them away. But they are a very important part of the puzzle. When we place them in the context of the whole picture, they help us see how things interconnect. Our lives will begin to make sense!

Learn How to Trust Our Truth Recognition Response

To help us accomplish the task of putting the truth together about ourselves, God has built inside each of us what I call a *truth recognition response*. When we recognize a part of the truth that is our puzzle, our heart knows it and we feel it. People describe this response in different ways: "It's like a bell going off," "It was like a curtain opened and I saw the truth," "It was like a light turning on and I could see it." Some people have described it as a sensation that says, "That's it! That fits!" or "I just knew it. I knew it was true." Some describe it as an "ah ha" experience or they say, "I just realized something about myself." Experiencing the sensation of self-understanding is truly a life-giving feeling. It is a feeling of growth. It may be sad, heavy, and painful at times, but it brings freedom and healing.

Jesus said that truth sets us free (John 8:32). Accepting the truth about our lives is freeing. Accepting His truth is absolutely freeing. When we learn to be more accepting of ourselves we will discover the wonder and awe of our inner world, no matter how pretty or ugly some parts of the picture may be.

As we improve in our understanding of ourselves, we can see how we became the person we are today. This is why self-acceptance, compassion, and forgiveness are so important and necessary if we are to be successful. Self-hate and self-condemnation will never allow us to understand ourselves.

If we become aware of certain attitudes, beliefs or behaviors we want to change, we can. Insight and self-understanding can help us do that. But what really gets us moving is making new choices—today! Self-understanding helps us "loosen up" our inner world and lets us accept ourselves more honestly. But it's the new choices we make today that bring about life-giving changes. One of the ways our self-awareness and self-acceptance can help us become a healthier person is learning how to be a good friend to ourselves. We can choose whether we will become one of our own best friends or remain our own worst enemy.

Becoming Our Own Best Friend

I want to put a question before you. If you treated me on the outside like you treat yourself on the inside, how long could I be around you before I would have to get away from you? Said another way, if I treated you like you treat yourself, how long would you hang around me? Many of us are so self-abusive that if someone else treated us the way we treat ourselves, we would have nothing to do with them.

One of the best ways we can become a healthier and happier person is to learn how to become a friend to ourselves. *If we don't learn how to become one of our own best friends, we will be our own worst enemy.*

Trust is an important part of any developing friendship. If we can't love and trust ourselves, we will have a hard time trusting others. The two people we need to learn to trust the most—without the fear of being rejected or abandoned—is Jesus and ourselves. Once these two friendships are in place, we will experience an inner acceptance and security we never thought possible. Then we can learn how to trust others more honestly and realistically. The characteristics that would be found in any good friendship with someone in our outer world would also be found in the way we treat ourselves in our inner world. We can become our own best friend.[4]

When we begin to treat ourselves as we would treat a good friend, life changes. We can learn how to be self-supporting, self-encouraging, self-forgiving, self-accepting, self- confrontive, self-disciplined, and self-caring. This is biblical self-love at its best.

Learning to Love Our Inner Child of the Past

Another way we can work with our self-awareness in a healthier way is to learn how to identify and love the kid we used to be. I will never forget the first time I became aware that the boy I once was was still a part of the man I had become. It happened one evening back at Wheaton in 1967. I was quietly talking with God and thinking back over my life when this picture formed in my mind. It was a metaphor of my life.

I was a young boy playing on a school grounds with a bunch of other kids. Several of us had formed a big circle by holding hands. Suddenly, this boy came up behind me on my right side and wanted to join the circle. He was the most repulsive kid there: dirty, stinky, and unkempt. My instant reaction was, "No Way! Not by me! You're welcome to join the circle, but you have to do it some place else." I knew intuitively that he was me! He represented what I hated about myself and I didn't want him near me. But I also knew that I had a decision to make: Was I going to accept him beside me and let him in the circle, or was I going to continue to turn my back on him, reject him, and act like he wasn't there, hoping he would just go away.

In those few quiet moments when I sensed all this, the Holy Spirit had a thought (from the Bible) cross my mind: "If you love the lovely, you love as the world loves. But if you love the unlovely, then you love as God loves" (Luke 6:31-36).

I knew in my heart I needed to love and accept that boy if I wanted my life to improve. Gradually, I made the decision to accept him into the circle next to me, so I let go of the hand holding mine, reached back, and put my arm over his shoulder and welcomed him into the circle beside me. The moment I felt the sensation of having accepted him as myself, I burst into tears and sobbed with relief. It was as if two family members had finally made peace with each other after so many years of dislike and hate. It was like two parts of myself becoming friends and knowing that things were going to be okay now, things were going to be better.

This was the beginning of my commitment to accept and love the boy in me (the boy I once was) no matter what age I looked at, no matter what memory I had of my past, no matter what the "ugly" parts of my puzzle were that needed to be put into the whole picture of myself.

Did I accept myself with all my history in a day, a week, a year? No. But I had to start somewhere, sometime, and my commitment to become my own best friend had begun.

Not long after this experience, I found the remarkable book *Your Inner Child of the Past* by W. Hugh Missildine. God knew what I needed at the time, and He helped my find it. What Dr. Missildine said reinforced my commitment to accept the boy I once was who was very much a part of the man I had become. He wrote:

> Somewhere, sometime, you were a child. This is one of the great obvious, seemingly meaningless and forgotten common denominators of adult life. Yet the fact that you were once a child has an important bearing on your life today. In trying to be adults we mistakenly try to ignore our lives as children, discount our childhood and omit it in our considerations of ourselves and others. . . . *What happened to the child you once were? Did he or she die? Was he outgrown and cast aside, along with old toys, overshoes and sleds? Was he somehow abandoned? Was he lost somewhere in Time, eventually forgotten?* . . . Whether we like it or not, we are simultaneously the child we once were, who lives in the emotional atmosphere of the past and often interferes in the present, and an adult who tries to forget the past and live wholly in the present. . . . You are already dealing with your "inner child of the past" in one way or another. . . . You can't turn against yourself and have inner security.[5]

Learning how to become a true friend to the child or teenager we once were can begin to transform our lives. We can begin to feel the healing power of self-love as we begin to accept the kid side that so many of us have ignored, hated and rejected. We can become one of their best friends.

We can also feel the healing power of Jesus' love as the kid side of us begins to accept and trust Jesus' love for us as a person. We can take him and his love into the secret, ugly places of our heart. **We can begin to trust Jesus Christ with our worth just as we can trust him for our salvation.**

For years I had wondered why becoming a Christian had not taken away the negative feelings I had about myself and about my past. I was told that when a person became a Christian he was a new creation in Christ and the old was gone and all things were new (2 Corinthians 5:17). I was told that because I was a Christian I didn't have to think about my past because it was gone, it was forgiven.

While this is absolutely true in how God looks at us, I mistakenly thought I could continue to "forget" my past. But it wasn't working. For years I felt torn, guilty, and confused until I learned this truth: to accept and love the kid I once was and to accept Jesus' love for him not just because he was a sinful kid, but because he was a person first—a person made in the image and likeness of God. When I took this attitude toward myself, the value and meaning of the Christian life took on another whole dimension.

David Seamands wrote a most helpful book integrating Christian thought with the healing of our inner child. He expressed it this way in his book, *Putting Away Childish Things*:

> When the dormant inner child of the past is thus aroused, he can take over the person's attitudes, reactions, outlook, and behavior. The submerged emotions rise up and express themselves in feelings of deep depression, rage, uncontrollable lust, inferiority, fear, loneliness, and rejection.
>
> These painful memories are not automatically evicted or transformed by an experience of conversion or even by the filling of the Holy Spirit. They are not necessarily changed by growth in grace. In fact, these memories are often great hindrances to spiritual growth. And until a person receives deliverance from them, he does not really mature. It is as if one part of his person is in a deep freeze, or in a time machine. His body matures and his mind develops but that one particular area is still frozen. He remains a little boy, she is still a little girl, locked into the childhood stage of life. . . .
>
> Often what is required is prayer for the healing of memories—the healing of that little child or teenager who underwent certain experiences which made him stop growing, experiences which imprisoned him, froze him at one stage in his growth. All those memories need to be offered in a prayer for healing, so that the person can be freed from his pain and compulsion. . . . My experience is that the inner child of the past which most needs healing is usually one of four kinds: he is the hurting child, the hating child, the humiliated child, or the horrified child.[6]

Today because of the growth of the Recovery Movement, the idea of the healing of the inner child of the past has touched our society in ways never believed possible a few years ago. Names like John Bradshaw,[7] Charles Whitfield,[8] Pia Mellody,[9] Sharon Wegscheider-Cruse, Melody Beattie[10] are well-known for their work on inner-child healing.

The Bible has always taught the importance of taking the love of God into the deepest corners of our heart and experiencing its redeeming and transforming effect. Sadly, the church has not been able to communicate as clearly about the need for self-love as it has about the need for God's love and the need for salvation.

God's love is foundational to all love, but we need to learn that self-love is also important and needed. We confuse self-love with selfishness, so what do we mean when we say, "You need to learn how to love yourself?"

Developing the Art of Self-Love

Much has been written about the notion of self-love, but many people in the church still seem to be confused about it. This notion goes back to the time when a Pharisee asked Jesus which commandment in the Law was the greatest? Jesus answered:

> Love the Lord your God with all your heart and with all your soul and with all your mind. This is the first and greatest commandment. And the second is like it: Love your neighbor as yourself. All the Law and the Prophets hang on these two commandments (Matthew 22:37-40).

For centuries the Church has taught that self-denial and self-sacrifice (or dying to self) were Christian virtues, and they are, when properly understood. But with the rise of modern atheistic humanism, the Human Potential Movement, and now the New Age and Recovery Movements, a greater emphasis has been placed on loving ourselves than in any other age in history. The church has been forced to define its position on self-love and many people struggle with how to apply it to their Christian life.

Healthy love for oneself implies having beliefs, attitudes, and behaviors which demonstrate self-caring by meeting one's own physical, emotional, social, and spiritual needs. It means having a positive commitment to oneself to promote and encourage one's own emotional and spiritual growth. It means having a heart for oneself, just like we would have a heart for others. If we do not understand and accept our selves, we will fail at self-loving. We won't have a clear sense of what we feel, want, or need. In time, we will show the results of self-neglect or self-abuse even if we are Christians.

Self-love is not self-centeredness; it is not self-glorification; it is not being narcissistic; it is not being arrogant and stuck on one's self; it is not being selfish. Erich Fromm wrote a classic on understanding love. In his book *The Art of Loving*, he talks about the meaning of self-love.

> If it is a virtue to love my neighbor as a human being, it must be a virtue—and not a vice—to love myself, since I am a human being too. There is no concept of man in which I myself am not included. A doctrine which proclaims such an exclusion proves itself to be intrinsically contradictory.

> The Idea expressed in the Biblical "love thy Neighbor as thyself!" implies that respect for one's own integrity and uniqueness, love for and understanding of one's own self, cannot be separated from respect and love and understanding for another individual. The love for my own self is inseparably connected with the love for any other being *Selfishness and self-love, far from being identical, are actually opposites.*[11]

If it is right to love our neighbor as a person made in God's image, it is right for us to love ourselves, since we are made in God's image too.

Learning to love ourselves is learning to love the child or the person at any age we use to be. One of my friends, Marty Fuller, wrote a poem that captures the essence of learning how to become a friend to the child we once were. The title of her poem is "My Own Best Friend."

I ran into my room and cried.
I could not stop the tears.
But no one came and no one cared
To try to calm my fears.

"They must not care," I was convinced,
Or they would come to me.
They let me cry all by myself.
My worth I could not see.

"I'm in the way, no good to them,
I'll run away from home."
But I just cried upon my bed
And bore the pain alone.

But then she came into my room
Someone I did not know.
She sat beside me and she said,
"My dear, I love you so."

I looked at her, she smiled at me.
Her arms were open wide.
I stared in utter disbelief
At love she did not hide.

"Come here," she said, "and hold my hand.
Your tears I do not mind.
For I have cried and share your pain."
Her eyes were more than kind.

I looked away, I dared not trust
Those eyes as blue as mine.
"Could it be? Was she a friend
Whose heart with mine aligned?"

I looked again into her eyes
And recognized something.
I felt I'd known her all my life.
My heart began to sing.

I crawled up on her lap and sighed.

She held me close to her.
We cried until the tears were gone
And then I knew for sure.

I recognized the love we shared
It always was you see.
For when I looked into her eyes,
I saw that she was me.

(used by permission)

Self-love is valuing and caring for the real person in our inner world with the same kind of love we would show to a person in our outer world. Love for others as we would have love for ourselves, is best described by the apostle Paul in his letter to the Corinthian people.

> Love is patient, love is kind. It does not envy, it does not boast, it is not proud. It is not rude, it is not self-seeking, it is not easily angered, it keeps no record of wrongs. Love does not delight in evil but rejoices with the truth. It always protects, always trusts, always hopes, always perseveres.

> Love never fails. . . . Now we see but a poor reflection as in a mirror; then we shall see face to face. Now I know in part; then I shall know fully, even as I am fully known.

> And now these three remain: faith, hope and love. But the greatest of these is love (I Corinthians 13:1-8, 12-13).

God is love. When we begin to take this truth to heart and love ourselves as God loves us, it can heal the feelings and memories of our inner child of the past.

Jesus Christ Loves the Child We Used to Be

Knowing that Jesus loved children—and that He loves the inner child that we use to be—can be another encouragement for developing a healthy sense of self-awareness.

The four Gospels record the care and kindness Jesus displayed toward children. I believe He saw them as little Imagebearers and He treated them with the love and respect they were entitled to as persons made in the image of God.

On one occasion, when Jesus and His disciples were going to Capernaum, the disciples were arguing about who was the greatest (this sounds like self-esteem stuff to me). Later, Jesus asked what they had been arguing about but they were embarrassed and "kept quiet." Jesus knew what had been going on and this is how He answered their argument.

Sitting down, Jesus called the Twelve and said, "If anyone wants to be first, be must be the very last, and the servant of all." He took a little child and had him stand among them. Taking him in his arms, he said to them, "Whoever welcomes one of these little children in my name welcomes me; and whoever welcomes me does not welcome me but the one who sent me" (Mark 9:35-37).

Jesus took a child in His arms and told us that the truly great person is one who can love children. To love a child is to welcome Christ in disguise and to welcome God who sent him. When we learn to hold the child we once were in our arms, even as Jesus would hold them, then we are being Christ-like.

On another occasion, people were bringing little children to Jesus to have Him bless them. But the disciples got upset and rebuked the people. When Jesus saw this, He became indignant and said to them:

"Let the little children come to me, and do not hinder them, for the kingdom of God belongs to such as these. I tell you the truth, anyone who will not receive the kingdom of God like a little child will never enter it." And he took the children in his arms, put his hands on them and blessed them (Mark 10:13-16).

Can you imagine what it would have been like if as a child we were held in Jesus' arms? Hugs can be so affirming, so reassuring, so comforting, so healing. Jesus loves children and I know He loves the child hidden in all of us. I know He would hold us and whisper to us that we are loved, that we are valued and that everything is going to be okay. But can we trust Him? Not without a struggle. We have found safety in not trusting.

Because Jesus loves us, we are free to love ourselves and in turn to love our neighbor as ourselves. When we learn how to accept our inner world with all its good and bad memories—its good and bad sides—we will love ourselves as Jesus loves us. It is learning how to understand and accept the different sides of ourself. Learning how to love ourself is learning how to let Jesus become one of our best friends.[12]

Accepting the Many Sides of Ourselves

Years ago at a baseball game, my son Kent was called on to pitch with the bases loaded and no outs. It was the ninth inning and his team was ahead by three runs. He was under a lot of pressure to do a good job and he did, saving the game by one run which earned him the game ball. At home his mom said, "Kent, I didn't know you could pitch under pressure. I've never seen that side of you before."

Many of us have said something similar, but most of us have never taken a positive attitude about accepting and working with the different sides of ourselves. Mostly, we criticize and condemn certain aspects about ourselves that we dislike. This shuts down our self-awareness.

Another way to learn how to work with self-awareness and self-acceptance is to recognize the positive benefits of accepting the many sides to ourself. They make up the whole person we call ourself. I will list a few just to give us a picture of what I am referring to. We have:

• a fearful side	• a cold side
• a caring side	• an insecure side
• an adventurous side	• a mischievous side
• a loving side	• a lazy side
• a sensuous side	• a tender side
• a selfish side	• a tough side
• a playful side	• a mean side
• a rebellious side	• a curious side
• an optimistic side	• a skeptical side

Elizabeth O'Conner taught classes on self-discovery for a church coffee house in the 1970s. She taught that self-observation was the starting point for self-knowledge. When we learn how to observe ourselves and identify the many different sides we have of ourselves, we are in a position to grow and change. In her book *Our Many Selves*, she wrote:

> If I respect the plurality in myself, and no longer see my jealous self as the whole of me, then I have gained the distance I need to observe it, listen to it, and let it acquaint me with a piece of my own lost history. In this way I come into possession of more of myself and extend my own inner kingdom. . . . The concept of the many selves gives the detachment and distance that we need to name and understand all the happenings in us. It is a simple handle for identifying the contradictions and ambivalences that Scripture and Dostoevsky and Freud talk to us about in other terms. With it we can stand back and get the distance we need in order to see the division and multiplicity in our own inner worlds.[13]

When we begin to identify, accept, and work with the many sides of ourselves, we begin to work on our being. We can take every part—every thought, feeling, mood, hurt, dream, desire, failure, or sin—and see that they are just that, they are only part of the whole. As we accept and work with each part, we can begin to become a whole person. Self-rejection and self-condemnation keeps us divided against ourselves, and people divided against themselves will not be stable, emotionally or spiritually.

One technique we can use to help us with this is to imagine we're sitting in the front row in the balcony of a theater. The actors on the stage represent different aspects of ourselves. Sometimes one actor has center stage and the lights and attention are focused on him. But in the background are standing all the other actors in the play. When we observe the different sides of ourself on the stage, we can get a better sense of the whole picture. We can see what is going on. Then we can redirect the players in their parts if we so choose.

Observe yourself when you are around certain friends and see if you can identify which part of you takes the spotlight and which part of you fades into the shadows. If your shy side comes forward, but you would rather have the friendly side take center stage, then gently but firmly change it. If you want it to be different, you can change it, because you are the director. You're in charge.

Sometimes there are sides to ourself we hate. Jesus said we are to love our enemies, and some of our greatest enemies are found within. They need to be brought under the love of the cross.

The Cross of Jesus Was a Two-Armed Cross

An honest and realistic acceptance of ourselves means that we learn to accept both our bad side and our good side, both the ugly stuff and the pretty stuff, both our weaknesses and our strengths, both our failures and our successes, both our bad qualities and our good qualities, both our sins and our virtues. It is more typical for us to either deny, reject or condemn the "bad things" about us as well as not accept the "good things" about us.

An important perspective that can help us accept the different parts of our lives and to stop condemning ourselves is to remember this: *the cross of Jesus Christ was a two-armed cross.* It covered everything about us—our past, present and future, the things we are ashamed of and the things we are proud of, the sins we have committed and the good things we have done—everything. The apostle Paul wrote to the Christians in Rome and said, "There is now no condemnation for those who are in Christ Jesus" (Romans 8:1). The illustration on the following page helps us picture this.

When I imagine myself standing at the foot of the cross, looking up at Jesus with His arms nailed to the cross bars and grasp even a small inclination of what He accomplished for me and for all mankind, I feel released from some of my own self-pity and self-hate. How foolish for us to doubt our worth when He demonstrated His great love for us.

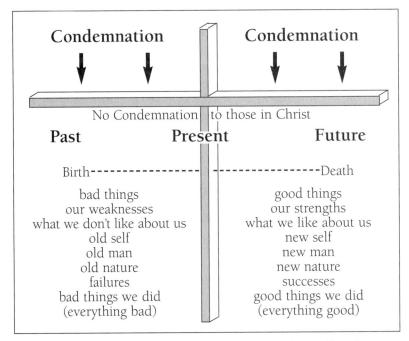

The two armed cross provides a safe place where all judgment and condemnation are gone and where unconditional love and acceptance are available. We can come out from hiding behind all our crazy-games and come into the light of God's grace and love. We can accept by faith that His cross covers everything about our life—from the most horrible part to the best—and discover a new lease on life. We are free to learn how to accept and work with everything about ourselves in new and life-giving ways.

In summary, our ability to be self-aware is an amazing piece of God's creative handiwork. It is a part of the wonder of our design as a person made in God's likeness. It is what gives us innate and intrinsic worth as a person. We are free to work with our ability to be self-aware, and in doing so find the beauty and wonder in one of our unique imagebearing abilities. We are fearfully and wonderfully made and the results of learning how to work with our self-awareness will affirm it.

Suggested Reading

1. Leman, Kevin, and Randy Carlson. *Unlocking the Secrets of Your Childhood Memories*. Thomas Nelson Publishers, 1989.
2. Seamands, David. *Putting Away Childish Things*. Victor Books, 1982.
3. Psalm 119:58-59; Proverbs 14:15; Proverbs 20:27; 2 Corinthians 13:5; 2 Timothy 2:7.

BECOME MORALLY AWARE

Many of us have very much *wanted* to get rid of moral values, to believe that reality is ethically neutral, and that experience or action is good or bad only insofar as it is followed by pleasure (lust) or displeasure (unlust). But gradually we are rediscovering that there is more to human existence than mere biology and that social systems (and, indeed, personality itself) cannot exist without prescribed and proscribed patterns of feeling and conduct.

O. Hobart Mowrer,
The Crises of Psychiatry and Religion [1]

A sinister inhumanity clouds all life. We have forgotten who we are, and no remembrance of an absolute obligation brings us back to our lost origin; all obligation simply intensifies the gulf which lies between us and our origin in the Word of God. . . . It is the Christian faith . . . which once again discloses to us the meaning of responsibility, and with it restores to us true humanity.

Emil Brunner, *Man in Revolt* [2]

The "image of God" means also that man is a moral being, a being made in the likeness of God spiritually and morally, as well as personally. . . . This is brought out in the New Testament, where the image of God is represented as being restored in regeneration. "Put on the new man, which after God is created in righteousness and true holiness" (Ephesians 4:24).

Earl Martin, *Toward Understanding God* [3]

CHAPTER 21

Moral Awareness:
Its Blessing and Burden

PERMISSION

Can you recall the earliest incident in your childhood when you became aware of right and wrong? Asked another way, can you remember the first time you stole something or told a lie and from that experience learned that you had done something wrong? The memory that connects a behavior with a sense of rightness and wrongness is the beginning of our awareness of our conscience.

I was about three years old when I first made the connection. I had been shopping with my mother at the corner grocery store. After returning home, I pulled out of my pocket a package of carmel candies and asked if I could have them.

Lovingly but firmly, I remember being walked back to the store to tell the clerk I was sorry. After paying for the candy (which I got to keep) we went home, but I still remember how I learned that stealing was wrong. That day I connected with one of our unique human characteristics—we are moral beings.

Many years later when I was traveling through various countries during my world trip, I became even more aware of the awesomeness of the human conscience. By hitchhiking most of the trip, I got to talk to a lot of people and stay in their homes.

One day while traveling through the Middle East, I realized that everyone I had met was struggling with their conscience—but what they felt guilty about varied from culture to culture. This was the first time in my life I separated the fact that we have a conscience from the content that informed our conscience (moral awareness ◄——► content).

That everyone has a conscience is universal, but the content that is educated into the conscience is cultural. Certain moral values are shared in common by all peoples and C. S. Lewis gives examples of this in his book *The Abolition of Man.* But the vast majority of things that make people feel guilty varied from country to country. In conversations with people, I remember thinking that the things I felt guilty about didn't seem that important to them, and what they felt guilty about certainly was no big deal to me.

What emerged from these experiences was a new and deeper appreciation for the wonder and awe of the human conscience. I met people who seemed free and happy and yet held firmly to a code of moral values. Some of these people were atheists, but most had a religious life—whether they were Christian, Muslim, or Jewish—and they honored the moral values found in their faith.

I met other people who were being crushed under the burden of a guilty conscience. They were trying so hard to live up to all the expectations of what it meant be be a good person in their culture, but their conscience only condemned their efforts. They couldn't be perfect enough!

I also met people whose lives were a testimony to how life deteriorates when we betray our conscience and behave in ways that are wrong and immoral. The deadening of their conscience in the quest to "live it up" was evident in the wrong ways they treated themselves and others. Paul described them as people "whose consciences have been seared as with a hot iron" (1 Timothy 4:2). Their conscience had become so deadened that what they said or did no longer bothered them. It was like they had experienced a "conscience-anectomy"—they seemed like people without a conscience.

The Affirmation of Our Conscience

Have you ever wished you could get rid of your conscience so you wouldn't have to feel guilty? I have. But no matter how hard we try to ignore or deny it, we can't escape it—it's an essential part of our Being. It is part of what makes us human. In his book *Somewhat Less than God,* Leonard Verduin expressed it this way:

> Conscience is a strange phenomenon, almost weird. Man does not acquire a conscience; he finds himself already in possession of one. He can no more escape from conscience than from awareness of self; he can no more eliminate out of his soul the sense of right and wrong than the sense of before and after.

> It must be added at once, however, that as to the content of a given conscience the matter is quite different. That the still small voice

approves or disapproves is native; what it approves or disapproves is a quite different matter.[4]

When we separate the fact that humans are moral beings from the moral values that inform the conscience, we take an important step in understanding a Christian view of self-esteem, ethics, and spirituality. That moral awareness is one of the identifiable marks of our humanness is attested to by many people. But many of us have suffered so much from a guilty conscience, we have failed to appreciate the uniqueness and dignity that is bestowed on us because we are moral creatures. So before we talk about how to work with our conscience, I want to elevate our appreciation for the wonder of this amazing attribute.

The Conscience—A Mark of Human Dignity

Anywhere we read, we will discover that moral awareness is a distinguishing characteristic of, our being human. In his book *Conscience*, Professor O. Hallesby described it this way:

> Conscience is the simplest and clearest expression of the exalted character and dignity of human life. Here we touch upon something which makes man a man and exalts him above the animal; we come in contact with the vital mystery of human life.[5]

The words "exalted" and "dignity" are strange words for those of us who have constantly walked in the shadow of guilt and self-condemnation. Our eyes have been so fixed on the Doing side of the human conscience, we have lost our appreciation for the Being side of moral awareness. To appreciate the mystery of moral awareness is to step into the light of being an Imagebearer of a Moral Creator. Eric Sauer helps bring this into clearer focus in his book *King of the Earth.*

> The Image of God as an endowment is found in the fact that man is a moral personality with self-consciousness and intelligence. . . . This is revealed by his look directed upwards, his faculty of speech, and by his ability to reflect his inner feelings in his face by blushing, laughing and crying. . . . It is revealed by his self-consciousness, his mental powers and his reason, and above all by his moral capacity, viz. his ability to judge what is good and evil. It is further seen in his conscience, acting as the inner law-giver. . . . All these are not something added at some time to human nature; they are the *essential basis and substance of his personality.* They enable him to live a personal, spiritual life, the "essence" of the concept of his being man. Without them he would cease to be man.[6]

Animals do not have a conscience. They are unable to be either moral or immoral. They just act out of instinct or from what they have learned. Because some animals have been domesticated, they have learned how to react to punishments or rewards for their actions. But they don't sit around and talk to themselves about how good they have been or about what kind of terrible animal they are for the bad ways they have been thinking or acting. Humans do.

Neither do animals blame others for their behaviors; they have no awareness of a sense of self, no self-esteem concerns, no ego, no conscience to protect. Humans blame others so they can shift the burden of responsibility and guilt away from themselves. This has been done since the beginning of human life when Adam blamed Eve and Eve blamed the serpent for their wrong choices (Genesis 3:12-13). There is a moral gulf between humans and the animal world and this frees animals from having to find and follow a code of ethics.

Moral-Awareness Is Universal and Human

To appreciate the phenomenon of the conscience is to realize that no matter where we go in the world or what age in human history we study, we find that human-beings have always had a sense of conscience. There is a moral line in the conscience that tells humans when they are acting right or wrong, good or bad, nobel or cruel. C. S. Lewis calls this the Law of Human Nature, Moral Law, or the Rule of Decent Behaviour. In his book *Mere Christianity*, he presents two things as a clue to understanding life.

> First, that human beings, all over the earth, have this curious idea that they ought to behave in a certain way, and cannot really get rid of it. Secondly, that they do not in fact behave that way. They know the Law of Nature; they break it. These two facts are the foundation of all clear thinking about ourselves and the universe we live in.[7]

This sense of "ought" is the conscience. It is that unique part of our humanness that becomes activated when we are facing a choice. This "ought" feeling can be called by other names like "fair play," "decency," "integrity," "goodness," or a sense of "rightness." It's that "small voice" inside each of us that tries to encourage us to act in a morally good way, praising us when we do and rebuking us when we don't.

The conscience is what makes us moral beings. When we work with our conscience in a healthy way, we bring glory to God and honor to ourselves. God created us in His image so we could represent the moral character of our Creator in our decisions. Eric Sauer expressed it this way:

> God's holy nature can be glorified and shine out of His creation only in and from such beings. Thus, applying this to ourselves, the

moral will of God as it reveals itself will lead of necessity to man's appointment to bear His image.[8]

The conscience is our God given capacity for developing ethical attitudes and actions and ultimately a healthy personality. John Drakeford saw the conscience as one of the most exciting aspects of human life. He expressed his views on its value in his book *Integrity Therapy*:

> It is the most wholesome and creative aspect of personality and helps men achieve their highest possibilities. . . . [Integrity Therapy] views conscience as not only awesome in its power but persuasive in its influence, rewarding in its returns for cooperation, and exacting in its penalties for indifference. Conscience makes us into real persons, capable of reaching untold possibilities. . . .[9]

Professor Hallesby also reaffirms the positive nature of the human conscience. He feels it brings a richness and quality to life for both the Christian and the nonChristian. He wrote:

> A good conscience imparts a new worthwhileness to a person's whole life, gives it a new richness and fullness, and a quiet, peaceful joy which transcends all other joys. It gives new meaning to even the little details of our temporal existence, giving us a peculiar zest for living, which should be "proof" enough of the truth and validity of the moral life.

> Just as an evil conscience affects adversely our whole life, both physically and mentally, . . . so a good conscience is a source of strength. In fact, in many instances it has a definite healing effect, not only mentally but physically as well. . . .

> This has been ordained by that God who "maketh his sun to rise on the evil and the good, and sendeth rain on the just and the unjust" (Matthew 5:45). God wills to give good gifts to men, because He is Love.[10]

There is something honorable about recognizing this special faculty as an important feature of our being fearfully and wonderfully made in God's image. Few of us have been thankful to God for our conscience because it feels more like a burden than a blessing. We lose this sense of appreciation when we focus primarily on what we should have or should not have done (Doing) and then become distracted by the guilt that rules our lives.

The Feeling of Guilt Is a Self-Esteem Feeling

The Christian view of life sees the conscience as originating from God as a gift—as part of our being created in His likeness. Moral awareness is by design and human worth and identity are directly linked to our being moral creatures.

But if we turn from a divine origin to a chance beginning for life, then all that has been said makes us only super animals burdened with a conscience. In his book *Escape from Evil*, Ernest Becker argued that the root causes of human evil are our attempts to deny our mortality and to achieve a "heroic" self-image. We want to become cosmic heroes. These urges are in response to not knowing our origin—not knowing our roots. Life created by chance has its own kind of guilt. He wrote:

> Guilt is a reflection of the problem of acting in the universe; only partly is it connected to the accidents of one's birth and early experiences. Guilt, as the existentialists put it, is the guilt of being itself. It reflects the self-conscious animal's bafflement at having emerged from nature, at sticking out too much without knowing what for, at not being able to securely place himself in an eternal meaning system.[11]

For years, I have maintained that when we are unable to experience being released from the feeling of guilt, it is because we have not dealt with the self-esteem issue involved.

Feeling guilty is a self-esteem feeling. We are not just dealing with the psychological effects of our wrong doing; we are dealing with the philosophical issue of the worth of human life—our life specifically. If we do not view our worth as separate from our actions, then if we do something "bad" enough, we will not accept forgiveness. We will not forgive ourselves. In our heart, we just can't believe we deserve it. We don't believe we are worth it!

When we do something that is truly wrong (true moral guilt), it is normal and healthy to feel pain, remorse, regret and sorrow. We know it's wrong and we feel badly about it. These are what I call "clean feelings" because they are healthy, appropriate, and right to feel. This is the healthy response to true moral guilt. They prompt us to make confession, to make appropriate apologies and to make amends if possible. The apostle Paul calls it a Godly sorrow that brings repentance and leads to salvation (2 Corinthians 7:10).

But the feeling of guilt that most of us suffer from appears when we make a moral judgment, not about our actions or thoughts, but about the worth of our personhood—the worthiness of our existence. This can be seen in the kinds of sentences that run though our mind. It might go something like this: "Why did I do that? I've really blown it this time. I am a stupid idiot for what I've done! I'm a no good. I am bad." It's the last couple of sentences that are the guilt-producers because the "I am" sentences are value-judgments against our personhood.

Guilt is a self-condemnation feeling. In the Recovery Movement, this kind of guilt is called "shame." It is the feeling that comes when we feel we don't deserve to be alive, that we are no good, that nothing about us is decent or worthwhile. Our existence is bad, evil, and wicked. Until we resolve the self-esteem issue, the feeling of guilt (shame) will remain because our conscience is not only condemning our behaviors, it is also speaking against our being.

This is why so many Christians know in their head that God has forgiven them but they don't feel it in their heart. The unresolved self-esteem and self-identity questions fill the heart.

It is hard to experience the awesomeness of God's love and forgiveness as found in Christ if the heart is full of self-doubt, self-hate, and self-condemnation. His love and forgiveness is always available, but we close it out because of our own self attitude—our sense of shame. As Ernest Becker said, "Self-knowledge is the hardest task because it risks revealing to the person how his self-esteem was built."[12]

The ideas that we are made in God's image, that we are sinners in need of forgiveness (salvation), and that we are saints because we can be redeemed by faith in Jesus Christ is truly the heart of the Christian message. To accept all three would free our conscience from the guilt that holds it hostage. We would see the value and worth of our human life (Genesis 1), we could admit we are sinners (Genesis 3), and we could accept forgiveness and the new life as found in Jesus Christ (the Gospels). In our heart we can know and feel, "I am somebody—I am made in God's image; I am somebody—I belong to Jesus Christ." When the self-esteem issue in our conscience is resolved, we are free to learn how to live in peace with God, ourselves, and others. We can celebrate life and organize life around moral values that have eternal meaning. A redeemed conscience is a liberated conscience.

The Importance of Moral Values

Appreciating our conscience and the moral code we choose to live by helps us organize life in both our inner and outer world.

It helps us live in harmony with ourselves, each other, and with God. It helps the individual and the human race keep on course by living in ways that promote life the way it was intended by the Creator. This is true for everyone, whether they believe in God or not. In her controversial book *The Virtue of Selfishness*, atheist Ayn Rand makes it clear how important moral values are to human life.

What is morality, or ethics? It is a code of values to guide man's choices and actions—the choices and actions that determine the purpose and the course of his life. . . . The first question that has to be answered, as a precondition of any attempt to define, to judge or to accept any specific system of ethics, is: Why does man need a code of values? . . . Is the concept of value, of "good and evil" an arbitrary human invention, unrelated to, underived from and unsupported by any facts of reality—or is it based on a metaphysical fact, on an unalterable condition of man's existence?[13]

She claims that no philosopher has ever given a "rational, objectively demonstrable, scientific" answer to the question of *why* human beings need moral values. Consistent with her world view as an atheist, she then gives her answer and it rests solely in the individual's personal need to experience life. This need for life becomes the standard for determining those values. "An organism's life is its standard of value: that which furthers its life is the good, that which threatens it is the evil."[14] Even though I disagree with her about man being the sole standard for deciding his moral values, I agree with her when she said that moral values are related to an "unalterable condition of man's existence" and that that which furthers life is good and that which takes away life is evil.

As we shall see in a moment, her point makes even more sense when we know that God is good and He wants the best for us. He gave the Golden Rule as an expression of His goodness and love because He designed life and he knows best how it morally functions. His commandments are rational and life-giving. True Christian ethics combines faith and reason.

Her close friend and fellow atheist, Nathaniel Branden, also made a strong claim for the rational importance of ethical values. He honors the human side but misses the spiritual connection to moral values. He wrote:

The existence of neurosis, of mental and emotional disturbances, is, I submit, one of the most eloquent proofs that man *needs* an integrated, objective code of moral values—that a haphazard collection of subjective or collective whims and precepts will not do—that a rational ethical system is as indispensable to man's psychological survival as it is to his essential survival.[15]

Erich Fromm also dealt with the search for "objectively valid norms of conduct." In his book *Man for Himself: An Inquiry Into the Psychology of Ethics,* he expressed it this way:

I have written this book with the intention of reaffirming the validity of humanistic ethics to show that our knowledge of human nature does not lead to ethical relativism but, on the contrary, to the conviction that the source of norms for ethical conduct are to be found in man's nature itself; that moral norms are based upon man's inherent qualities, and that their violation results in mental and emotional disintegration. . . . The choice between life and death is indeed the basic alternative of ethics. It is the alternative between productiveness and destructiveness, . . . between virtue and vice. For humanistic ethics all evil strivings are directed against life and all good serves the preservation and unfolding of life.[16]

If man is a moral being only by chance and not by design, then these writers have still given us some helpful standards on which to build our moral codes. If evil is that which tries to destroy life and good is that which tries to promote life, then at least we have a bottom line: *Moral living is choosing life, not death.* If God does not exist, then we can do our best to be good people (by some standard) and we can work hard to hold back the tidal wave of hate, cruelty, and immoral living; but there is no spiritual power to help us achieve it.

If life on this planet is the result of chance, then ultimately it won't make any difference anyway—and sadly, we have many examples of people who have shown us what this looks like. It is ugly, frightening, and destructive. Man's inhumanity to man can be absolutely mindboggling. On one of his news broadcasts, Paul Harvey reported about a man that had killed several young men and had eaten parts of their bodies. He said this was another example of the "depravity of the human animal."

On the other hand, if we are moral beings by design then there are real morals and moral absolutes to guide our decisions—and to honor them with our choices is life-giving. To violate them is death-producing emotionally, spiritually, and socially.

God Is Our Reference Point for Moral Values

A Judeo-Christian view of the world believes that God created us in His image to be moral beings and it is God Himself and His character which is the moral reference point for the moral values of life. God and our relationship to Him form the basis for moral living. Dr. Francis Schaeffer says this is the only view that can help solve our moral dilemma—our nobility and our cruelty.

Being finite means we are not a sufficient reference point for determining moral values. It's too easy to rationalize wrong to make it "look right" but the consequences of choosing to do wrong still leads to death-producing results. This is what happened when Adam and Eve chose death and the human race has never been the same. Human nature changed so that now we have a sinful nature, a cruel side to ourselves, and we need a renewed spiritual life to help us deal with evil. Human reasoning is an important part of moral development but we also need something outside ourselves to provide a life-giving moral code for us to follow. In his book *He Is There and He Is Not Silent*, Dr. Schaeffer expressed it this way:

> Men have always felt that things are right and things are wrong. . . .
> All men have this sense of moral notions. You do not find man without
> them anywhere back in antiquity. . . . It is God himself and his
> character which is the moral absolute of the universe.[17]

The Christian world view believes God is there and that He revealed His moral character to us through revelation (the Bible) and through Jesus Christ. We can know and follow moral norms based on God's inherent goodness and we can be confident that they were given so that life can be good. William Jennings Bryan had a picturesque way of saying it:

> There is that in each human life that corresponds to the mainspring
> of a watch—that which is absolutely necessary if the life is to be
> what it should be, a real life and not a mere existence. That necessary
> thing is *a belief in God*. Religion is defined as the relation between
> God and man, and Tolstoy has described morality as the outward
> expression of this inward relationship.[18]

Being conscious of God's presence in our life gives spiritual value and meaning to life. It also gives moral meaning to our relationship. Our sense of moral respect to our Creator and to people is based on the quality of our inward relationship with God. This truly honors our "inherent qualities" as human beings made in God's image. True morality is based on our having a personal relationship with God.

But we can take it one step further. Dietrich Bonhoeffer held that the foundation of Christian ethics is found in the reality of God as revealed in Jesus Christ.[19] This means Christian morality is the outward expression of our inward relationship with Jesus Christ. To cut ourselves off from our Judeo-Christian heritage regarding moral values is to create what Elton Trueblood called "a cut-flower civilization." In this kind of society, human dignity is lost. This is how he described it in his book *A Place to Stand*.

> What we meant was that it is impossible to sustain certain elements of
> human dignity, once these have been severed from their cultural roots.
> The sorrowful fact is that, while the cut flowers seem to go on living
> and may even exhibit some brightness for a while, they cannot do so
> permanently, for they will eventually wither and be discarded. The

historical truth is that the chief source of the concepts of the dignity of the individual and equality before the law are found in the Biblical heritage.

Apart from the fundamental convictions of that heritage, symbolized by the idea that every man is made in the image of God, there is no adequate reason for accepting the concepts mentioned. . . . men have broken laws; that is nothing new. What is new is the acceptance of a creed to the effect that there really is no objective truth about what human conduct ought to be.[20]

Human dignity, self-worth, and true morality find their meaning in the Judeo-Christian view of the world. Going back to the question raised by Ayn Rand, "Why does man need a code of values?" a more important question to ask first would be, "How did we humans acquire our sense of moral awareness in the first place which makes it necessary for us to look for a code of values to follow?" As we have seen, we find its origin in God who created us in His likeness.

In his book *Believe in the God Who Believes in You*, Dr Robert Schuller discusses the relationship between self-esteem and the Ten Commandments. He calls them the "Divine Design for Dignity." This is what he wrote:

These ten *commands* are *meant*—not to take the freedom out of life—but to build a positive faith in life that can free us from shame and spare us the oppression imposed by guilt and low self-esteem. . . . these ten *commands* are *meant*—not to inflict shame on humans— but to put liberating pride back into our lives! . . . Each of the ten rules is a *command meant* to:

- Protect us from shame.
- Reserve our self-respect.
- Point us to a positive pride that will let us lift our heads, poised to praise and worship the Creator![21]

Since 1960 I have been interested in how Christianity and psychology work together to make life real, healthy, rewarding and worthwhile. Since that time, I have received two degrees in the Bible, a doctorate degree in psychology and I have been in private practice for nearly thirty years. That is why I was very interested in what Dr. Laura Schessinger had to say about moral values in her book titled, *The Ten Commandments: The Significance of God's Laws in Everyday Life*.

For years Dr. Laura (as she is known by her listeners) has been a popular radio talk show host who has brought back into our cultural thinking the importance of moral values and behaviors. As a former licensed Marriage and Family therapist, she now reaches millions of people on her radio show "preaching, teaching and nagging" about morals, values, ethics, and principles.

Thousands of lives have been changed for the better as a result of her work on moral clarity in everyday life.

In her journey to understand the "authority behind" these moral values, she was "changed dramatically" once she "absorbed the significance" of the covenant God made with the Children of Israel at Mt. Sinai.

> You yourselves have seen what I did to Egypt, and how I carried you on eagles wings and brought you to myself. Now if you obey me fully and keep my covenant, then out of all nations you will be my treasured possession. Although the whole earth is mine, you will be for me a kingdom of priests and a holy nation. These are the words you are to speak to the Israelites (Exodus 19:4-6).

Dr. Laura then gives a clear and meaningful interpretation of what this covenant meant.

> "The Jewish understanding of "chosen" does *not* mean favorite child or a teachers pet . . . The Israelites were basically, given an assignment. By their adherence to a unique way of life, with laws of holiness, justice, generosity, mercy, ethics and compassion, the world would come to know, love, and obey the One and Only God. The Jews were to be role models, and their behavior in personal and public life, as commanded by God, would draw others to follow: ultimately resulting in God's kingdom on earth. God loves all people. We are all made "in His image". [22]

Her co-author, Robbi Stewart Vogel, also gave a clear testimony to the importance of our worth as human beings and its connection to the gift of moral awareness. He wrote:

> To believe in God is to believe that humans are more than accidents of nature. It means that we are endowed with purpose by a higher source, and that our goal is to realize that higher purpose. . . . Without God there is no *objective meaning* to life, nor is there an *objective morality*. . . . the purpose of religion is to lead us to holiness, a relationship with God, and an inspiration to live up to being "made in the image of God".[23]

In summary, we have looked into the wonder and awe of such a remarkable faculty as the human conscience. We have seen how our conscience finds its greatest meaning and value in its connection to our Divine Creator. To appreciate this is to celebrate the wonder of God's design in us as bearers of His likeness. It is what gives us innate worth as a person and makes it worthwhile when we learn to live in harmony with our conscience and in cooperation with divine moral values.

It is a marvelous gift and we can be assured that our conscience will function. It will do so based on truth and reality, or it will function under the burden of distortions, errors, lies, and falsehoods. How to work with our conscience in positive, healthy ways is the subject of the next chapter.

Suggested Reading

1. Schaeffer, Francis A. *He Is There and He Is Not Silent.* Tyndale House Publishers, 1972.
2. Schlessinger, Laura. *The Ten Commandments: The Significance of God's Laws in Everyday Life.* Harper Collins Publishers, 1998.
3. Genesis 9:6; Deuteronomy 5:29; 1 Samuel 24:5, 25:31; 1 Kings 3:9; Psalm 7:14; 19:7-11, 58:11; Proverbs 2:6,9; 5:22-23; 28:5; Isaiah 4:20; Matthew 15:14; 1 Corinthians 8:7-13; 15:33; 2 Corinthians 8:21; Titus 1:15; 3:8.

The Creator of the earth is the owner of it. He gives us being. . . . He is kind and merciful to his creatures; . . . as far as true love influences our minds, so far we become interested in his workmanship and feel a desire to make use of every opportunity to lessen the distresses of the afflicted and to increase the happiness of the creation.

John Woolman,
The Journal of John Woolman[1]

If any human being were ever to respond to God in harmony with His Word, and upon the basis of His Word, in believing love, he would be truly human. He would know what human existence means, and he alone would express and represent this knowledge in his life. In this human being the riddle of humanity would be solved, both in theory and in practice.

Emil Brunner, *Man in Revolt*[2]

But where can wisdom be found? Where does understanding dwell? . . . God understands the way to it and he alone knows where it dwells, for he views the ends of the earth and sees everything under the heavens. . . . And he said to man, "The fear of the Lord—that is wisdom, and to shun evil is understanding.

Job (Job 28:12,23-24,28)

CHAPTER 22

Trust Your Conscience:
It Can Become Your Friend

HOW TO

*T*he book *Situation Ethics* caused quite a stir when it was first published in 1966. The American culture was going through major changes, among them was a shift in belief from absolute moral values to relative ethics. Joseph Fletcher wanted people to understand how to make moral decisions based on individual situations.

"Love only is always good," became the catch phrase that was to govern the conscience. As Joseph Fletcher put it, "There are no universals of any kind. . . . If a lie is told unlovingly it is wrong, evil; if it is told in love it is good, right."[3] Said another way, whatever was the most loving thing to do in the situation was the right and good thing, because there were no moral absolutes outside of love to direct one's decisions.

Love became the only absolute—but love no longer found its meaning in the person and character of a Creator. The "God is Dead" movement, combined with the growing acceptance of atheistic evolution, caused many people to turn away from a personal faith in God. We began to see the eclipse of morals.

So Where Did We Go Wrong?

Why did the Western world reject the Judeo-Christian God and the moral absolutes that had governed our decisions for thousands of years? At the risk of being simplistic, I want to point out at least two of the reasons. First, rejecting moral absolutes was a logical step for a person or a society to take which has lost faith in the existence and importance of God.

Second, by ridding ourselves of any external moral absolutes to which we are held accountable, we mistakenly thought we could free ourselves of the burden of a guilty conscience. "Everybody's doing it, so it can't be wrong."

Anybody holding to traditional moral values was considered old fashioned and out of touch with life in a modern world. The pressure to compromise, to go along with the new morality, was tremendous—but the psychological and spiritual casualties for leaving our moral roots are enormous.

Many of those who maintained their faith in God and tried to be faithful to the important moral values of their church or synagogue described their moral position by the phrases, "I have to," "I can't," or "I should." These self-talk statements often made them feel trapped, restricted, and forced to conform to what was right and wrong. They did not experience real freedom in their heart. In addition, religious legalism made going to movies, playing cards, drinking coffee, eating meat on Friday, or not wearing a tie to church as serious an issue as lying or committing adultery. Christians felt so much guilt and pressure that it often overshadowed the joy in their faith.

On the other hand, those who turned away from God and embraced the philosophy of relative ethics often felt a great sense of relief and freedom. They felt in charge of their choices and they could choose to do whatever they wanted. They were not trapped by "have to's" and "shoulds" because nothing existed "above them" that could call them into account—not God, not tradition, not parents, not police, not any authority. They were the sole determiners of their moral values and actions. If anyone tried to tell them that what they were doing was wrong, they answered, "You don't have a right to tell me what to do. It's just your opinion. We have a right to decide for ourselves what we think is right or wrong."

The sexual revolution and the drug movement of the sixties and seventies provided plenty of opportunity for people to live out their concept of freedom of choice. But as the consequences of one's choices began to accumulate, many of these people began to rebuild a set of moral standards to guide their decisions for living a good and decent life. In an interesting kind of way, their "ten commandments" looked quite similar to God's without their acknowledging His existence or His importance for life.

Experience taught them what instruction failed to do. Free love, open marriages, and the erosion of self-respect carried to there logical conclusions left people broken and lost. Human beings cannot violate their conscience, their true sense of integrity, and not pay a price for it.

We Can Have Both Moral Absolutes and Free Choice

What do we do if we want and need moral absolutes that give life meaning and structure but also want to feel the freedom that comes from discarding the absolutes? Can we have it both ways? Can a person honor their conscience and learn how to work with their conscience in positive ways?

The answer is yes! It is found in moving to a third position. It is found in moving away from the "I have to, I can't, I should" mentality to the view that says, "I choose," "I am willing to," "I am not willing to."

Freedom does not come from discarding moral values. Freedom comes from accepting and appreciating that we are in charge of our choices. We are free to choose because God gave us free will and self-determination. The idea of "I have to be truthful," changes to "I choose to be truthful," or "I can't steal," or "I can't commit adultery," changes to "I am not willing to steal or commit adultery." The following diagram illustrates this change of thinking.

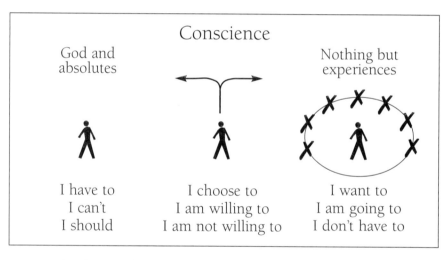

True freedom in life comes from accepting both moral absolutes and free will. Sometimes the realities of life force us into terrible situations where making a moral decision is complex and difficult. Living in a fallen world, sometimes lying is necessary such as when people lied to Nazi solders to protect the lives of other human beings. This was certainly a loving and right thing to do, but decisions like this only make sense if there is ultimate value to human life and human morality. It is situational but it is not the kind of situational ethics advocated by Fletcher. Knowing God, His love, and the moral laws He designed to govern our decisions is the key to being free as a moral being.

Moral Decisions Based on Relationship Value

Love is relational. One of the ways we can begin to work with our conscience in a healthy way is to regain a deeper appreciation for who God is and who we are as people made in His image. To believe that "God is Love" (1 John 4:8) is not just a nice thing for children to learn in Sunday school. Any true definition of love and its expression for others has its ultimate meaning in Divine love. Every action we take can rise from these two great truths—God is love and we are His Imagebearers.

God is the source of both love and moral values; He is the origin of human life and human worth. Love and moral values can become an integral part of the fabric of a person's character when they are open to God and open to learning how to see life from God's point of view.

John Woolman, the great Colonial Quaker, experienced the connection between loving God, human worth, and moral values when he had to personally deal with human slavery. A major turning point in his life occurred when he was asked to write out a bill of sale for an African slave. The year was 1743, a time when few white people in Christendom saw the injustice of slavery.

His faith in God had been growing and maturing when suddenly he realized how wrong slavery was. It was inconsistent with the religious teaching on human equality—that all human beings are made in God's image. As his love for God grew, he also grew to love what God created. Here's how he wrote about it in his journal.

In reading the Scriptures and other good books, [I] was early convinced in my mind that *true religion consisted in an inward life*, where-in the heart doth love and reverence God the Creator, and learns to exercise true justice and goodness, not only towards all men, but also toward the brute creatures; . . . As I lived under the cross, and simply followed the opening of truth, my mind, from day to day, was more enlightened. . . . I had many fresh and heavenly openings in respect to the care and providence of the almighty over his creatures in general, and *over man as the most noble amongst those which are visible*. And being clearly convinced in my judgment that to place my whole trust in God was best for me, I felt renewed engagements that in all things I might *act on an inward principle of virtue*. . . . My employer, having a negro woman, sold her, and desired me to write a bill of sale, the man being waiting who bought her. The thing was sudden; and though I felt uneasy at the thought of writing an instrument of slavery for one of my fellow-creatures, yet I remembered that I was hired by the year, that it was my master who directed me to do it . . . so through weakness I gave way, and wrote it; but at the executing of it I was so *afflicted in my mind*, that I said before my master and the Friend that I believed slave-keeping to be a practice inconsistent with the Christian religion. This, in some degree, abated my uneasiness; yet as often as I reflected seriously upon it I thought I should have been clearer if I had desired to be excused from it, *as a thing against my conscience*; for such it was (italics mine).[4]

This story encapsulates all the major variables of moral living and moral decision making—the existence of a personal God who loves; the valuing of a human life as people made in God's image; the establishment of a moral standard stemming from a personal relationship with God as found in Jesus Christ and in Scripture; and the struggle of a person, using the human attributes of reason, feeling, speech, choice, and conscience, to make a moral decision that honored life.

The moral decisions we make in daily life are directly related to our awareness of these great truths. John Woolman was dealing with slavery, but his insights would be just as true if we talked about the moral issues raised by Jesus when he said:

For from within, out of men's hearts, come evil thoughts, sexual immorality, theft, murder, adultery, greed, malice, deceit, lewdness, envy, slander, arrogance and folly. All these evils come from inside and make a man unclean (Mark 7:20-23).

True moral maturity begins in our heart—a heart that is open to God who is the source of moral values. This inner attitude can then manifest itself in our outward behavior toward those around us. Reinhold Niebuhr affirms this idea in his book *Moral Man and Immoral Society*:

The religious conscience is sensitive not only because its imperfections are judged in the light of the absolute but because *its obligations are felt to be obligations toward a person. The holy will is a personal will. . . . Moral attitudes always develop most sensitively in person-to-person relationships. . . .* In religion all the higher moral obligations . . . are felt as obligations toward the supreme person. Thus both the personality and the holiness of God provide the religious man with a reinforcement of his moral will and a restraint upon his will-to-power (italics mine).[5]

We haven't discussed a specific list of rights and wrongs or do's and don'ts because it's always easier to conform to a list of rules than to live by moral principles based on a healthy relationship with God and others. The prophet Isaiah saw this fact when he wrote:

> The Lord says: "These people come near to me with their mouth and honor me with their lips, but their hearts are far from me. Their worship of me is made up of rules taught by men" (29:13).

Following a list makes sense only if what we do or don't do enhances life rather than destroys it. True moral living is based on the quality and health of a personal relationship with God, ourselves, and others. Healthy relationships point to the need for moral absolutes that come from what Martin Buber called the "I and Thou" relationship.

In his book *Good and Evil*, he gives us a fascinating look into five psalms which deal with the struggle between good and evil (Psalms 1,12,14,73, and 82). He talks about the relation between right doing and wrong doing, between rightdoers and wrongdoers. Dr. Buber shows how a personal encounter with God kept the psalmist (Psalm 73) from sinking into despair because of the evil that surrounded him. He envied the prosperity of the wicked until he entered the sanctuary of God and understood the big picture. Buber says this about the psalmist:

> Then unexpectedly, under the influence of an unprecedented illumination, there takes place in him a change which leads him on the way of God, towards His presence. *With the change of heart there is a change of eye*, and to his new view there is meaning in what for long was meaningless. (italics mine).[6]

A present day testimony of moving from meaningless to meaningful is the life change that took place in Dr. Laura when she saw with new eyes the significance of God's covenant with man. She wrote:

> I had spent my whole life trying to find *meaning*–in being a "good kid," in doing well in school, in being intelligent, in being successful. Though it was all important, it didn't fill some special empty space, where meaning needed to be. Realizing that I had a God–mandated responsibility to represent His character, love, and ethical will was the meaning I'd been searching for.[7]

A change of heart brings about a change of view. Life in general and moral living specifically takes on new meaning and value when seen with new eyes—with spiritual eyes. Living in the presence of a loving, moral God can touch the innate moral chord in our being. Our actions toward others, like John Woolman, will then take on deeper meaning and significance. *As we treat others in the way Christ would treat them, we become like Christ. We bear his image in our character.* This is how our conscience is renewed and reeducated to what true moral values are for daily life.

Our Conscience Can Be Retrained

One of the most positive things to learn about our conscience is that it can be renewed and reeducated. Even though the human conscience is a universal phenomenon, the content poured into the conscience is culturally determined. The "still, small voice" in every human being that approves or disapproves, that praises or rebukes, is innate. It is there by design.

But what it approves or disapproves is shaped by the moral education we receive from our family, religious group, and society. If our conscience has been trained to respond by errors, distortions, or falsehoods, then we can reeducate our conscience to respond to the truth.

The education of the conscience was a major concern for C. S. Lewis when he wrote *The Abolition of Man*. In it he examines the role of education in the moral development of students. He was especially concerned about the moral shift he observed taking place in the classroom. He pointed out that until modern times people believed there were universal values that guided man's decisions.

But now he saw a shift away from these time-tested laws. He feared that education which failed to teach such values would produce what he referred to as "men without chests." We destroy moral absolutes, and yet expect people to do what is right and good, and we become upset when they don't. He believed that when people stepped away from these "Natural Laws" they lost their true humanity. He wrote:

> They are, if you like, men who have sacrificed their own share in traditional humanity in order to devote themselves to the task of deciding what "Humanity" shall henceforth mean. . . . Stepping outside the Tao [his word for universal moral values], they have stepped into the void. Nor are their subjects necessarily unhappy men. They are not men at all: they are artifacts. Man's final conquest has proved to be the abolition of Man.[8]

The renowned psychiatrist Dr. Karl Menninger was also concerned about the lack of moral definition and instruction in society. In his book *Whatever Became of Sin?*, he talked about how we acquire real psychological health through belief in true moral values. He noted that the word "sin" has all but disappeared from use except for some religious groups.

He gave an interesting historical overview on how this happened. He believed that the disappearance of the word "sin" involved a "shift in the allocation of responsibility for evil." Sin is a breaking of God's moral law and he supported the use of the word "sin" as appropriate for acts that are wrong. He writes:

> I believe there is "sin" which is expressed in ways which cannot be subsumed under verbal artifacts such as "crime," "disease," "delinquency," "deviancy." There is immorality; there is unethical behavior; there is wrongdoing. . . . We suspect—indeed we know—that there are still some plain old-fashioned homemade sins lying around which go unmarked. And for most of us, believers and nonbelievers, there is always that still small voice of our conscience.[9]

Dr. Menninger encouraged a return to the classical moral laws that have been time-tested for centuries.

When we begin to reaffirm the important moral values of life and spend less time arguing over trivialities, we will begin to appreciate again the beauty and value of our moral life. It may take time to reeducate our conscience, but the exciting thing about it is it can be done. It can begin today. We can begin to sort through the content of our conscience and keep the moral values we know to be true, good, and healthy even while we let go of the thoughts and ideas that are of no significance. One of the benefits we will gain is a renewed trust in our conscience. We can let our conscience be our guide.

The Value of the Bible in Moral Decision-Making

That God is there and that He has revealed His moral will in the Bible gives us another positive reason for working with our conscience. Moral stability in the ever-changing world of ethical values is possible because God has not been silent.

The conscience does not have its own criteria for moral living. It does not forge the rules by which it measures what is good and what is evil. As Leonard Verduin says:

> It does not spin out of its own innards the yardstick by which it allows or disallows. It assumes that this has been done for it. . . . In the Christian vision the "Fall" of man was basically a venture into autonomy. For the conscience this meant the surrender of the idea of a pre-existent norm and the saddling of conscience with a task for which it is not equipped—the positing of norms.[10]

The conscience was designed to be an innate part of the human personality, and deep within the conscience is the need for healthy moral norms. This explains why human beings are unable and unwilling to live without morals or laws. If they are not provided by God, we will attempt to create our own—or they will be provided for us by a single authority figure, an elite group, or a 51 percent majority vote of the people.

The Bible is a most important resource for finding moral values to guide our choices. The writer of Psalm 119 gives us a positive picture of how this works.

> How can a young man keep his way pure? By living according to your [God's] word. . . . I have hidden your word in my heart that I might not sin against you. . . . Open my eyes that I may see wonderful things in your law. I am a stranger on earth; do not hide your commands from me. . . . Your statutes are my delight; they are my counselors (Psalm 119:9,11,18-19,24).

When we mix true moral values with man-made religious legalisms, cultural legalisms or family legalisms things become confusing. What people are taught about right or wrong, good or evil can become a mixture of true and false norms. Man made do's and don'ts are often given more weight than God-given commands.

And what happen to us? We are left carrying a heavy burden of false guilt. Many people feel more guilt for missing church on a Saturday or Sunday than they do for molesting their children, committing adultery, or cheating another person on a business deal. Paul wrote about this in his letter to the Christians in Rome. He made an important distinction between true moral values and those that were disputable.

> Let us behave decently, as in the daytime, not in orgies and drunkenness, not in sexual immorality and debauchery, not in dissension and jealousy. Rather, clothe yourselves with the Lord Jesus Christ, and do not think about how to gratify the desires of the sinful nature.

> Accept him whose faith is weak, without passing judgment on *disputable matters*. . . . One man considers one day more sacred than another, another man considers every day alike. *Each one should be fully convinced in his own mind.* . . . Why do you look down on your brother? For we will all stand before God's judgment seat. . . . each of us will give an account of himself to God. Therefore let us stop passing judgment on one another. . . . Let us therefore make every

effort to do what leads to peace and to mutual edification. . . . So whatever you believe about these things keep between yourself and God. *Blessed is the man who does not condemn himself by what he approves* (Romans 13:13; 14:1,5,10,12-13,19,22, italics mine).

Human beings will argue over what goes on which list, but God and His Word will always be the ultimate authority. Our conscience can trust this! Our conscience can become a valued friend when it is not working as a measure for self-esteem or for salvation, but as a measure for our respect for God and for life as God designed it. Then when we do something that is truly wrong, there is something we can do about it.

The Therapeutic Value of Confession

One of the most positive ways we can work with our conscience is to rediscover the healing effect of confession. Confession means the recognition of one's true responsibility in acting wrongfully.

As long as we blame, deny, or rationalize our wrongfulness, we remain caught in true moral guilt and our conscience suffers. In his book *The Crises of Psychiatry and Religion*, O. Hobart Mowrer wrote:

> Recovery (constructive change, redemption) is most assuredly attained, not by helping a person reject and rise above his sins, but by helping him *accept them*. This is the paradox which we have not at all understood and which is the very crux of the problem. Just so long as a person lives under the shadow of real, unacknowledged, and unexpiated guilt, he *cannot* (if he has any character at all) "accept himself;" and all *our* efforts to reassure and accept him will avail nothing. He will continue to hate himself and to suffer the inevitable consequences of self-hatred. But the moment he (with or without "assistance") begins to accept his guilt and his sinfulness, the possibility of radical reformation opens up; and with this, the individual may legitimately, though not without pain and effort, pass from deep, pervasive self-rejection and self-torture to a new freedom, of self-respect and peace.[11]

Healing and forgiveness are released when we own our wrongdoing—in saying, "I was wrong. I owe you an apology. I am sorry for what I did." There is Divine forgiveness and healing available to those who can say to God, "God, have mercy on me, a sinner" (Luke 18:13). Clearing our conscience of sin or wrong doing is healing to the soul. It is hard to do and it is humbling, but the healing of the conscience is worth it. What Dr. Mourer said about the return of self-respect and peace was affirmed by King David more than three thousand years ago when he wrote about his own experience:

> Blessed is the man whose sin the Lord does not count against him and in whose spirit is no deceit. When I kept silent, my bones wasted away through my groaning all day long. For day and night your hand was heavy upon me; my strength was sapped as in the heat of summer. Then I acknowledged my sin to you and did not cover up my iniquity. I said, "I confess my transgressions to the Lord"—and you forgave the guilt of my sin. . . . Many are the woes of the wicked, but the Lord's unfailing love surrounds the man who trusts in him (Psalm 32:2-5,10).

Confession and forgiveness cleanse our conscience, heal our spirit, and restore our relationship with God, with ourselves, and with others. Solomon wrote, "He who conceals his sins does not prosper, but whoever confesses and renounces them finds mercy" (Proverbs 28:13).

But the word "confession" becomes too narrow if we only apply it to admitting our sins. If we want to deepen our appreciation for this word, we need to widen its meaning and application. To confess means to acknowledge, admit, or to own. It means to come clean, to plead guilty, to disclose, to profess, or to make known (*The Synonym Finder*).[12]

When we bring the truth (any truth) about ourselves out into the open—whether it is to God or to other people—we are confessing. If we admit openly that we are alcoholics, survivors of sexual abuse, or adult children from alcoholic homes, we are confessing.

Those of you in recovery programs know first-hand the spiritual and psychological healing and transformation that can come from opening up about your secrets.

Being open, honest, and transparent about what we know to be true (*to those who can be trusted*) is to practice confession in the best sense of the word. Our conscience will know this because the truth will set it free.

Do You Have a Healthy or an Unhealthy Conscience?

A healthy conscience is a conscience that judges whether or not a thought, behavior, or attitude is good or bad, right or wrong—but *it does not condemn the person*. A healthy conscience convicts but does not condemn.

A healthy Christian conscience is also a conscience that has been healed from trying to earn self-worth or salvation by works. It has been reeducated with the knowledge of what Jesus Christ has accomplished on our behalf as our Savior and Mediator.

Paul gives us an example of this in the church at Corinth, Greece. As people became Christians, they stopped performing the practices of their particular religion. But their new Christian conscience was sensitive to eating food that had been offered to idols then later sold at the public market. Paul wrote, "Some people are still so accustomed to idols that when they eat such food they think of it as having been sacrificed to an idol and since their conscience is weak, it is defiled" (1 Corinthians 8:7).

Paul goes on to illustrate that it's their lack of knowledge and faith in what Jesus Christ has accomplished for them that makes their conscience over-sensitive to their old way of life—to religious works as a means of obtaining the favor of God. As these new believers gained a deeper understanding and appreciation for the truth that their righteousness was in Christ, their conscience would become both renewed and freed.

A healthy conscience is one that allows a person to be true to their moral convictions and yet show compassion and tolerance for those who believe and act differently.

Religious legalism reflects a weak conscience, not a healthy, freed conscience. Even though the person may be right about a particular concern, their spiritual self-esteem has become attached to the need to always be right. They feel superior to others and condemn them for not conforming to a particular set of beliefs and values. In reality, this reveals both a false sense of self-worth and their immature conscience.

The renowned Christian psychiatrist from Switzerland, Dr Paul Tournier, does a masterful job discussing this in his book *The Strong and the Weak*. He calls it the "reaction of the righteous." Even though these people are sincere, it is difficult to have any real human contact with them because of their judgmentalism. He wrote:

> I do not deny, however, that there is a certain grandeur in the moral austerity which some believers impose upon themselves. They abstain from drink, smoking, gambling, theater-going, and dancing; they impose upon themselves a religious discipline . . . it is a means of reassuring oneself through one's pride in observing a strict discipline, a means of appearing strong and impressing others with one's reputation for virtue. . . . Everybody praises them, everybody thinks them strong; but in the privacy of my study they confess in tears how weak they feel.[13]

This sounds similar to what Paul pointed out to the Colossian people. Many of them must have been trying to appear strong in conscience when in fact they were weak. They were still living under the notion of a works-oriented religion. Paul wanted their conscience to be freed from such a burden. He wrote:

> Since you died with Christ to the basic principles of this world, why, as though you still belong to it, do you submit to its rules: "Do not handle! Do not taste! Do not touch!"? These are all destined to perish with use, because they are based on human commands and regulations. Such regulations indeed have an appearance of wisdom, with their self-imposed worship, their false humility and their harsh treatment of the body. . . . Since, then, you have been raised with Christ, set your hearts on things above, where Christ is seated at the right hand of God. Set your mind on things above . . . put on the new self, which is being renewed in knowledge in the image of its Creator (Colossians 2:20-23, 3:1-2,10).

A person with a healthy and mature conscience is one who holds to true moral values but whose conscience is freed from a works-based self-esteem or salvation. They are freed from the bondage of legalistic religious regulations. They are able to treat themselves and others the way Jesus Christ would have treated them. Jesus displayed love and compassion while at the same time holding firm to his moral convictions.

We can see this in the way Jesus dealt with the Pharisees when they brought to him the woman caught in adultery. They wanted Jesus to condemn her but He turned to them and said, "If any one of you is without sin, let him be the first to throw a stone at her" (John 8:7). To the Pharisees Jesus might have appeared morally weak because he did not condemn the woman. But being confronted with their own life, they left the woman with Jesus.

Jesus was both a kind and strong person with them and with the woman when He said to her, "Then neither do I condemn you. . . . Go now and leave your life of sin" (John 8:11). True moral strength can be assertive and compassionate at the same time. It can take a stand against wrong, yet love the person who did the wrong.

A kind and strong Christian is one who has learned to let their conscience be their guide. This is a person whose moral strength comes from a relationship with Jesus Christ. It is a person who may choose to adhere to a set of religious rules and regulations, but they do not conform to them in a rigid way as an attempt to earn or retain their acceptance with God, or to earn or prove their esteem, or to win browny points with others.

Christ's Ministry as High Priest Frees Our Conscience

Another important Christian belief that can help us work with our conscience in a positive way is seeing what Jesus Christ is doing for us. Most of us miss the significance of this truth because we are too busy condemning ourselves for not being good enough. Self-condemnation reflects a weak and unhealthy conscience.

When we take on the task of condemning ourselves, we are taking on a job that even Jesus Christ is not willing to do at this time. The New Testament points to the fact that after Jesus' death, burial, and resurrection, He ascended into heaven and now stands before God as our Intercessor and High Priest. A look at a few Bible verses may help us see with new eyes how the burden of our conscience can be lifted if we can get a better picture of what Jesus Christ is doing on our behalf.

Who is he that condemns? Christ Jesus, who died—more than that, who was raised to life—is at the right hand of God and is also interceding for us (Romans 8:34).

My dear children, I write this to you so that you will not sin. But if anybody does sin, we have one who speaks to the Father in our defense—Jesus Christ, the Righteous One. He is the atoning sacrifice for our sins, and not only for ours but also for the sins of the whole world (1 John 2:1-2).

Therefore, since we have a great high priest who has gone through the heavens, Jesus the Son of God, let us hold firmly to the faith we profess. For we do not have a high priest who is unable to sympathize with our weaknesses, but we have one who has been tempted in every way, just as we are—yet was without sin. Let us then approach the throne of grace with confidence, so that we may receive mercy and find grace to help us in our time of need (Hebrews 4:14-16).

Jesus lives forever, he has a permanent priesthood. Therefore, he is able to save completely those who come to God through him, because he always lives to intercede for them. Such a high priest meets our needs—one who is holy, blameless, pure, set apart from sinners, exalted above the heavens (Hebrews 7:24-26).

Whether we believe in Jesus or not, one of the major reasons our conscience condemns us is because we think that by our own religious efforts, we can make ourselves more perfect, more acceptable to God.

I have seen this in every religion I have studied. Trying to clear our conscience by not doing wrong or by trying always to do right will ultimately fail. Our conscience will condemn us when our efforts fail or fall short of the standards and expectations we think God demands. The writer of Hebrews made it clear that practicing "external regulations" could never be enough to "clear the conscience of the worshiper" (Hebrews 9:9).

A sensitive person who feels the need to be perfect is going to be in bondage to the condemnations of their conscience. Life becomes guilt-ridden and gradually the joy of life is worn away by the constant effort to try to "measure up." The conscience will become the master of the person; guilt and self-condemnation become the norm. Self-hate and depression cannot be far behind. Martin Luther described it best when he said, "Though I lived as a monk without reproach, I felt that I was a sinner before God with an extremely disturbed conscience."[14]

What can free our conscience from the tyranny of condemnation? The answer is found in realizing what Jesus Christ is doing as our High Priest. When He entered heaven, He offered himself as a payment (sacrifice) for sin once for all, for all time, for all people, to take away the guilt of sin. A person who knows in his heart that Jesus Christ has settled the problem of guilt for them for all time is truly free from a condemning conscience. This is how the writer of Hebrews stated it:

> Because Jesus lives forever, he has a permanent priesthood. Therefore he is able to save completely those who come to God through him, because he always lives to intercede for them. . . . When Christ came as high priest . . . he entered the Most Holy Place once for all by his own blood, having obtained eternal redemption. . . . How much more, then, will the blood of Christ, who through the eternal Spirit offered himself unblemished to God, *cleanse our consciences from acts that lead to death, so that we may serve a living God!* . . . since we have a great priest over the house of God, let us draw near to God with a sincere heart in full assurance of faith, having our hearts sprinkled to cleanse us from a guilty conscience (Hebrews 7:4-25, 9:11-12,14, 10:21-22, italics mine).

Our worth is secure in our being created in God's image. Our righteousness is complete in being in Christ. Most of us have never grasped the significance of these two truths. Imagine the scope of it—that Jesus Christ died for every human being that has ever lived or will live, to free us from the guilt of every sin that has ever been or ever will be committed, so that we can be freed from a guilty conscience to love and serve a living God. And He did this because He believes we are worth it.

In the light of ten thousand years of human history, what crimes, sins, or failures have you committed that would not be already covered by Jesus? Asked another way, what memories in your conscience keep you in bondage to self-condemnation and self-hate? What wrongs and sins have been committed by you or by another person against you that are so bad they would go beyond what Christ accomplished on your behalf?

If this picture ever captures our imagination, it would transform our lives. It would free us from a condemning, guilty conscience to live life the way God desires it to be—fully human and truly Christian. This can happen when the truth of the Christian world view touches the human conscience at our deepest need. This gives us the freedom to learn to trust and follow our conscience in life-giving ways. God gave it to us for a reason. Let's learn to work with it for the benefit of ourselves and others. If this has not happened, it may be due to having too small a view of God. We will look into this in the next chapter.

Suggested Reading

1. Tournier, Paul. *The Strong and the Weak*. Westminster Press, 1963.
2. Smedes, Lewis. *Forgive and Forget: Healing the Hurts We Don't Deserve*. Harper and Row Publishers, 1984.
3. Exodus 20:1-17; Psalm 34:14; 97:10; 106:3; Proverbs 8:13; 14:31; Isaiah 48:17-18; Amos 5:14-15; Acts 23:1; 24:16; Romans 16:19b; 1 Corinthians 4:4; Hebrews 5:14.

BECOME SPIRITUALLY AWARE

7

6

5

8

4

1

3

2

·HUMAN BEING·
·IMAGEBEARER·
·PERSON·

Man has gods, and he renders them homage. He has *religion*. Whatever may be said of the dividing-line between him and the other living creatures known to us, this at any rate is his special preserve; it has been characteristic of him from his earliest beginnings, and seems to be an inseparable part of his existence. . . . He can no more rid himself of this dimension of his existence than he can rid himself of the dimensions of time: past, present, and future.

Emil Brunner, *Man in Revolt* [1]

───────── ❧ ─────────

God is love. This means: . . . there is someone who faces us as benevolent and absolutely reliable: . . . not an empty, unechoing universe, not a merely silent infinite, . . . still less an anonymous interpersonal something . . . [God is] one who speaks to us and to whom we can speak. And in being addressed by this one, man learns the dignity of his own person.

Hans Küng, *Does God Exist* [2]

───────── ❧ ─────────

Now there are many ways in which we experience the divine likeness within us more specifically than we do with the three faculties, intellect, will and memory. . . . [Man] looks to God and to the words of God, thus signifying that by nature he is . . . far more like God . . . which undoubtedly derives from the fact that he is created in the divine image.

Zwingli, 1484-1531 A.D. [3]

CHAPTER 23

Human Beings:
The God Seekers

PERMISSION

In 1953, when I finished eighth grade, our family went through a personal tragedy that dramatically changed the course of our lives. On the evening of July 4, my Dad was involved in a terrible single-car accident. He had sustained so many broken bones and internal injuries he should not have survived.

While in the hospital, Dad had plenty of time to think. He decided that if he had to live in this lousy world he mighty as well figure out "what the hell it was all about." As he reflected on his life, he remembered a simple Bible verse he had learned in Catholic catechism as a boy—"God is Love" (1 John 4:16).

God began to bring loving people into our lives to help us spiritually, physically, and financially. One of those people was a big, six-foot-three Swede who was the minister of the Valley Bible Center in Cascade, Idaho. Ole Olson—himself crippled with severe arthritis—put his big arms around our family (Mom and Dad were only five-foot-three) and he *loved* all five of us into the Christian Faith.

Cascade had a population of just over a thousand people and Dad was well known for being a hard-working, hard-drinking, hard-fighting man. He had a big heart but he was also as tough as raw-hide and nobody tangled with him. So when he and Mom began to go to church the news spread through the valley like wild fire. Foggy Day had become a Christian.

Dad studied the Bible and the Christian faith with the same fervor he displayed in his partying days. Eventually, he began to preach at some of the little churches in the area and God opened up a new way of life for all of us as we grew in our understanding of the Christian faith.

In 1953 when I became a Christian as a freshman in high school, my world was really small. Thirteen years later, I had traveled all the way around the world and had visited some of the great religious centers both ancient and modern. I visited the great Protestant centers of northern Europe, the center of the Roman Catholic world at the Vatican in Rome, the ancient Greek center for religion on Mars Hill, and the Parthenon in Athens.

I visited the famous Muslim Mosque of Omar in Istanbul, Turkey, the ancient temples of Balbec in the Bacca Valley in Lebanon, and the beautiful Dome of the Rock mosque in Jerusalem, one of the Muslims' most holy places.

I stood with the Jews in prayer at the Wailing Wall, the only remaining part of the magnificent temple that King Solomon built in Jerusalem. I walked the courtyards of the Bahai Temple in Haifa and visited the historical sites of the Old Testament and of the Christian faith where Jesus was born, lived, died, was buried, and was resurrected.

And what amazing truth was I to gain from all this? At first, I experienced a lot of pain and confusion about my spiritual views of life. The world was so big, so diverse! Religion and all its various demands and practices were everywhere, sometimes helping, sometimes harming the people who embraced them.

Meeting some wonderful people who were "committed" atheists and seeing how successful their lives appeared to be only added to the confusion. All these religions, all these questions, all these contradictions pressed in upon me, forcing me to think, to question, to reevaluate, and to decide. It was like the old wine skin of my mind could not hold the new wine of my thoughts and questions and I felt like the wine skins might burst. What would I believe in; what could I commit my life to in regards to a spiritual view of the world.

Human Beings Are Innately Spiritual Beings

One of the most important conclusions I came to was that we human beings are innately religious. There is something deep inside us that makes us seek out and develop some kind of religious faith. Every culture until modern times has had some kind of a system of religious beliefs that included some concept of God or gods, a creation story, a concept of the origin of human life, the origin of evil, etc.

Only in modern times have humans experimented with cultural atheism such as seen in atheistic humanism or the political atheism of communism (as seen in the former communist countries of Europe and in present day China).

The human spirit cannot live long without some kind of spiritual perspective. Why? Because there is something innate in human beings that makes us God-conscious. That we are spiritual beings is one of the most distinctive characteristics of our being human. It is a faculty not found in any other part of creation.

Animals don't concern themselves with religious beliefs. They do not think about God, sin, worship, life after death, heaven or hell, salvation, or repentance. Humans do.

No one was probably more widely read or listened to on the subject of comparative religions, than was Joseph Campbell. His books *The Masks of God* and *Myths to Live By* provide rich reading for anyone wanting to grasp a sense of the innate spirituality of human beings. To summarize this amazing fact, he wrote:

> Man, apparently, cannot maintain himself in the universe without belief in some arrangement of the general inheritance of myth [his word for religious beliefs]. In fact, the fullness of his life would even seem to stand in a direct ratio to the depth and range not of his rational thought but of his local mythology.[4]

Our religious or spiritual view of the world is going to have a deep influence on the way we live. This same theme is clearly expressed by A.W. Tozer in his book *The Knowledge of the Holy*. He specifically speaks about how our concept of God shapes our lives and our cultures. He said;

> What comes into our minds when we think about God is the most important thing about us. The history of mankind will probably show that no people has ever risen above its religion, and man's spiritual history will positively demonstrate that no religion has ever been greater than its idea of God. Worship is pure or base as the worshiper entertains high or low thoughts of God. For this reason the gravest question before the Church is always God Himself, and the most portentous fact about any man is not what he at a given time may say or do, but what he in his *deep heart* conceives God to be like. *We tend by a secret law of the soul to move toward our mental image of God* (italics mine).[5]

Human beings are spiritual beings. To narrow this subject, I want us to deal with two main topics: How did we humans acquire this innate characteristic to be spiritual creatures? And second, how do our ideas and feelings about God relate to spiritual and psychological health?

Finding Spiritual Meaning for Life on This Planet

In an earlier chapter we talked about the fun we could have if we used a time machine to visit anywhere in time we wanted. Imagine with me again that we could enter such a machine and decided to take a trip back to the beginning of time. We are on a trip to learn about the origin of man—the beginning of human history. As we travel back through the centuries, we eventually reach the time when human life comes into being. Imagine that we stop the machine at the edge of time. We get out and look out into space before human life began—and we learn that NOTHING is there.

After staying for a few moments, we reverse the time machine and run forward to the very end of time, when the last human being dies and the last memory of human life on this planet dies with them. Imagine that we stop the machine, get out and look out into space and again learn that NOTHING is there.

How would you imagine you would feel about human life in general and your personal life specifically? The feelings most often expressed by others are these:

- "Life would be meaningless."
- "Life would feel empty and cold."
- "I would feel so utterly alone and lonely."
- "I would feel afraid and powerless because chance and fate would rule life."
- "I would feel relieved because I would not have to deal with God as I perceive Him to be.
- "Life would have no ultimate purpose because the end is nothingness."

J. B. Phillips gives us a good description of his thinking about this view of life in his book *God Our Contemporary*. He points out some of the consequences of this perspective. He wrote:

What really puzzles me is the attitude of mind adopted by the humanist who denies the existence of God. He claims that his own life has a purpose, and that other people's lives have their various purposes, but he emphatically denies that there is any purpose in the whole. Moreover, since he also denies any further existence beyond that of this planet, there can be no sense whatever of ultimate purpose of any kind. For the whole of man's struggles, discoveries, achievements, insights and aspirations ends automatically when this little planet becomes either too hot or too cold to support human life. I honestly find it impossible to believe that men who are otherwise quite intelligent can seriously think, as they appear to do, that the end of the whole vast human experiment is sheer nothingness.[6]

Temporarily setting aside these feelings, let's repeat the same trip. Imagine that we get into our time machine again and go back through the centuries to arrive at the beginning of time. We stop, get out and look out into space—and we see that GOD IS THERE AND HE IS GOOD! We wait for a few moments and then reverse the machine and travel forward to the end of time, when the last person dies. We stop and get out and look out into space—and find that GOD IS THERE AND HE IS GOOD! How would you imagine you would feel differently about life? Here is what others have said:

- "I would feel there is a purpose for my life and for everyone's life."
- "I would feel that life has meaning and value."
- "Life would be sacred."
- "I would feel like Someone is there and cares about what happens to me and what happens to others on this earth."
- "I would not feel so totally alone. I would know that Someone is always there with me."
- "I would feel more secure, more like I belong here rather than it doesn't make any difference anyway."

There is something at the core of our being that wants a reasonable answer for the meaning and purpose of life. I believe this longing is the evidence of God's image in each of us when God created us to be spiritually aware creatures. Viktor Frankl sees the spiritual nature of man as one of the things that make us human and not animal. In his book *The Doctor and the Soul*, he writes:

Man lives in three dimensions: the somatic, the mental, and the spiritual. The spiritual dimension cannot be ignored, for it is what makes us human. . . . Three factors characterize human existence as such: man's spirituality, his freedom, his responsibility. The spirituality of man is a thing-in-itself. It cannot be explained by something not spiritual; it is irreducible.[7]

Our ability to be spiritually aware is part of what makes us human, makes us unique in this world. This unique characteristic is there by design and finds its greatest fulfillment when connected to the Creator who designed us. Believing that God is there and that He created us in His likeness gives intrinsic worth to human life. This is how J. B. Phillips expressed it:

The intrinsic value of the individual, his dignity and his freedom become meaningful to us only when we see him standing in the same relationship to the Creator as we do ourselves. . . . I believe the time may come when it will seem ludicrous for men to discover layer after layer of truth which bears all the marks of pattern and design, and then categorically to declare that there is no Designer![8]

By looking objectively at the life-giving results that spring from faith in the spiritual reality of God, we can reasonably move forward in a step of faith in our own walk with God. We can affirm our own worth and value as an Imagebearer of God just as we can affirm the worth of others. Our worth rests in who we are rather that what we do.

What Is the Origin of Man's Religious Sentiment?

Why are human beings so religious? Why are they God-seekers? What is the origin of the urge that motivates us to display our spiritual capacity in all its religious forms? Read any book on the origin of our need for a religious faith and you will find all kinds of theories to explain it. If human beings are spiritual beings by chance then all the theories point to us as the creators of the gods. These are what Martin Buber calls "intra-psychic" processes and they explain how man created the gods or God in our own image based on psychological or social fears and needs. Gordon Allport gives us a concise description of this in his book *The Individual and His Religion.*

> Man's life, *bracketed between two oblivions,* is haunted by fear—of enemies, of nature, of sickness, poverty, ostracism; most of all of death, for of all creatures on earth man alone knows that he will die. Do we invoke the protection of an amulet, do we trust ourselves to the everlasting arms, do we discipline ourselves to seek Nirvana and so escape the threats that hover over us? To demand some form of reassurance is a spontaneous response to insecurity (italics mine).[9]

Many of the theories of the origin of our God-seeking focus on the psychological responses to life's needs and demands because human life is "bracketed between two oblivions." In his book *The Future of an Illusion,*[10] Freud taught that the origin of religion was found in man's helplessness to deal with the external forces of nature and the instinctive forces of sex and aggression found within. To control the emotions of fear, sex, and anger, man eventually creates gods or a god, projects them "out there" and then relates to them "as if" they existed. This is why belief in God is an illusion because God does not exist.

Carl Jung is another well-known writer widely-read on the subject of spiritual awareness. He is positive and affirming about the importance of religion in life. But if we look only at what he says about God concept, we would discover that God exists only as "the God within" and does not exist independent of our mind.[11]

He sees God as an archetype, formed in mankind's primordial past and resided only in man's unconscious mind. Eventually, it became conscious and manifested itself in all the various religious forms we see in the world. Even though he has written some of the most interesting material on the spiritual nature of man, the end result is the same—as an archetype, God does not exist outside one's own inner self.

Erich Fromm also makes a strong affirmation for the spiritual awareness of humankind. He believed that there was "no one without a religious need, a need to have a frame of orientation and an object of devotion." He believed that the need for a religious faith was an intrinsic part of what makes us human. He expressed it this way:

> Because the need for a system of orientation and devotion is an intrinsic part of human existence we can understand the intensity of this need. . . . The question is not religion or not but which kind of religion, whether it is one furthering man's development, the unfolding of his specifically human powers, or one paralyzing them.[12]

Like others mentioned earlier, Dr. Fromm believes man's spiritual awareness is "an intrinsic part of human existence", but he says nothing about how we acquired this unique gift. In fact, his position leads us to conclude that it's the result of chance. Like many others, he talks about "God" but does not believe God exists in reality outside the human mind. He made this point quite clear in his book *You Shall Be as Gods*.

> I believe that the concept of God was a historically conditioned expression of an inner experience. I can understand what the Bible or genuinely religious persons mean when they talk about God, but I do not share their thought concept; I believe that the concept "God" was conditioned by the presence of a socio-political structure in which tribal chiefs or kings have supreme power. . . . "God" is one of many different poetic expressions of the highest value of humanism, not a reality in itself. . . . If I could define my position approximately, I would call it that of a nontheistic mysticism.[13]

His support for the important feature of man's sense of spiritual awareness is positive and clear. But what he calls "Nontheistic mysticism," I would call atheistic spirituality. J. B. Phillips calls it "a de-personalized Something." In his remarkable little book *Your God Is Too Small*, he wrote:

> There are those who would make this "Something" the God of the future. Building up a mental concept from known values like

Goodness, Truth, and Beauty, they would have us hold in our minds and worship in our hearts the Source of Supreme Values. Such a God is not a Person in any sense, and though such an idea seems to satisfy some of the most intellectual of our time it does not, and probably will never, satisfy the ordinary man. . . . To worship, to love, and to serve, implies for most of us a Person with whom we can establish some personal relationship, although one cannot help pointing out that one great attraction of a non-personal God is that no claim can be made upon us! He (or It) may be used as much or as little as we like![14]

Phillips has brought out some important thoughts about the need for God to be a Person. Let's see what some others have to say about it.

Spiritual Awareness Is by Design

In contrast to those who believe that God is non-personal and exists only in our mind, there are those who believe God exists independent of what we think or don't think about him. God is seen as a Person and has a personal existence totally separate from us. A fascinating book that discusses this difference is the *Eclipse of God* by Martin Buber. To read his book is to hear a clear voice confirming the necessity and importance of a personal God who is there.

Like an eclipse of the sun, he shows how the view of God as existing independent of our mind has been temporarily blocked out by those who would have us believe that God exists only as a product of our imagination. But in time these views of God—the ones Pascal called "the God of the Philosophers" (and I would also call the God of many psychologists)—will pass by. Then God, the Great I AM—the God of Abraham, Isaac, Jacob, and Jesus—will shine in all His glory. But what a price we will have paid for this temporary blackout! Martin Buber expressed it this way:

Eclipse of the light of heaven, eclipse of God—such indeed is the character of the historic hour though which the world is passing. . . . An eclipse of the sun is something that occurs between the sun and our eyes, not in the sun itself. . . . [So] Man may even do away with the name "god,". . . yet He who is denoted by the name lives in the light of His eternity. But we, "the slayers," remain dwellers in darkness, consigned to death.[15]

Dr. Buber believed that all human-to-human relationships found their meaning and significance in the human-to-God relationship—the I and Thou relationship. A relationship with God is basic to true humanity.

God is not just a principle, a metaphor, "a poetic expression for the highest value of humanism." God is not an impersonal "force," or "universal cosmic consciousness." God is a Person, a Being that engages us in a personal relationship with him as a person. This distinction is essential if we are to come to a deeper appreciation of the worth of human life (self-esteem) and the value of interpersonal relations. It is also essential if we are to become truly human and truly Christian. In his book, *I And Thou*, Dr. Buber wrote:

> The description of God as a Person is indispensable for everyone who like myself means by "God" . . . him who—whatever else he may be—enters into a direct relation with us men in creative, revealing and redeeming acts, and thus makes it possible for us to enter into a direct relation with him. . . . As a Person God gives personal life, he makes us as persons become capable of meeting with him and with one another.[16]

This move from an impersonal idea about God to God as Person helps us be clear in our understanding and conversation about what we mean when we use the word "God." This means there is a reality about God that exists independent of ourselves and is not changed by our own inventions and inaccurate perceptions of Him. This diagram illustrates this important difference.

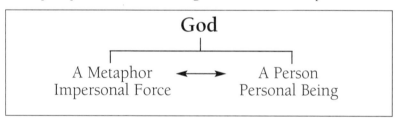

The Bible affirms this personal nature of God when it says, "I the Lord do not change. . . . Return to me and I will return to you" (Malachi 3:6-7), and again, "Jesus Christ is the same yesterday and today and forever" (Hebrews 13:8).

In his travels, the apostle Paul noted how religious humans were. While waiting for his friends Silas and Timothy to join him in Athens, he had walked around the city and noted all the religious centers around Mars Hill. He talked with people about the good news of Jesus and his resurrection. A group of Epicurean and Stoic philosophers heard Paul and brought him to a meeting of the Areopagus to have him explain what he was teaching. Luke, a physician traveling with Paul, wrote about what Paul said to those who came:

> Paul then stood up in the meeting of the Areopagus and said: "Men of Athens! I see that in every way you are very religious. For as I

walked around and looked carefully at your objects of worship, I even found an alter with this inscription: TO AN UNKNOWN GOD. Now what you worship as something unknown I am going to proclaim to you.

The God who made the world and everything in it is the Lord of heaven and earth and does not live in temples built by hands. And he is not served by human hands, as if he needed anything, because he himself gives all men life and breath and everything else. From one man he made every nation of men, that they should inhabit the whole earth, and he determined the times set for them and the exact places where they should live. God did this so that men would seek him and perhaps reach out for him and find him, though he is not far from each one of us. For in him we live and move and have our being. As some of your own poets have said, 'We are his offspring.'

Therefore, since we are God's offspring, we should not think that the divine being is like gold or silver or stone—an image made by man's design and skill. In the past God overlooked such ignorance, but now he commands all people everywhere to repent. For he has set a day when he will judge the world with justice by the man he has appointed. He has given proof of this to all men by raising him from the dead" (Acts 18:22-31).

Paul was so clear in his statement. The idea of God and our sense of spiritual awareness finds its origin in God who created us as spiritual beings—"spiritual offspring". This unique human characteristic is not the result of cosmic chance. Humans are spiritual beings by design. God created us in His image to be able to have an awareness of Him and to have the personality skills—such as reason, self-awareness, and speech—necessary to have a relationship with Him. This is why Augustine said, "You have made us for yourself, and our hearts are restless until they can find peace in you."[17] Pascal is credited with having said:

There is a God-shaped vacuum in the heart of every man that can not be satisfied by any created thing except by God himself known through the person of Jesus Christ.

God as Creator has made a God-shaped place in the heart of every human being and there is something deep inside of us that knows this. We may deny it, ignore it, fight it, even reject it, but it is there.

It may be cluttered up with all kinds of distorted ideas and mixed feelings about who God is and what He expects from us, but underneath it all we know—we know that He is there and we know we need Him. This can easily be seen when people are faced with a major crises. We turn to God in prayer during such times, like what happened on September 11, 2001. In his book *Your God Is too Small,*   J. B. Phillips summarizes it so well.

> No one is ever really at ease in facing what we call "life" and "death" without a religious faith. The trouble with many people today is that they have not found a God big enough for modern needs. While their experience of life has grown in a score of directions, and their mental horizons have been expanded to the point of bewilderment by world events and by scientific discoveries, their ideas of God have remained largely static. It is obviously impossible for an adult to worship the conception of God that exists in the mind of a child of Sunday-school age, unless he is prepared to deny his own experience of life. . . . Many men and women today are living, often with inner dissatisfaction, without any faith in God at all. This is not because they are particularly wicked or selfish or, as the old-fashioned would say, "godless," but because they have not found with their adult minds a God big enough to "account for" life, big enough to "fit in with" the new scientific age, big enough to command their highest admiration and respect, and consequently their willing cooperation.[18]

His book is an attempt to help us recognize our inadequate impressions of God which "linger unconsciously in many minds" and to help us develop a true and healthy sense of who God is.

Will the Real God Please Stand Up!

Hannah Whitall Smith also looked into how inadequate views of God have affected our personal lives. While still a new Christian, she spoke with an agnostic who wondered why people who were unhappy with God were at the same time not willing to get rid of Him. She said it was like having a headache. We don't want to get rid of our head, but we would like to stop the pain.

Many of us have one view of God in our head and another view in our heart. It is our feeling view of God that gives many of us a *heartache*. We think of God as loving, but we feel God to be disapproving and angry. We think of God as forgiving, but we feel him as harsh, punitive, and demanding. Hannah Smith wrote a most descriptive picture of this painful dilemma in her book *The God Who Is Enough*:

> It is our ignorance of God that does it all. Because we do not know Him, we naturally get all sorts of wrong ideas about Him. We think

He is an angry Judge who is on the watch for our slightest faults, or a harsh Taskmaster determined to exact from us the uttermost service, or a self-absorbed Deity demanding His full measure of honor and glory, or a far-off Sovereign concerned only with His own affairs and indifferent to our welfare. Who can wonder that such a God can neither be loved nor trusted? And who could expect Christians, with such ideas concerning Him, to be anything but full of discomfort and misery?[19]

For years, I have been interested in learning about people's impressions of God. I did my doctoral dissertation on how our concept of God relates to mental health.[20] One of the things I observed was that there is often a discrepancy between the concept of God we have in our head and the one we have in our heart. What we think about God can be quite different from what we feel about God.

People find it hard to admit the presence of this discrepancy. It can be embarrassing and painful to face the truth about how we feel toward God or how we think God feels towards us. Fear and guilt cause us to turn away from what we know to be true. If our heart sees God as unsafe, impulsive, judgmental or punitive, we try to deny what we sense is there, but it won't work. We will be unhappy people, unhappy Christians. Hannah Smith gave us a good example of how people's distorted view of God can effect them emotionally to the point they find no joy in knowing God. The following diagram shows this difference.

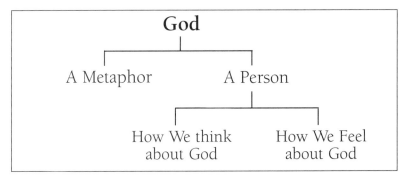

And how does this discrepancy develop? At the risk of being simplistic, we generally develop our thinking view of God from what we are taught about God in Sunday school, church, from Bible reading, from listening to sermons or conversations, and from reading books.

Our feeling view of God—how we feel toward Him and how we *think* He feels toward us—develops out of our personal relationships and experiences with one another. How we treat one another sets up the emotional climate of a person-to-person relationship. For example, I could teach you that God is love and that He loves you, but if I mistreat you, you are more likely to think negatively about God because I am supposed to be representing Him. How I treat you is going to leave more of a lasting impression on your life than what I might tell you. Actions can speak louder than words.

Our feeling impression of God is also shaped by how we *interpret* what happens to us in life. When bad things happen to us, many of us emotionally see God as uncaring, indifferent, mean, or outright punishing. This is why I have come to believe there are no intellectual atheists (this does not mean they are not highly intelligent because most of them are). They are emotional atheists. Some kind of tragedy, hardship or rigid religious training has caused them to develop an impression of God that is so bad, so sick, so unapproachable, so inaccurate, that it's easier not to believe in any God at all than to try to have faith in a monster-god.

Everyone in the world has a concept of God, even atheists. It's just that they can't possibly believe in the kind of God they envision. The move to Atheism is then a short step. Let me tell you about a person who did just that.

One Man's Journey from Atheism to Christianity

The book *Surprised by Joy* is the story of the Christian conversion of the renowned atheist and Cambridge professor C. S. Lewis. I want to tell his story because many of us are familiar with his writings, *Chronicles of Narnia*, or *Mere Christianity*, and *The ScrewTape Letters*. But even more importantly, it shows how certain impressions of God can move a person away from God to embrace atheism.

It's also important because it shows the journey back to a *faith in a healthy view of God*. It helps us see why the Christian life is not a blind, ignorant leap of faith into religion, but rather a reasonable step of faith into a personal relationship with God and with Jesus Christ. It rests upon an intelligent search for truth and the willingness to surrender to the truth when it appears. Hannah Whitall Smith said it best when she wrote:

> I can assert boldly, and without fear of contradiction, that it is impossible for anyone who really knows God to have such uncomfortable thoughts about Him. . . . The kind of knowing I mean is just the plain matter-of-fact knowledge of God's nature and character that comes to us by believing what is revealed to us in the Bible concerning Him.[20]

No one is called upon to commit intellectual suicide to become a Christian or to live the Christian life. Our hearts and our minds were designed to work in harmony with our spiritual awareness. There is no greater need for this harmony than in a person's understanding of their impressions of God.

C. S. Lewis was a young child when his mother died of cancer. He wrote, "With my mother's death all settled happiness, all that was tranquil and reliable, disappeared from my life. There was to be much fun, many pleasures, many stabs at Joy; but no more of the old security. It was sea and islands now; the great continent had sunk like Atlantis."[21]

Before her death the child Lewis believed that prayers offered in faith to God would be granted. He tried by "will power" to hold a firm belief that his prayers for his mother's recovery would be successful. When she died, the shock waves of grief began to distort his impression of God even more than they already were. He described what he thought about God before her death.

> I had approached God, or my idea of God, without love, without awe, even without fear. He was, in my mental picture of this miracle to appear neither as Savior nor as Judge, but merely as a magician; and when He had done what was required of Him I supposed He would simply—well, go away.

> It never crossed my mind that the tremendous contact which I solicited should have any consequences beyond restoring the status quo.[22]

As time passed after her death and through a series of steps, Lewis grew anxious to rid himself of his Christian religion. He was tired of "the ludicrous burden of fake duties." This, combined with rising doubts about religion and a deeply ingrained pessimism about the universe, led Lewis to embrace atheism. "And so, little by little, with fluctuations which I cannot now trace, I became an apostate, dropping my faith with no sense of loss but with the greatest relief."[23]

As adolescence passed, Lewis began to live his life "like so many Atheists and Antitheists, in a whirl of contradictions. I maintained that God did not exist. I was also very angry with God for not existing. I was equally angry with Him for creating the world."[24]

Atheism and pessimism were the most characteristic features of Lewis's world view. He continued to gather fresh ammunition for the defense of the position he had chosen. The materialistic universe became his cathedral. On one side, it freed him from all the doubts, confusions, and contradictions he found in religion.

But on the negative side, Lewis felt he had to accept the logical consequences of his position. He wrote:

One had to look out on a *meaningless dance of atoms* . . . [to] realize that all the apparent beauty was a subjective phosphorescence, and to relegate everything one valued to the world of mirage. That price I tried loyally to pay (italics mine).[25]

As Lewis continued to read, he was shaken by the thought that "perhaps" there was, after all, "something else" behind the world and "perhaps it had nothing to do with Christian Theology." At that moment, Lewis says, "a drop of disturbing doubt fell into my materialism."[26]

Lewis now found himself in an awkward position. He wanted to try to have it both ways: "To get the comforts both of a materialist and of a spiritual philosophy without the rigors of either."[27] The experiences of his life had taught him many things, and once again he was moving into a new area of search—and he was ready. This is how he described it.

What I like about experience is that it is such an honest thing. You may take any number of wrong turnings; but keep your eyes open and you will not be allowed to go very far before the warning signs appear. You may have deceived yourself, but experience is not trying to deceive you. The universe rings true whenever you fairly test it.[28]

And this is what Lewis did. In his pursuit of knowledge, he first read a volume of Chesterton's essays. Lewis reported, "I did not know what I was letting myself in for. A young man who wishes to remain a sound Atheist cannot be too careful of his reading."[29]

While teaching English and Philosophy at Oxford University, Lewis continued to read extensively. Books, people, and hours of discussions moved and shaped his reasoning. As he read Christian authors, he could ease his mind by referring to their material as "the Christian Myth." But the integrity of his mind would not allow it to rest. All over the chessboard of life Lewis said he saw his pieces in the most disadvantageous positions. God was beginning to make his final moves.

Two books and one conversation finally jolted Lewis from the safety of his failing materialistic philosophy. He read Alexander's *Space Time and Deity* and Chesterton's *Everlasting Man*. Also in 1926 the most hardheaded atheist Lewis had ever known remarked that "the evidence for the historicity of the Gospels was really surprisingly good." Lewis wrote:

The odd thing was that before God closed in on me I was in fact offered what now appears a moment of wholly free choice. . . . Without words and (I think) almost without images, a fact about myself was somehow presented to me. I became aware that I was holding something at bay, or shutting something out. Or, if you like, that I was wearing some stiff clothing, like corsets, or even a suit of armor, as if I were a lobster. I felt myself being, there and then, given a free choice. I could open the door or keep it shut; I could unbuckle the armor or keep it on.

Neither choice was presented as a duty; no threat or promise was attached to either, though I knew that to open the door or to take off the corset meant the incalculable. The choice appeared to be momentous but it was also strangely unemotional. I was moved by no desire or fears. In a sense I was not moved by anything. I chose to open, to unbuckle, to loosen the rein.[30]

Lewis describes his choice to open his spirit (his heart) and to accept God as the Creator of life in this manner.

You must picture me alone in that room in Magdalen, night after night, feeling, whenever my mind lifted even for a second from my work, the steady, unrelenting approach of Him whom I so earnestly desired not to meet.

That which I greatly feared had at last come upon me. In the Trinity Term in 1929 I gave in, and admitted that God was God, and knelt and prayed; perhaps, that night, the most dejected and reluctant convert in all England. I did not then see what is now the most shining and obvious thing; *the Divine humility which will accept a convert even on such terms.* The Prodigal Son at least walked home on his own feet. *But who can duly adore that Love which will open the high gates to a prodigal who is brought in kicking, struggling, resentful and darting his eyes in every direction for a chance of escape?* . . . The hardness of God is kinder than the softness of men, and His compulsion is our liberation (italics mine).[31]

Lewis does not give us much detail about his transition from mere Theism to Christianity, but certain steps played an important part. Believing in God and praying to Him took Lewis out of his self-preoccupation. He could now relate to God as a sovereign Being.

Soon afterward, he started attending a church on Sunday and a college chapel on weekdays—not because he believed in Christ or Christianity yet, but he thought "one ought to 'fly one's flag' by some unmistakable overt sign." This helped him move in the Christian direction because he began to think about the historical claims of Christ as found in the Gospels.

The God he had come to acknowledge was a righteous God; and if Jesus were the incarnation of the Person of God, then "here and here only in all time the myth must have become fact; the Word, flesh; God, man. This is not a 'religion,' nor 'a philosophy.' It is the summing up and actuality of them all."[32] Every step Lewis had taken to a belief in God brought him a step closer to a belief in Jesus Christ. He wrote:

> To accept the Incarnation was a further step in the same direction. It brings God nearer, or near in a new way. . . . I know very well when, but hardly how, the final step was taken. I was driven to Whipsnade one sunny morning. When we set out I did not believe that Jesus Christ is the Son of God, and when we reached the zoo I did.[33]

The one thing we can be confident of is that C. S. Lewis would have only taken this step of faith in accepting Jesus Christ as the incarnation of God if there were rational integrity and truth in doing so.

Who Do You Think Jesus Christ Is?

Once when Jesus was with His disciples, He asked them who did the people think He was. They answered, "Some say John the Baptist; others say Elijah; and still others, Jeremiah or one of the prophets." Then Jesus asked them, "Who do you say I am?" Peter answered, "You are the Christ, the Son of the living God" (Matthew 16:13-16).

Many people like to think of Jesus as a great moral teacher or as only another great prophet of God, or as the ideal model for a fully self-actualized human being, or as a person who had achieved a higher consciousness of God, or as one of the great figures of human history.

While all these are true, Jesus did not claim to be any of them. He claimed to be God (John 10:33-38). He claimed to be the Messiah (John 4:25-26) and a King (John 18:37). He claimed to be the light of the world (John 8:12), the way, the truth and the life (John 14:6), the good shepherd who would lay down his life for the sheep (John 10:14-15), the living water (John 7:37-38), the resurrection and the life (John 11:25). He also claimed to be able to forgive sin (Luke 5:24), that He came to give his life as a ransom for many (Matthew 20:28), that He and God the Father were one (John 10:30), and that if we have seen Him we have seen the Father (John 14:9). C. S. Lewis draws an interesting conclusion from all this in his book *Mere Christianity*.

> A man who was merely a man and said the sort of things Jesus said would not be a great moral teacher. He would either be a lunatic— on the level with the man who says he is a poached egg—or else he would be the Devil of Hell. You must make your choice. Either this man was, and is, the Son of God: or else a madman or something worse. You can shut Him up for a fool, you can spit at Him and kill Him as a demon; or you can fall at His feet and call Him Lord and

God. But let us not come with any patronizing nonsense about His being a great human teacher. He has not left that open to us. He did not intend to.[34]

J. B. Phillips also saw the significance of Jesus' claim to be God. If Jesus is the incarnation of God, then by learning about Jesus ("whom our hands have handled and eyes have seen") we learn about who God is (who is unseen). *This is how we can develop a healthy and life-giving impression of what God is like.* J. B. Phillips expressed it this way:

> It is, of course, a very big step intellectually (and emotionally and morally as well, it will be found) to accept this famous figure of history as the designed focusing of God in human life. . . . Yet if for one moment we imagine the claim to be true the mind almost reels at its significance. It can only mean that here is Truth, here is the Character of God, the true Design for life, the authentic Yardstick of values, the reliable confirming or correcting of all gropings and inklings about Beauty, Truth, and Goodness, about this world and the next. Life can never be wholly dark or wholly futile if once the key to its meaning is in our hands.

> Although an honest adult study of the available records is essential, to decide that Jesus really was the embodiment of God in a human being is not a merely intellectual decision. Our unconscious minds will sense (even if the conscious mind does not) that to accept such a unique Fact cannot but affect the whole of our life. We may with complete detachment study and form a judgment upon a religion, but we cannot maintain our detachment if the subject of our inquiry proves to be God Himself.[35]

When we open our heart to have a personal relationship with Jesus, we open our heart to God. It is such a simple thing and yet so profound. Even Jesus' disciples had to learn this. Once Philip said to Jesus, "Lord, show us the Father and that will be enough for us." Here is what Jesus answered:

> Don't you know me, Philip, even after I have been among you such a long time? Anyone who has seen me has seen the Father. How can you say, 'Show us the Father'? Don't you believe that I am in the Father, and that the Father is in me? The words I say to you are not just my own. Rather, it is the Father living in me, who is doing his work. Believe me when I say that I am in the Father and the Father is in me; or at least believe on the evidence of the miracles themselves (John 14:8-11).

The apostle Paul talked about this same idea when he wrote to the people at Colossi. This is how he described who Jesus was.

> He [Jesus] is the image of the invisible God. . . . For by him all things were created: things in heaven and on earth. . . . He is before all things, and in him all things hold together. . . . For God was pleased to have all his fullness dwell in him, and through him to reconcile to himself all things, whether things on earth or things in heaven, by making peace through his blood, shed on the cross. . . . For in Christ all the fullness of the Deity lives in bodily form. . . . God made you alive with Christ. He forgave us all our sins, having canceled the written code, with its regulations, that was against us and that stood opposed to us; he took it away, nailing it to the cross. And having disarmed the powers and authorities, he made a public spectacle of them, triumphing over them by the cross (Colossians 1:15,16, 17,19-20, 2:9,13-15).

The writer of Hebrews gives us this same picture of Jesus and what Jesus accomplished for mankind. He wrote:

> The Son [Jesus] is the radiance of God's glory and the exact representation of his being . . . After he had provided purification for sins, he sat down at the right hand of the Majesty in heaven (Hebrews 1:3).

Human beings are unique creatures and our need to have a spiritual life is universal. Knowing that God is there, that we are made in His image, and that Jesus Christ is who He claimed to be and what He claimed to do are spiritual truths that can change any life. These truths are absolute truths. They stand on their own. It is on these truths that life, psychologically and spiritually, can find meaning and worth.

Human worth, your worth, my worth and human salvation are intrinsically linked to these great truths. They can be embraced by faith with confidence by anyone who is searching. We can accept them as personally ours because this is how God designed it to be and how He wants it to be.

We may have given away or had taken away our permission to be spiritual beings but we can reclaim it at any time. It is God's gift to us as people made in His likeness. How does a person do this? How can a person work more positively with their spiritual life? The answer to these questions is the subject of the next chapter.

Suggested Reading

1. Phillips, J. B. *Your God Is Too Small.* Macmillan Publishing Co., 1961.
2. Lewis, C.S. *Mere Christianity.* Macmillan Publishing Co. 1960.
3. Deuteronomy 10:14,17; Job 12:10; Psalm 14:1a; 47:2; Romans 2:4.

A direct question: Why should one be a Christian? Why not be human, truly human? Why, in addition to being human, should we be Christian? . . . And the answer is equally direct: In order to be truly human. . . . Being Christian cannot mean ceasing to be human. But neither can being human mean ceasing to be Christian. . . . The true Christian is not a split personality.

Hans Küng, *On Being A Christian*[1]

[It is] dangerous for man to know God without knowing his own wretchedness, and to know his own wretchedness without knowing the redeemer who can free him from it. The knowledge of only one of these points gives rise either to the pride of philosophers, who have known God, and not their own wretchedness, or to the despair of atheists, who know their own wretchedness, but not the Redeemer.

Blaise Pascal, *Pascal's Pensées*[2]

In the doctrine of the divine image in man lies the ground of that *receptiveness* of man for the new divine life which the Spirit imparts—a life which, once imparted, becomes the individual's own life. . . . In the positive realization of the divine image in Christ, we have the *model* or *pattern* to which his redeemed nature is now to be conformed.

James Orr, *God's Image in Man*[3]

CHAPTER 24

Keys to Spiritual Maturity

How To

Sara was just a young girl when an event happened that shaped her impression of God for decades. The memory of that night was as fresh in her mind at age seventy as it was the day it happened.

She and her family attended a "hellfire and brimstone" church where the minister flailed his arms and pounded the pulpit as he preached. He wore a long, black robe with black velvet stripes on the sleeves, and his booming voice and piercing eyes gave him the appearance of a mean judge.

One night after the sermon, she and her family were riding home in their horse-drawn carriage when a terrible storm broke. The road became muddy, and the wind and rain beat against the frail canopy on the carriage. Suddenly, a bolt of lightning struck a tree near where they were riding. The sound was deafening, the flash of light blinding as it pierced the darkness, and the sheer power that split the tree sent the horses into a panic. It was total chaos!

In the midst of this, Sara's mind flashed back to the "big, stern-looking preacher" and his fiery sermons about God. *This is what God must be like!* she thought. *This is what the preacher meant by the awesomeness of God's power!*

Instantly, this terrifying impression of God imbedded itself deep in her young heart. She was to live in terror of God from that moment on. All future sermons on the love, patience, and grace of God could not dislodge this "feeling picture." Her Christian life became one of duty, fear, and deep spiritual insecurity as she tried in vain to please this menacing God. Not until she reached her seventies did she begin to experience God's love. This developed slowly as she felt loved by the people in the church she attended.

Most of us do not remember how our first negative impressions of God were formed. We may not understand how they continue to influence our mental and spiritual life even today. We just know that "something is not right." There is some kind of inconsistency between what we know about God and what we feel about God, but we don't like to think about it. To do so makes us feel worse, so we have learned to live with the uneasy feelings.

How to Discover Our Feeling Impressions of God

One positive way we can work with our spiritual awareness is to know it's okay for us to accept both our negative or positive feeling impressions of God. They are trying to tell us something important about ourselves—about our past religious experiences, our present religious attitudes, etc.

Even though most of us have forgotten how these early negative impressions of God were formed, they *cause us to feel unhappy in our Christian life.* Time may correct them, but it's not uncommon for our heart to remain closely tied to our early feelings about God.

These faulty pictures can be changed if we're willing to take an honest look at them. We need to see them for what they are—distortions or exaggerations of what God is truly like. We need to change these heart pictures if we are to develop a healthy spiritual life.

We can do this by asking ourselves two questions. The first question helps us recall the earliest impression of God we can remember. The question is: *To the best of your ability, what is the earliest felt memory you have of God and what was He like?* What picture did you have of Him? Where were you when this impression formed? What were the circumstances? How old were you? Were you alone or with someone? Was your impression of God negative, neutral, or positive? And did it have any lasting influence on the way you thought or felt about God in the future?

Many times my heart has been touched by the stories I've heard in response to this question. I have felt a sense of wonder, awe, and at times sorrow as I have listened to how childhood pictures of God were formed. These stories have deepened my appreciation for the innate sense of spiritual awareness that children have as Imagebearers of God. They reveal how sensitive children are to spiritual things.

I stand in awe when I hear how a teenager or an adult can remember when they prayed to God about something or when they "asked Jesus into their heart"—and they were only two, three, or four years old! How many of us can remember anything at that age, let alone remember decisions we made? Yet, when God's Spirit connects to the human spirit, the memory is clear and detailed.

While many people have positive first time impressions of God, many do not. In one of my seminars, a man was listening to others tell their stories when he remembered his own:

> As I was listening to everyone tell of their wonderful God who was full of love and understanding, I recalled a little boy about seven or eight years old who viewed God as a large and powerful man carrying a big club. As soon as I got out of line, that was it for me, punishment and then down the road to hell you go.
>
> To make matters even worse, while I was trying to recover from that question, Larry asked an even more startling one: "What is your current feeling concept of God?" I was shocked to realize it had not changed. I still had a "Policeman" type feeling concept of God which I somehow developed as a young boy.

This story validates the growing body of evidence supporting the idea that our feeling views of God as adults often can be traced back to our childhood. If our childhood impressions of God were positive and healthy, then our adult life psychologically and spiritually is generally healthy. But if our childhood views of God were distorted, negative or unhealthy, then there is a good chance our Christian life today is unhappy.

Growing Up Has an Effect on Our God Concept

Our childhood impressions of God may or may not be adequate for the challenges that face us as we grow up. The second question we can ask ourselves about our impressions of God helps us identify how our views of God were reinforced, challenged, or changed as we grew older. How was our faith in God affected by an ever-expanding world of reality? The question is: *Looking back over your life, what are five or six of the most significant times in your life when your impressions of God were shaped or changed in some way?* How old were you? What were the circumstances? Were you alone or with someone? Was your impression of God negative, neutral, or positive? And did it have any direct influence on the way you thought or felt about God in the future?

Years ago, while teaching a class on the Psychology of Religion at a local Christian college, I had my students discuss this question and then write a statement about it. Here's what one bright student wrote about his struggle with his impressions of God.

> The God of my early years was everything a Sunday school could make Him. Endowed with all His patent attributes: omnipotence,

omnipresence, omniscience, etc.: yet still kind, gently, thoroughly and effectively involved in my child's world. My God was tailor made for the convenience of an innocent box. . . .

With the advent of my adolescence things began to change. My thought patterns were maturing and what had previously been a secure (however restricted) view of my Christianity could no longer accommodate my religious demands. . . . I needed a God who would help me cope with what to me was the incredible sinfulness of high school, a God who knew about dope, sex, and sports. So as my perspective of God enlarged, so did my God-box.

In moving beyond my childhood God into my adolescent God, I also began to drift away from the God the church sought to impress upon me. . . . the God of church seemed static, a narrow projection of the church's molding.

After the traumatic experience of having all vestiges of my God-boxes shattered by serious intellectual doubting and temporary rejection of God, I was faced with the task of reconstructing a workable, personal view of God. . . .

I think that by realizing and accepting the fact that God has selectively revealed specific aspects of Himself both corporately, through the Bible and His incarnation, and personally, through my private experience, that He will share of Himself that which is truly pertinent to the maturing of my faith.

If I am able to integrate that specific revelation with my beliefs, then I think I will have taken (or set forth on) a great step towards God as He wishes me to see Him.

With skill, honesty, and transparency, he has been a voice for thousands of us, both Christian and nonChristian, who find that moving from our childhood impressions of God to mature, adult impressions is not an easy transition. And yet during this time, God is closer to us than we realize.

Developing an honest, healthy, mature relationship with God takes this kind of courage—the courage to face our immature impressions of God, to face ourselves, our doubts, the realities of life, and by faith to continue to relate honestly with a personal God who is there for us even when we are searching.

God Welcomes Doubters—God Is Not Shockable!

To feel free to learn how to develop a healthy Christian life, we need to know that searching and doubting are okay.[4] God has a heart for human beings who are searching! This is the central theme of a most insightful book by Eugenia Price titled *What Is God Like?* She knows that more of us than are willing to admit it "live uneasily beneath a row of universal question marks about God." She knows because she was searching and questioning, and as she came to know who God really was, her life was transformed. Here is what she says about the positive side of doubting and searching.

> God is the only living Person who can bear complete inspection. And He lovingly invites it. . . . I am convinced that when for any reason a Christian becomes discouraged in his spiritual life he is forgetting or falling a victim to his own ignorance of what God is really like. . . . I am inclined to believe that anyone who never doubts is not really thinking. *God is not confused by our honest doubts.* . . . Jesus Christ is every moment ready and willing to reveal Himself to those who seek honestly to know Him. . . . The more I read of Him in the Gospel accounts, the more I am convinced that He prefers to be confronted by an honest doubter who wants to see Him as He is. . . . Once and for all, we should have it straight that *God is never surprised, discouraged or shocked by us. He is realistic with us at all times* (italics mine).[5]

What a healthy picture of God she has painted for us! For years, I felt I was a "bad Christian" for having the doubts and questions I silently carried inside. This never changed until I began to look at them as areas for spiritual healing and growth.

Two stories in the Bible can help us approach searching and doubting with a positive attitude. The first incident involved John the Baptist. While in prison facing the possibility of his own death, he heard reports about the great things Jesus was saying and doing. Wanting assurance that Jesus was the promised Messiah, John sent his disciples to ask Jesus if he was the one. Instead of answering yes or no, Jesus pointed to the evidence and told them to report this to John. Jesus wanted John to come to his own conclusion. Believing is faith built on evidence. Jesus replied:

> Go back and report to John what you hear and see: The blind receive sight, the lame walk, those who have leprosy are cured, the deaf hear, the dead are raised, and the good news is preached to the poor. Blessed is the man who does not fall away on account of me (Luke 7:22-23).

As John's disciples were leaving, Jesus turned to the crowd and honored John rather then putting him down. A healthy faith always leaves room for some doubts, questions, and uncertainties.

Years ago I found a most interesting book by Leslie Weatherhead titled *The Christian Agnostic.* Even though I totally disagree with how far he has gone with some of his conclusions, I really like the encouragement he gives to those who are doubting and searching. I like the room he gives people to grow in their walk with Christ. He wrote:

> I am writing for the "Christian agnostic," by which I mean a person who is immensely attracted by Christ and who seeks to show his spirit, to meet the challenges, hardships and sorrows of life in the light of that spirit, but who, though he is sure of many Christian truths, feels that he cannot honestly and conscientiously "sign on the dotted line" that he believes certain theological ideas about which some branches of the church dogmatize, churches from which he feels excluded because he cannot "believe." His intellectual integrity makes him say about many things, "It may be so. I do not know." . . . Don't exclude yourself from the fellowship of Christ's followers because of mental difficulties. If you love Christ and are seeking to follow him, take an attitude of Christian agnosticism to intellectual problems at least for the present. . . . Accept those things which gradually seem to you to be true. Leave the rest in a mental box labeled, 'awaiting further light.'"[6]

The other incident occurred after Jesus' resurrection. The disciples were meeting in a room when Jesus appeared to them. He showed them His hands and side and they were overjoyed to know Jesus was alive. But one disciple, Thomas, was absent. Later, when the others told him about the incident, he said, "Unless I see the nail marks in his hands and put my finger where the nails were and put my hand into his side, I will not believe it" (John 20:19-21).

In my Christian upbringing, the talks I heard about Thomas never encouraged questioning or doubting. A doubter was labeled "a doubting Thomas" and no sensitive Christian would ever want to carry that label—especially if they are struggling with self-esteem problems.

Today, I have a more healthy view of this story. I believe Jesus felt compassion for Thomas and responded to him in a kind but straightforward manner. A week passed before Jesus again visited his disciples. This time Thomas was present. After greeting everyone, Jesus turned to Thomas and said, "Put your finger here; see my hands. Reach out your hand and put it into my side. Stop doubting and believe" (v.27). Jesus invited Thomas not only to look at the evidence, but to touch him. Thomas didn't need to. His experience with Jesus restored his faith and he replied, "My Lord and my God!" (v.28).

Taking a positive attitude toward our doubts and questions gives us the freedom we need to admit to ourselves and to others our true feelings about our spiritual life—about God, the world, or different aspects of the Christian faith. We can talk to God in prayer and lay before Him our doubts, confusions, and questions, and find that He does help us in life-giving ways. Sometimes the most helpful thing God does is accepting us just where we are. We need to know this is okay too.

Keep Your Christian Faith Simple

Everyone in the world deals with their impressions of God. This is true no matter what their religion, whether they believe in God or not, or whether they are particularly interested in their spiritual life. We are spiritual beings and we cannot escape it. Ask anyone about their impressions of God and you will discover some fascinating things.

Unfortunately, religious doctrines and practices (as good as they may be) can be given such a high priority that our ideas and feelings about God and about Jesus Christ become lost in the shuffle. The mind can become so overwhelmed with all the details about the doctrines, rules, regulations, and rituals of our faith that we can become confused in our walk with God. This is especially true if our life circumstances should suddenly change.

When I was a teacher at Wheaton Christian High School, three new students came to the school from New York. They were from the section of the city known as Hell's Kitchen, and as new Christians, their faith in Jesus Christ was simple, sincere, and real. They were used to living on the streets where drugs, gangs, pimps, and prostitution was the everyday way of life. To deal with this, their Christian life had to be simple and practical.

Now they were living in a Christian boarding school located in the country and surrounded with green fields. They felt a lot of love from Christian teachers, staff, and fellow students, but they also were exposed to more Christian thinking and teaching than they could absorb and apply. And it blew their minds!

I was the assistant dorm parent in the boys' dorm, and one night I heard a knock on my door. One of my New York boys came to talk and, in tears, poured out his heart about how confused he was becoming. The more he learned about Christianity, the further away he felt from Jesus. In Hell's Kitchen everything he knew about Jesus was alive and personal—it was connected to his heart. It had to be! The old way of life was all around him, constantly trying to pull him back into the old ways. Now he was gaining more head knowledge than he could understand or handle—and he was losing the simplicity of his faith in Christ.

Almost two thousand years earlier, the apostle Paul was concerned that the same thing might happen to the new Christians at Corinth. A lot of religions and even false teachings about Jesus and the Christian way were being circulated. Paul was afraid that their minds would become confused and that they would be led astray from the "simplicity that is in Christ" (King James version). Paul expressed it this way: "But I am afraid that just as Eve was deceived by the serpent's cunning, your minds may somehow be led astray from sincere and pure devotion to Christ" (2 Corinthians 11:3).

One of the ways we can improve the quality of our Christian life is to *simplify our faith*: our faith is in the person of God and in the person and work of Jesus Christ, not primarily in some elaborate system of dogma and doctrine. Yes! we all need some kind of "theological package" to believe in and practice, but it is secondary to our single-hearted acceptance and faith in God as a person as revealed in Jesus Christ.

This is why true Christianity is a relationship and not a religion. A Christian is a person who has opened their heart to having a relationship with Jesus Christ. They have made a personal connection with the Savior, the Messiah and have chosen to follow him as their Lord. All the variables that make for a healthy human relationship—faith, trust, openness, honesty, caring, communication, commitment, cooperation, respect, responsibility, safety— are to be found in our relationship with God. It's always easier to play roles and live by rules and rituals than to live in a healthy relationship.

Keeping our Christian life simple is one of the ways we can walk more quietly and confidently with Christ. One technique I use to simplify my faith when I begin to feel bogged down is to ask myself the question, "If I were to be executed for my Christian faith, would I be willing to be put against a wall and shot for this belief, this doctrine, this religious practice, this religious rule, or regulation?" Asking myself this question has helped me sort out those really important truths from those that are not so important.

Like the concentric circles of a target, I would be willing to die for those truths in the bull's eye; I might be willing to die for those truths in the ring next to the bull's eye; but I doubt I would be willing to die for ideas and rules that are further from the bull's eye.

At the center of this simplifying process is our thoughts about God. What do we really believe about God in the secret chambers of our heart? Who do we really believe Jesus Christ to be and what do we believe He accomplished on our behalf? Are we willing to give our life for the answers to these questions?

How to Overcome Religious Abuse

Nowhere is a discussion about our impressions of God more interesting, sad, and heartbreaking than to talk to someone whose feelings about God are messed up because of abuse—sexual, physical, or religious abuse. The current material in abuse recovery shows that our concept of God and our concept of ourselves (self-worth) are deeply affected by abuse.

I believe that religious abuse may be the most difficult abuse to overcome. It effects the very center of our sense of spiritual awareness. It distorts and twists our impressions of God at the deepest level of our experience, robbing us of one of our most important sources for healing—our faith in a loving, caring God. It wounds both our psychological and spiritual sense of well-being.

In the last few years religious abuse has begun to receive more attention. The more blatant forms, as found in cults and sects, have often been discussed —Jim Jones and his religious group in Guiana is one example. But in my opinion, it is also possible to experience religious abuse in a Christian home or church.

It sounds contradictory to put "abuse" and "Christian" in the same sentence. In reality, a home or church that is abusive is not being Christian. It is unhealthy and dysfunctional. Religious abuse in the Christian home or church occurs when religious ideas, beliefs, and practices are used to dominate, control, manipulate, or intimidate others into thinking, feeling, or behaving in certain ways. It occurs when parents or Christian leaders act toward others in judgmental, critical, and punitive ways for what they believe to be justifiable causes. Charles Swindoll calls these people "grace killers." A Christian family or church is dysfunctional when rigid, legalistic, and dogmatic thinking creates feelings of anxiety, guilt, fear, shame, anger, and depression in its people. Religious abuse impacts one's sense of self-esteem. One's faith in God is also hurt because it distorts our impressions of Him.

An unhealthy Christian home is one where a person (child, teen, or adult) can't talk, can't trust, can't feel, can't question, can't be human, can't be different for fear of being punished, criticized, or rejected because of religion.

Openness, trust, caring, respect, tolerance, acceptance, honesty, and age-appropriate rules are found in the healthy Christian home. In contrast, the unhealthy religious family is characterized by distrust, poor communi-cation, disregard for feelings, disregard for the needs or desires of others, and conformity to prescribed religious practices, with little or no room for individual differences.

The Reoccurring Nightmare

Elizabeth grew up in a religious abusive home. Like all children, her innate sense of spiritual awareness toward God made her tender and sensitive to Him. She tried to be what she was told a "good Christian" was supposed to be, but the religious perfectionism and the emotional crazy-games in the home made it impossible. The psychological and emotional unhealthiness become so intermixed with "Christian stuff" that any hope of developing a healthy faith in God or a healthy respect for herself was lost.

For years, beginning as a child and lasting until her mid-twenties, she had a recurring nightmare about the return of Jesus. She was always about to be "left behind" because she was not good enough to be accepted by God into heaven. In her dream, Jesus would appear in the sky and all the Christians would begin to rise from the earth to meet Him. She would run and grab onto the leg of another Christian and hang on for dear life as they rose into the air. But the higher they got, the harder it was to hold on.

Eventually, she would lose her grip and begin to fall. In her dream, the sensation of falling was so terrifying she would awake in a state of panic. Then, for the next several weeks, she would try to do her best to be the perfect Christian girl she was supposed to be. It never lasted and eventually the nightmare would recur.

This is not the kind of Christianity that represents the God I know and honor.[7] This is not the kind of Jesus the Gospels tell us about. This is the kind of religious faith Stephen Arterburn calls toxic religion. In his book *Toxic Faith*, he describes it.

> Toxic faith is a destructive and dangerous relationship with a religion that allows the religion, not the relationship with God, to control a person's life. . . . It is a defective faith with an incomplete or tainted view of God. . . . [It is] a counterfeit for the spiritual growth that can occur through a genuine relationship with God. The toxic faithful find a replacement for God. Acts of religion replace steps of growth. A facade is substituted for a heart longing to know God. The facade forms a barrier between the believer and God, leaving the believer to survive with a destructive addiction to religion.[8]

God is the author of life! Our deepest heart-felt impressions of Him need to be life-giving, not death-producing. Our faith in God can only move toward Him in healthy and life-changing ways when we see Him as a God who cares, who is safe, who loves, who welcomes, who is faithful, who is patient, who affirms us in our attempts to trust Him. Yes, God is just, pure, holy, and righteous. And these are absolutely necessary if we are to have a realistic, truthful concept of God. But when a person has been oppressed, they need a view of God that promotes healing and growth both psychologically and spiritually.

When people are in recovery, sometimes the most healing impression of God their faith can embrace is what I call a "generic view of God"—a Divine Being undefined by the traditional characteristics we so quickly attach to

Him. I know some Christians who disagree with AA's encouragement to those in alcohol recovery to "have faith in their higher power as they understand it." I also know this idea has been used by people to go off in all kinds of wrong directions. But I also believe God knows the heart and is not offended when He sees that someone's faith in Him has to begin "somewhere"—and He meets them there. God will work in them to bring about a growing faith in Him as revealed in the Bible. Renowned Christians such as C. S. Lewis and Francis Schaeffer had to begin their walk of faith with "perhaps Something is there" before their steps of faith could ultimately lead them to a faith in the personal God of the Bible. Eventually, it can lead to believing in Jesus Christ as the Son of God, the Savior, the Messiah.

The God I believe in is a God who will allow our faith in Him to start simply so that it can grow and mature into something deeper, something healthy as we learn more about Him. God gives us the freedom to start toward Him from a place of honest faith because He knows the wounds of our heart. He is a "God of all Grace" (1 Peter 5:10).

Picture God as the God of Grace

Joseph Cooke was a missionary in Thailand when he had to return home because of a nervous breakdown. He believed that God was a gracious God and he loved to teach and preach about Him. But deep down in his heart, Joseph lived with a non-gracious God (This is an example of the discrepancy I mentioned earlier). He knew that God's grace was there for him when he first became a Christian, and he believed that God's grace would be there for him at the end of his life. But day-by-day life "was one long, deadly grind of trying to be perfect to earn the daily pleasure of a God who simply could not be pleased." Deep down in his heart, Joseph experienced God as a demanding God, a God who had such high expectations of him he could never hope to live up to them. He also saw God as a nag. This is how he described it.

> Another characteristic of my non-gracious God was his nagging. I don't know whether you've ever lived with someone who nagged, but if you have, you know what it feels like. They nag you about how you eat and dress. They fuss about how you walk and spend your time. They're constantly after you to do this and not to do that. And it doesn't matter how hard you try, it's never quite good enough.

> Well, imagine living with a God like that. All day long it was, "Why don't you pray more? Why don't you spend more time in the Word? Why don't you witness? When will you ever learn self-discipline? How can you allow yourself to indulge in such wicked thoughts?

Do this! Don't do that! Yield! Confess! Work harder! On and on and on. The worst thing about it all was that you couldn't get away; there was no place to hide.[9]

This is a good example of someone trying to get their worth and identity from doing. So many times our self-worth and our feelings about God become so entangled we don't know which one we are struggling with the most. Look at the self-esteem picture Joseph paints of himself as he describes his feeling view of God.

Finally, I had a God who really, deep down underneath, considered me to be less than dirt. Oh yes, he made a great to-do about loving me enough to die for me. . . . But I believed the day-by-day love and acceptance I longed for could only be mine if I'd let him crush nearly everything that was really me. When you come right down to it, there was scarcely a word, feeling, decision, motive or thought of mine that God really liked. All had to be brought down to absolute zero so that he could pull the strings of my life and make me into a marionette, dancing to the will of a divine puppeteer.

The fact was that I really knew very little about the God of the Bible—the God Paul tells us about and the one Jesus came to reveal. *I had hardly even met the God who created me in his image, who deeply cherished what he created* and who longed to free me to be a mature son and heir (italics mine).[10]

Joseph's healing, growth, and recovery took time and there were many things he had to learn to accept about himself—his feelings, his history, his thoughts, his failures. But underneath it all, he began to place his faith in a newly developing impression of God as a God of grace and of himself as a person made in the image of God.

God's favor, kindness, love and grace are extended to us, not because we deserve it, not because we earn it, but because we are worth it as people made in His likeness. God extends it to us with no strings attached because it comes as evidence of His unconditional love. All we can do is accept it by faith and *experience it* and then from a grateful heart thank Him for His gifts.

God Is a Big God

So what is God like? We will never be able to describe who God is in His entirety, and that is right and good. If we could, God would not be God. But a brief look at a few Bible verses can begin to give us a few pictures of what God is like—the kind of God we can approach, the kind of God that can be loved and trusted, that is good, the kind of God that is just, moral, and fair. Here are a few examples.

> Know therefore that the Lord your God is God; he is the faithful God, keeping his covenant of love to a thousand generations of those who love him and keep his commands (Deuteronomy 7:9).

> This is what the Lord says: "Let not the wise man boast of his wisdom or the strong man boast of his strength or the rich man boast of his riches, but let him who boasts boast about this: that he understand and knows me, that I am the Lord, who exercises kindness, justice and righteousness on earth, for in these I delight," declares the Lord (Jeremiah 9:23-24).

> He prayed to the Lord, "O Lord, is this not what I said when I was still at home? . . . I knew that you are a gracious and compassionate God, slow to anger and abounding in love, a God who relents from sending calamity (Jonah 4:1).

> The Lord is compassionate and gracious, slow to anger, abounding in love (Psalm 103:8).

> And he will be called Wonderful Counselor, Mighty God, Everlasting Father, Prince of Peace (Isaiah 9:6).

> By faith we understand that the universe was formed at God's command, so that what is seen was not made out of what was visible. . . . And without faith it is impossible to please God, because anyone who comes to him must believe that he exists and that he rewards those who earnestly seek him (Hebrews 11:3,6).

One year I read the Bible through looking for only those places that dealt with concepts and impressions of God. It was fascinating reading. What was most interesting was reading the Gospels and learning about Jesus' concepts of God.

If our views of God are distorted and unhealthy, we can correct them by believing in the view of God that Jesus both believed in and taught. We can't go wrong if the man we learn from not only had a life-giving view of God himself, but was also the "visible image of the invisible God" (Colossians 1:15)—"the exact representation of God's being" (Hebrews 1:3). J. B. Phillips is right when he wrote:

> We shall never want to serve God in our real and secret hearts if He looms in our subconscious mind as an arbitrary Dictator or a Spoil-sport, or as one who takes advantage of His position to make us poor mortals feel guilty and afraid. We have not only to be

impressed with the "size" and unlimited power of God, we have to be moved to genuine admiration, respect, and affection, if we are ever to worship him. . . . . It is a fascinating problem for us human beings to consider how the Eternal Being—wishing to show men His own Character focused, His own Thought expressed, and His own Purpose demonstrated—could introduce Himself into the stream of human history without disturbing or disrupting it. There must obviously be an almost unbelievable "scaling-down" of the "size" of God to match the life of this planet. . . . If it is to be done at all God must be man.[11]

Jesus Christ is that man. To know Jesus and to live in a personal relationship with him is to see God refocused. It is also to see the freedom we have to grow emotionally and spiritually because of God's grace as seen in the finished work of Christ at the cross.

It Is for Freedom That Christ Has Set Us Free

Another positive way we can work with our spiritual awareness is to join the grace movement. This is a movement that embraces God's grace as a way to deal with the realities of living in a sinful world. The award winning journalist Philip Yancey wrote about this grace as applied to what he called, "street level living." In his enlightening book, *What's So Amazing About Grace*, he gives us some pearls of wisdom to ponder about God's gift of grace. He wrote:

- Grace is Christianity's best gift to the world...
- Guilt exposes a longing for grace...
- The world starves for grace...
- Grace comes free of charge to people who do not deserve it...
- [Grace] has about it the maddening quality of being undeserved, unmerited, unfair...
- Grace means there is nothing I can do to make God love me more, and nothing I can do to make God love me less...
- God yearns to see in people something of his own image reflected; at best he sees shattered fragments of that image. Still, God cannot—or will not—give up...
- God gave up His own Son rather than give up on humanity...
- Where society saw only a bum and a whore, grace saw "a little kid," a person made in the image of God no matter how defaced that image had become.[12]

One man that embraced that grace was the captain of an African slave ship. The wretchedness of his business drove him to his knees to ask for God's forgiveness. Later John Newton wrote the classic Christian hymn, *Amazing Grace*, as a testimony to his newly found freedom in the Christian life.

The grace movement is also a movement to embrace God's grace as a way to deal with the bondage of man-made regulation and restrictions of legalistic religion. The apostle Paul wrote about the grace and freedom that can be ours because of what Jesus Christ accomplished on our behalf. This is what he wrote in his letter to the Galatian people.

> It is for freedom that Christ has set us free. Stand firm, then, and do not let yourselves be burdened again by a yoke of slavery. . . . You, my brothers, were called to be free. But do not use your freedom to indulge in the sinful nature; rather, serve one another in love. The entire law is summed up in a single command: "Love your neighbor as yourself" (Galatians 5:1,13-15).

Charles Swindoll encourages everyone to become part of this grace movement. In his book *The Grace Awakening*, he expressed it this way.

> People need to know that there is more to the Christian life than deep frowns, pointing fingers, and unrealistic expectations. . . . If you find yourself yearning to be . . . truly liberated from those who would hold you captive, free to be free and to challenge the world to embrace grace's liberties, all I ask for is your time and attention. . . . But I should warn you, once the smoldering embers burst into full flame, you'll not be able to extinguish them. Having joined the ranks of the freedom movement, you will never again be satisfied with slavery.[13]

We Christians talk a lot about our freedom in Christ, and yet so few of us experience it. Our religious expectations have become so closely tied to our self-esteem that we find ourselves in bondage to religion—to religious performance. Grace gives us the room to enjoy life as God intended.

The Freedom to Be Fully Human, Fully Christian

God's grace also gives us the freedom to be a human and a Christian at the same time. With our worth secure in being made in God's image and our salvation secure in being in Christ, we are free to grow, develop, and become the kind of Christian that is alive and real. We can be fully human and fully Christian. Hans Küng gives us some interesting insight into this.

> It is evident from the history of the Christian Church, of theology and spirituality, that being Christian has meant all too often being less than human. But is this really being Christian? For many then

the only alternative was to be human and therefore less Christian. But is this being truly human? . . . In fact is it not the failure to be fully human which so often makes being a Christian seem inadequate? Is not the lack of genuine, complete humanity the reason why being a Christian is disregarded or rejected as an authentically human possibility? Must we not strive for the best possible development of the individual: a humanization of the whole person in all his dimensions, including instinct and feeling? Being human ought to be complementary to being a Christian. The Christian factor must be made effective, not at the expense of the human, but for the benefit of the latter.[14]

Life gets exciting when we realize the freedom we have in Christ to grow and be truly human and truly Christian. Life becomes an adventure rather than a contradiction or a burden. A Christian is free to know this better than anyone else in the world and yet, so many of us are missing it. We need to take to heart what Jesus said: "I have come that they may have life, and have it to the full" (John 10:10).

Our being human can compliment our being Christian; our being Christian can authenticate our being human. Truly, this would be life at its fullest.

What Does It Mean to Be Like Jesus? A Quiet Walk with Mother Teresa

If anyone has ever been truly human and truly spiritual, it is Jesus Christ. To read the Gospels is to be touched by how much He loved God and by how much He loved and cared for people. For two thousand years people have wanted to emulate His life. One of those was Mother Teresa of Calcutta. Her love for Christ and for people received world recognition when she was awarded the Nobel Peace Prize. I point to her as an example of what it means to be like Christ because she is one of the most visible. I could say the same for Billy Graham, and many others. Yet, there are millions of people who reflect the Spirit of Christ in their little corner of the world who someday will be honored by Jesus with the words, "Well done, good and faithful servant" (Matthew 25:14).

To be like Christ means to look at life from Jesus' point of view and then act in harmony with that view. To be like Christ, we would need to spend time with Him, learn from Him, feel and know what He thinks and feels, and then to act accordingly—to walk as He walked. Our life would reflect His life in our values, morals, perspectives, and beliefs. Our outer actions would demonstrate our inner world of thought and spirit. Mother Teresa expressed it this way:

We need to find God, and he cannot be found in noise and restlessness. God is the friend of silence. See how nature—trees, flowers, grass—grow in silence; see the stars, the moon and sun, how they move in silence. . . . The more we receive in silent prayer, the more we can give in our active life. We need silence to be able to touch souls. The essential thing is not what we say, but what God says to us and through us. All our words will be useless unless they come from within—words which do not give the light of Christ increase the darkness.[15]

There are many things we could discuss about being like Christ but I want to point out only a few. First, to be like Christ means to have a secure sense of self-worth even as He did. The apostle Paul wrote:

If you have any encouragement from being united with Christ, if any comfort from his love, if any fellowship with the Spirit, if any tenderness and compassion, then make my joy complete by *being like-minded. . .*

Your attitude should be the same as that of Christ Jesus: Who, being in very nature God, did not consider equality with God something to be grasped, but made himself nothing, taking the very nature of a servant, being made in human likeness. And being found in appearance as a man, he humbled himself and became obedient to death— even death on a cross! Therefore God exalted him to the highest place and gave him the name that is above every name, that at the name of Jesus every knee should bow, in heaven and on earth and under the earth, and every tongue confess that Jesus Christ is Lord, to the glory of God the Father (Philippians 2:1-11, italics mine).

Jesus knew who he was. His sense of personal worth and identity was secure in being the Son of God. He didn't have to prove anything to himself or to anybody. This gave Him the freedom to willingly become a servant, and eventually, to give His life on the cross on our behalf.

We become like Christ when we develop a secure sense of self-worth and identity because of our being made in God's image. This gives us the freedom to love and serve others from a healthy position of self-respect and self-love. We are free to give, sacrifice, and work hard because we are NOT trying to prove anything. We will be more balanced in considering our own interests and needs even as we consider the interests and needs of others.

Second, to be like Christ means to see the worth and value of every human life—no matter what their condition, no matter how bad they have been. I am convinced that Jesus saw people from the view of Genesis 1:26-27

—He saw them as people created in God's image and likeness—and he responded to them from this view. He knew their Divine origin. They were fearfully and wonderfully made and they needed to be loved and respected.

In his television interview with Mother Teresa, the renowned author and broadcaster, Malcolm Muggeridge asked her if it was "worth while trying to salvage a few abandoned children who might otherwise be expected to die of neglect, malnutrition, or some related illness." He wrote:

> In the film we made in Calcutta, there is a shot of Mother Teresa holding a tiny baby girl in her hands; so minute that her very existence seemed like a miracle. As she holds this child, she says in a voice, and with an expression, of exaltation most wonderful and moving: "See! there's life in her!" Her face is glowing and triumphant; as it might be the mother of us all glorying in what we all possess—this life in us . . . Either life is always and in all circumstances sacred, or intrinsically of no account . . . The God Mother Teresa worships cannot, we are told, see a sparrow fall to the ground without concern. For man, made in God's image, to turn aside from this universal love, and fashion his own judgements based on his own fears and disparities, is a fearful thing, bound to have fearful consequences.[16]

We become like Christ when we see people as having innate worth and value because they are made in God's image—and love them as He would love them.

Third, to be like Christ means to develop a way of looking at life that captures the essence of what Jesus thought and taught in the Gospels about God, morals, faith and behavior. It is developing a comprehensive view of the world from a spiritual perspective that is like the one Jesus had. In preparing his disciples for the future, Jesus told them about the coming of the Holy Spirit who would be with them and who would teach them about the things of God. This is what He said:

> And I will ask the Father, and he will give you another Counselor to be with you forever—the Spirit of truth. . . . All this I have spoken while still with you. But the Counselor, the Holy Spirit, whom the Father will send in my name, will teach you all things and will remind you of everything I have said to you (John 14:16,25-26).

The apostle Paul echoed these same thoughts about the work of the Holy Spirit when he wrote to the church at Corinth.

> The Spirit searches all things, even the deep things of God. . . . We have not received the spirit of the world but the Spirit who is from

God, that we may understand what God has freely given us. . . . We have the mind of Christ (1 Corinthians 2:10,12,16).

We become like Christ when we think about life the way Jesus thought about it. The Holy Spirit works with us to help us learn God's ways of thinking about life.

Fourth, to be like Christ means to learn how to love people the way Jesus loved them. Jesus is love, and we become like him when we can love as He loved. Jesus said: "A new command I give you: Love one another. As I have loved you, so you must love one another. By this all men will know that you are my disciples . . ." (John 13:34-35).

During his interview with Mother Teresa, Muggeridge asked, "What exactly are you doing for these dying people? I know you bring them in to die there. What is it you are doing for them or seeking to do for them?" This was her answer:

> First of all we want to make them feel that they are wanted, we want them to know that there are people who really love them, who really want them, at least for the few hours that they have to live, to know human and divine love. That they too may know that they are the children of God, and that they are not forgotten and that they are loved and cared about. . . .[17]

Love is practical. Love moves into the realities of life and makes a difference for God and for good. To be like Christ is to make a difference in our little corner of the world. It may not seem like much in comparison to others, but it is just as vital, just as significant, just as necessary. When we do this, we bring God's kingdom on earth even as it is in heaven. If we all did this, maybe our little worlds would overlap, and together we could make a big difference. And how do we do this? Jesus gave us the answer and it was simple and practical:

> I was hungry and you gave me something to eat,
> I was thirsty and you gave me something to drink,
> I was a stranger and you invited me in,
> I needed clothes and you clothed me,
> I was sick and you looked after me,
> I was in prison and you came and visited me.
>
> (Matthew 25:35-36)

We become like Christ when we see people as made in God's image and likeness and show love, kindness, and caring to them in all the little ways that make life better. *When we choose life for ourselves and for those around us, we are being like Christ.* Learning how to do this is working with our sense of spiritual awareness in a positive way—the way God intended.

We are not alone in this process. God is working in us to transform us into the image of His Son. Here is how the Scriptures state it:

> Now the Lord is the Spirit, and where the Spirit of the Lord is, there is freedom. And we, who with unveiled faces all reflect the Lord's glory, are being transformed into his likeness with ever-increasing glory, which comes from the Lord, who is the Spirit (2 Corinthians 3:17-18).

We become **Imagebearers of Christ in our life and character** when we learn how to think as He thought, value what He valued, believe as He believed, and love as He loved. These changes come from within as we spend time with Jesus getting to know Him—becoming one in spirit with Him. Then our outward actions can reveal these inward transformations through our unique personality, interests, talents, and skills. As Lynn Hough said earlier, "Individual character is the crystallization of free choice into permanence." Repeated choices become habits and habits shape character. We bear Christ's image in our character as we choose to be like him.

In summary, we have seen how our sense of spiritual awareness is a valued gift from God. It is part of what makes us human beings—made in His image. It is a unique human faculty that God created in us so that we could enjoy a relationship with Him.

The joy of the Christian life is found in the freedom that comes from knowing and experiencing God's grace and Christ's love and redemption. When we give ourselves permission to open our spiritual world to the love of Jesus Christ, life will never be the same. We can learn how to grow and mature in our spiritual life the way God intended for us to grow.

Suggested Reading

1. Price, Eugenia. *What Is God Like?* Zondervan Publishing House, 1960.
2. Yancey, Philip. *What is so Amazing About Grace.* Zondervan Publishing House, 1997.
3. Exodus 15:11,13; Nehemiah 9:13,17-18; Psalm 46:1-3; 119:105,130; Proverbs 9:10; Isaiah 30:15,18; 40:18-22; 42:5; Romans 8:28-29; Galatians 6:1; Ephesians 2:8-10; Colossians 3:12-15; 1 Timothy 6:6.

BE
CREATIVE

We are giving the world back to man, and man back to himself. Man shall no longer be vile, but noble. We shall not destroy his mind in return for an immortal soul. Without a free, vigorous and creative mind, man is but an animal, and he will die like an animal, without any shred of a soul. We return to man his arts, his literature, his sciences, his independence to think and feel as an individual, not to be bound to dogma like a slave, to rot in his chains.

Irving Stone, *The Agony and the Ecstasy*[1]

As Christians we often speak of men being "made in God's image." This formula only remains a set of words until given further meaning and definition. If there is one area that surely sets man clearly apart from the rest of the animal kingdom and gives meaning to these words "made in the image of God," it is the area of creativity.

Franky Schaeffer, *Addicted to Mediocrity*[2]

We express our being by creating. Creativity is a necessary sequel to being. . . . The creative process must be explored not as the product of sickness, but as representing the highest degree of emotional health, as the expression of normal people in the act of actualizing themselves.

Rollo May, *The Courage to Create*[3]

CHAPTER 25

~ひひ~

Creativity:
Privilege Reclaimed

PERMISSION

What comes to mind when you think of names such as Walt Disney, Charles Shultz, Bill Gates, Grandma Moses, Thomas Edison, Michelangelo, or Mozart? Most people identify them as highly creative people who became famous because they were successful in what they did. For example, Edison invented the light bulb, the phonograph, the electric locomotive, a telegraph signal box, and contributed to the Bell telephone. And yet, it was reported that his teacher described him as a boy who day-dreamed too much and would probably never succeed in life.

All of us are innately creative, but most of us find it hard to believe that this applies to us. Lack of opportunity, loss of interest, the lack of vision or little outside encouragement may have convinced us to settle for being less creative than we really are.

But for most of us, childhood negative experiences are the biggest reasons for the lack of belief in our creative abilities. Our creative efforts failed to gain someone's approval or didn't measure up to their expectations and standards. Feeling hurt and discouraged we concluded, "I am not any good at doing things like this. I must not be very creative or I would have done better." Sadly, many of us decided to quit.

The moment this happened, unknown to us, we betrayed ourselves and turned away from one of the most unique and remarkable characteristics of our humanity. We gave away our permission (our right) to be creative and our lives have never been the same since.

I believe this has happened to all of us to some degree leading to a drastic reduction in our creative expressions. In my self-esteem classes many touching stories have been told by those who have experienced some really unhappy circumstances. One man revealed how in high school he sang in the choir for one entire year, never once vocalizing any songs, "just so I could belong to the choir." His choir teacher said he could attend but he was not to vocalize the music. The pain and humiliation of that experience took him years to overcome before he finally joined a church choir and sang just for the joy of it.

Whenever our creative desires become inhibited, stifled, squashed, or shut down, our BEING falls victim to our DOING. Our future suffers when we focus on *how well* we do something creative rather than on *just being* creative. Let me describe how this happened to me.

The Story of the Papier-Mâché Owl

My self-betrayal took place in the fourth grade when the teacher had us make papier-maché animals. We had great fun tearing the old newspapers into long strips to be dipped in paste, which of course some of us had to taste. When we actually started making our animals, my mind went blank. But the longer I sat and the more anxious I became, the less I could think.

Finally, I decided to make a ball so I could at least look busy. Finishing a grapefruit sized ball, I thought, *Now what do I do?* Again, my mind went blank, so I decided to make another ball, which turned out smaller than the first. Soon I was sitting there with two papier-maché balls, feeling totally lost as to what to do next.

Feeling nervous, pressured and a little dumb by then (everybody else looked like they knew what they were doing), I began experimenting with different configurations. Suddenly, the image of a snowman popped into my imagination. I quickly rejected it because we had six feet of snow outside our school building in Cascade, Idaho. How original is a snowman in that kind of climate?

After what felt like an eternity, a picture of an owl emerged in my mind. Feeling relieved and excited about its possibility, I began shaping the two balls into the appearance of an owl. I pasted on the two ears, a beak and a tail. I painted the owl brown with big yellow eyes and beak. When I finished, the owl was so real to me I felt it could almost fly. Years later I learned that when Michelangelo finished his marble sculpture of Moses, it was reported that he stood in front of it and yelled, "Now Speak!"

Here comes the sad part. Friday night the parents were invited to attend an open house to admire our masterpieces. Arriving at school early, I found our sculptures lined up in a row on a long table. From right to left, the teacher had arranged them, first, second, and third prize and then all the rest. I am sure she had no idea how a nine-year-old kid was going to interpret this arrangement.

As I stood in front of the table, looking at my owl placed second from the left end—second to the worst in my mind—feelings of dismay, hurt, and failure filled me. In a sentence, I was devastated! Deeply discouraged by the results of my creative effort, I *concluded* I was not any good at doing creative things and *decided* I would never again make another serious attempt at being creative.

This decision lasted for twenty-three years! I was thirty-two years old before I finally stepped out from behind the memory of this incident and *purposefully chose* to carve a frog out of a block of wood.

It happened one afternoon in Denver while visiting my long-time friends, Jim and Elaine Hay. We had decided to make some wooden toys we had seen in a store when suddenly I was faced with a deep inner battle. One side of me was saying, "I can't do that. I am no good at doing that kind of thing. Besides, it will look dumb and if I can't do it perfect, I won't do it." The other side was saying, "But I want to make something just for the fun of it. It doesn't matter if anyone else likes it, I just want to do it. So what if it's not perfect? Who cares?"

I felt like I was in fourth grade again, facing the papier-mâché owl and the decision I had made to cope with my hurt and disappointment. Would I choose to do what I really wanted to do and carve the frog, or would I continue to react to my feelings and turn away from a chance to overcome my past?

Reminding myself that God had made me in His likeness to be a creative person, I gave myself permission to be what I was designed to be. I carved the frog. In choosing life at that moment, I gained both a personal and spiritual victory over a painful childhood memory. Healing, growth, and change began when I shifted the weight of my choice away from performance and on to my God given gift to be creative. I still have the frog as a symbol of my "coming-out party"—my choosing to be a creative person.

Over the years I have continued to make new choices, take new risks, experience new successes (I call them confidence builders), and working through new failures until I finally decided to write a book. It's a long way from a frog to a book, but as Paul Harvey would say, "And now you know the rest of the story."

Human Creativity: By Chance or by Design?

I know that many of you have a story of how your belief in your ability to be creative was shaken. You may still be standing in the shadow of your past, not realizing *you no longer have to remain there*. The truth is you are free as an Imagebearer of God to express yourself through the creative activities that fit your interests, talents, and desires.

This is a good thing to do because both natural observation and scientific study have shown that we are innately creative Beings. Abraham Maslow spent years studying human creativity. In his book *Toward a Psychology of Being*, he describes two different kinds of creative activities. One he called the "special talent of the genius type." This referred to the special talents and gifts people possess which are expressed in the conventionally accepted forms of poetry, art, painting, writing, sculpturing, theories, experiments or music.

The other kind of creativity is what he called "self-actualizing (SA) creativeness." He believed this kind of creativity sprang more directly from the personality and was demonstrated in peoples' lives in the ordinary affairs of life. It is a kind of creativity "which is the *universal heritage of every human being that is born*, and which seems to co-vary with psychological health"[4] (italics mine).

This kind of creativity is found in every person because it is innate within our being. Watch children at play anywhere in the world and they will demonstrate that creativity is one of our strongest human desires. They are the greatest testimony to the natural, uninhibited creativity we all possess. Dr. Maslow emphasized this relationship between children and creativity when he wrote:

> SA [self-actualizing] creativeness was in many respects like the creativeness of all happy and secure children. It was spontaneous, effortless, innocent, easy, a kind of freedom from stereotypes and cliches. . . . Almost any child can compose a song or a poem or a dance or a painting or a play or a game on the spur of the moment, without planning or previous intent. . . . In any case, this all sounds as if we are dealing with a fundamental characteristic, inherent in human nature, a potentiality given to all or most human beings at birth, which most often is lost or buried or inhibited as the person gets enculturated.[5]

What an encouraging picture Maslow gives of the uniqueness and naturalness of creativity in children! It's sad that as we get older, we lose so much of what makes us truly human. But like the phrase, "universal heritage," the statement "inherent in human nature" says that creativity is built into the very nature of our personhood. It is an ability and potential we all possess that can either be encouraged to develop or can remain inhibited or buried.

Maslow is not alone in believing that creativity is a unique and universal characteristic of the human being. Eugene Raudsepp, president of the Princeton Creative Research Inc. stated in his book *How Creative Are You?*:

Creativity, contrary to firmly entrenched folklore, is not the province or preserve of only a few talented individuals in the arts, the sciences and certain other "creative professions." Many experiments conducted over the past decade have conclusively proven that *creative ability is well-nigh universal*, that it is *built into the human species* and that in almost everything we do we can be creative (italics mine).[6]

His phrase, "built into the human species," affirms again that creativity is innate, and like Dr. Maslow, he says nothing about how this happened, nothing about its origin. Was it built in by mother nature, by chance and time, by the gods, or by God our Creator? Is this unique human ability the product of cosmic chance or is it the evidence of God's image in us? The answer we choose is going to make a significant difference on our outlook on life.

For years Dr. Rollo May was fascinated with the subject of creativity. Many questions ran through his mind as he read, observed and participated in art and science. In his book *The Courage to Create*, he made two important points I believe are at the heart of understanding human creative ability. First, he clearly believed that creativity was a unique characteristic of human beings; and two, it takes courage to be a creative person. This is how he expressed it:

> Is it not the distinguishing characteristic of the human being that in the hot race of evolution he pauses for a moment to paint on the cave walls at Lascaux or Altamira those brown-and-red deer and bison which fill us with amazed admiration and awe? . . . We express our being by creating. Creativity is a necessary sequel to being. Furthermore, the word courage in my title refers . . . to that particular kind of courage essential for the creative act.[7]

From his statement and those we saw earlier, there is not much doubt that creativity is a remarkable characteristic found in all human beings and demonstrated only by human beings. Creating is an expression of our being, a mark of human distinction. After all, what other creature would "pause to paint?" But if the origin of human creativity is the result of chance, then death robs life and creativity of any ultimate value and meaning. This is vividly illustrated by Dr. May.

> We may look at an autumn tree so beautiful in its brilliant colors that we feel like weeping; or we may hear music so lovely that we are overcome with sadness. The craven thought then creeps into our consciousness that maybe it would have been better not to have seen the tree at all or not to have heard the music. Then we wouldn't

be faced with this uncomfortable paradox—knowing that "time will come and take my love away," that everything we love will die. But the essence of being human is that, in this brief moment we exist on this spinning planet, we can love some persons and some things, in spite of the fact that time and death will ultimately claim us all.[8]

Facing this condition—that there is no God and no life after death—creates the feelings of what atheistic existentialists call "the anxiety of nothingness," or "existential despair." According to Dr. May, courage is not the opposite of despair but "it is, rather, the capacity to move ahead in spite of despair."[9]

According to this view creative activity becomes our savior. It helps us "reach beyond our death" to give life momentary meaning before nothingness. We can become all that we can be for our few brief years of life on this "spinning planet".

We Are Creative by Design

What a different picture we get of life and human creativity when we believe that life finds its origin and meaning in a relationship with a Personal God who exists and who created us in His image! The Christian view of life affirms the uniqueness of human creativity as the evidence pointing to God who is also creative and who made us like Himself.

A better explanation for how we acquired this unique gift is that it was given to us by design. This perspective affirms the enjoyment of life and encourages us to be creative because it has both temporal and eternal meaning and value. We are not wasting time when we engage in creative activities! They can be acts of worship honoring the One who gave us such a wonderful gift. What a positive outlook on life Franky Schaeffer gives regarding creativity and Christianity. He expressed it this way in his book *Addicted to Mediocrity*:

> Creativity, human worth, the arts, cultural endeavor, the media, communication, enjoyment of beauty and creativity in others, enjoyment of our own creativity, enjoyment of God's creativity—all of these need no justification. They are a good and gracious gift from the Heavenly Father above. This, like so much of biblical teaching, is something which brings tremendous freedom—not guilt, back-ward-looking fear, but freedom. Freedom that is brought through Christ's redemption, to go fuller, to go deeper, to go broader, to experience more. . . .[10]

As we can see, creativity, and human worth—as well as freedom and enjoyment of life—are all significantly linked to God and a Christian understanding of life. Are these ideas new? Are they just a contemporary answer to the modern world that battles with despair, hopelessness, meaninglessness and worthlessness? Listen to what Augustine said almost two thousand years ago.

> See, there are the heaven and the earth. They cry aloud that they were created. . . . They cry aloud also that they did not create themselves.

> It was you, Lord, who made them, you who are beautiful (for they are beautiful), you who are good (for they are good), you who are (for they are).

> It was you who made for the craftsman his body, you who, made the mind that directs his limbs, the material out of which he makes anything, the intelligence by which he grasps the principles of his art and sees inwardly what he is to make outwardly; you made his bodily senses by which he translates what he is doing from the mind to the material and then reports back again to the mind what has been done, so that the mind may within itself consult the truth presiding over it as to whether the work has been well done or not. All these things praise you, the Creator of all.[11]

Affirmation, reverence and worship of God, esteem for life, esteem for self and others replaces despair and nothingness when creativity is seen as evidence of God's image in us. It is human, it is healthy, and it is Christian to be creative. This is the way God designed it. It is not just an end in itself.

We Christians need to understand that if we do not affirm the arts specifically and creativity in general, then other world views, especially the New Age Movement, will fill that need. New Age philosophy offers a spiritual meaning to life—but if God is only a metaphor and not a person, then the end is no different than that espoused by atheistic humanism or existentialism. In case we have forgotten what that end is, let's look at a very eloquent picture painted for us over fifty years ago by the atheist Bertrand Russell in his book *Why I Am Not a Christian:*

> That man is the product of causes which had no prevision of the end they were achieving; that his origin, his growth, his hopes and fears, his loves and his beliefs, are but the outcome of accidental collocations of atoms; that no fire, no heroism, no intensity of thought and feeling, can preserve an individual life beyond the grave; that all the labor of all the ages, all the devotion, all the noonday brightness of human genius, are destined to extinction in the vast death of the solar system, and that the whole temple of man's achievement must inevitably be buried beneath the debris of a universe in ruins—all

these things, if not quite beyond dispute, are yet so nearly certain, that no philosophy which rejects them can hope to stand. Only within the scaffolding of these truths, only on the firm foundation of unyielding despair can the soul's habitation henceforth be safely built![12]

This is probably one of the finest pieces of writing I have read representing the atheistic world view carried to its logical conclusion. The creative use of words is inspiring but the picture he paints is death producing. What a different picture the Judeo-Christian world view offers to those who look upon its truths—that God is there; that God created us in His image; that God has shown His love for us in the person of Jesus Christ; that our acceptance of Christ brings new life; that daily life has ultimate meaning and purpose as we choose to be creative in life-giving ways for ourselves and for others.

Read again Franky Schaeffer's statement and see the beauty, hope, and life found in his word painting. It takes courage to choose to be creative but the burden is lighter. Jesus promised this when He said, "Come to me, all you who are weary and burdened, and I will give you rest. Take my yoke upon me and learn from me, for I am gentle and humble in heart, and you will find rest for your souls. For my yoke is easy and my burden is light" (Matthew 11:28-30).

The Need for Courage

I will never forget the day I welcomed Jesus Christ into my life and chose to commit my life to Him. Neither will I ever forget the day I decided to carve the frog. That day I took a courageous step toward life. I want to encourage and challenge you to come with me on this journey of rediscovering our creative ability. We will have to exercise both faith and courage, but this courage is not moving ahead in spite of despair; it is moving ahead despite our past failures and present fears. Its moves ahead, accepting risks, because our worth is not attached to the outcome. It is attached to our being made in the image of God.

The courage we need is the courage to step out from behind the memories of our past and begin to become the creative person God designed us to be. Maslow summarized it so well when he said:

SA [self-actualizing] creativeness stresses first the personality rather than its achievements. . . . It stresses characterological qualities like boldness, courage, freedom, spontaneity, perspicuity, integration, self-acceptance, all of which make possible the kind of generalized SA creativeness, which expresses itself in the creative life, or the creative attitude, or the creative person.[13]

Carl Rogers also emphasized the important distinction between the *person* and the *product*. He believed that creativity could emerge if a person felt a sense of unconditional worth. A person's creative *ability* needed to be separated from their creative *doing*. Dr. Rogers explained it this way in his book, *On Becoming a Person*:

> From the very nature of the inner conditions of creativity it is clear that they cannot be forced, but must be permitted to emerge. The farmer cannot make the germ develop and sprout from the seed; he can only supply the nurturing conditions which will permit the seed to develop its own potentialities. So it is with creativity. . . . My experience in psychotherapy leads me to believe that setting up conditions of psychological safety and freedom, we maximize the likelihood of an emergence of constructive creativity. . . . Whenever a teacher, parent, therapist, or other person with a facilitating function feels basically that this *individual is of worth in his own right* and in his own unfolding, no matter what his present condition or behavior, he is fostering creativity. . . .
>
> In a climate of safety, a person gradually learns that he can be whatever he is, without shame or façade, *since he seems to be regarded as of worth no matter what he does*. Hence he has less need of rigidity, can discover what it means to be himself, can try to actualize himself in new and spontaneous ways. He is, in other words, moving toward creativity (italics mine).[14]

What exciting possibilities lie ahead for us when we separate our personhood from our achievements (Creative Being ◄———► Creative Doing) and begin to express creativity in our own personal way. In the next chapter we will learn more about how to become the creative Imagebearer we were designed to be.

Suggested Reading

1. Schaeffer, Franky. *Addicted to Mediocrity.* Cornerstone Books, 1981.
2. Raudsepp, Eugene. *How Creative Are You?* Perigee Books, 1981.
3. Exodus 31:3-6; I Kings 4:32; Psalm 19:1-6.

Christianity is about the renewal of life. Therefore it is also about the renewal of art. This is how art can be shown its validity through Christianity. . . . It is for Christians to show what is meant by life and humanity; and to express what it means for them to have been 'made new' in Christ, in every aspect of their being.

Dr. H.R. Rookmaaker,
Modern Art and the Death of a Culture [1]

His image is woven into the fabric of everything we are. His thumbprint on our lives affects us in ways we will never begin to understand. His divine beauty . . . is part of our essence . . . which explains our drive to create things which are beyond us and which we don't always understand.

Michael Card,
Scribbling in the Sand [2]

My feeling is that the concept of creativeness and the concept of the healthy, self-actualizing, fully human person seem to be coming closer and closer together, and may perhaps turn out to be the same thing. . . . Is then creativeness part of the general human heritage? It does very frequently get lost, or covered up, or twisted or inhibited, or whatever, and then the job is of uncovering what all babies are, in principle, born with.

A. H. Maslow,
The Farther Reaches of Human Nature [3]

CHAPTER 26

How to Turn the Rembrandt
Loose in Yourself

How To

In 1987 Pope John Paul II visited the United States. Television coverage provided us with several stories of the Pope's interaction with a number of groups.

On one occasion he attended a large youth rally to challenge Catholic young people on issues of Christian belief and morality. Special music was provided by an armless guitarist. Anyone watching that event will probably never forget the scene of the Pope embracing the young musician at the conclusion of his song.

On a separate platform, a few feet from the Pope, sat Tony Melendez, a young man who was born without arms and hands. It was reported that as a boy he wanted to become a priest, but instead decided to minister to people through music. So he began to learn to play the guitar with his feet and toes while the guitar rested on the floor.

In those early days of awkward, frustrating, and discouraging times of practice, I am sure he never dreamed he would be given the opportunity to play for the Pope. Yet because of his love for music combined with hard work, persistence, patience, and the willingness to learn, his musical skills began to develop. In time his playing and singing began to touch peoples' lives. One day he was given an opportunity to do a solo for the youth rally where the Pope was the featured speaker.

The national news covered only a brief moment of Tony's singing and playing. When he finished, the crowd rose as one in a standing ovation. To everyone's surprise, the Pope stepped down from his platform, walked over to Tony, and hugged him. Tears filled Tony's eyes as the Pope returned to his chair.

Tony's eyes were not the only eyes filled with tears. I was deeply touched by Tony's example of being truly human and alive despite his physical handicap. By expressing his Christian faith and his creativity through music, he allowed God's image to shine through him in a clear and life-giving way. It truly brought glory to God. It also brought honor to Tony and inspiration and encouragement to his listeners.

Overcoming Our Creative Handicaps

Like Tony, we all have creative desires, interests, and talents. God would love to see us develop them. But we also have our handicaps to overcome— some are physical, but most are emotional, spiritual, or psychological. Each of us have innate creative ability and potential, but various blocks and barriers inhibit, intimidate, and discourage us from being creatively active. To become more of a creative person, we need to recognize our handicaps, face them honestly, accept them, and then give ourselves permission to be creative in spite of them. Eugene Raudsepp describes some of the blocks and barriers to creativity by dividing them into three categories: personal blocks, problem solving blocks, and environmental-organizational blocks. All three affect us, but I want to list those in the personal category so we can better identify them and change them.

1. Faulty attitude toward problems.
2. Lack of self-confidence.
3. Fear of criticism.
4. Mistaken notions about success.
5. Tendency to compare.
6. Early negative conditioning.
7. Lack of self-knowledge.
8. Lack of positive feelings and emotions.
9. Need for the familiar.
10. Desire or enforcement to conform.
11. Excessive togetherness/fear of solitude.
12. Excessive future/past orientation.
13. Emotional numbness.[4]

It shouldn't be difficult to see which of these personal blocks have prevented us from being as creative as we would like to be. Writing down an example for each one on the list could help us know specifically which ones we need to overcome to become more creative. For instance, under "faulty attitudes towards problems," I used to believe that "spiritual Christians" didn't have problems. I had problems, so I concluded it was because I wasn't spiritual *enough*. This perspective prevented me from doing any creative thinking about how to change the things that made me unhappy.

Later, as I began to give myself permission to do more creative thinking and creative problem-solving, I discovered many new ways to understand and change the things that bothered me. Overcoming the blocks to our creativity will have a positive impact on our life.

Characteristics of a Creative Person

One of the positive changes we will discover is the power and freedom to be ourselves that comes from living creatively. The more creative we become, the more we'll like the kind of person we are becoming. Eugene Raudsepp has given us a valuable description of what a creative person is like. It's helpful to have a clear idea of what to work toward in becoming that kind of person.

1. Fluency.
2. Flexibility.
3. Sensitivity to problems.
4. Originality.
5. Curiosity.
6. Openness to feelings and the unconscious.
7. Motivation.
8. Persistence and concentration.
9. Ability to think in images.
10. Ability to toy with ideas.
11. Ability to analyze and synthesize.
12. Tolerance of ambiguity.
13. Discernment and selectivity.
14. Ability to tolerate isolation.
15. Creative memory.
16. Background of fundamental knowledge.
17. Incubation.
18. Anticipation of productive periods.
19. Ability to think in metaphors.
20. Aesthetic orientation.[5]

By reading this list, we get a feel for what a creative person is like? They are people that are alive and involved in life! They express their creativity in all areas of life, which may include the classical arts like music, poetry and painting.

They are people who are creative in their personal lives whether they are a teacher, a custodian, a dog breeder, a minister, a counselor, an athlete, or a law officer. They are also people who can be creative in their relationships with their friends, spouse or children. Edith Schaeffer calls this "Hidden Art." This is art which expresses creativity in one's home life: interior decorating, flower arrangements, food preparation, gardening, clothing, and recreation.[6] Maslow described such a woman who convinced him that creativity can be demonstrated in the everyday areas of life.

> One woman, uneducated, poor, a full-time housewife and mother, did none of these conventionally creative things and yet was a marvellous cook, mother, wife and homemaker. With little money, her home was somehow always beautiful. She was a perfect hostess. Her meals were banquets. Her taste in linens, silver, glass, crockery and furniture was impeccable. She was in all these areas original, novel, ingenious, unexpected, inventive. I just had to call her creative. I learned from her and others like her that a first-rate soup is more creative than a second-rate painting, and that, generally, cooking or parenthood or making a home could be creative while poetry need not be. . . .[7]

How do we become more creative in life? By allowing ourselves to develop the characteristics mentioned above—like being flexible, open-minded, imaginative, and aware of feelings. By identifying our interests, desires, and abilities and then committing ourselves to doing something about it.

Creativity and the Healthy Personality

Another idea that can encourage us to become more creative is to better understand the relationship between creative activity and the development of a healthy personality. Research continues to support the idea that the creative approach to life is directly related to the development of a happier and healthier person.

At first we might not think so because we have heard stories of famous scientists, painters, writers or musicians who became destitute, depressed, even psychotic. Some tragically ended their lives by suicide.

But the kind of creativity that is linked to a healthy person is the creativity that promotes the development of the natural facets of our personality. Here's how Raudsepp described it:

> It has also been demonstrated that the more fully creative a person's experiences and activities are, the more fulfilling they are of his life. The creative approach is a direct, positive, assertive, involved approach to life. It helps a person to become more than he is now, or could become, without exercising his inherent creative ability.

The creative approach to life is at the core of healthy maturation and personality development. All healthy people want to grow, expand, develop, and express all the capacities they possess. That is why, in psychologist Erich Fromm's words, "education for creativity is nothing short of education for living."[8]

These men are not alone in their belief that creativity and healthy living are interrelated. Carl Rogers also felt that the motivation for creativity was innate and was the same force that promoted psychological health and healing. That force is the aspiration to become all that we desire to be. In his book *On Becoming a Person*, he wrote:

> The mainspring of creativity appears to be the same tendency which we discover so deeply as the curative force in psychotherapy—*man's tendency to actualize himself, to become his potentialities*. By this I mean . . . the urge to expand, extend, develop, mature—the tendency to express and activate all the capacities of the organism, or the self. This tendency may become deeply buried under layer after layer of encrusted psychological defenses; it may be hidden behind elaborate facades which deny its existence; it is my belief however, based on my experience, that it exists in every individual, and awaits only the proper conditions to be released and expressed.[9]

We saw a great example of this earlier when we talked about Joni's recovery from the accident that made her a quadriplegic. She reported that her drawing became more of a therapy than she had anticipated. She grew and blossomed into the person we know her to be today. A commitment to creativity is a commitment to health and life.

Fulfilling Childhood Dreams

Each of us have childhood dreams and desires of wanting to be creative in some way. As kids, these desires awakened our natural urge to express ourselves in creative ways—in bead work, number painting, sewing, wood burning, baking cookies.

One of the most significant steps we can take to become creative again is choosing to fulfill some of our childhood desires. Like treasured toys left forgotten on a closet shelf, we can rediscover them, bring them out into the light and enjoy them again. This allows us to recover lost childhood hobbies and interests. We can let the little girl or little boy side of ourselves step into freedom and do some of the creative things we use to do or that we have always wanted to do but never did.

Some of you might think you're too old to do this, but age is no barrier. In his book *Applied Imagination*, Alen Osborn tells about people who did wondrous things, and age was not an issue. For example, Oliver Wendell Holmes literary fame started with the writing of *Autocrat of the Breakfast Table* when he was near 50. Chief Justice Holmes wrote his first great book, *The Common Law*, when he was 72.

Milton lost his sight at age 44. He wrote *Paradise Lost* at age 57 and wrote *Paradise Regained* at 62. Mark Twain wrote two books at age 71. Julia Ward Howe wrote "The Battle Hymn of the Republic" when she was 43. Alexander Graham Bell perfected his telephone at age 58 and when he was past 70, he solved the problem of stabilizing the balance in airplanes.

People can enjoy creative living at any age if they will just be brave and have fun. Mr. Osborn encourages us to be creatively active by saying, "Even if our native *talent* should not grow, our creative *ability* can keep growing year after year in pace with the *effort* we put into it".[10] Whatever our age, our creative life will begin to change the moment we decide to change it.

Creativity Is a Choice

One of the greatest enemies of creativity is passivity. Doing nothing drains the will and the heart of the desire to be creative. If we value conformity, stereotyped thinking, constant order, compliance to the norm, or unchanged routines, we are not likely to nurture or encourage creativity in ourselves or others.

Creativity requires choice-making. It just doesn't happen by sitting back and doing nothing. We choose to make it happen when we want more out of life than what we are experiencing. As we have seen, creative living is a direct, positive, assertive, involved approach to life. Creative living stimulates feelings such as "aliveness," joy, fun, energy, power, satisfaction, accomplishment, adventure, excitement, purposefulness, and happiness. These feelings are produced by good choices in how we think and act in creative ways. Sometimes to make these choices we need the support of others who understand the value of a creative life-style.

The Value of Community Encouragement

Another thing we can do to become more creative is to associate with people and agencies that encourage creative expression. Being around creative people and feeling their enthusiasm is contagious. Soon we will find ourselves entertaining ideas of things we would like to do.

We can also begin to fill our minds with new and stimulating experiences by traveling, visiting with people, attending craft fairs, wondering through hobby shops, reading, listening to lectures, attending concerts and conferences, and by writing.

I have often wondered what would happen if our homes, schools, synagogues, and churches became positive agencies for the development of creativity in all their members. What impact would they have if they became places where people were encouraged to develop their creative interests and talents? They could be the "galleries" where the results could be displayed for all to enjoy.

I saw an example of what could happen several years ago at a church craft-fair. My booth was located between that of a pretty twenty-year-old girl with exceptional talent in painting and that of a seventy-five-year-old man who had just learned to toll paint on porcelain. I will never forget the warm-hearted grin spreading across the face of this slender, shaky, wrinkled old man when he was given a compliment about his work. The quality of his work was poor in comparison to the young girl's talent but that didn't matter to anyone. There was love, warmth, and encouragement for everyone simply because they had expressed their creativity.

Creativity as Self-Expression

One of my favorite psalms is Psalm 19. It talks about the creative handiwork of God and how it reveals who He is: "The heavens declare the glory of God; the skies proclaim the work of his hands" (Psalm 19:1). All of creation displays God's creative activities and speaks a language understood around the world. It says, "God is here; He is creative and He loves beauty and variety."

Creative accomplishments are one of the ways we can express ourselves —who we are, what we value, what we believe, and how we think and feel about life. Creative expression gives outward proof of what otherwise would remain hidden. It would remain unshared, unknown, and unappreciated. But when a person expresses themselves, others can be touched. Edith Schaeffer said it this way:

> Whatever form art takes, it gives outward expression to what otherwise would remain locked in the mind, unshared. . . . One area of art inspires another area of art, but also one person's expression of art stimulates another person and brings about growth in understanding, sensitivity and appreciation.[11]

Creating makes us visible and most of us have a natural desire to "be seen." In the past when my son Kent would come home from school, he often brought home one of his creative projects. One especially caught my attention because he had titled it, "A Rainbow Chasing a Man." What I saw in this single piece of work was not just his individual accomplishment; I saw a young Imagebearer standing in front of me demonstrating his likeness to God.

By exercising his creative ability, he made visible both his personhood and his product. Who knows where this will lead? I am sure Thomas Edison had no idea what things he would accomplish when he first began to express himself creatively. Yet every time we turn on a light bulb we witness one of his creative achievements.

To stifle our creativity is to stifle our personhood and become less visible as a person. It is to be hidden behind a facade, displaying only a partial image of what God originally designed. This too can change by choice.

The Art of Self-Creation

The most creative decisions we will ever make are the ones that create the kind of person we become. We have heard someone say in anger, "Just look at the kind of person you have turned into!" Our choices do have a direct impact on the the way we develop as a person. Our choices have shaped us into the person we are today. I agree with Rollo May when he said we have a great deal to say about how we create ourselves. He wrote:

> Human freedom involves our capacity to pause between stimulus and response and, in the pause, to choose the one response towards which we wish to throw our weight. The capacity to create ourselves, based upon this freedom, is inseparable from consciousness or self-awareness.[12]

Our life is a mosaic of the choices we make: our choice of values, goals, beliefs, dreams, morals, ideals, attitudes, and behaviors. In a unique and creative way we have assembled these choices into the kind of person we are now. Our lives may be one of beauty, integrity, balance, energy, and life, or it may be a display of discord, chaos, darkness, pain, and death.

God wants life to be fulfilling, purposeful, adventurous, enjoyable, and productive. Creatively working on ourselves in partnership with Jesus Christ is one way to experience life the way God intended. Sadly, I have known many Christians who have sat back and passively waited for God to "zap" them into being happy, healthy people. Their dependency on God was a passive dependency resulting in little creative success or victory in making life become richer, fuller, and more fun. Carl Rogers observed this same experience in his work with people. It was directly related to our appreciation for our ability to choose. He wrote:

> In the therapeutic relationship some of the most compelling subjective experiences are those in which the *client feels within himself the power*

of naked choice. He is free—to become himself or to hide behind a façade; to move forward or to retrogress; to behave in ways which are destructive of self and others, or in ways which are enhancing; quite literally free to live or die, in both the physiological and psychological meaning of those terms (italics mine).[13]

I am convinced that God wants us to work *with Him* in finding creative ways to grow, change, heal, and become mature Christian human beings. For example we can be more creative in:

- Dealing with problems.
- Handling conflict.
- Working our way through hardship/tragedies.
- Disciplining our children.
- Making love with our spouse.
- Facing our past hurts.
- Accepting ageing.
- Experiencing the loss of a loved one.
- Paying for an education, etc.

Our creativity is only limited by our unwillingness to use it in any and every aspect of life. My own experience over the past forty years has convinced me that God wants us to be actively involved in creating the kind of person we want to become in all areas of our life. We need to do more creating and less complaining. This allows changes to happen and results to be achieved that could go beyond our wildest dreams. This will require some creative changes to be made in the way we talk to ourselves. In the past our self-talk has probably been limiting and negative.

Change the Negative Self-Talk

Only humans are aware they can be creative. That's why stifled creativity can almost always be traced back to self-esteem problems. It remains inhibited because only humans can say to themselves, "I am no good at being creative" or "I can't do that because I might fail and make a fool of myself." Negative self-talk keeps the natural desire to be creative imprisoned in the experiences of the past.

One of the keys that will open the prison cell and release us to be creative people is to begin to talk to ourselves in affirming and encouraging ways. Statements like, "It's okay for me to become creative because God made me that way," or "It's okay if it isn't perfect. Just have fun doing it," helps us overcome the negative self-talk we have listened to for years. It is reminding ourselves we have permission to be creative because *God loves seeing us be our creative selves.*

Creativity is learning how to put our trust in God's design and in ourselves—trusting our feelings, desires, ideas, and choices. It is coaching ourselves to move forward in enjoying our creativity and that "failing" is part of the learning process. The first steps may be small, but small steps in the right direction will begin to open up avenues of creativity, planned in advance by God to display his likeness in us. And we get to be creative just for the pure joy of it.

My desire is that we all awaken to our creative privilege, feel the revitalization of our creative desires, step out from behind the memories of our past and become the creative Imagebearers God designed us to be. When we choose to fulfill the creative potential given to us as a gift from God, we choose life.

Suggested Reading

1. Schaeffer, Edith. *Hidden Art.* Tyndale House, 1971.
2. Osborn, Alex. *Applied Imagination.* Charles Scribner's, 1953.
3. Psalm 33:3; 96:1.

1 - FEEL
2 - CHOOSE
3 - THINK
4 - COMMUNICATE
5 - BECOME SELF-AWARE
6 - BECOME MORALLY AWARE
7 - BECOME SPIRITUALLY AWARE
8 - BE CREATIVE

The glory of God is a human being who is fully alive!

Saint Irenaeus, 2nd century A.D.

———◦◦◦———

While it is not sane to defame human nature, it is idiot-ic to deify it. Between the two extremes of undue depreciation and exaggerated exaltation lies a safe middle where the high and lasting dignity of man even in the ruins of the fall appears and becomes at once the proof of what he was and the call to what he may yet become.

James I. Vance, *The Eternal in Man*[1]

———◦◦◦———

For this reason I kneel before the Father, from whom his whole family in heaven and on earth derives its name. I pray that out of his glorious riches he may strengthen you with power through his Spirit in your inner being so that Christ may dwell in your hearts through faith. And I pray that you, being rooted and established in love, may have power together with all the saints, to grasp how wide and long and high and deep is the love of Christ, and to know this love that surpasses knowledge—that you may be filled to the measure of all the fullness of God.

The apostle Paul, Ephesians 3:14-20.

CHAPTER 27

Be What We Were
Designed to Be

W e have just completed our orbit around our personhood—our creation in the image of God. The eight human qualities that make us a person have been invited into the spotlight. They have loudly proclaimed that *Our worth is in our design.* Self-esteem is by God's design.

When we view humankind from the Christian perspective, we affirm the imprint of our nobility stamped on our *being* by God Himself. It restores our innate worth and gives ultimate meaning and dignity to human life. We are Imagebearers of the Creator of life. We are fearfully and wonderfully made!

We are also fallen. His image in us has been twisted and marred by the effects of sin and of living in a fallen, sinful world. True Christianity is about renewal—a renewal of a healthy sense of worth and identity, a renewal of life in all its dimensions.

Christianity is also about restoration—the restoration of our ability to feel, choose, think, communicate, to be self-aware, morally aware, spiritually aware and creative. A growing person is alive in all areas of his being. This is an ideal, a goal toward which we can grow each day, one day at a time, one choice at a time–and lasting for a lifetime. In this way, the image of God in each of us is gradually restored and made whole again.

Christianity is also about the restoration of our relationships—with God, with Jesus, with ourselves, and with others. This is more easily done when we can see our worth and the worth of those around us. Seeing the worth of a person is seeing them through the eyes of Jesus. Something in our personhood was of great worth to Him. That something was our creation in God's likeness. This gives us a worth that is innate and rests in our Being rather than our Doing.

This book is a call to everyone to become what God created us to be. What a tragedy it would be to come to the end of our life and feel regret for not having chosen to become what God designed us to be. My Mom died in 1998. I found a poem she had written in 1991 that expressed that regret. As a high school senior in Caldwell, Idaho in the late 1930s, she had been awarded a full-ride scholarship to Stanford University in California but her foster mother would not let her go. So she married my father to get away and gave birth to me a year later. All her life she lived for her three boys but I know her journey to Stanford would have made her a completely different woman. Here is her poem. May it never be written about us.

Regret

When I die,
Don't grieve for the relic of the woman gone.
I am old and tired, disillusioned.

Instead grieve my grief with me—
For the woman I wanted to be—
For the woman I might have become.

Edythe Day

Our rescue by Jesus Christ gives us the freedom to live—really live as a whole person. In His love and grace we are free to step out from behind the memories of our past and grow each day to become a more healthy, whole person psychologically and spiritually. We are free to give ourselves permission to be what God created us to be, to be who Jesus saved us to be.

We began this book with the questions: "Who Me? I can feel good about myself and know I am a person of worth and importance?" I hope you can respond with a resounding "Yes!" I hope you have come into a new appreciation of *who you are* and of *what you're able to do*. I hope you can always keep these truths in mind:

We bear God's image in our Personhood.
We can bear Christ's image in our Character.

Our worth is secure in being made in God's image.
Our salvation is secure in being in Christ.

We can trust Christ for our Salvation.
We can trust Christ with our worth.

Our heart is the inner sanctuary for a living God. Our heart is also the hiding place of our self-opinions. May the light of the eternal truth that we are made in the image and likeness of God transform any unhealthy pictures into healthy ones. Then let us live to bear His image with dignity and joy.

Dear Fellow Imagebearer,

Congratulations! You have just completed a course on being an Imagebearer of God. Your graduation certificate on the following page is to remind you that you are entitled to all the rights and privileges of being a person created in the image of God. Put your name on the certificate, read it frequently, and then go and become all that God designed you to be. May your journey to your worth and identity be as rewarding and fulfilling as mine.

In His image and service,

Dr. Larry Day

Affirmation of Self-worth

This certificate is to affirm that you

_____

are entitled to enjoy the sense of worth and dignity bestowed on you by your Creator because of your being designed in His Image. You are encouraged to commit yourself to be fully what you are—an Imagebearer of God.

It is to be remembered that your worth is a settled issue and rests in the truth of Who You Are rather than what you do. Because your worth is secure in being made in God's image, you are free to grow in personal ways and thus demonstrate your individual uniqueness by what you do.

It is to be remembered that your emotional and spiritual growth is gradual and will be completed only at the Designer's return; therefore, you are free in God's love and Christ's redemption to grow each day in becoming more of a

Feeling	_Self-aware_
Choosing	_Morally aware_
Thinking	_Spiritually aware and_
Communicative	_Creative person._

You were designed for relationship. Becoming a whole person in a quality relationship with God and others is the purpose of life; therefore, you can glorify God not only by what you do but also by who you are. Being made in His Image is God's gift to you; your becoming a whole person is your gift to God.

© Dr. Larry Day 1983, 2004

If you have found this book to be a helpful resource and would like to contact Dr. Day about other materials on self-esteem, or to schedule a speaking engagement with him, please write or call:

Dr. Larry Day
P. O. Box 33524
Portland, Oregon 97292
Phone: 503-231-0202
www.drlarryday.com

Materials now available for purchase: (call for an order form and prices)
1. The book *Self-Esteem: By God's Design*.
2. Ten-week Self-Esteem class on audio cassette.
3. The "Affirmation of Self-Worth" certificate (5"x7").
4. Two different mugs: Imagebearer Mug and Stress Management Mug.
5. Individual Tapes covering a variety of topics.
- Self-Esteem: Rediscovering the Wonder of Your Worth.
- The Power to Choose: the Art of Creating a New Past.
- Self-Talk: What We Say to Ourselves Does Make a Big Difference.
- Why God: Understanding and Overcoming Hardships and Tragedies.
- Handling Difficult People Before They Drive You Nuts.
- Handling Frustration and Anger Successfully.
- Overcoming Fear and Worry.
- Co-Dependency: Can Christians Love Too Much.
- Habits: How to Overcome Bad Ones and Develop Good Ones.
- Overcoming the Tyranny of Perfectionism.
- Procrastination: God Help Me Overcome It—Tomorrow Maybe.
- Expectations: How They Help or Hinder Your Life.
- Encouragement: Is It Okay for Me to Accept a Compliment.
- Stop Being a Victim and Become a Victor.
- Sweet 16: Sixteen Skills to Help You Get Along with Almost Everyone You Meet.
- Overcoming Depression.
- Handling Stress Effectively to Prevent Burnout.
- The Secret of Contentment.
- God, Is It Okay If I Go Play?
- Survival Guide for Parents of Difficult Children.
- Hope: Its Meaning and Purpose in Life.
- Why am I the Way I am. God Did You Make Me this Way?

APPENDIX A

FEELING WORD LIST

Developed by Dr. Larry Day

"I feel _____ when _____."

"I have felt _____ when _____."

accepted	bubbly	deflated	envious	grateful
accused	burdened	degraded	evasive	gratified
adrift	burned out	dejected	evil	greedy
affectionate	calm	delighted	excited	grief
affirmed	cautious	determined	exhausted	grown up
afraid	cheated	dependent	exhilarated	guilty
aggravated	cheerful	depressed	expectant	gutless
aggressive	childish	deprived	exposed	handcuffed
aglow	childlike	despair	fatalistic	happy
aimless	clean	detached	fatherly	harassed
alarmed	cold inside	devalued	fearful	hard-hearted
alienated	comfortable	dignity	fed up	hateful
alive	committed	dirty	feminine	healthy
ambitious	communicative	disappointed	flattered	helpless
ambivalent	compassionate	discouraged	flexible	hollow
amused	competent	disenchanted	flirtatious	honored
angry	complacent	disinterested	fluffy	hopeful
annoyed	concerned	disgusted	forceful	hostile
antagonistic	condemned	disheartened	forgetful	humble
anxious	confident	dismayed	forgiven	humorous
apathetic	confused	disorganized	fortunate	hurt
appalled	content	disoriented	fragile	ignored
appreciated	contempt	displeased	frantic	immobilized
apprehensive	controlled	disrespected	free	impatient
arrogant	courageous	distracted	friendless	important
attractive	cowardly	distressed	friendly	impure
awkward	crazy	dominated	frustrated	inadequate
bad	creative	down	funny	incapable
baffled	critical	drained	furious	incompetent
beat	cruel	dreary	generous	inconsistent
beautiful	crushed	dumb	gentle	indecisive
belittled	curious	eager	genuine	independent
bewildered	dazed	easy going	giddy	indifferent
blue	deceitful	empty	glad	inferior
bothered	defeated	encouraged	gloomy	inhibited
brave	defenseless	energized	good	innocent

irritated
insane
insecure
insincere
intense
intimate
intimidated
involved
irreligious
isolated
jealous
joyful
judgmental
justified
kind
knotty
lazy
left out
liberated
lighthearted
like myself
lonely
loveable
loved
lovely
loving
lost
loyal
lucky
lustful
mad
made fun of
manipulated
manipulating
masculine
mean
melancholy
mischievous
miserable
mistaken
misunderstood
messed up
mocked
moody
motherly
myself
natural
needed
needy
negative
neglected
nervous

noble
numb
old
open
optimistic
organized
original
outgoing
out of control
outraged
overlooked
panicky
paralyzed
paranoid
passionate
passive
peaceful
penalized
persecuted
perturbed
pessimistic
phony
pity
pious
pleased
pleasure
positive
possessive
pouty
powerful
powerless
preoccupied
prejudice
pressured
prideful
productive
protective
proud
punished
puzzled
quiet
rage
rattled
rebellious
redeemed
refreshed
regretful
rejected
reliable
relieved
religious
repulsed

resentful
respective
restored
restricted
revengeful
reverent
rewarded
ridiculous
right
sad
satisfied
secure
seductive
selfish
self-reliant
self-respect
self-righteous
sensitive
sensual
sentimental
set free
sexual
shallow
shy
significant
silly
simple
sinful
sluggish
sociable
soft
sorrowful
sorry
speechless
special
spent
spiritual
spiteful
spooked
stifled
strange
stubborn
stupid
stunned
sullen
sunshiny
surprised
superior
supported
suspicious
sympathetic
tearful

tender
terrible
terrified
thankful
threatened
thrilled
timid
tired
tolerant
tongue-tied
tormented
torn
tranquil
trapped
ugly
unappreciated
uncertain
uncomfortable
understood
uneasy
unhappy
unique
unloved
unwanted
unsure
uplifted
upset
up-tight
used
useless
vain
valued
victimized
vindicated
vindictive
virtuous
violent
vulgar
vulnerable
wanted
warm inside
weak
weary
weepy
whole inside
witty
wonderful
worn out
worried
worshipful
worth
worthwhile

worthy
wrong
wronged
xenophobic
young
youthful
zany

NOTES

CHAPTER 1

1. Maxwell Maltz, *The Magic Power of Self-Image Psychology* (New York: Simon & Schuster, Inc., 1964), 4.

2. Cecil Osborne, *The Art of Understanding Yourself* (Grand Rapids, Mich.: Zondervan Publishing House, 1967), 161, 162-63.

3. Nathaniel Branden, *Honoring the Self* (New York: Bantam Books, 1983), 3.

4. J. Rodale, *The Synonym Finder* (Emmaus, Penn.: Rodale Press, 1978), 336. Revised by Laurence Urdang, Editor-in-Chief.

5. Maxwell Maltz, *Psycho-Cybernetics* (New York: Prentice-Hall, Inc., 1960), 2.

6. Nathaniel Branden, *The Psychology of Self-Esteem* (Los Angeles: Nash Publishing Corporation, 1969), 109-10.

7. For further reading, see Stanley Coopersmith, *The Antecedents of Self-esteem* (San Francisco: W. H. Freeman and Company, 1967).

CHAPTER 2

1. Branden, *The Psychology of Self-Esteem*, 110.

2. Robert Schuller, *Self-Esteem: The New Reformation* (Waco, Tex.: Word Books, 1982), 33-34.

3. James Dobson, *Hide or Seek* (Old Tappan, N.J.: Fleming H. Revell Company, 1974), 7, 12.

CHAPTER 3

1. Lynn Harold Hough, *The Dignity of Man*, New York: Abingdon-Cokesbury Press, 1950. 10, 11.

2. Dorothy Corkille Briggs, *Your Child's Self-Esteem* (Garden City, New York: Doubleday & Company, Inc., 1975), 3.

3. James Dobson, *Hide or Seek*, 47.

4. Branden, *Psychology of Self-Esteem*, vii.

5. Albert Ellis, *Reason and Emotion in Psychotherapy* (Secaucus, New Jersey: The Citadel Press, 1962), 153.

6. Mortimer Adler, *How to Think about God* (New York: Bantam Books, Inc., 1980), 156.

7. Francis A. Schaeffer, *He Is There and He Is not Silent* (Wheaton, Ill.: Tyndale House Publishers, 1972), 11.

8. Francis A. Schaeffer, *Genesis in Space and Time* (Downers Grove, Ill.: InterVarsity Press, 1972), 51-52.

9. For further reading, see G. C. Berkouwer, *Man in the Image of God* (Grand Rapids, Mich.: Wm. B. Eerdmans Publishing, 1962).

10. William Jennings Bryan, *In His Image* (New York: Fleming H. Revell Company, 1922), 13, 103.

11. Max Lucado, *You Are Special* (Wheaton, Illinois: Crossway Books, 1997).

CHAPTER 4

1. John Baillie, *Invitation to Pilgrimage* (London: Oxford University Press, 1942), 85.
2. Maxwell Maltz, *The Search for Self-Respect* (New York: Grosset & Dunlap Publishers, 1973), 5.
3. Hough, *The Dignity of Man*, 10.

CHAPTER 5

1. Maltz, *Psycho-Cybernetics*, 112.
2. Hough, *The Dignity of Man*, 10-11.
3. Jean Mouroux, *The Meaning of Man*. Translated by A. H. G. Downes. (Garden City, New York: Image Books, 1961), 242.
4. James Irwin, *To Rule the Night* (Philadelphia: A. J. Holman Company, 1973), 17.
5. Hans Küng, *Does God Exist* (New York: Progress Publishers, Inc., 1975), 641.

CHAPTER 6

1. Paul Tournier, *The Whole Person in a Broken World* (New York: Harper & Row Publishers, 1964), 36, 120, 168.
2. Earl Martin, *Toward Understanding God* (Anderson, Ind.: The Warner Press, 1942), 100.
3. Henri de Lubac, *The Drama of Atheist Humanism*. Translated by Edith M. Riley. (New York: The World Publishing Company, 1950), 3-4.
4. Schaeffer, *Genesis in Space and Time*, 58-59.
5. Lee Strobel, *The Case for a Creator* (Grand Rapids, Mich.: Zondervan Publishing House, 2004), 59.
6. Charles Colson, *Kingdoms in Conflict* (Grand Rapids, Mich.: William Morrow/Zondervan Publishing House, 1987), 73-74.
7. For further reading, see Randall N. Baer, *Inside the New Age Nightmare* (Lafayette, La.: Huntington House, Inc., 1989). Mr. Baer was a top New Age leader for fifteen years before his conversion to Christ.

CHAPTER 7

1. Blaise Pascal, *Pascal's Pensées* (New York: E. Dutton & Co., Inc., 1958), 111.
2. David Cairns, *The Image of God in Man* (London: SCM Press Ltd., 1953), 21, 248.
3. Josh McDowell, *Building Your Self-Image* (Wheaton, Ill.: Tyndale House Publishers, Inc., 1986), 41-42, 43.
4. Francis Schaeffer, *Genesis in Space and Time*, 100.

CHAPTER 8

1. Philip Yancey, *Disappointment with God* (New York: Harper Collins Publishers, 1988), 32.
2. Harold S. Kushner, *When Bad Things Happen to Good People* (New York: Schocken Books, 1981), 3.
3. C. S. Lewis, *The Problem of Pain* (New York: MacMillan Publishing Company, 1962), 46, 47-48.
4. Ernest Becker, *The Denial of Death* (New York: Collier MacMillan Publishers, 1973), 26.
5. Ibid., 87.
6. For further reading, see Robert Schuller, *Life's Not Fair but God Is Good* (Nashville: Thomas Nelson Publishers, 1991).
7. John Peter Lange, *Commentary on the Holy Scriptures: Chronicles—Job* (Grand Rapids, Mich.: Zondervan Publishing House, 1960), 215. A new rhythmical version of the book of Job, translated from the German by Philip Schaff.
8. Becker, *Denial of Death*, 90, 91.
9. Joni Eareckson, *Joni* (Minneapolis, Minn.: WorldWide Publications, 1976), 73, 82-83.
10. Ibid., 91-92.

11. Ibid., 132-33.

12. Ibid., 94.

13. Christopher Reeve, Still Me (New York: Random House, 1998) 12.

CHAPTER 9

1. Bryan, *In His Image*, 134, 135.

2. Dobson, *Hide or Seek*, 159.

3. Hough, *The Dignity of Man*, 26-27.

4. H. D . McDonald, *The Christian View of Man* (Westchester, Ill.: Crossway Books, 1981), 1, 2.

5. Hough, *The Dignity of Man*, 76, 77.

CHAPTER 10

1. Schaeffer, *He Is There*, 3.

2. Hough, *The Dignity of Man*, 35.

3. Schuller, *Self-Esteem: The New Reformation*, 20, 60.

CHAPTER 11

1. Branden, *Honoring the Self*, 158, 159.

2. Joan Jacobs, *Feelings! Where They Come From and How to Handle Them* (Wheaton, Ill.: Tyndale House Publishers, Inc., 1976), 15, 16.

3. David Viscott, *The Language of Feelings* (New York: Simon & Schuster, 1976), 9.

4. Jacobs, *Feelings! Where They Come From*, 15.

5. Viscott, *The Language of Feelings*, 9, 13, 19.

6. For further reading, see Carroll E. Izard, *Human Emotions* (New York: Plenum Press, 1977).

7. Jean-Paul Sartre, *Existentialism and Human Emotions* (New York: Philosophical Library, Inc., 1957), 15, 23, 52.

8. Benjamin Breckenridge Warfield, *The Person and Work of Christ*. ed. Samuel G. Craig (Philadelphia: The Presbyterian and Reformed Publishing Company, 1950), 139.

9. Willard Gaylin, *Feelings: Our Vital Signs* (New York: Harper and Row Publishers, Inc., 1979), 3, 7.

10. Branen, Nathaniel, The Disowned Self, (New York: Bantam Books, 1971), 71, 74.

11. Ibid., 4.

CHAPTER 12

1. Izard, *Human Emotions*, 18.

2. Joseph Hart, Richard Corriere, and Jerry Binder. *Going Sane: An Introduction to Feeling Therapy* (New York: Jason Aronson, Inc., 1975), 10-11, 26.

3. Jacobs, *Feelings! Where They Come From*, 19-20.

4. Gaylin, *Feelings: Our Vital Signs*, 11.

5. Robert Plutchik, *The Emotions: Facts, Theories, and a New Model* (New York: Random House, 1962), vii.

6. Viscott, *The Language of Feelings*, 10, 13.

7. Ibid., 11-12.

CHAPTER 13

1. Hough, *The Dignity of Man*, 83-84.

2. Andrew Murry, *How to Raise Your Children for Christ* (Minneapolis, Minn.: Bethany Fellowship, Inc., 1975), 128.

3. St. Thomas Aquinas, *Treatise on Man*. translated by James F. Anderson (Englewood Cliffs, N.J.: Prentice-Hall, Inc., 1962), 110.

4. Victor Frankl, *Man's Search for Meaning: An Introduction to Logotherapy* (New York: Pocket Books, 1963), 44, 51, 99.

5. Ibid., 104-105.

6. Brandon, *The Psychology of Self-Esteem*, 39.

7. Viktor Frankl, *Psychotherapy and Existentialism* (New York: Simon and Schuster, 1967), 35.

8. Wayne Dyer, *Your Erroneous Zones* (New York: Avon Books, 1976), 14.

9. William Glasser, *Control Theory* (New York: Harper & Row Publishers, 1984), 40.

10. Erich Sauer, *The King of the Earth* (Grand Rapids, Mich.: Wm. B. Eerdmans Publishing Co., 1962), 54.

11. Ibid., 58.

12. For further reading, see Margaret J. Rinck, *Can Christians Love Too Much* (Grand Rapids, Mich.: Zondervan Publishing House, 1989). A good book on helping a person understand what a healthy sense of self means.

13. Garry Friesen, *Decision Making and the Will of God* (Portland, Ore.: Multnomah Press, 1980), 16-17.

CHAPTER 14

1. Paul Tournier, *The Meaning of Persons* (New York: Harper & Row Publishers, 1957), 200, 201.

2. Sharon Wegscheider-Cruse, *The Miracle of Recovery* (Deerfield Beach, Fla.: Health Communications, Inc., 1989), 104.

3. Walter Abbott, gen. ed., Joseph Gallagher, trans. ed., *The Documents of Vatican II* (New York: The American Press, 1966), 214.

4. For further reading, see Robert E. Alberti and Michael L. Emmons, *Your Perfect Right*, Revised Third Edition (San Luis Obispo, Calif.: Impact Publishers, 1978).

5. For further reading, see Robert Hemfelt, Frank Minirth, and Paul Meier. *Love Is a Choice* (Nashville: Thomas Nelson Publishers, 1989). A helpful book on understanding codependency written by Christian authors.

6. Gloria Gaither, *Decisions* (Waco, Tex.: Word Books Publisher, 1982), 19.

7. Bruno Bettelheim, *The Informed Heart* (New York: The Free Press, 1960), 75.

8. Manuel Smith, *When I Say No I Feel Guilty* (New York: Bantam Books, 1976), 73ff.

9. A.H. Maslow, *The Father Reaches of Human Nature* (New York: Penguin Books, 1971), 44.

10. Harold Greenwald, *Direct Decision Therapy* (San Diego, Calif.: Edits Publishers, 1973), 13.

11. Phillip McGraw, *Self-Matters* (New York: Free Press, 2001), 157.

12. G. Gilmore, *Don The Freedom to Fail* (Westwood, N.J.: Fleming H. Revell Co., 1966), 13, 17, 22.

13. Leonard Verduin, *Somewhat Less than God* (Grand Rapids, Mich.: Wm. B. Eerdmans Publishing Co., 1970), 99.

14. Henry Cloud & John Townsend, *Boundaries* (Grand Rapids, Mich.: Zondervan Publishing House, 1992), 32, 33.

CHAPTER 15

1. Pascal, *Pensées*, 97.

2. Emil Brunner, *Man in Revolt: A Christian Anthropology* (Philadelphia: The Westminster Press), 42.

3. James Orr, *God's Image in Man* (Grand Rapids, Mich.: Wm. B. Eerdmans Publishing Co., 1948), 262, 263-64.

4. Mortimer Adler, *The Difference of Man and the Difference It Makes* (New York: Holt, Rinehart, and Winston, 1967), 54.

5. Branden, *The Psychology of Self-Esteem*. 5-6, 28.

6. Ibid., 35.

7. Descarte, *Philosophical Writings* (New York: St. Martin's Press, Inc., 1952), 140, 141, 205. Selected and translated by Norman Kemp Smith.

8. Adler, *The Difference of Man*, 55.

9. Ibid., 287.

10. Pascal, *Pensées,* 45, 97.

11. Ayn Rand, *Atlas Shrugged* (New York: Signet Books, 1957), 938, 939, 940.

12. Helmut Thielicke, *Being Human . . . Becoming Human: An Essay in Christian Anthropology.* Translated by Geoffrey W. Bromiley, Garden City (New York: Doubleday & Company, Inc., 1984), 129.

CHAPTER 16

1. Robert Schuller, *Moving Ahead with Possibility Thinking* (New York: Family Library, 1967), 15.

2. Albert Ellis, and Robert A. Harper. *A New Guide to Rational Living* (Englewood Cliffs, N.J.: Prentice-Hall, Inc., 1975), 13, 60.

3. Norman Vincent Peale, *The Power of Positive Thinking* (New York: Prentice-Hall, Inc., 1952), 13.

4. Ibid., 60.

5. Martin E. Seligman, *Learned Optimism* (New York: Pocket Books, 1990), 8, 16.

6. Ibid., 15-16, 44.

7. For further reading, see David Stoop, *Self-Talk* (Old Tappan, N.J.: Fleming H. Revell Co., 1982).

8. Albert Ellis, and Robert A. Harper, *A Guide to Rational Living* (N. Hollywood, Calif.: Wilshire Book Co., 1961), 21, 50.

9. Schuller, *Moving Ahead with Possibility Thinking,* 39.

10. For further reading, see Jerry A. Schmidt, *Do You Hear What You're Thinking* (Wheaton, Ill.: Victor Books, 1983). This is another helpful Christian book on understand self-talk.

11. Maltz, *Psycho-Cybernetics,* xi-xii.

12. Ibid., 39-40.

13. For further reading, see William Backus and Marie Chapian. *Telling Yourself the Truth* (Minneapolis, Minnesota: Bethany House Publishers, 1980).

CHAPTER 17

1. Aristotle. *The Politics.* Translated by Carnes Lord (Chicago: The University of Chicago Press, 1984), 37.

2. William James, *The Principles of Psychology.* Vol. II. (London: Macmillan and Co., Ltd., 1891), 355-56.

3. Schaeffer. *He Is There and He Is Not Silent,* 65.

4. Adler, *The Difference of Man,* 112.

5. Julian Huxley, *Man in the Modern World* (New York: Mentor Books, 1948), 8.

6. Charlton Laird, *The Miracle of Language* (Greenwich, Conn.: Fawcett Publications, Inc., 1953), 24.

7. Schaeffer. *Genesis in Space,* 58-59.

8. Ibid., 60.

9. Sidney M. Jourard, *The Transparent Self.* Revised Edition (New York: D. Van Nostrand Co., 1971), vii, 4.

10. Ibid., 32.

11. Jordan Paul and Margaret Paul, *Do I Have to Give Up Me to Be Loved By You?* (Minneapolis: CompCare Publishers, 1983), 155.

CHAPTER 18

1. Tournier, *The Meaning of Persons,* 162.

2. Verduin, *Somewhat Less Than God,* 123-24.

3. For further reading, see Matthew McKay, Martha Davis, and Patrick Fanning, *Messages: The Communication Book* (Oakland, Calif.: New Harbinger Publications, 1983).

4. For further reading, see Gary Smalley and John Trent, *The Language of Love* (Pomona, Calif.: Focus on the Family Publishing, 1988).

5. For further reading, see John Drakeford, *The Awesome Power of the Listening Ear* (Waco, Tex.: Word Books, 1967).

CHAPTER 19

1. Orr, *God's Image in Man,* 61.

2. David Abrahamsen, *The Road to Emotional Maturity* (Englewood Cliffs, N.J.: Prentice-Hall, Inc., 1958), 157.

3. Eric Fromm, *Psychoanalysis and Religion* (New Haven: Yale University Press, 1950), 22, 23.

4. Arnold Toynbee, *Surviving the Future* (New York: Oxford University Press, 1971), 6.

5. Brandon, *The Psychology of Self-Esteem,* 35.

6. James, *The Principles of Psychology,* 358-359.

7. Karen Horney, *Neurosis and Human Growth* (New York: W. W. Norton & Company, Inc., 1950), 21, 22, 23.

8. Robert McGee, *The Search for Significance* (Houston, Texas: Rapa Publishing, 1985).

9. Horney, *Neurosis and Human Growth,* 155.

10. Ibid., 86.

11. Toynbee, *Surviving the Future,* 38.

12. John Calvin, *Institutes of the Christian Religion.* Eighth American Edition, Vol. I, translated by John Allen (Grand Rapids, Mich.: Wm. B. Eerdmans Publishing Company, 1949), 47, 56, 265-66.

13. Gordon W. Allport, *Becoming* (New Haven, Conn.: Yale University Press, 1955), 23.

14. Maslow, *The Farther Reaches of Human Nature,* 44, 45, 46.

15. Clark Moustakas, *Creativity and Conformity* (New York: Van Nostrand Reinhold Company, 1967), 13.

16. For further reading, see H. Norman Wright, *Making Peace with Your Past* (Old Tappan, N.J.: Fleming H. Revell Company, 1985).

17. David Seamands, *Healing for Damaged Emotions* (Wheaton, Ill.: Victor Books, 1981), 12-13.

CHAPTER 20

1. Robert Schuller, *Self-Love* (New York: Hawthorn Books, Inc., 1969), 24, 25.

2. Abrahamsen, *The Road to Emotional Maturity,* 100.

3. Jean-Jacques Rousseau, *The Confessions of Jean-Jacques Rousseau* (New York: Pocket Books, Inc., 1956), 1.

4. For further reading, see Mildred Newman and Bernard Berkowitz, *How to Be Your Own Best Friend* (New York: Ballantine Books, 1971). An easy reading little book on what it means to become a friend to yourself.

5. W. Hugh Missildine, *Your Inner Child of the Past* (New York: Pocket Books, 1963), 3, 4, 10.

6. David A. Seamonds, *Putting away Childish Things* (Wheaton, Ill.: Victor Books, 1982), 19-20, 20-21, 22.

7. For further reading, see John Bradshaw, *Homecoming: Reclaiming and Championing Your Inner Child* (New York: Bantam Books, 1990). A very helpful book showing how to accept our past.

8. For further reading, see Charles L. Whitfield, *Healing the Child Within* (Deerfield Beach, Fla.: Health Communications, Inc., 1987).

9. For further reading, see Pia Mellody with Andrea Wills Miller and J. Keith Miller, *Facing Codependence: What It Is, Where It Comes From, and How It Sabotages Your Life* (San Francisco: Harper San Francisco, 1989).

10. For further reading, see Melody Beattie, *Codependent No More* (Center City, Minn.: Hazelden Educational Material, 1987).

11. Fromm, *The Art of Loving,* 49, 51.

12. For further reading, see Cecil G. Osborne, *The Art of Learning to Love Yourself* (Grand Rapids, Mich.: Zondervan Publishing House, 1976).

13. Elizabeth O'Conner, *Our Many Selves* (New York: Harper & Row Publishers, 1971), 23, 24.

CHAPTER 21

1. O. Hobart Mowrer, *The Crises of Psychiatry and Religion* (New York: Van Nostrand Reinhold Co., 1961), 130.

2. Brunner, *Man in Revolt*, 51-52.

3. Martin, *Toward Understanding God*, 100.

4. Verduin, *Somewhat Less Than God*, 51.

5. O. Hallesby, *Conscience*. translated by C. J. Carlsen (London: InterVarsity Fellowship, 1950), 9.

6. Sauer, *King of the Earth*, 144-145.

7. C. S. Lewis, *Mere Christianity* (New York: MacMillan Publishing Co., Inc., 1943), 21.

8. Sauer, *King of the Earth*, 56.

9. John Drakeford, *Integrity Therapy* (Nashville, Tenn.: Broadman Press, 1967), 14-15.

10. Hallesby, *Conscience*, 19-20.

11. Ernest Becker, *Escape from Evil* (New York: The Free Press, 1975), 158.

12. Ibid., 163.

13. Ayn Rand, *The Virtue of Selfishness* (New York: Signet Books, 1961), 13-14.

14. Ibid., 17.

15. Branden, *The Psychology of Self-esteem*, 228.

16. Eric Fromm, *Man for Himself: An Inquiry into the Psychology of Ethics* (Greenwich, Conn.: Fawcett Publications, Inc., 1947), 17, 216.

17. Schaeffer, *He Is There and He Is Not Silent*. 23, 33.

18. Bryan, *In His Image*, 86.

19. For further reading, see Dietrich Bonhoeffer, *Ethics*. ed. by Eberhard Bethge (New York: Macmillan Publishing Co., Inc., 1955).

20. Elton Trueblood, *A Place to Stand* (New York: Harper & Row Publishers, 1969), 14-15.

21. Robert Schuller, *Believe in the God Who Believes in You* (Nashville: Thomas Nelson Publishers, 1989), Preface.

22. Laura Schlessinger, *The Ten Commandments: The Significance of God's Laws in Everyday Life* (New York: Harper Collins Publishers, 1998), xxii-xxii.

23. Ibid., xxix.

CHAPTER 22

1. John Woolman, *The Journal of John Woolman* (New York: Corinth Books, Inc., 1961), 226-27.

2. Brunner, *Man in Revolt*, 53.

3. Joseph Fletcher, *Situational Ethics* (Philadelphia: The Westminster Press, 1966), 64, 65.

4. Woolman, *The Journal of John Woolman*, 8, 9, 13, 14.

5. Reinhold Niebuhr, *Moral Man and Immoral Society* (New York: Charles Scribner's Sons, 1932), 53, 54.

6. Martin Buber, *Good and Evil* (New York: Charles Scribner's Sons, 1952), 5.

7. Laura Schlessinger, *The Ten Commandments*, xxii

8. C. S. Lewis, *The Abolition of Man* (New York: Macmillan Publishing Co., Inc., 1947), 76, 77.

9. Karl Menninger, *Whatever Became of Sin* (New York: Bantam Books, Inc., 1973), 54, 155-56.

10. Verduin, *Somewhat Less Than God*, 54.

11. Mowrer, *The Crises of Psychiatry*, 54.

12. Rodale, *The Synonym Finder*, 212.

13. Paul Tournier, *The Strong and the Weak* (Philadelphia: The Westminster Press, 1963), 145-46.

14. Martin Luther, *Martin Luther's 95 Theses*. Kent Aland, Editor (Saint Louis, Missouri: Concordia Publishing House, 1976), 31.

CHAPTER 23

1. Brunner, *Man in Revolt*, 25.

2. Küng, *Does God Exist*, 634.

3. Zwingli and Bullinger, Vol. XXIV. Selected translations by G. W. Bromiley (Philadelphia: The Westminster Press [n.d.]), 61, 62.

4. Joseph Campbell, *The Masks of God: Primitive Mythology* (New York: Penguin Books, 1959), 4.

5. A. W. Tozer, *Knowledge of the Holy* (New York: Harper & Row Publishers, 1961), 9.

6. J. B. Phillips, *God Our Contemporary* (New York: The Macmillan Company, 1960), 23.

7. Victor E. Frankl, *The Doctor and the Soul* (New York: Vantage Books, 1955), x, xviii.

8. Phillips, *God Our Contemporary*, 40-41, 45.

9. Gordon W. Allport, *The Individual and His Religion* (New York: Macmillan Publishing Co., Inc., 1950), 10.

10. For further reading, see Freud, "Totem and Taboo," and "The Future of an Illusion," in J. Strachey (editor and translator), *The Standard Edition of the Complete Psychological Works of Sigmund Freud*, Vol. XIII and Vol. XXI (London: The Hogarth Press, 1961).

11. For further reading, see Carl G. Jung, *Psychology of the Unconscious*. B. M. Hinkle, translator (New York: Dodd, Mead & Co., 1952).

12. Erich Fromm, *Psychoanalysis and Religion* (New Haven: Yale University Press, 1950), 24, 26.

13. Erich Fromm, *You Shall Be As Gods* (Greenwich, Conn.: Fawcett Publications, Inc., 1966), 18.

14. J. B. Phillips, *Your God Is Too Small* (New York: Macmillan Publishing Co., Inc., 1961), 64.

15. Martin Buber, *Eclipse of God* (New York: Harper & Brothers Publishers, 1952), 23-24.

16. Martin Buber, *I and Thou*. Second edition translated by Ronald Gregor Smith (New York; Charles Scribner"s Sons, 1958), 135, 136.

17. Augustine, *Confessions of Augustine* (New York: Mentor-Omega Books, 1963), 17.

18. Phillips, *Your God Is Too Small*, 7, 8.

19. Hannah Whitall Smith, *The God Who Is Enough* (Chicago: Moody Press, 1956), 11, 12.

20. For further reading, see Larry Gene Day, *The Relationship of Self-Disclosure and Self-actualization to Cognitive and Affective God Concepts*. Unpublished dissertation. Rosemead Graduate School of Psychology, La Mirada, California, 1979.

21. C. S. Lewis, *Surprised by Joy* (New York: Harcourt, Brace & World, Inc., 1955), 21.

22. Ibid., 21.

23. Ibid., 66.

24. Ibid., 115.

25. Ibid., 172-73.

26. Ibid., 175.

27. Ibid., 178.

28. Ibid., 177.

29. Ibid., 191.

30. Ibid., 224.

31. Ibid., 228-29.

32. Ibid., 236.

33. Ibid., 237.

34. Lewis, *Mere Christianity*, 56.

35. Phillips, J. B. *Your God Is Too Small*, 82-83.

CHAPTER 24

1. Hans Küng, *On Being a Christian*. Translated by Edward Quinn (New York: Wallaby Books, 1976), 27, 601.

2. Pascal, *Pensées*, 153.

3. Orr, *God's Image in Man*, 279.

4. For further reading, see Os Guinness, *In Two Minds* (Downers Grove, Ill.: InterVarsity Press, 1976). A good book to read to help understand the problem of doubt.

5. Eugenia Price, *What Is God Like* (Grand Rapids, Mich.: Zondervan Publishing House, 1960), 5, 33-34.

6. Leslie D. Weatherhead, *The Christian Agnostic* (New York: Abingdon Press, 1965), 15, 21.

7. For further reading, see Juan Arias, *The God I Don't Believe In*. Translated by Paul Barrett (St. Meinrad, Ind.: Abbey Press, 1973).

8. Stephen Arterburn and Jack Felton. *Toxic Faith: Understanding and Overcoming Religious*

Addiction (Nashville: Oliver-Nelson Books, 1991), 31, 32.

9. Joseph Cooke, "My God Was Too Small," *Faith at Work*, April 1979, 14.

10. Ibid., 15.

11. Phillips, *Your God Is Too Small*, 63, 73.

12. Philip Yancey, *What's So Amazing About Grace?* (Grand Rapids: Zondervan Publishing House, 1997), 27, 32, 36, 37, 79, 62, 57, 59, 255.

13. Charles R. Swindoll, *Grace Awakening* (Dallas: Word Publishing, 1990), xv, xvi.

14. Hans Küng, *On Being a Christian*, 530-31.

15. Malcolm Muggeridge, *Something Beautiful for God: Mother Teresa of Calcutta* (San Francisco: Harper & Row Publishers, 1971), 66.

16. Ibid., 29-30.

17. Ibid., 91-92.

CHAPTER 25

1. Irving Stone, *The Agony and the Ecstasy* (New York: Doubleday and Company, 1961), 119.

2. Franky Schaeffer, *Addicted to Mediocrity* (Westchester, Ill.: Cornerstone Books, 1981), 11-12.

3. Rollo May, *The Courage to Create* (New York: W. W. Norton and Company, Inc., 1975), viii, 38.

4. Abraham H. Maslow, *Toward a Psychology of Being*. Second Edition (New York: D. Van Nostrand Company, 1968), 135.

5. Ibid., 138.

6. Eugene Raudsepp, *How Creative Are You* (New York: G. Putman's Sons, 1981), 11.

7. May, *The Courage to Create*, vii-viii.

8. Ibid., 19.

9. Ibid., 3.

10. Franky Schaeffer, *Addicted to Mediocrity*, 39.

11. Augustine, *The Confessions of St. Augustine*, 260-61.

12. Bertrand Russell, *Why I Am Not a Christian* (New York: Simon and Schuster, 1957), 107.

13. Maslow, *Toward a Psychology of Being*, 145.

14. Carl R. Rogers, *On Becoming a Person* (Boston: Houghton Mifflin Company, 1961), 356-57.

CHAPTER 26

1. H. R. Rookmaaker, *Modern Art and the Death of a Culture* (Downers Grove, Ill.: InterVarsity Press, 1970), 229.

2. Michael Card, *Scribbling in the Sand* (Downers Grove, Ill.: Intervarsity Press, 2002), 39, 44.

3. A. H. Maslow, *The Further Reaches of Human Nature*, 55, 76.

4. Raudsepp, *How Creative Are You*, 7.

5. Ibid., 8.

6. Edith Schaeffer, *Hidden Art* (Wheaton, Ill.: Tyndale House Publishers, 1971), 31.

7. Maslow, *Toward a Psychology of Being*, 136.

8. Raudsepp, *How Creative Are You*, 12.

9. Carl R. Rogers, *On Becoming a Person*, 350-51.

10. Alex F. Osborn, *Applied Imagination*. Third Revised Edition (New York: Charles Scribner's Sons, 1953), 19, 70.

11. Edith Schaeffer, *Hidden Art*, 14.

12. May, *The Courage to Create*, 117.

13. Carl R. Rogers, *On Becoming a Person*, 192.

CHAPTER 27

1. James I. Vance, *The Eternal in Man* (New York: Fleming H. Revell Company, 1907), 22, 23.

AUTHOR INDEX

SUBJECT INDEX

Memory cont.
    Seamonds on, 290, 301
    secrets of, 78
Mind
    biblical teaching, 233
    conclusions of, 81
    healthy, 218, 231
    renewing of, 232-33
    waste of, 212-14
Moral values
    biblical teaching, 342-44
    absolutes, 333-40
    awareness, 315-30
    Branden on, 325-26
    decisions, 336-40
    frame of reference, 327-30
    free choice and, 335-36
    Fromm on, 326
    guilt and, 321-24
    importance of, 324-27
    judgments, 323
    Menninger on, 341-42
    Mowrer on, 314
    Niebuhr on, 339
    Rand on, 325
    Schaeffer on, 328
    Schuller on, 330
    self-talk, 334
    and sexuality, 335
    Trueblood on, 329
    v. relative ethics, 333
    Woolman on, 337-38
Mother Teresa, 404-9
New Age Movement
    creativity and, 422
    philosophy of, 74
Nobility
    mark of, 211
    Sauer on, 166-67, 169
    Schaeffer on, 108
Past
    creating a new, 197-98
    Greenwald on, 198
Personhood
    authenticating, 35-39, 455-57
    creativity and, 436
    Tournier on, 68
Prayer
    answered, 109-10

Prayer cont.
    Peale on, 224
    therapeutic, 273-75
    and thinking, 224
    unanswered, 122
Pride: basis of, 81
Reality, 232, 234, 237
Reasoning
    ability, 211-18
    Adler on, 209, 210-11
    Branden on, 209
    Brunner on, 206
    Descarte on, 210
    gift from God, 210-12
    Orr on, 206
    Pascal on, 206, 211
    Rand on, 214-15
    Thielicke, 215-16
    to think or not to think, 214-16
    uniqueness of, 208-12
Repentance: remorse and, 94
Self-acceptance
    communication and, 255
    restored, 122
Self-awareness
    Allport on, 287
    Becker on, 323-24
    being v. doing, 286
    Calvin on, 284-85
    and faith in God, 283
    and frame of reference, 46, 280, 284
    friendship with self, 297-98
    Fromm on, 278
    and image of God, 284-85
    of inner child, 298-312
    loss of, 285-86
    many sides of, 308-10
    missing pieces and, 294-96
    Moustakas on, 289
    O'Conner on, 309
    Orr on, 278
    present v. past, 288-91
    past, 298-312
    Rousseau on, 292
    and self-esteem, 281-83
    Toynbee on, 279, 283
    uniqueness of, 279-81
    v. self-centeredness, 280-81

SCRIPTURE INDEX

PERSONAL NOTES

ABOUT THE AUTHOR

Dr. Larry Day is a Christian counselor in Portland, Oregon. He has been in private practice since 1975. His teaching and counseling on self-esteem and Christian living have helped thousands of people.

He received his Th.B. degree in Bible from Multnomah Bible College and a B.A. degree in Sociology-Anthropology from Western Washington University. At Wheaton Graduate School of Theology, he received his M.A. degree in New Testament, and from Rosemead School of Psychology, a Ph.D. in Counseling Psychology.

Dr. Day has traveled to over thirty five countries around the world, studying one summer under Dr. Francis Schaeffer at L'Abri in Switzerland, and has spent two summers studying and living on a Kibutz in Israel. He enjoys running, mountain climbing, reading, remodeling projects, traveling and photography.

As a speaker, educator, author, consultant, former High School teacher and youth minister, Dr. Day is highly recognized for his important work on self-esteem and currently speaks on the subject across the country.

Larry and his wife Gail live in Portland, Oregon.

"Your book is inspirational, wonderful . . . your insights are helpful and uplifting. . . . Since I read your book I have been noticing things all around that remind me how valuable I am to God."

Alyssa, Oregon

"This is one outstanding book, one that I shall treasure as long as I live."

Shari, Oregon

"Excellent book . . . after reading it several times, I was able to use it as a tool to develop a series of messages for my congregation on the topics of Dignity. The feedback has been positive."

Pastor Rich, Oregon

"I have just finished my second reading of your book, and the underlining, arrows, scribbled notes and general dog-eared quality of the pages attest to its worth."

Wendy, Oregon

"For ten years, now, Larry's book has challenged, encouraged and directed me towards a better understanding of myself and how God's Word may be applied to my heart, my thinking, and my free will to – choose life."

Little Brother, Bron, S.A.D. (Self-Appointed Dean)
Brother's Keeper Philosophical Society, Sawtooth County, Idaho